pop art

an international perspective

Exhibition selected by Marco Livingstone with Norman Rosenthal
assisted by Simonetta Fraquelli
The Fluxus section selected by Thomas Kellein

This exhibition was organised by the Royal Academy of Arts, London

The Royal Academy of Arts is also grateful to Her Majesty's Government for its help in agreeing to indemnify the exhibition under the National Heritage Act 1980 and to the Museum and Galleries Commission for their help in arranging this indemnity

edited by Marco Livingstone

an international perspective

with contributions by
Dan Cameron • Constance W. Glenn • Thomas Kellein • Marco Livingstone
Sarat Maharaj • Alfred Pacquement • Evelyn Weiss

Exhibition
Exhibition and Catalogue Coordinator: Simonetta Fraquelli
Assistant Coordinator: Susan Thompson

Catalogue
Sub-Editors: Stephen Stuart-Smith (essays); Samantha Roberts (anthology and bibliography); Kevin Halliwell (biographies)
Biographies compiled by: Elizabeth Brooks, Philip Cooper, Simonetta Fraquelli, Caroline Odgers, Joanna Skipwith
Translations from the French and German: David Britt (Alfred Pacquement, Evelyn Weiss, Thomas Kellein)
Photographic Copyright Coordinator: Miranda Bennion

Copyright of all other documents, see p. 306

House editor: Alice Millington-Drake
Catalogue Design: Malcolm Garrett, Assorted Images

First published in the United States of America in 1992 by
RIZZOLI INTERNATIONAL PUBLICATIONS, INC.
300 Park Avenue South, New York, NY 10010

First published in Great Britain in 1991 by
George Weidenfeld & Nicolson Ltd

ISBN 0-8478-1475-0 Hardcover
ISBN 0-8478-1476-9 Paperback
LC 91-62786

Printed and bound in Great Britain

Cover illustration: James Rosenquist, *Look Alive (Blue Feet, Look Alive)*, 1961 (Detail; cat 205)

contents

SPONSORS' PREFACES

Thirty years on, Pop Art still appears fresh, witty, iconoclastic. It remains a strong influence on contemporary artists and designers. This exhibition is thus a significant cultural event.

The Independent has supported numerous arts events in its short history and it will continue to place great emphasis on them in the future. As we approach *The Independent*'s fifth anniversary, we are delighted to be involved in such an important event as The Pop Art Show.

We give our support enthusiastically. We know the show will engage the interest of our readers.

Andreas Whittam Smith
Editor, *The Independent*

Mercury Communications is a long distance and international telecommunications company that provides UK business and residential users with a full range of products and services.

Formed in 1981, Mercury was granted its first government licence to provide services in competition with BT in 1982. Telephone services were first offered in 1983, and the company was granted a full licence by the government in 1984. Half a million business and residential lines have been supplied by Mercury, 100,000 residential lines in the last year. Mercury access areas already reach 75% of the population. Mercury subscribers enjoy savings of 10–20% on their long distance calls (calls over 35 miles).

The Pop Art Show is Mercury Communications's first major association with the visual arts, and the company looks forward to an exciting and productive partnership with the Royal Academy of Arts. The assembling of such an important, comprehensive and prestigious international exhibition is a challenging task and one of which the Academy can feel justly proud.

In March 1991 Mercury Communications announced its sponsorship of The Prince's Trust's Fifteenth Anniversary Year, a partnership of great benefit to both organisations. Mercury's contribution of a million pounds is being used to finance grants for young people and further fundraising activities.

Mercury's support for The Prince's Trust and for the Royal Academy of Arts is linked through fundraising events, sales of special edition Mercurycards and publicity surrounding the exhibition. Through both of these complementary sponsorships, Mercury Communications is pleased to be able to contribute in different ways to the community in which it has grown.

Peter van Cuylenburg
Chief Executive

ACKNOWLEDGEMENTS

We would like to thank the following who have contributed in so many different ways to the organisation of the exhibition and the preparation of the catalogue:

Michael D Abrams
William Acquavella
Thomas Ammann
Victoria Atkinson
Bruno Bischofsberger
William Bodine
Rainer Borgemeister
Irving Blum
Maria Brassel
Richard Brown Baker
Susan Brundage
Veronica Bulgari
Cherise Chen
Beverly Coe
Candy Coleman
Sadie Coles
Michael Compton
Ina Conzen-Meairs
James Corcoran
Keith Davey
Jeffrey Deitch
James Demetrion
Anthony d'Offay
Caroline Douglas
Stephen Dunn
Rhona Edelbaum
Richard Feigen
Mark Francis
Vincent Fremont
Constance W Glenn
William Goldsten
Deborah Goodman
Martin Guesnet
Agnes Gund
Hildegard Hahn
Walter Hayes
Frances Hazlehurst
Joseph Helman
Sophie Hicks
Antonio Homen
Walter Hopps
Michael Hue-Williams
Jasper Jacob
David Janis
Hugues Joffre
Piet de Jonge
Deborah Jordy
John Kasmin
Karen S Kuhlman
Mark Lancaster
Richard S Lane
Graham Langton
David Levy
James Lingwood
Cassandra Lozano
Chris Lycett
Liz McCrae
Tom MacGregor
Michael Maegraith
Anders Malmberg
Giò Marconi
Giorgio Marconi
Bill Maynes
Hans Mayer
Helen van der Meij
Paul Moorhouse
Richard Morphet
Peter Nestler
Hans Neuendorf
Thomas Neurath
Sasha Newman
Caroline Odgers
Cathal O'Doherty
Gisèle Ollinger
Lorcan O'Neill
Alfred Pacquement
Patrick Painter
Jonathan Pratt
Odyssia Quadrani
Marlee Robinson
Nan Rosenthal
David Ross
Jane Rubin
Lawrence Rubin
Klaus Runkel
Charles Saatchi
Paul Schimmel
Ian Spero
Nikos Stangos
Hans Strelow
Blake Summers
Sarah Taggart
Linda Tanner
Vicente Todoli
Sarah Tooley
Samuel Lorin Trouwer
Gabriele Uelsberg
Daniel Varenne
Johanna Vogt
Robin Vousden
Christopher Webb
David White
Heather Wilson
William S Wilson
Daniel Wolf
Charles Wylie

We are also deeply grateful to all those artists who have generously agreed to waive copyright fees for reproductions of their works in the catalogue.

foreword

Pop Art, one of the most influential of twentieth-century art movements, made its first appearance in London and New York over thirty years ago. Those cities acted as poles of attraction for artists, whether they came from the provinces of England, the hinterland of the United States or the Continent of Europe. Pop Art was always infectious in its vitality and has affected contemporary art since its first exhibitions, even if only by provoking a reaction. It still continues to do so as we now see a new generation of artists transform and revitalise the idiom of the 1950s and '60s. This exhibition will be the first time that artists from Continental Europe who were working in a Pop idiom in the Sixties are shown in strength alongside their American and British contemporaries.

The exhibition has been selected by Marco Livingstone, whose writings have contributed enormously to the scholarship of Pop Art, with Norman Rosenthal, Exhibitions Secretary at the Royal Academy; they have been ably assisted by Simonetta Fraquelli. The Fluxus material has been selected by Thomas Kellein, Director of the Kunsthalle Basel.

The Royal Academy is particularly delighted that this exhibition will travel to the Museum Ludwig in Cologne – home to what is probably the greatest single collection of Pop Art in the world, formed by Dr Peter Ludwig. We are especially grateful for the personal interest that Dr Ludwig has shown in this project and we wish to thank him, as well as Dr Siegfried Gohr and Dr Evelyn Weiss, for their enthusiastic support. We are equally delighted that the exhibition will be seen at the Centro de Arte Reina Sofía in Madrid, the contemporary art centre inaugurated in 1989 which has already provided a programme of twentieth-century art exhibitions of international significance. It is particularly pleasing that this exhibition should be seen in Madrid in the year when that city is Cultural Capital of Europe and we are most grateful to its Director, Maria de Corral, for her commitment to this project.

Many individuals have contributed to the exhibition. First, we thank the artists themselves, who have been unfailingly helpful and enthusiastic throughout (the Academy is fortunate in having among its Members some of the artists who pioneered Pop Art in the 1950s and '60s). We are also indebted to all the institutions and individuals who have lent us important works from their collections: particular mention should be made of two of the greatest art dealers in New York, Leo Castelli and Ileana Sonnabend, who have done so much over the years to establish the careers of many of the artists. In London, Leslie Waddington and James Mayor, in Berlin, Mr and Mrs Reinhard Onnasch and, in Zurich, Thomas Ammann have been especially cooperative in helping us to trace several key works. Nicholas Serota and his staff at the Tate Gallery have been extremely supportive in making loans available and providing facilities for research.

Finally, the Royal Academy is deeply indebted to the sponsors of the exhibition: Mercury Communications, whose outstanding generosity has made it possible to present such an ambitious show, and to *The Independent*, which has provided additional funding as well as editorial support. Radio One has also supported the exhibition and is the official radio station. London was one of the original centres of Pop Art; the sponsors' commitment expresses their confidence in the culture of our capital city and its continuing vitality, just as Pop Art itself did during the Sixties.

Sir Roger de Grey, KCVO
President

introduction

in glorious technicuIture

MARCO LIVINGSTONE

Pop Art emerged slowly, insidiously from the mid-1950s through to the early 1960s, not with a bang or a manifesto but as a series of manoeuvres by artists as far afield as New York, Los Angeles, San Francisco, London, Paris, Düsseldorf, Milan and Rome. Working at first independently and in ignorance of each other, each of the artists conceived of ways of making an assault on cherished notions of good taste and decorum and also of challenging the modernist stance that postulated the hermetic inviolability of the work of art.

fig 1 Installation view of 'The New Realists' at the Sidney Janis Gallery, New York 1962

Pop artists were first called New Realists, after their Paris-based counterparts the Nouveaux Réalistes, when their work was exhibited together at the Sidney Janis Gallery, New York, in 1962[1] (fig. 1). The participants here included the Americans Jim Dine, Robert Indiana, Roy Lichtenstein, Claes Oldenburg, James Rosenquist, George Segal, Wayne Thiebaud, Andy Warhol and Tom Wesselmann; the British artists Peter Blake, John Latham and Peter Phillips; and a strong European contingent featuring, among others, Arman, Enrico Baj, Christo, Oyvind Fahlström, Tano Festa, Raymond Hains, Yves Klein, Martial Raysse, Mimmo Rotella, Mario Schifano, Daniel Spoerri, Jean Tinguely and Per-Olof Ultvedt. The first show was a fully-international manifestation of a movement that only retrospectively became treated as a largely American and (somewhat grudgingly) British phenomenon. The New Realist label that it conferred on the artists concentrated attention on their gritty engagement with contemporary life in all its banal familiarity. The eventual suppression of the term in favour of the shorter, snappier, Pop Art, with its connotations of popular culture and identification with the new forms of pop music as signs of teenage rebellion, shifted the emphasis from subject-matter to one of attitude. Whatever its shortcomings as an umbrella term covering such a heterogeneous collection of approaches, Pop remained a useful way of identifying an outward-looking art wholly immersed in the urban visual culture from which it sprang.

Although the Nouveaux Réalistes were included in the Sidney Janis group show, they were subsequently treated as a largely separate phenomenon. Critics, artists and dealers – American and British – defined the unifying characteristics of their aesthetic partly in opposition to that of the Europeans; but the Europeans allowed this to happen because they, too, were conscious of the differences. While artists working along similar lines in various parts of the world became increasingly aware of each other's work during the 1960s – for instance through the exhibitions by American Pop artists held at the Galerie Sonnabend in Paris, or in one-man shows by Raysse, Alain Jacquet and other Europeans in America – the separate circumstances shaping the art in each country seem to have made it difficult at the time to recognise more than a distant kinship. Indeed to Americans Pop remained an artistic manifestation almost completely circumscribed by their own culture, to the

1 A similar grouping had been shown in Paris in July 1961 at the Galerie Rive Droite, 'Le Nouveau Réalisme à Paris et à New York'.

fig 2 **Jasper Johns** Target with Four Faces 1955; encaustic on newspaper over canvas 66 × 66 cm (26 × 26 ins) surmounted by four tinted plaster faces in wood box with hinged front, box closed 9.5 × 66 × 8.9 cm ($3\frac{3}{4}$ × 26 × $3\frac{1}{2}$ ins), overall dimensions with box open 85.3 × 66 × 7.6 cm ($33\frac{5}{8}$ × 26 × 3 ins) The Museum of Modern Art, New York, Gift of Mr and Mrs Robert C. Scull

fig 3 **Jim Dine** My Tuxedo Makes an Impressive Blunt Edge to the Light 1965 Courtesy Pace Gallery, New York

fig 4 **Richard Artschwager** Table and Chair 1963–64 Tate Gallery, London

extent that British artists, too, were excluded from virtually all the major Pop Art shows held in the USA.

Pop Art had no prescriptive programme, and it would thus be misleading to ascribe identical intentions to all the artists who have been bracketed together under the term. The most cursory reading of the original Pop texts reprinted in this volume will make it evident that among the American artists alone there were discrepancies of attitude as marked as the variations of imagery and technique. This is the case even when one can point to direct links among the artists, for example with regard to the influential role played by Jasper Johns and Robert Rauschenberg. As early as the mid-1950s Johns had presented painted canvases or cast sculptures as replicas of familiar things such as flags, targets (fig. 2) and even light bulbs or tin cans, and Rauschenberg had incorporated printed ephemera and actual objects into his 'combine' paintings as the flotsam of life collected on expeditions through the streets of New York. To this moment one can ascribe the later concern of Pop artists, especially in America, with the object. Johns remained especially close in spirit to Marcel Duchamp's aesthetic of the ready-made, preferring to find the most typical representative of a class of object, such as a flashlight, to be made into art.

Dine also used objets trouvés, in his case usually tools or items of clothing, but for him they functioned consistently as a personal sign; the clothing in a work such as *The Green Suit* (1959, cat. 33) was plainly a stand-in for himself, while he had loved tools since his childhood and had grown to think of them as extensions of his hands. When elaborating a given image, such as that of the Valentine's heart or of a bathrobe spied in an advertisement printed in *The New York Times,* there is again a sense of a subjective motivation lurking within the apparent anonymity of the source, with each motif giving form to a succession of emotions and experiences (fig. 3). Oldenburg, Pop's most assiduous master of the common object, used equally familiar things as a starting-point but subjected them always to a process of refabrication that emphasises not only the forms as the end product of a particular process but also their mysterious and often almost human presence. His 'soft sculptures' in particular, sewn from a variety of materials including vinyl and canvas, have anthropomorphic connotations: they are the size of people, and their limp shapes, weighed down by the force of gravity, often assume 'exhausted' poses.

A similarity can be discerned between certain works by Oldenburg, notably his *Bedroom Ensemble* of 1963, and the furniture sculptures made out of formica on wood by Richard Artschwager in the mid-1960s (fig. 4). Although the two artists had met, they arrived independently at superficially similar solutions, each artist reshaping domestic objects from synthetic materials and playing on their connotations of use. Artschwager's art, unlike Oldenburg's, was essentially one of surface, in that he explored the image potential of a flat pattern composed from a single substance printed to give the illusion of different textures. Although formica, too, had inescapable social connotations as a cheap, readily available material used especially in lower-middle-class houses to give an impression of greater luxury, such a reading now seems less important than the subterfuge of simulation as an end in itself. At its most tantalising, American Pop remains stubbornly resistant to interpretations that uncover only one level of meaning.

The advent of Pop as an unstoppable movement was greeted by many with dismay. In one of the most celebrated early attacks on American Pop, all the more outraged for recognising the intentions of many of its adherents, the critic Max Kozloff remarked: 'The truth is, the art galleries are being invaded by the pin-headed and contemptible style of gum-chewers, bobby soxers, and, worse, delinquents. Not only can't I get romantic about this; I see as little reason to find it appealing as I would an hour of rock and roll into which has been inserted a few notes of modern music'.[2] Kozloff later modified his views, admitting to having responded emotionally out of contempt for the commercial imagery featured in the work of these artists, but others were less forgiving. Many artists and critics alike, especially those associated with the lofty ideals of Abstract Expressionism, clearly saw the movement as a betrayal of the long-fought battles of modernism. Mark Rothko is said to have spoken scathingly of the newcomers as 'Pop-sicles'. Pop's sometimes vulgar sense of humour was like a slap in the face to artists who had spent their lives trying to persuade their potential audience that modern art was not a joke but a serious business (fig. 5). The wilful crudeness and vulgarity apparently celebrated by these 'gum-chewers', who seemed to find in their society only the shallowness of the inveterate shopper and the literacy of comic-book fanatics, seemed offensively inured to the moral values held dear by the liberal intellectual establishment. To the presentation of the creative act as a heroic struggle of the individual, or as the fragile evidence of the artist's refined sensibility, the Pop artists countered with comic-strip emotions, second-hand imagery and mechanical or pseudo-mechanical processes apparently drained of all signs of personality.

fig 5 **Mel Ramos** A. C. Annie 1965 Collection of Hirshhorn Museum and Sculpture Garden, Washington, DC

Like earlier terms used to describe modern art movements, Pop remained for many years such a term of abuse that even many of its leading exponents were reluctant to have it applied to their work. Some of the artists who helped shape the terms of this art in Britain in the early 1960s, such as R. B. Kitaj and David Hockney, were quick to disassociate themselves from it and to invent a new lineage for their art from older figurative traditions. Conversely, even the early work by the American artists who were most comfortable with the label now sits much more easily within the artistic framework that it seemed at first to be overturning. With time it has become possible to recognise the sense of the tragic in Warhol's dispassionate treatment of images of fame and death as interchangeable signs, or the classicism of Lichtenstein's studied formality and emotional reticence. The dreamlike quality of Rosenquist's fragments of floating imagery now seems to take precedence over their associations with the matter-of-fact displays of billboard advertising, just as Oldenburg's re-creations of the ordinary now delight with their formal inventiveness, humanity and intimacy rather than shocking by their banality. The incorporation of real objects in works by Dine, Wesselmann and others, which may at first have seemed like a lazy way out, in retrospect takes shape as part of a dialogue about the twin roles of invention and representation.

Yet one of the great achievements of all these artists, like that of the first-generation Dadaists to whom some of them were at first compared, was to shake up complacency by acting as *agents provocateurs*. Artists at the forefront of the early modernist movements had sought to rid art of the stultifying effects of academicism by recourse to imagery and techniques that were wholly of their time. Such was the case with the literal fragments of everyday life inserted into the collages of the Cubists, or with the related notions of the objet trouvé and the ready-made espoused by Duchamp and the Dadaists. Similar concerns were at the root of the machine aesthetic investigated not only by Fernand Léger and his disciples but also by the Purists in Europe and the Precisionists in America. The Surrealists were among the first twentieth-century artists to embrace the debased popular taste of kitsch, reviled by the American critic Clement Greenberg as the antithesis of genuine 'high culture'.[3]

2 M. Kozloff, 'Pop Culture, Metaphysical Disgust, and the New Vulgarians', *Art International*, March 1962, reprinted in M. Kozloff, *Renderings: Critical Essays on a Century of Modern Art*, London, 1970, p. 221.

3 C. Greenberg, 'Avant-Garde and Kitsch', *Partisan Review*, 6, Fall 1939, pp. 34–9.

Pop artists injected a new vitality into each of these approaches, often basing their work on the principles of collage and assemblage as a way of opening their art to the plethora of sources equally available to everyone through the mass media. Whether using these objets trouvés in their raw form, copying them by hand or replicating them by recourse to mechanical techniques such as photography or screenprinting, they made a point of drawing attention to the fact that they were merely recycling motifs and artifacts that already existed. Their iconography was borrowed in large measure from ubiquitous signs of their culture such as advertisements and billboards (fig. 6), photographs and comic books, magazines and newspapers, the cinema and television; with this they forged an art that was genuinely democratic in the accessibility of its imagery and that functioned as a clear mirror to the culture in which it originated. As Warhol later recalled, the stunningly simple strategy devised by him and his colleagues now seems so obvious as to have been inevitable: 'The Pop artists did images that anybody walking down Broadway could recognize in a split second – comics, picnic tables, men's trousers, celebrities, shower curtains, refrigerators, Coke bottles – all the great modern things that the Abstract Expressionists tried so hard not to notice at all'.[4]

fig 6 **Allan d'Arcangelo** June Moon 1963 Sidney and Frances Lewis Collection

The challenge posed by the ready-made to conventional notions of artistic invention and creativity was taken up by Pop artists with an almost ferocious enthusiasm. It was above all in their defiant refusal to take responsibility either for their imagery or for their processes that they most outraged the sensibilities of those nurtured on the idea of the work of art as a subjective and personal intervention on the world by an individual. Making do with what was already available, they drew attention to the glut of information and visual stimuli assaulting each of us as we go about our business. In their apparent reluctance to add to the existing range of choices, they suggested that the world was in no need of further inventions from them, and that a more useful function lay in reordering this otherwise bewildering barrage of sensations. Paradoxically, of course, they fulfilled this aim by creating more objects, that is to say by themselves contributing to the feverish production and consumerism characteristic of post-war industrialised society.

The ambivalence implicit in much Pop Art is especially evident in its relationship to kitsch. Although refusing to succumb to the superior attitude towards areas of popular taste displayed by the protectors of 'high culture', the purveyors of Pop cannot be said to have adopted a uniform tone towards their borrowed styles or material. An openly celebratory approach can be found only rarely, for instance in the circus and fun-fair pictures painted in the 1950s by Peter Blake, which are free of condescension towards their sources. As a general rule it was British artists who found it easiest to convey their enthusiasm for popular culture. Such is the case with the paintings made in the early 1960s by Peter Phillips, then in his early 20s, which convey the excitement he felt as a young man when confronted by the signs of the new teenage culture, although the disquieting overtones evident even in these exuberant works have become more pronounced as he has grown older. The paintings of Allen Jones, while often compared in their frank eroticism to those made in America by Wesselmann, go much further in acknowledging their specific sources in pin-up imagery and in sexually-based illustrations of the 1940s and 1950s. Eduardo Paolozzi's screenprints of the 1960s, leading on from the collages he had made in the late 1940s and early 1950s, display his magpie collector's instinct for every conceivable kind of modern printed ephemera, sifted, collated and then presented as a dizzying sign of his own consciousness.

Pop Art in Britain was no more consistent in this or other respects than it was

4 A. Warhol, *POPism: The Warhol '60s*, New York, 1980, p. 3.

in America or on the Continent. In fact the investigations of the Independent Group in London, which contained some of the first stirrings of Pop ideas in the early 1950s, provide vivid evidence of an inherently sceptical approach to popular culture almost as a condition of their insatiable curiosity for it. Their wide-ranging approach to culture was reflected in the membership itself, consisting of painters and sculptors (notably Paolozzi and Richard Hamilton), architects such as Alison and Peter Smithson, and critics and historians such as Reyner Banham, Toni del Renzio and Lawrence Alloway, who is credited with the first published use of the term 'pop' in 1958.[5] This small group, which met almost in secrecy at the Institute of Contemporary Arts on Dover Street, set themselves on a kind of mission to examine subjects that would have been considered beneath contempt by the establishment that ran the ICA itself, as personified by Herbert Read. Between 1952 and 1955 they held sessions, for example, on automobile styling and helicopter design, advertising and Italian product design, fashion and science fiction, and also on more purely artistic topics such as the machine aesthetic.

fig 7 **John McHale** Machine-made Man 1967
Magda Cordell McHale, Buffalo

In spite of the variety of their interests, however, the Independent Group maintained a certain critical distance appropriate both to their essentially intellectual appreciation of these subjects and to their sense that they were examining foreign cultures of which they were not strictly a part. Of the little finished art that came out of the Independent Group at the time, much of it – notably Paolozzi's rough-hewn figures cast in bronze from found fragments and John McHale's anthropomorphic collages of machine imagery culled from magazines (fig. 7) – was dominated by the example of Jean Dubuffet and his notion of Art Brut. It was only in Hamilton's work that a full-blown Pop aesthetic began to emerge, notably in *Just what is it that makes today's homes so different, so appealing?* (1956, cat. 99), a small collage made for reproduction as a poster for the exhibition 'This is Tomorrow' at the Whitechapel Gallery in London. This compact work, with its compendium of motifs later explored more fully by Hamilton and other Pop artists, is perhaps the closest that the British side of the movement came to producing a work comparable in importance to Picasso's *Demoiselles d'Avignon* in relation to Cubism. Yet even when Hamilton himself began in 1957 to produce collage-based paintings that satisfied in some respects the prophetic definition of Pop he had formulated in that year in a letter to the Smithsons,[6] he treated the evidence of popular culture with a certain mistrust. One of the first of these works, *Hommage à Chrysler Corp* (1957, cat. 100), already tempers a genuine admiration of modern design with a suspicion towards the manipulative role of advertising. While stopping short of satire, the very title of *Glorious Techniculture* (1961–64, cat. 101) reveals a less than reverential attitude towards the brave new world of modern technology.

The attitude of American Pop artists towards their source material was so fundamentally ambivalent that critics and other spectators could read whatever they wanted into the works. In this, as in so much else, Warhol proved a prime example, seen variously as mindlessly glorifying consumer culture, as gently satirising it and even – according to one of the first published monographs on his work – as offering a Marxist critique of it.[7] Warhol himself consistently protested that he intended no social comment, but that he was simply painting 'the things I know best' as 'symbols of the harsh, impersonal products and brash materialistic objects on which America is built today'.[8] Such a deliberately neutral stance seems closer to the truth, although there are still many critics, 30 years later, who would prefer to see Pop as either confirming a 'correct' social or political view – that is to say, their own – or on the contrary as embodying everything that is wrong with the society in which it originated.

5 L. Alloway, 'The Arts and the Mass Media', *Architectural Design*, XXVIII, 2, February 1958.
6 Quoted in *Richard Hamilton*, exhibition catalogue by R. Morphet, Tate Gallery, London, 1970, p. 31.
7 R. Crone, *Andy Warhol*, Frankfurt am Main, 1970; English translation, New York, Washington and London, 1970.
8 A. Warhol, *America*, New York, 1985, p. 8; 'New Talent U.S.A.', *Art in America*, I, 1, 1960, p. 42, quoted in K. McShine, ed., *Andy Warhol: A Retrospective*, exhibition catalogue, Museum of Modern Art, New York, 1989, p. 458.

This is not to say that a satirical flavour never enters into any of the work, nor that Pop promoted an extreme form of amorality out of a constitutional inability ever to declare a point of view. Rather it would seem that the social meanings that can be extrapolated from American Pop are as various and contradictory as the reactions that we as individuals may have towards that society itself. If Warhol's work conveys a sense of the frenetic pace and consumerism of life in a modern capitalist state, or the deadening and depersonalising quality of its repetitive tasks and conformism, one can never be sure that these are his intentions rather than simply one's own responses. If Lichtenstein's art touches on the contrary impulses of romantic love and aggression without appearing to yield to emotion except as an abstract concept, this may be because the artist wishes us to remain as conscious as he is of the ways in which our responses can be manipulated (fig. 8). In presenting images as objets trouvés, therefore, rather than as signs of personal preference, Lichtenstein and other Pop artists can be said to have recourse to a device comparable to Bertolt Brecht's 'alienation effect' in the theatre.

fig 8 **Roy Lichtenstein** Kiss II 1962 Private Collection

However varied in form, Pop from the English-speaking world can be seen as a coherent movement with certain shared concerns, especially with regard to the use of familiar objects and existing flat images replicated in a literal manner, often by reference to the methods of mass production. It was to such ends that Pop artists throughout the world played such an influential role in the revival of printmaking – indeed, in the substantial redefinition of what constituted an 'original' print in terms of technique – that took place during the 1960s. The case made thus far for the studied neutrality of much of this art, however, begins to fall apart when one seeks to make similar generalisations for its equivalents in Europe. An important contribution to this dialogue was made as early as the 1950s by European artists, particularly by those who joined together as the Nouveaux Réalistes in 1960. Yet the situation for artists working in France, Germany or Italy, let alone for those based in less industrialised nations, was clearly not the same as for those in America or even in Britain. Pop artists accorded a central role to the post-war consumer boom and the pervasiveness of the mass media. Given that these economic and cultural changes were most enthusiastically embraced in America, it is natural that even those European artists who were drawn to such subject-matter would take a more overtly critical stance, as in the case of Fahlström, who divided his time between New York and Sweden.

The political dimension evident in much Pop-related work made in Europe during the 1960s first made itself felt within the ranks of the Nouveaux Réalistes in the previous decade, especially in the work of the *affichistes* Rotella, Hains and Jacques de la Villeglé. These artists, along with Wolf Vostell in West Germany, made their pictures by tearing off the layers of posters from public hoardings, a technique known as *décollage*. Since these posters were as likely to advertise political matters as consumer products or feature films, such subject-matter could again be regarded as intrinsic to the situation in which they were working. In this sense they were reflecting their society in much the same way as the Americans. Among the sculptors it was above all Arman, especially in his *Accumulations* of particular types of mass-produced objects, who broached themes of repetition and surplus production comparable to those implicit in the work of an American Pop artist such as Warhol. But there are strong similarities, too, between the use of objets trouvés by such sculptors as Spoerri, Tinguely and Niki de Saint Phalle and the 'junk art' engaged in by Rauschenberg and Dine but also by others less closely associated with Pop. Furthermore, the sculptures of consumer products and packaging made as early as 1960 by one of the youngest of the Nouveaux Réalistes, Raysse, presaged the *Brillo Boxes* and related sculptures made by Warhol four years later, with an important distinction: Raysse, following Duchamp, presented the things themselves as the elements of his sculptures, rather than remaking them in another material.

Even before the dissemination of Pop in the early 1960s, European artists not linked with the Nouveaux Réalistes were exploring territory that had much in common with Pop. As early as the mid-1950s the German painter Konrad Klapheck, working in a meticulously illustrative idiom reminiscent of *Neue Sachlichkeit* of the 1920s, produced studiously mute images of banal objects such as typewriters and sewing machines. In Italy Baj assaulted all notions of good taste in deliciously kitsch paintings called *Modifications* (fig. 9), while in another group of works, *Personnagi in legno,* he produced frontal portraits of ordinary pieces of furniture recreated with maximum literalness from pieces of veneered wood glued onto backgrounds made from patterned wall coverings. In the late 1950s the Danish painter Asger Jorn, a prominent member of the Neo-Expressionist Cobra movement but also a co-founder with Baj of the Mouvement pour un Bauhaus Imaginiste in 1954, also produced a series entitled *Modifications,* which consisted of routine junk-shop landscapes hastily overpainted with images in a wilfully jarring style.

fig 9 **Enrico Baj** Susanna 1959 Courtesy Studio Marconi, Milan

The reaction by other Europeans to their first sightings of American or British Pop brought further waves of more clearly Pop-oriented work. Italy, for instance, contributed among other things the immaculate sign-paintings of Valerio Adami, the mirror pictures and *Oggetti in meno* sculptures of Michelangelo Pistoletto, the stencilled motifs of Mario Schifano (fig. 10), Domenico Gnoli's painted close-ups of banal objects and Pino Pascali's two- or three-dimensional responses to familiar things. In France one can cite above all the luridly coloured photographically-based paintings made by Raysse as early as 1962 and the 'Mec Art' devised by Jacquet, and the more politically oriented work of the painters associated with a development termed *Figuration narrative,* such as Bernard Rancillac and Hervé Télémaque. In 1963 Sigmar Polke and Gerhard Richter, after moving to Düsseldorf from East Germany, devised Kapitalistischer Realismus with Konrad Lueg as an ironic response to the consumer culture of Pop in the shadow of Socialist Realism. Vostell, who was known not only for his *décollages* but also as a maker of Happenings and as a leading figure within the Fluxus movement, turned in the 1960s to other methods of recycling found images, particularly by screenprinting. Even in Spain, a less likely breeding ground for Pop, there emerged the paintings of Eduardo Arroyo, layered in their references to twentieth-century art, as well as the pointedly satirical collaborative works of the Equipo Crónica group, based in Valencia.

The immense variety of European responses to Pop makes a vivid story in itself, but the fragmentary nature of such isolated occurrences make them difficult to contain under the same rubric as the mainstream of American or British Pop. As has already been remarked, however, much of this work adopts a more clear-cut stance with regard to subject-matter, coming very close at times to the polemical style of the political poster. Among British and American Pop artists perhaps only Colin Self, in his frequent allusions to nuclear annihilation, or Hamilton – for example in his *Kent State* screenprint of 1970 or in the more recent reference in *The Citizen* (1982–83) to the conflict in Northern Ireland – have so unequivocally stated a political position. Whether such work by Europeans can be referred to as a new category of political Pop, or whether Pop, as a 'cool' style, remains in any sense a suitable term for such hot passions, remains a moot point. In making so plain their subjectivity they have in a sense transgressed one of the essential features of Pop, that of its dispassionate ambiguity. This is not a value judgement, simply an observation of the ways in which artists such as these directed the formal language of Pop to very different ends.

Just why is it that Pop, after three decades, retains so much of its youthful exuberance and vibrant appeal? On the most immediate level, it remains as accessible as ever to the general public whose terms of reference it shares. It is alluring and glamorous, yet we can recognise in it many of the circumstances that inform our daily lives, as seen in our possessions and through the pervasive presence of the mass media. It communicates through humour and in ordinary voices, without pandering to us and without suggesting that one area of culture is superior to others simply because it is labelled 'art'. The directness and immediacy of its forms of representation, together with the unapologetic decorative appeal of its strong formal sense and often brash range of colours, are stimulating and sometimes electric in their effect. Pop revels in the modernity of the culture from which it arises and delights in the still shocking effect of its own contemporaneity. If it slips occasionally into nostalgia, it is not from a desire to retrieve a golden past that never existed except in fantasy, but from an affection for the origins of our synthetic modern world with all its imperfections.

fig 10 **Mario Schifano** Exterior Detail 1962 (Location unknown)

Pop would not have had such a long shelf life, however, simply if it were a joy for the spectator to behold, or for that matter only because it had such support in the market-place, though its linked critical and commercial success is certainly another factor that should be taken into account. Nor has it continued to attract new converts and to hold the attention of its original exponents merely by opening up huge new areas of subject-matter. The possibilities thus suggested, however, for a representational art that acknowledges both the formal force of abstraction and its crisis of content, without retreating into an anti-modernist stance, have been essential to the very survival of modern art.

Pop has lasted above all because of its radical redefinition of the attributes of the work of art. While free to make reference to a great variety of themes and images, to adopt at will the disguise of virtually any style and to make use of almost any technique or medium imaginable, from the most hand-made to the most mechanistic, the practitioners of Pop have continued to contribute to a debate concerning the most pressing philosophical issues facing artists today. In response to modernism's emphasis on originality as an end in itself, they have proposed numerous ways in which artists can absolve themselves of the need to invent anything – their styles, techniques or imagery – yet still produce something that is new and marked by a distinct identity. They have shunned the cult of the artist as a heroic isolated individual, preferring to declare their sense of oneness with their society by eliminating the evidence of their own personalities and by appealing to the lowest common denominators of taste; yet in doing so, they have paradoxically produced as many variants of Pop as there are adherents to the movement. Finally, in assaulting conventions of taste by subjecting their own sensibility to that of their sources, they have in turn modified our own perceptions and created an indelible record of the spirit of our time.

pop art's pharmacies
kitsch, consumerist objects and signs

SARAT MAHARAJ

Poison and cure in one dose? Derrida stages the startling idea of the 'pharmakon' as both a lethal and remedial drug. We face an 'undecidable' – a force shuttling between opposites, seeming to be both at once.[1] We may take this as a metaphor of Pop Art's gear-switching modes and shifting stances. Would it serve to concentrate on Pop Art's more radical ambivalences rather than the overwhelming tendency to read it in terms of strict, reductive oppositions, as either truth-drug or the opiate of mass culture, as critical purge or kitsch palliative?

The dead-ends of an either/or approach, its steely divisions and separations, were unsettlingly dramatised and probed in Eduardo Paolozzi's *Kitsch Cabinet* (1970), an 'installation' made for his 1971 Tate retrospective (fig. 1). On the one hand, it seemed little more than a jam-packed display of vulgar knick-knacks from the vast Krazy Kat Archive he had built up steadily since the 1940s. On the other, individual pieces in the Cabinet were marked out as different, singled out as works of art, inventoried as such in the catalogue.[2] Snow White, Bugs Bunny, Batman – figurines from the ever-expanding archive of consumerist objects, bric-à-brac of the amusement industry – are surmounted on a mirrored bathroom wall cabinet. He entitles this ready-made *Three American Heroes* (1971), a tongue-in-cheek comment on kitsch war memorials and monuments. But the innocent figures also speak as an image of earnest, all-American patriotism, as part of an icon of harmless fun and fantasy and its flip side, which in the period often meant the grim realities of American involvement in Vietnam. In the 1970s the *Kitsch Cabinet* 'undecidables' might have seemed controversial, easy to shrug off as a devil-may-care extravaganza at Pop Art's tail-end. But what was consigned to its fringes came to be played centre stage with a vengeance towards the 1990s, especially by Jeff Koons and Haim Steinbach. Koons's *Pink Panther* (1988) or *Ushering in Banality* (1988; fig. 2) flaunt their excessive display of slick craftsmanship even as they insist on presenting themselves as works of art. Another example of this double-stance is Steinbach's *Untitled (shoes with braces, wooden boots)* (1987; fig. 3), which places the everyday commodity on a pedestal/shelf, an ambiguous space where it might be looked at both as itself and as something aspiring to the condition of the art object.

The Pop Art indeterminate refuses to relinquish its flagrantly non-fine art look but at the same time it thus holds up the possibility of being read exclusively as fine art object. In dragging its feet over which genre it belongs to, in deferring decision about its identity, it seems at one with the high Modernist ready-made and its 'hesitations'. Duchamp's *Large Glass* (1915–23), subtitled

fig 1 **Eduardo Paolozzi** Kitsch Cabinet 1970 Installation for 1971 Tate Gallery retrospective, London

fig 2 **Jeff Koons** Ushering in Banality 1988 Courtesy Sonnabend Gallery, New York

1 J. Derrida, *Dissemination*, London, 1981, pp. 70–71; *Positions*, Chicago, 1981, pp. 42–4.
2 E. Paolozzi, 'Iconography of the Present', *The Times Literary Supplement*, 8 December 1972, pp. 1479–80; *Eduardo Paolozzi*, exhibition catalogue by F. Whitford, Tate Gallery, London, 1971.

fig 3 **Haim Steinbach** Untitled (shoes with braces, wooden boots) 1987 Collection of the Artist

fig 4 **Roy Lichtenstein** Art 1962 Locksley Shea Gallery, Minneapolis

a 'delay in Glass', signposts such a holding back. It seeks by every non-painterly ruse it is able to muster to put off for as long as possible the idea of being taken as traditional fine art statement.[3] However, Duchamp's 'snapshot inscribing' of the objet trouvé as a ready-made does point to something like the unveiling of a heightened, more conceptual experience. It involves a stripping bare of the bride-object's mundaneness, even if he makes this a deliberately fumbled and fraught affair. It is not unlike the Joycean linguistic ready-made, the epiphany: a vulgar phrase, a foul-mouthed expression evokes a split-second illumination, revealing exhilarating possibilities. Hamilton's *Epiphany* (1964; cat. 103) may hint at such a revelation by acknowledging its debt to Duchamp and Joyce. But it also puts it off until further notice. The badge's risqué colloquialism, 'Slip It To Me', its brash, exciting colour, mix of 'seedy joke shop tone' and sentimentality are calculated to engage our attention for their own sake.[4] Similarly, Warhol's *Brillo Boxes* – in showing themselves off as scandalously bare, brute, commodities – might be seen as a reversal of Duchamp's reciprocal ready-made, by which a painting by Rembrandt was to be used as an ironing board.

Such Pop Art objects might be considered lightweight, in that they recoil from gravity of theme or weighty meaning in their conspicuous mundaneness. But they do not altogether shake off a certain ponderousness, for they make heavy weather of the glamorous look increasingly assumed by everyday objects and, conversely, of the exaggerated identification of fine art objects with ordinary commodities. Their chameleon quality makes their weight and worth difficult to estimate and fix, thus bringing into question the methods or criteria by which artistic value and non-value are determined. Consequently they dramatise an inversion of generally accepted standards of taste, worth and sensibility.

The redemptive interpretation of Pop Art voiced by writers such as Umberto Eco, who claimed that 'in Pop Art kitsch is redeemed and elevated into a new state of esthetic dignity',[5] has tended to hold sway in the controversy as to the extent to which such art transforms its consumerist sources into true art statement rather than simply enjoying them.[6] Its either/or framework was defined by the period's formidable jargon of authenticity in a variety of local forms: in Britain, Leavisite criteria of the primacy of unsullied, lived experience; in the United States, a cult of pure expressivity with Abstract Expressionism's ascendancy;[7] in Europe, the predominance of existentialist, phenomenological perspectives and the quest for the authentic.[8] Whether 'authenticity' was meant in philosophical Heideggerian terms or in political Marcusian terms it entailed a reading of Pop Art either as a transvaluation of kitsch values or as utterly tainted by them.[9] If the early, Marcusian reception of Pop Art in Germany tended to see it as a drive towards a sphere of values which transcends the status quo, in England much the same critical perspective came to opposite conclusions.[10] Perhaps this again highlights Pop Art's double-coding and undecidable element, which resists totalising in a grand dialectical scheme. This tight-rope walk sets into motion an open-ended review of artistic values, definitions of art and object, orders of taste and pleasure.

Pop Art's images and signs speak volumes even as they are passed over to us without comment, with lips sealed. The word 'Art' emblazoned across the canvas in Lichtenstein's *Art* (1962) holds forth without pause about art's condition as advertising, as commodity, as sign standing in for the real thing (fig. 4). At the same time it seems to protest too much, falling silent as redundant lettering, as blank, transparent sign. If the textures and tensions of this double-movement were sensed by critical responses to Pop Art from

3 *The Writings of Marcel Duchamp*, ed. M. Sanouillet and E. Peterson, New York, 1989, pp. 22, 32.

4 *Richard Hamilton*, exhibition catalogue, Hanover Gallery, London, 1964.

5 U. Eco, 'Lowbrow Highbrow, Highbrow Lowbrow', *The Times Literary Supplement*, 8 October 1971, pp. 1209–11.

6 For a full documentation of the American side of this controversy see C. Mahsun, *Pop Art and The Critics*, Ann Arbor, 1987, pp. 41–61.

7 S. Foster, *The Critics of Abstract Expressionism*, Michigan, 1980, pp. 75–96; M. Kozloff, 'The Critical Reception of Abstract Expressionism', *Arts*, 40, 2, 1965, pp. 27–33.

8 J. Keller, 'De l'inauthentique à l'authentique', *Pop Art et Evidence du Quotidien*, Paris, 1979, pp. 153–6.

9 D. Kuspit, 'Pop Art: A Reactionary Realism', *Art Journal*, vol. 36 (1), 1976, pp. 31–8; H. Read, *The Origins of Form in Art*, London, 1965, pp. 174–87.

10 A. Huyssen, 'The Cultural Politics of Pop', *New German Critique*, 4, 1975, pp. 77–98; H. Read, op. cit., pp. 174–87; P. Fuller, *The Naked Artist*, 1983, pp. 118–24.

the outset,[11] the tendency has been to treat it either as talkative or as taciturn sign; to see in it either a flood of associations with the world-text of consumerism or a drying up of meanings in favour of a purely formalist pictorial syntax.[12] Our reading shuttles between these poles with Warhol's *Before and After* (1960), in which the raw, grainy state of the advertising image is mimicked in a minimal transformation that hovers between artwork and source (fig. 5). But it is inescapably about transformation, about re-designing the profile, bringing the nose in line with the norms of good looks, as was the case with a much earlier painting by Warhol, *The Broad Gave Me My Face, But I Can Pick My Own Nose* (*c.* 1948).

fig 5 **Andy Warhol** Before and After 1960 The Andy Warhol Foundation for the Visual Arts Inc., New York

Do Pop Art signs simply replay the scene of consumerist desire, or do they prise open a critical gap in it? Hamilton's *Just what is it that makes today's homes so different, so appealing?* (1956; cat. 99) draws us into a world of overspilling consumerist abundance, its promise of blissful gratification and well-being. We are borne along by the suggestive surfaces and textures, the glamorous look of things, glowing bodies, but not without a pang of awareness that the interior might be half-styled as a Vanitas, an allegory of the five senses, a cautionary tale of acquisitiveness, exhibitionism, surfeit. The collage composition suddenly seems both quite askew and too perfect to ring true. The seductive spell breaks: is it after all no more than an advertisement telling us that 'ordinary cleaners only reach this far'? But the scene's allure, its pleasures and thrills quickly close in. Prefiguring Pop Art's classic strategies, everything seems to be both endorsed and questioned. A similar process is suggested in Wesselmann's interiors, both inviting and unnerving in their luxurious excess, and in the realm of the vanities suggested by the verbal plays of Robert Indiana's work – 'Eat, Hug, Err, Love, Die' – in which a brisk and didactic moralising force is not easily untangled from an accepting, affirming play. Though Lichtenstein parodies consumerist representations, he feels for them too.[13]

Unlike satire, which confronts its targets from a superior position, Pop Art appears as a subversive force emanating from within the very consumerist myths and representations that it calls into question. As such it seems by turns doubting and credulous, ready to take things at face value, with a roundabout and yielding form of address. As with the 'persuasion techniques' of worldly-wise advertising, it invites our participation by giving us at least the illusion that we have the option of making up our own minds. In the more openly critical work produced in the 1960s and '70s by the Situationists the consumerist sign is pirated and made to speak against itself,[14] but in Pop Art the attitude is rarely so clear-cut. Since the 1970s, however, consumerist culture, with its systemic capacity to take over any representation, however oppositional, seems to have used Pop for its own ends. When a Gaulloise ad meticulously mimics Lichtenstein's cool style, is Pop Art caught in its own trap?[15]

As we look back from the 1990s, Pop Art strategy seems to be largely tied to a particular phase of consumerist culture out of which we now appear to be passing, that of sheer spectacle.[16] At any rate, a phase when it still seemed possible for the Pop Art gaze to read and cross-check the order of 'brute objects, things and goods' against the order in which they are displayed as commodities styled and pictured in terms of advertising myths and fantasies. Its gaze could wander and shift between objects and how they are dramatised in the consumerist space, as images and signs meant to excite needs and appetites in a drugstore theatre of desire.[17] We watch Pop Art watching this theatre of the commonplace object as aphrodisiacal commodity. We see the Independent Group looking at the way the motor car is styled in advertising

11 P. Selz, 'A Symposium on Pop Art', *Arts Magazine*, 37, April 1963, pp. 36–45.
12 For the classic texts on these positions see R. Rosenblum, 'Pop and Non-Pop Art', *Art and Literature*, 5, 1965, pp. 80–93; J. Russell and S. Gablik, *Pop Art Redefined*, London, 1969, pp. 6–9; New York 1974, *American Pop Art*, exhibition catalogue by L. Alloway, Whitney Museum of American Art, 1974, p. 7; see also D. Crane, *The Transformation of the Avant-garde*, Chicago, 1987, pp. 64–83.
13 *Roy Lichtenstein*, ed. J. Coplans, New York, 1972, pp. 52–3.
14 G. Debord and G. Wolman, 'Methods of Détournement', in K. Knabb, ed., *Situationist International Anthology*, Berkeley, 1981, p. 9.
15 J. Keller, op. cit., p. 156.
16 G. Debord, *Society of the Spectacle*, Detroit, 1970, Theses 1–22.
17 J. Baudrillard, *La Société de la consommation*, Paris, 1970, pp. 17–26.

idiom and imagery as 'vehicle of desire' (Banham), 'amorous object' (Barthes), as the 'mechanical bride object' or the 'Love-Goddess Assembly Line' (McLuhan). We watch its gaze scan commodity styling to see how the contours of a woman and the chassis of a motor car coalesce, how the woman/automobile association is constructed as 'dreamboat', a metaphor for an object of transporting delight.[18] It is this kind of advertising, which pictured and styled the motor car as 'orgasm in chrome',[19] that Hamilton plays off in *Hommage à Chrysler Corp* (1957; cat. 100) against a reworking of imagery borrowed from Duchamp's *Large Glass*. If the smudgy, smeary passages of paintwork mimic and decode fine art and demotic modes of representation they also evoke the fleshy, erotic world of the Bride's and Bachelors' search for satisfaction. Duchamp's reflections on the orgasmic cycle – promise, fulfilment, frustration – are set off against the way commodity styling dramatises much the same through the 'desirable look of things'.

This readable relationship between the order of the object and the order of its styling as commodity sign seems to become less clear by the 1980s. In the swirling, saturation effect of the media communication circuit, they seem to telescope more and more into each other. The everyday object, consumerist jargon, advertising idiom, Pop Art commentary all appear to mix and flatten into a seamless flow of images, as if they were all of the same order.[20] For evidence of this tendency we need only glance at how fashion advertising mimics and appropriates similar devices for constructing femininity in a knowing, tongue-in-cheek way. As the orders of consumerist representation close in on Pop Art by the 1990s, our attention shifts to its focus on waste, the excremental, precisely what consumerism – as a vast digestive, gustatory system – finds too disgusting to mention openly. Yet where there is consumption, there must be excretion. For consumerism, however, the spotlight remains on the former. It banishes the excremental from sight for fear it might disrupt its seductive spell. If the spoilsport is brought back into the arena of representation at all it is in the guise of something glamorous, eroticised, titillating – as part of the consumerist theatre of desire.

At the edge of Pop Art, Arman's installation 'Le Plein' (1960) and his *Poubelles* series (1960–71) present consumerism with its other face by putting on display collections of decomposing refuse and junk as if they were data on consumption habits of social groups and classes. From junk art of the 1950s, including Paolozzi's early 'metamorphoses of rubbish',[21] through to Pop Art's legacy – Tony Cragg, Bill Woodrow, Gilbert & George's scatological imagery – something of the unease about consumerist excess and its all-too-blinding splendour seems to be signposted, a focus on its litter, scrapheaps, its throwaway culture. *Soft Pink Landscape* (1971–72; cat. 106) belongs to a group of works in which Hamilton elaborates the excremental theme.[22] The piece centres on how Andrex toilet roll advertisements deal with 'the unmentionable'. It parodies their roundabout way of referring to basic bodily functions and needs, of never quite spelling them out. At any rate, it looks at how they displace as mundane a commodity as toilet tissue onto a plane of romantic reverie, making it part of a suggestive fantasy.

What the art world proper flings out, its leftovers, the 'excremental' world of mass culture gathers together under the blanket sign 'kitsch'.[23] With Pop Art it knocks on the door of the art world that has expelled it as improper excess, demanding to be included even as it stands apart by insisting on being no more than itself. The stance mirrors the medicine prescribed by Adorno: 'Kitsch is not the dregs and dross of art but a poisonous substance mixed in with it. How to discharge it is the difficult task today. . . . Kitsch may even be the true progress of art.'[24]

18 R. Banham, 'Vehicle of Desire', *Art*, no. 1, 1 September 1955; R. Barthes, 'The New Citroen', *Mythologies*, London, 1972, pp. 88–90; M. McLuhan, *The Mechanical Bride*, London, 1951, rev. 1967, pp. 84, 93–7; *Understanding Media*, London, 1967, pp. 217–25; R. Banham, *Man, Machine, Motion*, London, 1955, p. 14.

19 G. Gammage and S. Jones, 'Orgasm in Chrome: Rise and Fall of the Automobile Tail Fin', *Journal of Popular Culture*, VIII, no. 1, 1974.

20 U. Eco, op. cit., pp. 1209–11; J. Baudrillard, 'The Ecstasy of Communication', *Postmodern Culture*, ed. H. Foster, 1989, pp. 126–34; 'The Precession of Simulacra', *Art & Text*, 11, 1983, pp. 3–47.

21 'Metamorphosis of Rubbish – Mr Paolozzi Explains his Process', *The Times*, 2 May 1958; L. Alloway, 'Paolozzi and the Comedy of Waste', *Cimaise*, Paris, 1960, pp. 114–16.

22 For this group of works see *R. Hamilton – Studien 1937–77*, Kunsthalle, Bielefeld, Kunsthalle, Tubingen, Kunsthalle, Gottingen, 1978, pp. 189–219; see also R. Hamilton, *Collected Words*, London, 1982, p. 100.

23 U. Eco, op. cit., pp. 1209–11.

24 T. Adorno, *Aesthetic Theory*, London, 1984, pp. 339–40, 435.

american pop

2 american pop art a prologue

CONSTANCE W. GLENN

By British and French standards, the coalescence of Pop Art in America around 1960 was untidy. There was no 'club', as there had been during the Abstract Expressionist era, no manifesto paralleling that of Nouveau Réalisme, no generally accepted name for the phenomenon, and no neat list of proponents upon which the dealers, critics, collectors and curators could readily agree. The designation of shared attitudes and modes of expression that could assuredly be labelled 'Pop' was hasty in most instances and the artists were not necessarily anxious to share the title. In fact, most of those who later became the core disclaimed it at one point or another. However, by 1961, as Roy Lichtenstein, Andy Warhol, Tom Wesselmann, Jim Dine, James Rosenquist and Claes Oldenburg were more and more frequently singled out, it became apparent that two distinct strains of 'New Realism' or 'Neo-Dada' had been joined at the hip to comprise a twin-pronged American genre. Though all six artists were seeking ways to depersonalise their art, to strip it of Abstract Expressionism's grand gestures and hermeticism, they did not deliver the humanist or post-WPA[1] form of realism that had been predicted.

Lichtenstein and Warhol derived their imagery from the popular media, while Dine and Oldenburg applied painterly, expressionist techniques to material (subjects and objects) scavenged from the urban culture of Allan Kaprow's *Assemblage, Environments and Happenings.* Between the two camps Wesselmann and Rosenquist occupied less clear-cut territory, Wesselmann leaning towards the collage of commercially-printed and found elements, treating slick products of 1950s' advertising and street junk alike in an intentionally rough, even naive manner; Rosenquist favouring the gigantism of fractured billboard segments joined together by the luscious paint handling true to his sign-painter's skills. All trained and accomplished commercial artists in various arenas, they drew upon the new possibilities suggested by the work of Robert Rauschenberg and Jasper Johns, plus particular aspects of their low-art backgrounds, in order to find the high-art language which could be used to get on with the formal problems of making art. In general their earliest Pop work (1959–61) had a kind of ingenuous look that, in concert with a 'perverse' choice of imagery, such as washing machines (cat. 148), lurid fields of spaghetti (cat. 204) and green plaster shoes (cat. 159), seemed to flaunt bad taste and offer cause for vicious critical attack.

In terms of cohesion, 1961–63 were the decisive years. The artists began to recognise something of themselves in each other. They shared a modified interest in the return to a loosely-defined figurative art and the subject-matter associated with traditional themes – still-life, landscape and portraiture. Among the painters the emphasis was still on maintaining non-illusionistic, tightly-packed, edge-to-edge compositions characterised by an aggressive frontality

1 The Federal Arts Project/WPA (Works Progress Administration) was instituted by the United States Government in 1935–43 to assist artists who had been hit by the Depression and to deploy the artistic potential of the country in the decoration of public buildings and places.

and impenetrable flatness that forced the sense of movement forward into the viewers' space. In addition Oldenburg, George Segal, Wesselmann and Dine physically infiltrated that space through appendages, constructions and environments. Just as Johns had adopted red, white and blue from a dream, they too found reason to embrace severely limited, non-literal palettes (Lichtenstein: red, yellow and blue, plus black; Wesselmann: red, white and blue with khaki and yellow for accents; Oldenburg: the primary colours; Dine: grey mixed with more literal references). Rosenquist offered the most obvious exception, soon abandoning the early monochromatic schemes to explore the spectrum.

The question most often raised in criticism was the degree to which the artists, especially Lichtenstein and Warhol, transformed their appropriated subject-matter. It was seldom noted that transformation did occur, not by means of elaborate alteration of the images themselves, but as a result of their filtering through the highly individual choice of commercial processes. By 1962 Warhol's pictorial appropriations were accessible only through the repetitively squeegeed and smudged silkscreen; Lichtenstein's compositions were Benday-dotted, creating a unifying all-over surface pattern, achieved first by awkward hand, and then by stencil. Additionally, the sources for Lichtenstein's cartoons show how subtly and scrupulously he refined, repositioned, deleted, and heightened tension not found in his pulp sources.

At its most distant polarities art emphasises either the ornamental or the symbolic. By 1964, ornamentalism – characterised by stylistic quotation and/or a familiar pictorial language of curves, arabesques, circles and geometric forms – was a significant factor in full-blown Pop.[2] In its graphic clarity the work also nostalgically recalled the 1940s and '50s, especially in the advertising ephemera that gave it a come-hither look to its own generation, a media generation that never participated in the private, symbolic world of Abstract Expressionism, and whose environment Pop Art cannibalised. In its anti-theoretical, anti-analytical, anti-rhetorical stance that allowed the public in, it achieved its greatest popularity, often in spite of its formal brilliance.

Those who were classified as Pop artists were not that much at odds with contemporaries who sought to remake the old abstraction along the same anti-sensibility lines. When Frank Stella said, 'What you see is what you see', he spoke for the mood of the moment. It was, however, the ornamental aspect of Pop Art that separated it visibly, if not conceptually, from the early Minimalism of Stella, Donald Judd, Robert Morris, Dan Flavin and Carl Andre. Ordering Benjamin Moore flat wall paint in three arbitrary primary and secondary colours (as Stella did) is not particularly distant in concept from buying pre-printed billboard segments to use as collage materials (as Wesselmann did); but the look of the products was radically different. At its apogee (1964) Pop, however rigorous its formalism, became the most ornamental of American art forms: witness the arabesques that describe the hair and facial features of Lichtenstein's cartoon girls; the Matisse-inspired, succulent curves of Wesselmann's nudes; the classical tondos of both Wesselmann and Rosenquist; the curvaceous, sexy forms of Oldenburg's sculpture, from the breast-like soft light switches to the erect lipstick; the mosaic pattern of Wayne Thiebaud's deliciously-rendered gumballs; the movie-poster smile of Warhol's *Marilyn,* or his wallpaper-design parade of overly-bright blossoms. Of the core only Dine was a misfit. He would never abandon the expressionist surfaces (shared with Johns) and his art was too personal to partake of the ambiguity central to Pop. He found his images in his heritage, as did Segal, not in the mass media.

2 'Ornamentalism … provides a means of dealing in imagination with our culture, of filtering the monstrously contradictory facts of our existence … it is quite the opposite of what we call kitsch – [it may] recall historical styles or evoke nature, it may refer to folk art or to the human body; but it does so in a way that allows the audience to understand.' R. Jensen and P. Conway, *Ornamentalism,* New York, 1982, p. 19.

Originally seen as regional associates, expanding Pop Art from coast to coast, the southern Californians were, in that context, miscast as well. The popular culture to which Billy Al Bengston, Ed Ruscha and others made reference was the world of the Day-Glo Los Angeles landscape and the 'Finish Fetish': gas stations for hot cars and motorcycles, slicked up by the same sunny hues and light-reflective resins that occupied their counterparts in abstraction, such as John McCracken. Neither the straight appropriation of low-art sources nor the conceptual unification of a media-based visual language occupied them to any significant degree. They were aware of and influenced by Johns and Rauschenberg, but individually and collectively went on to develop an art that spoke first of California and then of their own experiences and agendas.

In 1968 *The New York Times* announced the death of Pop Art and, within months, a novel hallmark of the era disappeared as well: the Pop Art lifestyle that had flourished with it since about 1964. Warhol had set the tone during the Factory years in New York, followed by endless nightly appearances with his entourage at Max's Kansas City, and in 1966 by the début of 'The Silver Dream Factory Presents the Exploding Plastic Inevitable with Andy Warhol/The Velvet Underground/and Nico' at the Dom disco on St Mark's Place. The mood was 'party'. In lofts around Manhattan the various merits of the Beach Boys and the Beatles were hotly debated until the 'Motown Sound' drowned them out. *The New Yorker* magazine covered Pop-style parties in the real Kansas City; Courrèges boots and Pop-pattern Mondrian mini-dresses were rampant; Happenings migrated across the country to once-conservative museum bastions where locals lined up to take part. With an eye to Pop subject-matter, collections of American advertising ephemera, from Coke trays to Mickey Mouse, were assembled; the artists (Lichtenstein and Thiebaud among them) designed jewellery and dishes; hostesses set out Thiebaud displays of buffet food and papered their bathrooms with Warhol cows. It all jolted to a halt that week in June 1968 when Robert Kennedy was assassinated in Los Angeles (Tuesday, 4 June) and when Valerie Solanas marched into the Factory (Monday, 3 June) to fire the shots that put Andy Warhol on the front pages he might once have appropriated.

The Photo Realists quickly, if briefly, stepped into the void and the 'ex'-Pop artists, who had begun to go their individual ways as early as 1965, could at least be seen as discrete talents. Lichtenstein's work became initially more reductive, more economical of means, as he quoted from the areas of art history that engaged him intellectually. Abstract Expressionist *Brushstrokes* (cat. 153), *Greek Temples, Entablatures* (cat. 155), Art Deco sculpture, followed by School of Paris explorations and complex recombinations of his own earlier themes, all reflected the widening scope of interests that he continued to introduce through the language of commercial reproduction that remained *his* vernacular. Warhol, too, retained his trademark technology to single out increasingly banal subject-matter, including the ubiquitous society portrait and the parallel money symbols (cat. 247). While Lichtenstein's work of the 1960s and early 1970s signalled ongoing refinement, Warhol reverted to the brushiness of expressionism that, in effect, sweetened the images (cat. 248). Wesselmann took the nudes and still-lifes he had gleaned from the School of Paris into the realm of hard-edge, free-standing sculpture, and later into cut-steel drawings (cat. 254). Oldenburg's monuments began to people the landscape, becoming popular architecture in place of Pop Art. Rosenquist's paintings never lost their billboard scale, but by the late 1970s he had abandoned his Cubist-fragmented style for a hot, sharp-laced Floridian combination of flora and female that took him far from Times Square. Significantly Lichtenstein, Warhol, Wesselmann and Oldenburg never entirely abandoned the non-literal, metaphorical palettes ('yellow for hair') that characterised their early work, nor the idioms that informed their signature styles and became inseparable from their identities.

At the close of the 1960s it seemed there would be no second generation to stake out territory within the confines of ambiguity, high ornamentalism, common vernacular or appropriation. One seldom acknowledged bridge lay in architecture. In 1964 Philip Johnson, who not only championed Pop Art from the beginning but also internalised its possibilities, commissioned large outdoor works on an architectural scale for the New York World Fair. Then in 1966 Robert Venturi, reacting to Mies van der Rohe's dictum 'Less is more', proposed 'Less is a bore' in the course of inventing a post-modernist architectural vernacular derived in part from the vulgarity of Las Vegas and its gaudy commercialism. Venturi's brand of Pop post-modernism was soon followed by the equally controversial gains of Charles Moore, Frank Gehry[3] and a whole succession of architects who matured in the late 1970s, in time to give both name and continuity to a period that intervened between the first Pop artists and those who now constitute a second-generation-once-removed, a generation whose ascension through Conceptual Art and the post-modernist era was no more predictable than the original explosion of Pop Art itself.

3 'I think of myself as a realist. In my work I'm saying, "This is the real world – this is what it is, this is what it looks like." It's more interesting to work with it than pretend it doesn't exist. Trying to cover up your surroundings is like trying to catch all the water that comes over Niagara Falls in a glass. It's just not possible.' Frank Gehry, in interview with Scott Gutterman, *Journal of Art*, April 1991.

2 american pop art
inventing the myth

CONSTANCE W. GLENN

Spring 1963. Jim Dine is 27; James Rosenquist 29; Tom Wesselmann 32; Andy Warhol and Claes Oldenburg 34; and Roy Lichtenstein 39. By acclamation, confirmed by the frequency of their appearance in a chain of decisive exhibitions, these 'New Vulgarians' have become the most notorious practitioners of a new art form variously labelled 'Neo-Dada', 'New Realism', 'Neo-Surrealism', 'Common Object Painting', and, most consistently, 'Pop Art'.[1]

In New York, Washington, Kansas City and Houston museums are simultaneously delivering the message that this barely three-year-old phenomenon is not merely grist for New York intellectuals, who largely disdain the style and cling to more apparently serious modes of abstraction, but a genuinely accessible art wrenched from the stuff of our everyday surroundings and quite possibly destined for our suburban living rooms.

How did it all happen so quickly? Did these artists emerge from the heartland, unknown to each other, as legend would have it? Was Pop Art, by any definition, truly popular outside an exclusive circle of dealers, collectors and curators? And why, by 1964, was the pure phase over, almost as quickly as it had begun?

The stage was irrevocably set by the mid-1950s. From the far-reaching coverage of *Life* magazine and its counterparts to the household arrival of magical pictures on a bulbous electronic tube; from the relative ease of world-wide travel to college studies supported by the G.I. Bill; from economic euphoria to plentiful products flaunted via hyper-inventive, four-colour advertising, the end of World War II and the ensuing complacency of the early Eisenhower era bracketed a decade (1945–55) that spawned a new breed of artist and an expanded art audience. The war had set into motion a series of circumstances that shifted the focus of the art world from the School of Paris to the School of New York. A fresh generation of stolid, middle-class, American-born young men went to college, served in the military (but not on the battlefields), travelled abroad, and received formal training in both commercial and fine art. Of them, a small group, all in their 20s and 30s, invented a vernacular that brought them fame as the frontline Pop Art stars.

How different their group portrait is from that of the first-generation Abstract Expressionists: typically born in Europe; closely associated with the influential expatriate artists exiled in New York during World War II; seldom college graduates or academic affiliates; pessimistic, volatile, battle and Depression survivors with a mission to create an American art; often denied monetary success or even solo exhibitions until they were well into their 40s; outsiders all of their lives. The gap between the two generations was so vast that the

1 B. Rose, 'The New Realists, Neo-Dada, Le nouveau réalisme, Pop Art, The New Vulgarians, Common Object Painting, Know-nothing genre', *Art International*, VII 1, 25 January 1963, pp. 22–8.

breakthrough years of the 1950s were years of fermentation and linkage, a linkage absolutely dominated by the gains of Robert Rauschenberg and Jasper Johns.

The issue at hand was succinctly defined by Rauschenberg: 'I don't want a picture to look like something it isn't. I want it to look like something it is. And I think a picture is more like the real world when it is made out of the real world.'[2] Rauschenberg was the conduit for the aesthetic role of chance and indeterminacy fostered by John Cage at Black Mountain College in North Carolina,[3] while Allan Kaprow, at Rutgers University, was the pivotal figure in the emergence of the Environments and Happenings that produced a theatrical, ephemeral brand of 'junk' art.[4] 'If this rich "stew"', as George Segal called it, 'had any common denominator it was a non-hierarchical attitude toward the possible subject matter of art and a real love of the city: the city junk and refuse, the city materials, the city cacophony, the city symbols. The new generation, in one form or another, took these as their media.'[5] They also saw in Johns's flat, emblematic targets and flags (cat. 120, 121), and Rauschenberg's messy, permissive 'combines' (cat. 189) the opportunity to evade the hegemony of de Kooning in particular and the Abstract Expressionists in general, by introducing elements of the 'real world' and real-life experiences into their art. Tom Wesselmann spoke for more than one art student of the 1950s when he said that he felt suffocated by the power of de Kooning, 'who had already done all my art'.[6]

fig 1 **Roy Lichtenstein** Washington Crossing the Delaware II *c*1951 (Location unknown)

During the symposium on Pop Art held at the Museum of Modern Art in New York on 13 December 1962, Henry Geldzahler recounted what, by then, had become the accepted scenario:

> *About a year and a half ago I saw the work of Wesselman* [sic], *Warhol, Rosenquist and Lichtenstein in their studios [about July 1961]. They were working independently, unaware of each other, but with a common source of imagery. Within a year and a half they have had shows, been dubbed a movement, and we are here discussing them at a symposium. This is instant art history, art history made so aware of itself that it leaps to get ahead of art.*[7]

Geldzahler, along with, most importantly, Ivan Karp and Richard Bellamy, *was* influential in bringing the nascent Pop artists to the attention of future dealers and early collectors, but the story of isolation was and is popular fiction. Of what can be called the core group, most were known to each other, and all were active on the New York scene, both together and individually throughout the latter half of the 1950s.

Warhol was the first to arrive in New York, fresh out of the Carnegie Institute of Technology in Pittsburgh, in 1949 (with his classmate Philip Pearlstein). He quickly became one of the city's most successful illustrators and his drawings were shown regularly, even at the Museum of Modern Art in 1956 ('Recent Drawings'). He was acutely aware of both Johns and Rauschenberg by 1958 and wanted nothing so much as the success and acclaim they received in the 'real' art world of the new Leo Castelli Gallery.[8] Although he did not live in New York until 1963, Lichtenstein, a veteran with a Master's degree from Ohio State University and training in engineering drawing, had his first one-man show there in 1951 and exhibited his abstract/realist 'American History' and 'Far West' paintings as early as 1952 (fig. 1).[9] If anyone was isolated from day-to-day exchange he was, yet after a decade of exhibitions in New York Lichtenstein was a seasoned artist by the time he turned to Pop imagery in 1960 under the influence of Allan Kaprow and the Rutgers circle.[10] Next, in 1955, came Rosenquist from Minnesota. Having shown prodigious talent as a

2 C. Tomkins, *The Bride and the Bachelors*, New York, 1976, pp. 193–4.
3 Rauschenberg first arrived at Black Mountain College in 1948 and was there sporadically until 1952. During that time Josef Albers was head of the Fine Arts Department; John Cage and Jack Tworkov were among the faculty.
4 Kaprow was the central figure in the 'New Brunswick School', an informal group of students and faculty (including Kaprow, Segal, Samaras, Whitman, Watts and Brecht) at Rutgers, the State University of New Jersey at New Brunswick, where Lichtenstein joined the faculty of Douglass College in 1960.
5 Long Beach 1977, *George Segal: Pastels, 1957–1965*, exhibition catalogue by C. Glenn, The Art Galleries, California State University, Long Beach, 1977, p. 3.
6 Long Beach 1974, *Tom Wesselmann: The Early Years, Collages, 1959–1962*, exhibition catalogue by C. Glenn, The Art Galleries, California State University, Long Beach, 1974, unpaginated.
7 'A Symposium on Pop Art', *Arts Magazine*, April 1963, special supplement, p. 37.
8 V. Bockris, *The Life and Death of Andy Warhol*, New York, 1989, pp. 92–3.
9 For documentation of Lichtenstein's pre-Pop work see E. Busche, *Roy Lichtenstein Das Fruhwerk 1942–1960*, Berlin, 1988.
10 'The most immediate influences [1960–63] on my work were Allan Kaprow . . . and associates of his in happenings. Obviously, comic strips themselves were an influence, but the license to refer to them so directly came from work being done then by Kaprow, Oldenburg, Dine, Whitman, Rauschenberg and company.' Roy Lichtenstein in B. Diamonstein, *Inside New York's Art World*, New York, 1979, p. 212.

billboard painter he received a scholarship to the Art Students League and in the same year met Robert Indiana and Lee Bontecou. By 1957 he had also become acquainted with Johns, Rauschenberg and Ellsworth Kelly; and in 1959 he attended drawing classes, organised by Robert Indiana and Jack Youngerman, with Oldenburg and Henry Pearson. After attending Yale and the Art Institute of Chicago, and briefly working as a magazine illustrator, Oldenburg had moved to New York in 1956 and was working in the library at Cooper Union. In the same year Wesselmann (BA, Psychology, University of Cincinnati) received a scholarship to Cooper Union in order to develop the skills he needed to become a cartoonist, an ambition he developed during a dull stint of national service at Fort Riley, Kansas, during the Korean War. The youngest of the group, and the last on the scene, was Jim Dine, who landed in New York in 1958 after studying at the University of Cincinnati, the Boston Museum School and Ohio University in Athens.

fig 2 **Tom Wesselmann** Portrait Collage g 1959
Michael D. Abrams

1958 was a significant year. Two one-man shows, for Johns and then for Rauschenberg (at the Castelli Gallery), galvanised the young artists. Wesselmann and Dine (and their friend Marcus Ratliff) founded the Judson Gallery, where they soon included Oldenburg.[11] The three were initially quite close, and Dine and Oldenburg (with Lucas Samaras) regularly shared in aspects of the Happenings they conceived and presented at gallery co-ops. All three created rough, found-material 'junk' art and collages (fig. 2) indebted to Kaprow and to Rauschenberg, while Warhol eyed the iconic imagery of Johns with affection and envy.[12] It is indeed true that Warhol, in 1960, and Lichtenstein, in 1961, made large works derived from comic strip sources, each without knowledge of the other (cat. 236, 147). Ivan Karp saw Lichtenstein's work first and recommended him to Castelli. When he also put forward Warhol, Castelli decided the gallery could not exhibit both artists because of the similarity he perceived in their paintings. In dismay Warhol turned from cartoons and created the series of Campbell's Soup Cans shown in his first one-man Pop Art exhibition, which was presented by Irving Blum at the Ferus Gallery in Los Angeles, but not until July 1962.[13]

The clearest way of charting the meteoric rise of American Pop Art and its classic period from 1961 to 1964 is to examine a series of twelve crucial exhibitions conceived by a variety of individuals and presented across the entire country, from New York to California. Ten exhibitions form the core; a 1960 prologue stands as a prophetic introduction; a final exhibition confirms the international reputation of Pop Art in 1964. These are the shows that 'selected' the six artists – Warhol, Lichtenstein, Rosenquist, Dine, Oldenburg and Wesselmann – whose names became synonymous with the purest form of Pop. The artists might disagree with the categorisation but it stands nevertheless.

It is worth saying at this stage that the success of the ten 'High Pop' shows owed a great deal to the contribution of Ivan Karp of the Castelli Gallery and Richard Bellamy of the Green Gallery. These two individuals defined Pop Art by the work they made available, the studios where they arranged visits, the collectors they guided and pressed for loans, and the artists they championed. This is not to ignore singularly important contributions made by Leo Castelli, Alan Solomon, Lawrence Alloway, Eleanor Ward, Irving Blum, Henry Geldzahler, Virginia Dwan, John Weber, John Coplans and many others; it simply acknowledges that the history was incalculably influenced by the formidable team of Karp and Bellamy.

The Martha Jackson Gallery, where both men had worked and where John Weber became director in 1960–62, had presented the exhibition that signalled

11 *Tom Wesselmann: The Early Years*, op. cit.
12 *The Life and Death of Andy Warhol*, op. cit., pp. 92–3.
13 Ibid., pp. 105–6.

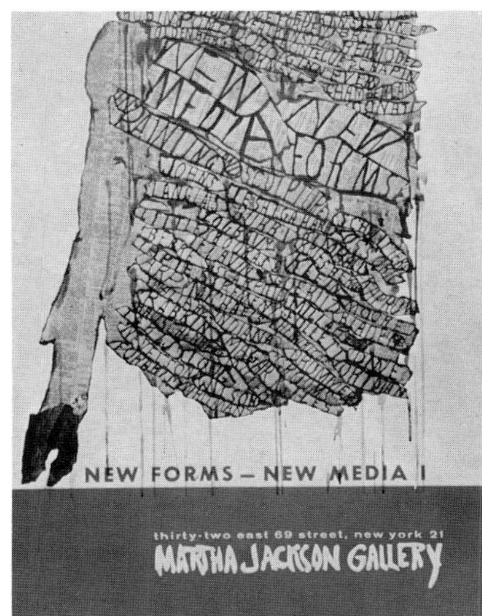

fig 3 **Claes Oldenburg** catalogue cover for 'New Forms–New Media I' at the Martha Jackson Gallery, New York 1960

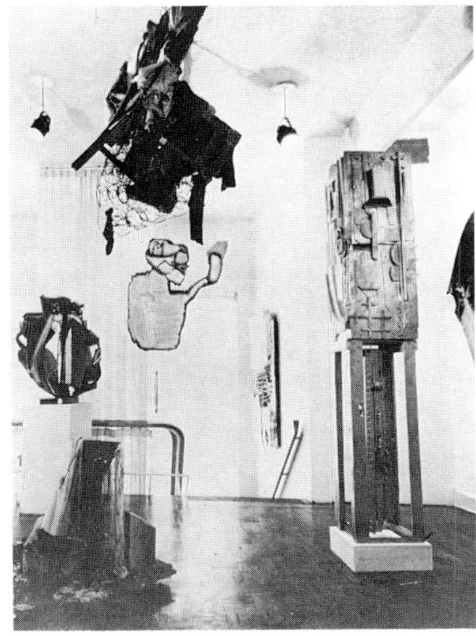

fig 4 Installation view of 'New Forms–New Media I' at the Martha Jackson Gallery, New York 1960

that a different New York art was at hand. It was titled 'New Forms–New Media' (first version, 6–24 June 1960; second version, 27 September–22 October 1960; catalogue with cover by Oldenburg [fig. 3]).[14] *The New York Times* critic John Canaday called it

> *... wild and wacky ... a kind of cherry on top of the banana split [end of the art season] ... The show is primarily neo-Dada or neo-Surrealist, according to which definition you apply to objects of morbid wit that are either intentionally senseless and anti-art (neo-Dada) or translatable into Freudian terms to make their own kind of bizarre sense .... [It] includes a lot of unabashed junk.*[15]

The two events at the Martha Jackson Gallery featured some 70 artists and the street-junk mode was the most assertive but by no means the only theme (fig. 4). Dine, Oldenburg, Johns and Rauschenberg were included; but so were such diverse talents as Hans Arp, Alexander Calder, Joseph Cornell, Jean Dubuffet, Dan Flavin, Red Grooms, Indiana, Louise Nevelson, Takis, Tàpies and Robert Whitman. In the catalogue Alloway, then still living in England and closely associated with the Independent Group, drew parallels between 'New York Junk Culture' and Dada/Futurism, describing 'the city' as their common source. He noted that 'We read the junk as traces of a life like our own ... The objects have an anonymous intimacy with our own lives.'[16] In the second catalogue essay Kaprow identified 'rawness and immediacy', as well as an 'indifference to the "beauty" of craftsmanship-like arrangement as characteristically common to work preoccupied with "the changeable" as its raison d'être ... Space is no longer pictorial', he said, 'but actual (and sometimes both), and sound, odors, artificial light, movement and time are now utilized ... We ought to begin to realize ... that there is no fundamental reason why a work of art should be a fixed object to be placed in a locked case.'[17]

In this context Rauschenberg was represented by *Odalisque,* composed of 'post, two pillows, box construction with collage and paint', from the collection of Leo Castelli; Johns by *Target,* also from Castelli's collection; Dine by a 'Chair with bedsprings, brightly colored fabric and unwoven cotton, freely used as original materials', priced at $300; and Oldenburg by *Mug,* an 'object drawing of corrugated board, cut, torn, nailed and strung together', available at $250.

After the big, ungainly adventure that was 'New Forms–New Media', things must have appeared, in large part, to have returned to normal; yet behind the scenes lines were being drawn, positions and galleries solidified, exhibitions planned and masterworks of the period created. In 1961 Lichtenstein painted his first cartoon canvases, *Look, Mickey* and *Popeye* (cat. 147), as well as a series of single-object 'dumb' household images, such as *Washing Machine* (cat. 148); and he joined the Leo Castelli Gallery, where Castelli himself had not only previously rejected Warhol but now passed over Rosenquist on the same grounds. Various advocates, including Karp and Geldzahler, were pursuing a dealer for Warhol and their efforts resulted in one-man shows in both California and New York (Eleanor Ward's Stable Gallery) in 1962, the same year that *Big Campbell's Soup Can (19 ¢)* (cat. 238), *Do It Yourself* (cat. 239), and *Fox Trot* were shown at the Sidney Janis Gallery, New York. In 1961 Bellamy was in the process of forming the Green Gallery, backed by the collector Robert C. Scull, and he offered shows to Rosenquist, Oldenburg and Wesselmann, who joined the gallery and were first seen there in solo shows in 1962. Rosenquist's *I Love You with My Ford* (cat. 204), which starred in three of the major Pop exhibitions, was completed in the same year. Dine and Oldenburg were actively involved in Happenings presented at the Judson and Reuben Galleries and even on Segal's chicken farm in

14 The confusion over the title of the exhibition was due to the fact that 'New Forms–New Media I' was printed on the catalogue cover and title page, but in the introduction and in the gallery press release Martha Jackson called it 'New Media–New Forms'.

15 J. Canaday, 'Art: A Wild, but Curious, End-of-Season Treat', *The New York Times,* 7 June 1960, p. 32:5.

16 New York 1960, *New Forms–New Media I,* exhibition catalogue by L. Alloway and A. Kaprow, foreword by M. Jackson, Martha Jackson Gallery, New York, 1960, unpaginated.

17 Ibid.

suburban New Jersey, while Dine himself was preparing for a 1962 exhibition at the Martha Jackson Gallery.

The positioning, the preparations, even the work emerging from the studios might have gone unnoticed in a pre-war America, but as Geldzahler was to note:

> *There is now a community of collectors, critics, art dealers and museum people, a rather large community, that has been educated and rehearsed to the point that there is no longer any shock in art. For the first time in this century there is a class of American collectors that patronizes its advanced artists. The American artist has an audience, and there exists a machinery ... to keep things moving and keep people on their toes.*[18]

Although early converts would argue that 'a rather large community' consisted of perhaps no more than 250–300 individuals who were intimately involved, by the autumn of 1962 museums and galleries were ready to showcase Pop Art from coast to coast.

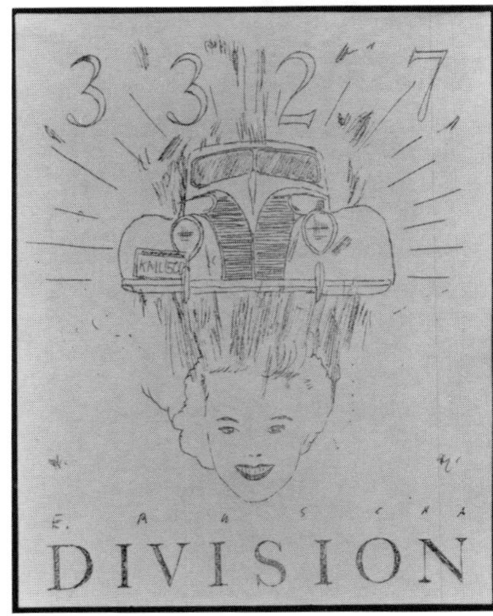

fig 5 **Ed Ruscha** Division 1962 mimeographed line drawing for 'The New Painting of Common Objects'

On 25 September 1962 'The New Painting of Common Objects' opened at the Pasadena Museum of Art in California (25 September–19 October). The exhibition was assembled by the newly appointed curator, Walter Hopps, previously a founder, with Edward Kienholz, of the Ferus Gallery in Los Angeles. Hopps's viewpoint was bicoastal and the show as eccentric as the curator himself. The artists included Dine, Robert Dowd, Joe Goode, Philip Hefferton, Lichtenstein, Ed Ruscha, Wayne Thiebaud and Warhol – southern Californians, northern Californians and artists labelled New Yorkers – each represented by three works. Instead of a catalogue there was a checklist accompanied by quirky, mimeographed line drawings by Ruscha (fig. 5), Goode, Dowd, Hefferton and Dine. Needing a poster, Hopps found a printer in the Yellow Pages and ordered a straightforward announcement over the telephone. Major works were included in the show, the majority of which had already entered private collections. Thiebaud's *Five Hot Dogs* (cat. 226) already belonged to its present owner; pioneering Los Angeles collectors such as Mr and Mrs Melvin Hirsch, Dr and Mrs Leonard Asher and Mr and Mrs Donald Factor lent works by Warhol and Lichtenstein. Other lenders included Irving Blum and the Ferus Gallery, which Blum now owned, and where he had already shown Warhol. But the prescience of these local collectors did not impress the local critic Henry Seldis, who observed: 'The overall impression of the exhibition does not so much point up the absurdity of some of the common objects literally depicted as the absurdity of those who would have us take these pictures seriously ...'[19] Yet in the same article Seldis reviewed a Llyn Foulkes exhibition at the same museum in rapturous language. Foulkes was, and still is, exhibited within the context of Pop Art.

Less than two weeks after the Pasadena exhibition closed, the Sidney Janis Gallery mounted 'The New Realists' (1 November–1 December 1962), the first exhibition to propose an international viewpoint. In addition to Dine, Indiana, Lichtenstein, Oldenburg, Rosenquist, Thiebaud, Warhol and Wesselmann, the selection included Arman, Enrico Baj, Peter Blake, Christo, Oyvind Falhström, Peter Phillips, Martial Raysse, Mimmo Rotella, George Segal and Jean Tinguely, among 29 artists. Warhol's works, mentioned above, were surrounded by Oldenburg's *The Stove* (1962), from the collection of Robert C. and Ethel Scull; Lichtenstein's *Blam* (cat. 149), lent by Richard Brown Baker; Dine's *Five Feet of Colorful Tools* (1962), then from the collection of Mr and Mrs Leon Mnuchin; Rosenquist's *I Love You with My Ford* (1961) and *Silver Skies* (1962); Thiebaud's *Salads Sandwiches and Desserts* (1962); and

18 'Symposium on Pop Art', op. cit., p. 37.

19 H. Seldis, 'Avant-Garde Theme Not Convincing', *Los Angeles Times*, 5 October 1962, Part IV, p. 5.

fig 6 Installation view of 'The New Realists' at the Sidney Janis Gallery, New York 1962

Wesselmann's *Still Life #17* and *Still Life #19* (both 1962). This exhibition of 54 works was so large that it spilled over into a second space at 19 West 57th Street (fig. 6). In the catalogue, with an introduction by Pierre Restany, Janis reiterated the urban theme: 'City-bred, the New Realist is a kind of urban folk artist . . . He is attracted to abundant everyday ideas and facts which he gathers . . . from the street, the store counter, the amusement arcade or the home.' He remarked upon the two traditions represented – one in which the 'common object becomes the common subject', and the other in which work is 'colored by other qualities in mass media. The billboard, magazine, comic strip, daily newspaper' – and he called the artists 'Factualists'.[20] *The New York Times* critic Brian O'Doherty thought the 'target [was] mass banality', but he alluded to 'an undercurrent of seriousness' in the cases of Thiebaud, Warhol, Wesselmann and especially Segal. 'Pop . . . art is a definite trend, a possible movement. At the moment, most of it fails under the heading of clever – very clever – journalism', he concluded.[21] 'With this show, "pop" art is officially here.'[22]

Pop's next important exhibition was at the Dwan Gallery in Los Angeles; it was memorably entitled 'My Country 'Tis of Thee' (18 November–15 December 1962), curated by Virginia Dwan and John Weber (who had moved to California in 1962), with a catalogue by Gerald Nordland. Virginia Dwan had been the first to show Rauschenberg in Los Angeles (1961); she had brought Yves Klein (1961), Arman (1962) and other French artists associated with Nouveau Réalisme, to Los Angeles, and, with Blum's Ferus Gallery, she introduced Pop Art to the area. She and Weber selected John Chamberlain, Charles Frazier, Indiana, Johns, Kienholz, Lichtenstein, Marisol, Oldenburg, Larry Rivers, Rauschenberg, Rosenquist, Warhol and Wesselmann, presenting not only the progenitors but also an increasingly tight-knit circle of younger artists that was achieving a consensus status.

Less than a year after 'My Country 'Tis of Thee', Weber loaded works by Rosenquist, Rivers, Lichtenstein and others, into a panel truck and set out to visit collectors in New Mexico, Texas, Missouri and beyond. In his catalogue essay Nordland had asked:

> *Why do our artists reserve special consideration for the nation's flag or presidents, hamburgers or movie queens? Are these subjects more worthy than others? I think not . . . these subjects are turned to not for the purpose of honoring them but in order to illustrate that anything can provide legitimate subject matter for the creative genius of the painter and sculptor.*[23]

His reverie was prompted by, among other works, Oldenburg's *Plaster Cup* (1962); Rauschenberg's 1961 'combine' *Co-existence*; Rivers's *Cedar Bar Menu* (1962); Rosenquist's *Hey, Let's Go for a Ride,* (1961; cat. 203); Warhol's *Marilyn Monroe* (1961); Wesselmann's *Great American Nude #10* (1961); Jasper Johns's *Flag on Orange Field* (1957); and Lichtenstein's *Takka Takka* (1962).

Back in New York Lawrence Alloway, transplanted in 1961 from England, curated the first major museum show, 'Six Painters and the Object', at the Solomon R. Guggenheim Museum (14 March–12 June 1963). Dine, Johns, Lichtenstein, Rauschenberg, Rosenquist and Warhol ('all born between 1923 and 1933') comprised Alloway's selection because they had 'in common . . . the use of objects drawn from the communications network and the physical environment of the city.'[24] Alloway's catalogue essay remains an early landmark, and his exhibition, replete with today's acknowledged masterworks, included: Johns's *Gray Flag, Target, White Numbers* and *0 Through 9*; Lichtenstein's stunning *Live Ammo* (1962), six panels presumably

20 New York 1962, *The International Exhibition of the New Realists,* exhibition catalogue by J. Ashbery, P. Restany and S. Janis, Sidney Janis Gallery, New York, 1962, unpaginated.

21 B. O'Doherty, '"Pop" Goes the New Art', *The New York Times,* 4 November 1962, p. 23:3.

22 B. O'Doherty, 'Exhibition at Sidney Janis Gallery', *The New York Times,* 31 October 1962, p. 41.

23 Los Angeles 1962, *My Country 'Tis of Thee,* exhibition catalogue by G. Nordland, Dwan Gallery, Los Angeles, 1962, unpaginated.

24 New York 1963, *Six Painters and the Object,* exhibition catalogue by L. Alloway, The Solomon R. Guggenheim Museum, New York, 1963, unpaginated.

never shown together since; Rosenquist's *Woman I* (1962); and Warhol's *Dick Tracy* (1960) and *200 Soup Cans* (1962). Already recognised as pre-Pop masters, Johns and Rauschenberg dominated only half of the exhibitions under consideration, but their presence was palpable in all. Reviewing the show, Stuart Preston of *The New York Times* proposed that Pop Art's

> *... weakness – preventing it from being truly popular – lies in the fact that its most gifted practitioners are of necessity sophisticated. It is a said* [sic] *irony that its public will also be a sophisticated one, comprising just the very persons searching for an amusing novelty who not so long ago were delighted by such esthetic absurdities such as white-on-white non-objective paintings ... The deep, dark secret of Pop art is that it is anti-popular with a vengeance.*[25]

On 18 April 1963 the focus shifted to the Washington Gallery of Modern Art in Washington, DC, for Alan Solomon's 'The Popular Image Exhibition' organised with Alice Denney (fig. 7). A brilliant scholar and highly engaging writer, Solomon curated exhibitions around the world and continued to write perceptively about Pop Art until his untimely death in 1970. In this first exhibition he presented Vern Blosum, George Brecht, Dine, Johns, Lichtenstein, Oldenburg, Rauschenberg, Rosenquist, Warhol, Robert Watts, John Wesley and Wesselmann. The combination was idiosyncratic, close to the Karp and Castelli view, and included two maverick artists (Brecht and Watts) who became more closely associated with Fluxus than with Pop Art. 'To put it as simply as possible', Solomon said,

fig 7 **Jim Dine** catalogue cover for 'The Popular Image' at The Washington Gallery of Modern Art, Washington, DC 1963

> *... the new artists have brought their own sensibilities and their deepest feelings to bear on a range of distasteful, stupid, vulgar, assertive and ugly manifestations of the worst side of our society ... They have done so not in a spirit of contempt or social criticism or self-conscious snobbery, but out of an affirmative and unqualified commitment to the present circumstance and to a fantastic new wonderland, or, more properly, Disneyland, which asserts the conscious triumph of man's inner resources of feeling over the material rational world, to a degree perhaps not possible since the middle ages.*[26]

Given the opportunity to see 56 works, most of lasting quality, a Washington paper blared, 'Modern Art Pop Show Is Strictly Dullsville',[27] while another critic hunted valiantly for precedents, beginning with the idea of the Madonna in secular Renaissance clothing, and then proceeding through a short course in art history, finally naming the genre 'neo-Ashcan'.[28]

Simultaneously, at the Nelson Gallery–Atkins Museum in Kansas City, 'Popular Art' was under way (28 April–26 May 1963) in the Sales and Rental Gallery of the Friends of Art. It was the project of Susan C. Buckwater, one of the earliest serious Pop collectors, and the museum curator Ralph T. (Ted) Coe. A number of works from the Buckwater collection are in the Nelson-Atkins Museum today. Her Lichtenstein, *The Kiss,* was acquired by Coe after her death, and remained in his collection for two decades. Beyond Coe's intelligent, graceful essay, the catalogue includes the original sales prices: Warhol's *Merce* cost $2,100; Lichtenstein's *Girl with Piano,* $1,800; and Oldenburg's *U.S. Flag,* $625. The exhibition included works by Dine, Miles Jensen, Lichtenstein, Oldenburg, Rosenquist, Thiebaud, Warhol and Wesselmann. Karp played a significant role in 'Popular Art'. He remarked at the opening that he was 'shocked by one of Kansas City's largest billboards which shows a woman chased by a monster rat', but on the other hand, said that 'the picture of Borden's cottage cheese was very well done and would not be [an] unlikely [subject for] a Pop Art construction.'[29] Karp took to Kansas City and Kansas City collectors took to Karp and Pop Art. As a result of 'Popular Art' Thiebaud's

25 S. Preston, 'On Display: All-Out Series of Pop Art', *The New York Times,* 21 March 1963, p. 8:2.

26 Washington, DC 1963, *The Popular Image Exhibition,* exhibition catalogue by A. Solomon, Washington Gallery of Modern Art, Washington, DC, 1963, unpaginated.

27 F. Geitlin, 'Modern Art Pop Show Is Strictly Dullsville', *Washington Star,* 21 April 1963.

28 L. Aklander, 'Washington Gallery Shows Pop Art', *The Washington Post,* 21 April 1963, p. G6.

29 G. Shane, 'Artists Save Various Bits of Buildings', *Des Moines Register Tribune,* 29 April 1963.

Jawbreaker Machine of 1963 (cat. 228) was among a number of works acquired by Jack and Connie Glenn, who at the age of 29 were the youngest of the early collectors.

'Pop! Goes the Easel', the third show held that month, took place in Houston at the Contemporary Arts Museum (from 3 April 1963) and, like the Kansas City exhibition, featured Dine, Lichtenstein, Rosenquist, Thiebaud, Warhol and Wesselmann. The addition of Vern Blosum, Konrad Klapheck, Mara McAfee, Mel Ramos, Tinguely and Idelle Weber, again reflected artists of special interest to Karp and Castelli. The catalogue essay by Douglas MacAgy concluded with the thought that 'When the present mode of Pop Art plays out, it will be due to the emergence of artists from the cover. Their voluntary hitch in the public's prefabricated service will have expired. Signs of their exodus are already appearing. On the other hand, the viewer who continues to prefer commercials to the program will go right on receiving them from the point of origin.'[30] Among the works shown were: Lichtenstein's *Girl with Beach Ball* (1961), *Brattata* (1962) and *Head-Red and Yellow* (1962) from the Albright-Knox Art Gallery, erroneously listed as *Head of Girl* (1963); Dine's *Two Panel Black Bathroom* (1962); Rosenquist's *Halved Apricots* (1962); Thiebaud's *Gumball Machine* (1962); six Warhol *Campbell's Soup Cans*; and Wesselmann's *Great American Nude #42* (1962). Ann Holmes of the *Houston Chronicle* observed that MacAgy's catalogue was

> *... such a thicket of gimmick phrases and plays upon words that the message scarcely comes through. But no matter. Pop Art speaks blatantly for itself ... even though the soup can [for example] reflects no artist's point of view, the very absence of an angle on the can or a surrealistic juxtaposition is an act of control and a powerful statement of banality. This is, in art, comparable to the stream of everyday dialogues used in modern plays to point up the vacousness* [sic] *of some modern life ... a curious show, and one which gives us renewed sensitivity to our surroundings – just when we'd learned to blot them out.*[31]

After the Houston show Alloway's 'Six Painters and the Object' travelled to the Los Angeles County Museum of Art (7 July–25 August 1963) with an extra section entitled 'Six More'. The six artists added (to develop a West Coast perspective) were Billy Al Bengston, Goode, Hefferton, Ramos, Ruscha and Thiebaud, a selection closely mirroring the earlier Pasadena show arranged by Hopps. The doyen of Los Angeles critics, Arthur Millier, more accustomed to serene California landscape painting, wrote a scathing review, finding 'a glimmer of discovery' only in Thiebaud's work,[32] while Virginia Laddey of the Long Beach *Independent-Press Telegram* focused on the jousting of curator Alloway and Peter Selz, then working at the Museum of Modern Art in New York: 'Selz tore into "Pop" art ... [as] non-art which is merely a garish, accepting reproduction of the banality of the world structured by Madison Avenue and the producers of comic strips ... Alloway rebutted ... with an attack on Selz and his standards, implying that he and these were bourgeois and on the whole rather passé.'[33] A local syndicated columnist summed up the event, noting 'Viewer reaction ranged from bewilderment to ridicule to amusement.'[34] Significantly, the critics did not acknowledge the fact that the exhibition was sponsored by the museum's recently formed Contemporary Art Council (one of the first such groups in the country), which included prominent local collectors. Among its members Frederick Weisman (and Marcia Weisman), Mrs Stanley Freeman, Mrs Leonard Asher, Donald Factor, and Mrs Melvin Hirsch were all actively collecting Pop Art before the exhibition.

From Los Angeles, West Coast attention turned north to the Bay Area and 'Pop Art USA' at the Oakland Art Museum (7–29 September 1963). Curated

30 MacAgy quoted in C. Geeslin, 'Art: About the pop people', *The Houston Post*, 7 April 1963.

31 A. Holmes, 'o pop, poor pop, macagy's hung you in the museum', *Houston Chronicle*, 14 April 1963, p. 9.

32 A. Millier, 'Pop Art? He'll Take Billboards', *Los Angeles Herald Examiner*, 4 August 1963.

33 V. Laddey, 'Controversial Pop Art at L.A. Museum', Long Beach *Independent-Press Telegram*, 28 July 1963, p. W11.

34 'County Museum to Show Two "Pop" Art Exhibits', nine community newspapers, from the archives of the Los Angeles County Museum of Art.

by John Coplans, a founder and later Editor-at-large of *Artforum*, 'Pop Art USA' featured one work each by 48 artists. Dine, Lichtenstein, Oldenburg, Rauschenberg, Rosenquist, Thiebaud, Warhol and Wesselmann made appearances, but so did almost every tangentially related New York figure, as well as the California contingent. More unusual inclusions were Jess Collins, Ray Johnson, Richard Pettibone, Peter Saul, Ernest Trova and less closely related artists such as William Copley, Stuart Davis and Gerald Murphy. In the catalogue Coplans was first to note the 'series of important museum exhibitions within the last year' and suggested that

> *Pop Art reveals a complete shift of emphasis in both geographical location and subject matter. The first body of work that has emerged from this new movement is widely dispersed between the two coasts – this simultaneous eruption is an important factor neglected by all the organizers of previous exhibitions, with the exception of Pasadena's 'New Painting of Common Objects' . . . The curious phenomenon, particularly in these times of easy communication, of a group of artists widely separated geographically, who, without knowing, for the most part, of the existence of the others, appear at roughly the same time with images startlingly different from those which dominated American painting for two decades . . . points to the workings of a logic within the problems of American painting itself rather than to the logic of dealers and pressure groups.*[35]

In retrospect it is hard to find fault with Coplans's concept of a new 'logic', but also hard to find in favour of the isolation theory, or of the equality of regional work. Jess's *The Tricky Cad* (1959), Johns's *Flashlight* (1958), Warhol's *Coca Cola* (1962) and Thiebaud's *Jawbreaker Machine* were among the works in the Oakland exhibition. Local press, in what was by now a familiar vein, observed that the show was a vast survey of the 'phenomenon which has exploded on both coasts from its early beginnings with Stuart Davis's dazzling expression of the American city . . . to current works by the most publicized and lesser-known adherents . . . Let's hope some of our truly creative artists are immune or survive this destructive "art" to build upon it and profit from its frightening significance.'[36]

The ninth of the key exhibitions, 'The Popular Image' (24 October–23 November 1963), was held not in the United States, but at the Institute of Contemporary Arts in London; it was important because it took Alan Solomon's viewpoint abroad. Solomon exported many of the same artists he had shown in Washington (Dine, Johns, Lichtenstein, Oldenburg, Rauschenberg, Rosenquist, Wesley, Wesselmann and Warhol) but he deleted Blosum, Brecht, and Watts in favour of Allan D'Arcangelo, Indiana, Ramos and Thiebaud, in effect moving away from work that now seemed less persuasively Pop and giving a nod to the West Coast. Johns's *Flag above White* of 1954 (cat. 120) and Wesley's *Olympic Field Hockey Officials* of 1962 (cat. 250) were presumably in this exhibition; however, as the catalogue did not include a list of works it is uncertain. In it Solomon's essay brought up an issue that critics have only recently begun to address seriously:

> *There has been a tendency to focus on the work of the artists . . . who use popular images (Lichtenstein, Warhol, Rosenquist, Wesselman* [sic], *etc.) without respect to the merit of their paintings, because the presence of the comic strips, soupcan labels and billboards titillates and is easy to accommodate on a superficial level. The fact that these images are 'fun' . . . has little to do with . . . the precarious balance between gross ugliness and exquisite beauty . . . which the public at large has not really been prepared to face.*[37]

The final American show in 1963, and the last of the core of ten, was a rollicking

35 Oakland 1963, *Pop Art USA*, exhibition catalogue by J. Coplans, Oakland Art Museum, Oakland, 1963, unpaginated.

36 M. Cross, 'Whatever "Pop Art" Is, You Cannot Ignore It', *Oakland Tribune*, 22 September 1963, p. 5 EL.

37 London 1963, *The Popular Image*, exhibition catalogue by A. Solomon, Institute of Contemporary Arts, London, 1963, unpaginated.

round-up at the Albright-Knox Gallery in Buffalo, New York, 'Mixed Media and Pop Art' (19 November–15 December). The totality was as eclectic as 'New Forms–New Media' had been in 1960, and more than 60 artists of every conceivable persuasion were judged appropriate to the double bill. The quintessential Pop Art material came from the museum's own collection, which had been acquired at an early date through the combined efforts of patron Seymour H. Knox, and the director, Gordon M. Smith. They were early on the scene, as the excellence of the collection testifies. The Albright-Knox was, in fact, a lender to many of the regional exhibitions of the period. Some of the artists travelled to Buffalo for the opening and most were quoted liberally in the *Buffalo Evening News.* Their reception was enthusiastic and press articles pointed with pride to the significant numbers of the works from Buffalo itself, a far cry from the sniping common in other cities and obviously due to local familiarity with the material. The year closed on a high note: only one more season remained before the central artists abandoned what they viewed as a contrived association and went off to pursue their own interests and personal visions.

The final exhibition, the postscript, stands for summation, broad consensus and the end of a magical period when American Pop Art seemed neatly definable and readily accessible. The show was 'Amerikansk pop-kunst', selected by K. G. Hulten for the Moderna Museet in Stockholm (29 February–12 April 1964). It included the artists of the consensus (Dine, Lichtenstein, Oldenburg, Rosenquist, Warhol and Wesselmann) as well as Segal. Of the ten core exhibitions, Lichtenstein and Warhol had appeared in all, Dine and Rosenquist in nine, Wesselmann in eight, and Oldenburg in seven. With one exception, all other artists fell below the 50% line.[38] The anomalies were Thiebaud (seen in eight), and Segal (in three). From the beginning Thiebaud's work was set aside and valued for formal qualities and luscious paint handling that had little or nothing to do with Pop Art *per se.* Thus his career came to be consciously viewed outside the traditional Pop milieu, despite his frequent participation. In the case of Segal, a humanist sculptor who was always closely associated with early Pop Art, there is the assumption that the difficulty of transporting his three-dimensional environments mitigated against his inclusion in many of the first venues, while his later work, like Dine's, has occupied the area of figurative expressionism.

The years of these 'lost' exhibitions – rebellious, sometimes profound spectacles – were the years that served to quantify American Pop Art. Predictably, there was a 'hurry of thought which attends the first perusal ... [when] the true characters of the style [were] little distinguished; the ... perfections and defects ... wrapped up in ... confusion'.[39] The distance of 30 years, and the magnitude of the careers in the interim, leave only the apologists wrapped in confusion.

38 Johns and Rauschenberg, not included in the core, appeared in six of the ten exhibitions.

39 D. Hume, 'Of the Standard of Taste', *Art Issues,* No. 14, November 1990, p. 25.

pop art in america
an anthology of sources

A Symposium on Pop Art

The Museum of Modern Art, New York, 13 December 1962, printed in *Arts Magazine*, 37, April 1963, pp. 37–9, 41–2.

Henry Geldzahler

... it seems that the phenomenon of pop art was inevitable. The popular press, especially and most typically *Life* Magazine, the movie close-up, black and white, technicolor and wide screen, the billboard extravaganzas, and finally the introduction, through television, of this blatant appeal to our eye into the home – all this has made available to our society, and thus to the artist, an imagery so pervasive, persistent and compulsive that it had to be noticed.

...

Both Clement Greenberg and Harold Rosenberg have written that increasingly in the twentieth century, art has carried on a dialogue with itself, art leads to art, and with internal sequence. This is true still, even with the external references pop art makes to the observed world.

...

Pop art is a new two-dimensional landscape painting, the artist responding specifically to his visual environment. The artist is looking around again and painting what he sees.

...

We live in an urban society, ceaselessly exposed to mass media. Our primary visual data are for the most part secondhand. Is it not then logical that art be made out of what we see? Has it not been true in the past?

...

The great body of imagery from which the pop artists draw may be said to be a common body, but the style and decisions of each are unmistakable. The choice of color, composition, the brush stroke, the hardness of edge, all these are personal no matter how close to anonymity the artist may aspire in his desire to emulate the material of his inspiration, the anonymous mass media. The pop artists remain individual, recognizable and separate. The new art draws on everyday objects and images. They are isolated from their ordinary context, and typified and intensified. What we are left with is a heightened awareness of the object and image, *and* of the context from which they have been ripped, that is, our environment. If we look for attitudes of approval or disapproval of our culture in this art, of satire or glorification of our society, we are oversimplifying.

...

Pop art is immediately contemporary. We have not yet assimilated its new visual content and style ... the point is too to realize that pop art did not fall from the heavens fully developed. It is an expression of contemporary sensibility aware of contemporary environment and growing naturally out of the art of the recent past.

Hilton Kramer

Pop art derives its small, feeble victories from the juxtaposition of two clichés: a cliché of form superimposed on a cliché of image. And it is its failure to do anything more than this that makes it so beguiling to talk about and write about – that makes pop art the conversation piece *par excellence* – for it requires talk to complete itself. Only talk can effect the act of imaginative synthesis which the art itself fails to effect.

...

Pop art carries out a moderately successful charade – but a charade only – of the two kinds of significance we are particularly suckers for at the present moment: the Real and the Historical. Pop art seems to be about the real world, yet it appears to its audience to be sanctified by tradition, the tradition of Dada. Which is to say, it makes itself dependent upon something outside art for its expressive meaning, and at the same time makes itself dependent upon the myths of art history for his aesthetic integrity. In my opinion, both appeals are fraudulent.

But pop art does, of course, have its connections with art history. Behind its pretensions looms the legendary presence of the most overrated figure in modern art: Mr Marcel Duchamp. It is Duchamp's celebrated silence, his disavowal, his abandonment of art, which has here – in pop art – been invaded, colonized and exploited. For this was never a real silence. Among the majority of men who produced no art, and experienced little or none, Duchamp's disavowal was devoid of all meaning ... it is only in the context of a school of painting which has radically deprived art of significant visual events that pop art has a meaning.

...

Pop art does not tell us what it feels like to be living through the present moment of civilization – it is merely part of the evidence of that civilization. Its social effect is simply to reconcile us to a world of commodities, banalities and vulgarities – which is to say, an effect indistinguishable from advertising art. This is a reconciliation that must – now more than ever – be refused, if art – and life itself – is to be defended against the dishonesties of contrived public symbols and pretentious commerce.

Dore Ashton

... here is the crux of the matter: the contemporary artist, weary and perplexed by the ambiguities of idealism (as in Abstract Expressionism, for instance) decides to banish metaphor. Metaphor is necessarily a complicating device, one which insists on the play of more than one element in order to effect an image. The pop artist wants no such elaborate and oblique obligation. He is engaged in an elementary game of naming things – one at a time.

Perhaps the movement can be seen as an exacerbated reaction to the Romantic movement, so long ascendant in modern art history, in which artists were prepared to endure an existence among things that have no name.

...

The attitude of the pop artist is diffident. He doesn't aspire to interpret or re-present, but only to present. He very often cedes his authority to chance – either as he produces his object, or as it is exposed to the audience which is expected to complete his process. The recent pop artist is the first artist in history to let the world into his creative compound without protest.

In the emphasis on randomness and chance, on the virtual object divested of associations, on the audience as participant, and in his rebellion against metaphor, the pop artist generally begs the question of reality. He refuses to take the responsibility of his choices.

...

To the extent that interest in objects and their assemblage in non-metaphorical terms signifies a reduction of individual choices, pop art is a significant sociological phenomenon, a mirror of our society. To the extent that it shuns metaphor, or any deep analysis of complex relations, it is an impoverished genre and an imperfect instrument of art.

...

I can see the movement as cathartic – art protecting itself from art. But catharsis is by no means an adequate response to the conundrum of contemporary life.

Stanley Kunitz

How does one explain the overnight apotheosis not of a single lonely artist but of a whole regiment wearing the colors of pop art, for whom the galleries and the museums immediately open their doors, and the collectors their pocketbooks? The best analogy I can think of is a blitz campaign in advertising, the object of which is to saturate the market with the name and presence – even the subliminal presence – of a commodity. 'Repetition is reputation,' said one of the great tycoons of American industry. The real artists in this affair, I submit, are the promoters, who have made a new kind of assemblage out of the assorted and not necessarily related works of dozens of painters and sculptors, to which they have given the collective title (substitute brand-name) 'pop art,' or the 'new realism.'

...

The world of pop art is a clean, well-lighted place where we can see a deliberately tidy arrangement of the most anonymous traces of collective man, persented to us as though they were things in themselves, now that they have been detached from our Western karma, the cycle of manufacture and consumption. The pop artist assiduously refrains from divulging his feelings while he is setting up his store. Perhaps he has had a hard day at the supermarket which is our world, but he is as reticent about his private responses as a newscaster on a network station. Perhaps he is saying that it is futile to attempt a new creation, given the facts of our situation, but we can only guess at that. All that we know is that he has limited himself to a rearrangement of familiar counters ... This is an art not of transformation but of transposition.

...

Pop art rejects the impulse towards communion; most of its signs and slogans and stratagems come straight out of the citadel of bourgeois society, the communications stronghold where the images and desires of mass man are produced, usually in plastic.

Condemning an aesthetic of process, the pop artist proposes to purify the muddied stream of art by displaying objects in isolation, the banal items of our day refurbished, made real, by their separation from the continuum. What a quixotic enterprise! Even a seventh-grade science textbook informs us that objects are the least solid of our certainties.

Richard Artschwager

Jan McDevitt, 'The Object: Still Life. Interviews with the New Object Makers. Richard Artschwager and Claes Oldenburg, on Craftsmanship, Art, and Function', *Craft Horizons*, 25, September–October 1965, p. 31.

... I'm making objects for non-use: by use, I mean cups to drink out of, a spoon to stir with. By killing off the use part, non-use aspects are allowed living space, breathing space. Things in a still life painting can have monumentality – and I don't think their monumentality has been lessened because their edibility or other use has been either taken away or not put into them. Instead, its focus is on other things.

And what is this?

It's a table with a tablecloth. There are a lot of wisecracks made about it – 'Well, you never have to send that to the laundry,' and so on, but it's called 'Table with Tablecloth,' and it's about the way a table with a tablecloth is in a painting, in a still life – a three-dimensional still life.

...

From the days when you were making useful furniture, how did you come to this notion?

... I started doing some work for a Catholic church. I made altars. I must have made thirty shipboard altars over about a year's time – portable altars with all kinds of brass fittings. I don't know if they did anything for me as far as ideas are concerned, but I was making something that, by definition, is more important than tables or chairs – that is, an object which celebrates something that is supposed to be more important than sitting down or eating or taking out garments or putting them away, which is what furniture does. The altars were good though. They opened up to show some words in Latin to help the priest remember the vital parts of the Mass – a sort of prompter arrangement. And beneath that there was a drawer and then a cabinet for vestments.

Allan D'Arcangelo

Allan D'Arcangelo: Paintings of the Early Sixties, exhibition catalogue preface, Neuberger Museum, State University of New York, Purchase, 1978.

The desire and need to imbue my work with content, my perceptions of the world I lived in, required other means: clarity and simplicity. I wanted to shorten the distance between meaning and metaphor. I had things to say about us and wanted to do this in the most direct way possible, while at the same time, divesting the work of references to art's immediate historical past in order to make the content more available and immediate. I looked for a visual language that would be broadly communicable, direct and clear and that was intimately part of my experience. I drew on a memory of 'real visualizations,' rather than 'art visualizations,' to find that common language. The particular look of these paintings comes from working in a way that was directly opposed to many of the sacred canons of expressionism, abstract or otherwise. They are without gesture, without brush stroke, without color modulation, without mysticism and without personal angst because these qualities would have obscured the intention of the paintings. The work is pretty much preconceived, and the execution is relatively mechanical. In this sense my art, as well as that of many other artists at that time, was being formed as part of a reaction to Abstract Expressionism.

Jim Dine

Interviews by G. R. Swenson, 'What is Pop Art?', part I, *ARTnews*, LXII, 7, November 1963, pp. 25, 61, 62.

What is your attitude to Pop Art?
I don't feel very pure in that respect. I don't deal exclusively with the popular image. I'm more concerned with it as a part of my landscape. I'm sure everyone has always been aware of that landscape, the artistic landscape, the artist's vocabulary, the artist's dictionary.

Does that apply to the Abstract-Expressionists?
I would think so – they have eyes, don't they? I think it's the same landscape only interpreted through another generation's eyes. I don't believe there was a sharp break and this is replacing Abstract-Expressionism. I believe this is the natural course of things. I don't think it is exclusive or that the best painting is being done as a movement . . . Pop Art is only one facet of my work. More than popular images I'm interested in personal images, in making paintings about my studio, my experience as a painter, about painting itself, about color charts, the palette, about elements of the realistic landscape – but used differently.

The content of a Pollock or a de Kooning is concerned with paint, paint quality, color. Does this tie you to them in theory?
I tie myself to Abstract-Expressionism like fathers and sons. As for your question, no. No, I'm talking about paint, paint quality, color charts and those things objectively, as objects. I work with the vocabulary that I've picked up along the way, the vocabulary of paint application, but also the vocabulary of images. One doesn't have to be so strict – to say, 'Let's make it like a palette,' and that's it . . . It always felt right to use objects, to talk about that familiarity in the paintings, even before I started painting them, to recognize billboards, the beauty of that stuff. It's not a unique idea – Walker Evans photographed them in 1929. It's just that the landscape around you starts closing in and you've got to stand up to it.

Your paintings look out and still make a statement about art?
Yes, but a statement about art the way someone else talks about new Detroit cars, objectively, as another kind of thing, a subject.

Not as both subject matter and content?
No.

Abstract-Expressionism tended to look in?
Yes.

Is this the difference between your work and theirs?
I don't know what the difference is. Certainly Abstract-Expressionism influenced me, particularly Motherwell. I think he's continually growing and making problems. His paintings meant a lot to me, especially *Pancho Villa Dead or Alive* and the *Je t'aime* paintings, although it now seems a bit strange to write it in French. Still, the climate Motherwell has to live in is rarer and he has to do that for his style, the idea of style, this hothouse flower – but really that's all frivolities compared to the real structures he sets up.

Style as a conscious striving for individuality?
I suppose so. I'm only interested in style, as content at least, if it makes the picture work. That's a terrible trap – for people to want to *have style*. If you've got style, that means you've only got one way to go, I figure; but if you've got art, if you've got it in your hands going for you, style is only an element you need to use every once in a while. The thing that really pulls a painting out is you, if you are strong, if it's your idea you're wanting to say – then there's no need to worry about style.

Do you feel related to Dada?
Not so much, although I never saw any reason to laugh at that stuff. It seemed the most natural thing in the world to have that fur-lined teacup.

It wasn't anti-art?

No, not at all. I thought it was just a beautiful object; it wasn't anti-art at all. Some of my friends used to say I was square because I was interested in art. Jan van Eyck and Rogier van der Weyden are great favorites of mine. I'm interested in the particular way they manipulate space. With Northern painting there's more than just seeing it ... And I love the eccentricity of Edward Hopper, the way he puts skies in. For me he's more exciting than Magritte as a Surrealist. He is also like a Pop artist – gas stations and Sunday mornings and rundown streets, without making it Social Realism ... it seems to me that those who like Hopper would be involved with Pop somehow. Or those who like Arthur Dove – those paintings of sounds, fog horns, the circle ideas that were meant to be other things. There's a real awareness of things, an outward awareness ...

Actually I'm interested in the problem and not in solutions. I think there are certain Pop artists who are interested mainly in solutions. I paint about the problems of how to make a picture work, the problems of seeing, of making people aware without handing it to them on a silver platter. The viewer goes to it and is held back slightly from being able to get the whole picture; he has to work a little to deal with the problems – old artistic problems, that particular mystery that goes on in painting.

You once said that your audience tends to concentrate too much on the subject matter in your work.

They can't get past it? Well, that's their tough luck. I was talking about the big audience. The smaller audience gets through it and lives with it and deals with it, just like things coming up all day – in a shooting gallery, you know, things keep popping up to shoot at. And some guys can't shoot, that's all; they can only stand there with a gun in their hands. I'm interested in shooting and knocking them all down – seeing everything ... But the statement about bridging the gap between art and life is, I think, a very nice metaphor or image, if that's what you'd call it, but I don't believe it. Everybody's using it now. I think it misleads. It's like the magic step, like – 'Oh, that's beautiful, it bridges art and life.' Well, that's not so. If you can make it in life – and I don't say that's easy to do – then you can make it with art; but even then that's just like saying if you make it with life then you can make it as a race-car driver. That's assuming art and life can be the same thing, those two poles. I make art. Other people make other things. There's art and there's life. I think life comes to art but if the object is used, then people say the object is used to bridge that gap – it's crazy. The object is used to make art, just like paint is used to make art.

Does Pop Art serve a social function? Is it a comment?

There are only a handful of people who seem to understand what I'm doing, so I'm certainly not changing the world. People confuse this social business with Pop Art – that it's a comment. Well, if it's art, who cares if it's a comment. If you write some fantastically obscene thing on a wall, that may be an even better comment, but I'm not sure *that's* art. I'm involved with formal elements. You've got to be; I can't help it. But any work of art, if it's successful, is also going to be a comment on what it's about. I'm working on a series of palettes right now. I put down the palette first, then within that palette I can do anything – clouds can roll through it, people can walk over it, I can put a hammer in the middle of it ... Every time I do something, the whole thing becomes richer; it is another thing added to the landscape. But once I've done something, I'm no longer interested in it as a problem. It just becomes another facet of my work. I'm interested in striving to do something tougher.

Öyvind Fahlström

'Manipulating the World', *Art & Literature*, 3, 1964

In my variable pictures the emphasis on the 'character' or 'type' of an element is achieved materially by cutting out a silhouette in plastic and sheet iron. The type then becomes fixed and tangible, almost 'live' as an object, yet flat as a painting. Equipped with magnets, these cut-outs can be juxtaposed, superposed, inserted, suspended. They can slide along grooves, fold laterally through joints, and frontally through hinges. They also can be bent and riveted to permanent three-dimensional forms.

These elements, while materially fixed, achieve their character-identity only when they are put together; their character changes with each new arrangement. The arrangement grows out of a combination of the rules (the chance factor) and my intentions, and is shown in a 'score' or 'scenario' (in the form of a drawing, photographs or small paintings). The isolated elements are thus not paintings, but machinery to make paintings. Picture-organ.

The finished picture stands somewhere in the intersection of paintings, games (type Monopoly and war games) and puppet theater.

Just as the cut-out materializes the type, the factor of time in painting becomes meaningful through the many, in principle infinite, phases in which the elements will appear. As earlier, in my 'world' pictures such as 'Ade-Ledic-Nander' and 'Sitting ...' a form would be painted on ten different picture places on the canvas, now it may be arranged in ten different ways during a period of time.

The role of the spectator as a performer of the picture-game will become meaningful as soon as these works can be multiplied into a large number of replicas, so that anyone interested can have a picture machine in his home and 'manipulate the world' according to either his or my choices.

Joe Goode

Essay by Marilu Knode, *LA Pop in the Sixties*, exhibition catalogue, Newport Harbor Art Museum, Newport Beach, 1989.

Joe Goode was interested in giving a 'common experience,' and he used formal painting conventions for a pop engagement with the object. For Goode it was important to provoke his viewers into feeling something about themselves . . .

In 1967–68 Goode drew and painted series of unmade beds and of cups and spoons. The house portraits generated all the later common-object series, for in 'looking through' the banal exterior of an American dream home, Goode extracted isolated parts to represent the whole. His concern for the intimate voice of common objects provided new and different comprehensions of the daily environment, engendering a change in the mind of the viewer. The 'common experience' was facilitated by objects, not only in the reassurance inherent in the familiar, but also in our emotional reactions to objects that function as human stand-ins.

Robert Indiana

Interviews by G. R. Swenson, 'What is Pop Art?', part I, *ARTnews*, LXII, 7, November 1963, pp. 27, 63, 64.

What is Pop?
Pop is everything art hasn't been for the last two decades. It is basically a U-turn back to a representational visual communication, moving at a break-away speed in several sharp late models. It is an abrupt return to Father after an abstract 15-year exploration of the Womb. Pop is a re-enlistment in the world. It is shuck the Bomb. It is the American Dream, optimistic, generous and naïve . . .

It springs newborn out of a boredom with the finality and over-saturation of Abstract-Expressionism which, by its own esthetic logic, *is* the END of art, the glorious pinnacle of the long pyramidal creative process. Stifled by this rarefied atmosphere, some young painters turn back to some less exalted things like Coca-Cola, ice-cream sodas, big hamburgers, super-markets and 'EAT' signs. They are eye-hungry; they pop . . .

Pure Pop culls its techniques from all the present-day communicative processes: it is Wesselman's TV set and food ad, Warhol's newspaper and silkscreen, Lichtenstein's comics and Ben Day, it is my road signs. It is straight-to-the-point, severely blunt, with as little 'artistic' transformation and delectation as possible. The self-conscious brush stroke and the even more self-conscious drip are not central to its generation. Impasto is visual indigestion.

Are you Pop?
Pop is either hard-core or hard-edge. I am hard-edge Pop.

Will Pop bury Abstract-Expressionism?
No. If A-E dies, the abstractionists will bury themselves under the weight of their own success and acceptance; they are battlers and the battle is won; they are theoreticians and their theories are respected in the staidest institutions; they seem by nature to be teachers and inseminators and their students and followers are legion around the world; they are inundated by their own fecundity. They need birth control.

Will Pop replace Abstract-Expressionism?
In the eternal What-Is-New-in-American-Painting shows, yes; in the latest acquisitions of the avant-garde collectors, yes; in the American Home, no. Once the hurdle of its non-objectivity is overcome, A-E is prone to be as decorative as French Impressionism. There is a harshness and matter-of-factness to Pop that doesn't exactly make it the interior decorator's Indispensable Right Hand.

Is Pop here to stay?
Give it ten years perhaps; if it matches A-E's 15 or 20, it will be doing well in these accelerated days of mass-medium circulation. In twenty years it must face 1984.

Is Pop esthetic suicide?
Possibly for those Popsters who were once believing A-Eers, who abandoned the Temple for the street; since I was never an acolyte, no blood is lost. Obviously esthetic 'A' passes on and esthetic 'B' is born. Pity more that massive body of erudite criticism that falls prostrate in its verbiage.

Is Pop death?
Yes, death to smuggery and the Preconceived-Notion-of-What-Art-Is diehards. More to the heart of the question, yes, Pop does admit Death in inevitable dialogue as Art has not for some centuries; it is willing to face the reality of its own and life's mortality. Art is really alive only for its own time; that eternally-vital proposition is the bookman's delusion. Warhol's auto-death transfixes us; DIE is equal to EAT.

Is Pop easy art?
Yes, as opposed to one eminent critic's dictum that great art must necessarily be *difficult* art.

Pop is Instant Art . . . Its comprehension can be as immediate as a Crucifixion. Its appeal may be as broad as its range; it is the wide-screen of the Late Show. It is not the Latin of the hierarchy, it is vulgar.

Is Pop complacent?
Yes, to the extent that Pop is not burdened with that self-consciousness of A-E, which writhes tortuously in its anxiety over whether or not it has fulfilled Monet's Water-Lily-Quest-for-Absolute/Ambiguous-Form-of-Tomorrow theory; it walks young for the moment without the weight of four thousand years of art history on its shoulders, though the grey brains in high places are well arrayed and hot for the Kill.

Is Pop cynical?
Pop does tend to convey the artist's superb intuition that modern man, with his loss of identity, submersion in mass culture, beset by mass destruction, is man's greatest problem, and that Art, Pop or otherwise, hardly provides the Solution – some optimistic, glowing, harmonious, humanitarian, plastically perfect Lost Chord of Life.

Is Pop pre-sold?
Maybe so. It isn't the Popster's fault that the A-Eers fought and won the bloody Battle of the Public-Press-Pantheon; they did it superbly and now there *is* an art-accepting public and a body of collectors and institutions that are willing to take risks lest they make another Artistic-Oversight-of-the-Century. This situation is mutually advantageous and perilous alike to all painters, Popsters and non-Popsters. The new sign of the Art Scene is BEWARE – Thin Ice. Some sun-dazed Californians have already plunged recklessly through.

Is Pop the new morality?
Probably. It is libertine, free and easy with the old forms, contemptuous of its elders' rigid rules.

Is Pop love?
Pop is love in that it accepts all . . . all the meaner aspects of life, which, for various esthetic and moral considerations, other schools of painting have rejected or ignored. Everything is possible in Pop. Pop is still pro-art, but surely not art for art's sake. Nor is it any Neo-Dada anti-art manifestation: its participants are not intellectual, social and artistic malcontents with furrowed brows and fur-lined skulls.

Is Pop America?
Yes. America is very much at the core of every Pop work. British Pop, the first-born, came about due to the influence of America. The generating issue is *Americasm* [*sic*], that phenomenon that is sweeping every continent. French Pop is only slightly Frenchified; Asiatic Pop is sure to come (remember Hong Kong). The pattern will not be far from the Coke, the Car, the Hamburger, the Jukebox. It is the American Myth. For this is the best of all possible worlds.

Jess

A Tricky Cad by Jess Collins, in John Russell and Suzi Gablik, *Pop Art Redefined,* London, 1969, p. 61.

One surprisingly curmudgeony Fraternity Sunday in 1953 Tricky Cad scrambled out of Chester Gould's *Dick Tracy,* afterwards to concentrate (undertaking 8 cases) in demonstration of the hermetic critique lockt up in Art, here Popular. Also here was a bad case of sincerest-form-of-flattery; later, not amusing to the originator.

Given the journalistic-fact, no augmentations were made of text, image, line, punctuation, excepting the underlying addition of paste. Yes: cutting compressions, with scissors via maxmister. Mimetic method kept true to material within arbitrary units – by episode, by day, week, month, or full story. During the *tantric* process, correspondences came in a counterpoint of rhymes echoing events of the World, personal events, and predictions of the crime.

Art is somehow getting-to-the-heart-of-it-all. Tricky Cad detected that in every aesthetic-analyst is a lay-anaesthetist, *c* being the speed of light.

(Feb 69)

Jasper Johns

Interviews by G. R. Swenson, 'What is Pop Art?', part II, *ARTnews,* LXII, 10, February 1964, pp. 43, 66, 67.

What is Pop Art?
There has been an attempt to say that those classified under that term use images from the popular representations of things. Isn't that so?

Possibly. But people like Dine and Indiana – even you were included in the exhibitions . . .
I'm not a Pop artist! Once a term is set, everybody tries to relate anybody they can to it because there are so few terms in the art world. Labeling is a popular way of dealing with things.

Is there any term you object to?
I object to none any more. I used to object to each as it occurred.

It has been said that the new attitude toward painting is 'cool.' Is yours?
Cool or hot, one way seems just about as good as another. Whatever you're thinking or feeling, you're left with what you do; the painting is what you've done. Some painters, perhaps, rely on particular emotions. They attempt to establish certain emotional situations for themselves and that's the way they like to work.

I've taken different attitudes at different times. That allows different kinds of actions. In focusing your eye or your mind, if you focus in one way, your actions will tend to be of one nature; if you focus another way, they will be different. I prefer work that appears to come out of a changing focus – not just one relationship or even a number of them but constantly changing and shifting relationships to things in terms of focus. Often, however, one is very single-minded and pursues one particular point; often one is blind to the fact that there is another way to see what is there.

Are you aspiring to objectivity?
My paintings are not simply expressive gestures. Some of them I have thought of as facts, or at any rate there has been some attempt to say that a thing has a certain nature. Saying that, one hopes to avoid saying I feel this way about this thing; one says this thing is this thing, and one responds to what one thinks is so.

I am concerned with a thing's not being what it was, with its becoming something other than what it is, with any moment in which one identifies a thing precisely and with the slipping away of that moment, with at any moment seeing or saying and letting it go at that.

What would you consider the difference between subject matter and content, between what is depicted and what it means?
Meaning implies that something is happening; you can say meaning is determined by the use of the thing, the way an audience uses a painting once it is put in public. When you speak of what is depicted, I tend to think in terms of an intention. But the intention is usually with the artist. 'Subject matter'? Where would you focus to determine subject matter?

What a thing is. In your Device *paintings it would be the ruler.*
Why do you pick ruler rather than wood or varnish or any other element? What it is – subject matter, then – is simply determined by what you're willing to say it is. What it means is simply a question of what you're willing to let it do.

There is a great deal of intention in painting; it's rather unavoidable. But when a work is let out by the artist and said to be complete, the intention loosens. Then it's subject to all kinds of use and misuse and pun. Occasionally someone will see the work in a way that even changes its significance for the person who made it; the work is no longer 'intention,' but the thing being seen and someone responding to it. They will see it in a way that makes you think, that is a possible way of seeing it. Then you, as the artist, can enjoy it – that's possible – or you can lament it. If you like, you can try to express the intention more clearly in another work. But what is interesting is anyone having the experiences he has.

Are you talking about the viewer or the artist?
I think either. We're not ants or bees; I don't see that we ought to take limited roles in relationship to things. I think one might just as well pretend that he is the center of what he's doing and what his experience is, and that it's only he who can do it.

If you cast a beer can, is that a comment?
On what?

On beer cans or society. When you deal with things in the world, social attitudes are connected with them – aren't they?
Basically, artists work out of rather stupid kinds of impulses and then the work is done. After

that the work is used. In terms of comment, the work probably has it, some aspect which resembles language. Publicly a work becomes not just intention, but the way it is used. If an artist makes something – or if you make chewing gum and everybody ends up using it as glue, whoever made it is given the responsibility of making glue, even if what he really intends is chewing gum. You can't control that kind of thing. As far as beginning to make a work, one can do it for any reason.

If you cast a beer can, you don't have to have a social attitude to beer cans or art?
No. It occurs to me you're talking about *my* beer cans, which have a story behind them. I was doing at that time sculptures of small objects – flashlights and light bulbs. Then I heard a story about Willem de Kooning. He was annoyed with my dealer, Leo Castelli, for some reason, and said something like, 'That son-of-a-bitch; you could give him two beer cans and he could sell them.' I heard this and thought, 'What a sculpture – two beer cans.' It seemed to me to fit in perfectly with what I was doing, so I did them – and Leo sold them.

Should an artist accept suggestions – or his environment – so easily?
I think basically that's a false way of thinking. Accept or reject, where's the ease or the difficulty? I don't put any value on a kind of thinking that puts limits on things. I prefer that the artist does what he does than that, after he's done it, someone says he shouldn't have done it. I would encourage everybody to do more rather than less. I think one has to assume that the artist is free to do what he pleases so that whatever he does is his own business, that he had choices, that he could do something else.

But shouldn't the artist have an attitude to his subject, shouldn't he transform it?
Transformation is in the head. If you have one thing and make another thing, there is no transformation, but there are two things. I don't think you would mistake one for another.

Does art change with time?
One can be content just to do something over and over again in a kind of blindness. But every aspect of a work of art changes in time, in five minutes or longer.

Some painters have tried to paint Ageless Art.
The whole business here in America, of my training and even more the people before me, was rooted in the mythology that the artist was separated and isolated from society and working alone, unappreciated, then dying and after that his work becoming very valuable, and that this was sad. That was part of the way I was trained. I think it's even less true than thinking that one is finding one's own values in the act of painting. One does it – paints – and wishes to do it. If not, you're making it into a kind of martyr situation which doesn't interest me very much.

With what has been called the 'New Audience' that situation seems reversed.
Things are picked up and publicized as quickly as the mediums for doing those things allow. To say it is bad one has to have some idea about the social role art *should* have, that communication about art should be restricted because artists have a secret weapon or something which shouldn't be announced for twenty years for some reason – or because it may go out of date or someone will find something better. It's silly to say that art shouldn't get to be so well known so quickly. How quickly should it get to be known? It should be publicized just as quickly as somebody wants to publicize it.

But weren't you just saying that art should not be used as a social force?
For myself I would choose to be as much as possible outside that area. It's difficult because we are constantly faced with social situations and our work is being used in ways we didn't ask for it to be used. We see it being done. We're not idiots.

Then is it being misused in a social situation?
My point of view tends to be that work is being misused in *most* situations. Nevertheless I find it a very interesting possibility, that one can't control the situation, the way one's work is viewed, that once one offers it to be seen then anybody is able to see it as he pleases.

Jasper Johns

Excerpts from an interview by David Sylvester recorded for the BBC in spring 1965, broadcast 10 October 1965, in *Jasper Johns Drawings*, exhibition catalogue, Arts Council of Great Britain, 1974.

What was it first made you use things such as flags, targets, maps, numbers and letters and so on as starting-points?
They seemed to me pre-formed, conventional, depersonalised, factual, exterior elements.

And what was the attraction of depersonalised elements?
I'm interested in things which suggest the world rather than suggest the personality. I'm interested in things which suggest things which are, rather than in judgments. The most conventional thing, the most ordinary thing – it seems to me that those things can be dealt with without having to judge them; they seem to me to exist as clear facts, not involving aesthetic hierarchy.

...

But what of the objects you begin with?
The empty canvas?

No. Not only the empty canvas; well, the motif, if you like, such as the letters, the flag and so on, or whatever it may be.
I think it's just a way of beginning.

In other words the painting is not about the elements with which you have begun.
No more than it is about the elements which enter it at any moment. Say, the painting of a flag is always about a flag, but it is no more about a flag than it is about a brush-stroke or about a colour or about the physicality of the paint, I think.

...

But all the same, when you are actually making a painting, you prefer to incorporate the real thing or a part of the real thing to representing it?
That's my tendency yes, so far.

Do you know why?
No, but I can make up a reason. I think my thinking is perhaps dependent on real things and is not very sophisticated abstract thinking. I think I'm not willing to accept the representation of a thing as being the real thing, and I am frequently unwilling to work with the representation of the thing as, you know, as standing for the real thing. I like what I see to be real, or to be my idea of what is real. And I think I have a kind of resentment against illusion when I can recognise it. Also, a large part of my work has been involved with the painting as object, as a real thing in itself. And in the face of that 'tragedy', so far, my general development, it seems to me, has moved in the direction of using real things as painting. That is to say I find it more interesting to use a real fork as painting than it is to use painting as a real fork.

...

What is the difference between seeing when you look about you and seeing when you look at a painting?
At its best there is no difference.

Ray Johnson

David Bourdon, 'An Interview with nosnhoJ yaR', *Artforum*, III, 1, September 1964, p. 29.

Great artists are said to present a new way of seeing and experiencing things. For me, papier collé *is a mirror which reflects the world around it, but is unable to offer a new image to the world. For you, have* papiers collés *ever offered more than a point of view?*
I was in a synagogue recently and I left as an offering a small wooden spoon in an envelope. I think that Schwitters collages and Rauschenberg silk screens should be put in envelopes and left as offerings in churches.

...

For the past few years, you have concentrated on the creation and dissemination of your 'mailings' (envelopes with miscellaneous clippings). This is, I know, a means of visual communication between members of your New York Correspondence School. Are these 'mailings' breakdown collages in the form of do-it-yourself kits? Is this an art form?
The contents is the contents; the stamp are the stamp; the address are the address. It is very clear. Your question 'Is this an art form' is the art form.

Jasper Johns

Walter Hopps, 'An Interview with Jasper Johns', *Artforum*, III, 6, March 1965, p. 32.

The target seemed to me to occupy a certain kind of relationship to seeing the way we see and to things in the world which we see, and this is the same kind of relationship that the flag had. We say it comes automatically. Automatically you tend to do this, but you see that there are relationships which can be made and those seem to me the relationships that could be made between two images. They're both things which are seen and not looked at, not examined, and they both have clearly defined areas which could be measured and transferred to canvas.

Allan Kaprow

Allan Kaprow, 'The Legacy of Jackson Pollock', *ARTnews*, LVII, 6, October 1958, pp. 56–7.

... Objects of every sort are materials for the new art: paint, chairs, food, electric and neon lights, smoke, water, old socks, a dog, movies, a thousand other things which will be discovered by the present generation of artists. Not only will these bold creators show us, as if for the first time, the world we have always had about us, but ignored, but they will disclose entirely unheard of happenings and events, found in garbage cans, police files, hotel lobbies, seen in store windows and on the streets, and sensed in dreams and horrible accidents. An odor of crushed strawberries, a letter from a friend or a billboard selling Draino; three taps on the front door, a scratch, a sigh or a voice lecturing endlessly, a blinding staccato flash, a bowler hat – all will become materials for this new concrete art.

The young artist of today need no longer say 'I am a painter' or 'a poet' or 'a dancer'. He is simply an 'artist'. All of life will be open to him. He will discover out of ordinary things the meaning of ordinariness. He will not try to make them extraordinary. Only their real meaning will be stated. But out of nothing he will devise the extraordinary and then maybe nothingness as well. People will be delighted or horrified, critics will be confused or amused, but these, I am sure, will be the alchemies.

Roy Lichtenstein

Interviews by G. R. Swenson, 'What is Pop Art?', part I, *ARTnews*, LXII, 7, November 1963, pp. 25, 62, 63.

What is Pop Art?
I don't know – the use of commercial art as subject matter in painting, I suppose. It was hard to get a painting that was despicable enough so that no one would hang it – everybody was hanging everything. It was almost acceptable to hang a dripping paint rag, everybody was accustomed to this. The one thing everyone hated was commercial art; apparently they didn't hate that enough either.

Is Pop Art despicable?
That doesn't sound so good, does it? Well, it *is* an involvement with what I think to be the most brazen and threatening characteristics of our culture, things we hate, but which are also powerful in their impingement on us. I think art since Cézanne has become extremely romantic and unrealistic, feeding on art; it is utopian. It has had less and less to do with the world, it looks inward – neo-Zen and all that. This is not so much a criticism as an obvious observation. Outside is the world; it's there. Pop Art looks out into the world; it appears to accept its environment, which is not good or bad, but different – another state of mind.

'How can you like exploitation?' 'How can you like the complete mechanization of work? How can you like bad art?' I have to answer that I accept it as being there, in the world.

Are you anti-experimental?
I think so, and anti-contemplative, anti-nuance, anti-getting-away-from-the-tyranny-of-the-rectangle, anti-movement-and-light, anti-mystery, anti-paint-quality, anti-Zen, and anti all of those brilliant ideas of preceding movements which everyone understands so thoroughly.

We like to think of industrialization as being despicable. I don't really know what to make of it. There's something terribly brittle about it. I suppose I would still prefer to sit under a tree with a picnic basket rather than under a gas pump, but signs and comic strips are interesting as subject matter. There are certain things that are usable, forceful and vital about commercial art. We're using those things – but we're not really advocating stupidity, international teenagerism and terrorism.

Where did your ideas about art begin?
The ideas of Prof. Hoyt Sherman [at Ohio State University] on perception were my earliest important influence and still affect my ideas of visual unity.

Perception?
Yes. Organized perception is what art is all about.

He taught you 'how to look'?
Yes. He taught me how to go about learning how to look.

At what?
At what, doesn't have anything to do with it. It is a process. It has nothing to do with any external form the painting takes, it has to do with a way of building a unified pattern of seeing ... In Abstract-Expressionism the paintings symbolize the idea of ground-directedness as opposed to object-directedness. You put something down, react to it, put something else down, and the painting itself becomes a symbol of this. The difference is that rather than symbolize this ground-directedness I do an object-directed appearing thing. There is humor here. The work is still ground-directed; the fact that it's an eyebrow or an almost direct copy of something is unimportant. The ground-directedness is in the painter's mind and not immediately apparent in the painting. Pop Art makes the statement that ground-directedness is not a quality that the painting has because of what it looks like ... This tension between apparent object-directed products and actual ground-directed processes is an important strength of Pop Art.

Antagonistic critics say that Pop Art does not transform its models. Does it?
Transformation is a strange word to use. It implies that art transforms. It doesn't, it just plain forms. Artists have never worked with the model – just with the painting. What you're really saying is that an artist like Cézanne transforms what we think the painting ought to look like into something he thinks it ought to look like. He's working with paint, not nature; he's making a painting, he's forming it. I think my work is different from comic strips – but I wouldn't call it transformation; I don't think that whatever is meant by it is important to art. What I do is form, whereas the comic strip is not formed in the sense I'm using the word; the comics have shapes but there has been no effort to make them intensely unified. The purpose is different, one intends to depict and I intend to unify. And my work is actually different from comic strips in that every mark is really in a different place, however slight the difference seems to some. The difference is often not great, but it is crucial. People also consider my work to be anti-art in the same way they consider it pure depiction 'not transformed.' I don't feel it is anti-art.

There is no neat way of telling whether a work of art is composed or not; we're too comfortable with ideas that art is the battleground for interaction, that with more and more experience you become more able to compose. It's true, everybody accepts that; it's just that the idea no longer has any power.

Abstract-Expressionism has had an almost universal influence on the arts. Will Pop Art?
I don't know. I doubt it. It seems too particular – too much the expression of a few personalities. Pop might be a difficult starting point for a painter. He would have great difficulty in making these brittle images yield to compositional purposes . . . Interaction between painter and painting is not the total commitment of Pop, but it is still a major concern – though concealed and strained.

Do you think that an idea in painting – whether it be 'interaction' or the use of commercial art – gets progressively less powerful with time?
It seems to work that way. Cubist and Action Painting ideas, although originally formidable and still an influence, are less crucial to us now. Some individual artists, though – Stuart Davis, for example – seem to get better and better.

A curator at the Modern Museum has called Pop Art fascistic and militaristic.
The heroes depicted in comic books are fascist types, but I don't take them seriously in these paintings – maybe there is a point in not taking them seriously, a political point. I use them for purely formal reasons, and that's not what those heroes were invented for . . . Pop Art has very immediate and of-the-moment meanings which will vanish – that kind of thing is ephemeral – and Pop takes advantage of this 'meaning,' which is not supposed to last, to divert you from its formal content. I think the formal statement in my work will become clearer in time. Superficially, Pop seems to be all subject matter, whereas Abstract-Expressionism, for example, seems to be all esthetic . . .

I paint directly – then it's said to be an exact copy, and not art, probably because there's no perspective or shading. It doesn't look like a painting *of* something, it looks like the thing itself. Instead of looking like a painting *of* a billboard – the way a Reginald Marsh would look – Pop Art seems to be the actual thing. It is an intensification, a stylistic intensification of the excitement which the subject matter has for me; but the style is, as you said, cool. One of the things a cartoon does is to express violent emotion and passion in a completely mechanical and removed style. To express this thing in a painterly style would dilute it; the techniques I use are not commercial, they only appear to be commercial – and the ways of seeing and composing and unifying are different and have different ends.

Is Pop Art American?
Everybody has called Pop Art 'American' painting, but it's actually industrial painting. America was hit by industrialism and capitalism harder and sooner and its values seem more askew . . . I think the meaning of my work is that it's industrial, it's what all the world will soon become. Europe will be the same way, soon, so it won't be American, it will be universal.

Claes Oldenburg

Jan McDevitt, 'The Object: Still Life. Interviews with the New Object Makers. Richard Artschwager and Claes Oldenburg, on Craftsmanship, Art, and Function', *Craft Horizons,* 25, September–October 1965, p. 31.

... I've never made the separation between, say, the museum and the hardware store. I mean, I enjoy both of them, and I want to combine the two.

I've been using a typewriter all my life. I used to be a reporter, and I used the telephone and so on, so I feel very close to these objects. I started with the telephone, went on to the typewriter, and then the toaster has always fascinated me, so I made a toaster. They are all made in vinyl. They were first made in muslin and then redone in vinyl because I wanted to get a yielding surface. That was one of the ways I felt I could remove the object from context, I mean to individualize it, and it was always a desire to control space, to shape space in sculpture in a different way because most sculptures are hard, even when they move. Also, if they are kinetic sculptures they usually have a very definite pattern of movement ...

... I wanted to have the informal possibility of movement so that you could push it in all different ways and it wouldn't look the same from one day to the next ... from there it was very easy to go to the larger objects in the home, such as the things that stand on the floor, the chair and then the bedroom.

... My intention is to make an everyday object that eludes definition. ... I'm happy if people smile at my work. I mean, I'm very happy if they enjoy it, because it can be enjoyed that way as a frustration of the expectations.

Claes Oldenburg

Claes Oldenburg, *Store Days,* New York, 1967, pp. 39–42

I am for an art that is political-erotical-mystical, that does something other than sit on its ass in a museum.
I am for an art that grows up not knowing it is art at all, an art given the chance of having a starting point of zero.
I am for an art that embroils itself with the everyday crap & still comes out on top.
I am for an art that imitates the human, that is comic, if necessary, or violent, or whatever is necessary.
I am for an art that takes its form from the lines of life itself, that twists and extends and accumulates and spits and drips, and is heavy and coarse and blunt and sweet and stupid as life itself.

I am for an artist who vanishes, turning up in a white cap painting signs or hallways.

I am for art that comes out of a chimney like black hair and scatters in the sky.
I am for art that spills out of an old man's purse when he is bounced off a passing fender.
I am for the art out of a doggy's mouth, falling five stories from the roof.
I am for the art that a kid licks, after peeling away the wrapper.
I am for an art that joggles like everyones knees, when the bus traverses an excavation.
I am for art that is smoked, like a cigarette, smells, like a pair of shoes.
I am for art that flaps like a flag, or helps blow noses, like a handkerchief.
I am for art that is put on and taken off, like pants, which develops holes, like socks, which is eaten, like a piece of pie, or abandoned with great contempt, like a piece of shit.

I am for art covered with bandages. I am for art that limps and rolls and runs and jumps. I am for art that comes in a can or washes up on the shore.
I am for art that coils and grunts like a wrestler. I am for art that sheds hair.
I am for art you can sit on. I am for art you can pick your nose with or stub your toes on.
I am for art from a pocket, from deep channels of the ear, from the edge of a knife, from the corners of the mouth, stuck in the eye or worn on the wrist.
I am for art under the skirts, and the art of pinching cockroaches.

I am for the art of conversation between the sidewalk and a blind mans metal stick.
I am for the art that grows in a pot, that comes down out of the skies at night, like lightning, that hides in the clouds and growls, I am for art that is flipped on and off with a switch.
I am for art that unfolds like a map, that you can squeeze, like your sweetys arm, or kiss, like a pet dog. Which expands and squeaks, like an accordion, which you can spill your dinner on, like an old tablecloth.
I am for an art that you can hammer with, stitch with, sew with, paste with, file with.
I am for an art that tells you the time of day, or where such and such a street is.
I am for an art that helps old ladies across the street.

I am for the art of the washing machine. I am for the art of a government check. I am for the art of last wars raincoat.
I am for the art that comes up in fogs from sewer-holes in winter. I am for the art that splits when you step on a frozen puddle. I am for the worms art inside the apple. I am for the art of sweat that develops between crossed legs.

I am for the art of neck-hair and caked tea-cups, for the art between the tines of restaurant forks, for the odor of boiling dishwater.
I am for the art of sailing on Sunday, and the art of red and white gasoline pumps.
I am for the art of bright blue factory columns and blinking biscuit signs.
I am for the art of cheap plaster and enamel. I am for the art of worn marble and smashed slate. I am for the art of rolling cobblestones and sliding sand. I am for the art of slag and black coal. I am for the art of dead birds.
I am for the art of scratchings in the asphalt, daubing at the walls. I am for the art of bending and kicking metal and breaking glass, and pulling at things to make them fall down.
I am for the art of punching and skinned knees and sat-on bananas. I am for the art of kids' smells. I am for the art of mama-babble.
I am for the art of bar-babble, tooth-picking, beerdrinking, egg-salting, in-sulting. I am for the art of falling off a barstool.

I am for the art of underwear and the art of taxicabs. I am for the art of ice-cream cones dropped on concrete. I am for the majestic art of dog-turds, rising like cathedrals.

I am for the blinking arts, lighting up the night. I am for art falling, splashing, wiggling, jumping, going on and off.
I am for the art of fat truck-tires and black eyes.
I am for Kool-art, 7-UP art, Pepsi-art, Sunshine art, 39 cents art, 15 cents art, Vatronol art, Dro-bomb art, Vam art, Menthol art, L&M art, Exlax art, Venida art, Heaven Hill art, Pamryl art, San-o-med art, Rx art, 9.99 art, Now art, New art, How art, Fire sale art, Last Chance art, Only art, Diamond art, Tomorrow art, Franks art, Ducks art, Meat-o-rama art.

I am for the art of bread wet by rain. I am for the rats' dance between floors. I am for the art of flies walking on a slick pear in the electric light. I am for the art of soggy onions and firm green shoots. I am for the art of clicking among the nuts when the roaches come and go. I am for the brown sad art of rotting apples.
I am for the art of meowls and clatter of cats and for the art of their dumb electric eyes.
I am for the white art of refrigerators and their muscular openings and closings.
I am for the art of rust and mold. I am for the art of hearts, funeral hearts or sweetheart hearts, full of nougat. I am for the art of worn meat-hooks and singing barrels of red, white, blue and yellow meat.
I am for the art of things lost or thrown away, coming home from school. I am for the art of cock-and-ball trees and flying cows and the noise of rectangles and squares. I am for the art of crayons and weak grey pencil-lead, and grainy wash and sticky oil paint, and the art of windshield wipers and the art of the finger on a cold window, on dusty steel or in the bubbles on the sides of a bathtub.
I am for the art of teddy-bears and guns and decapitated rabbits, exploded umbrellas, raped beds, chairs with their brown bones broken, burning trees, firecracker ends, chicken bones, pigeon bones and boxes with men sleeping in them.

I am for the art of slightly rotten funeral flowers, hung bloody rabbits and wrinkly yellow chickens, bass drums & tambourines, and plastic phonographs.
I am for the art of abandoned boxes, tied like pharaohs. I am for an art of watertanks and speeding clouds and flapping shades.
I am for U.S. Government Inspected Art, Grade A art, Regular Price art, Yellow Ripe art, Extra Fancy art, Ready-to-eat art, Best-for-less art, Ready-to-cook art, Fully cleaned art, Spend Less art, Eat Better art, Ham art, pork art, chicken art, tomato art, banana art, apple art, turkey art, cake art, cookie art.

add

Im for an art that is combed down, that is hung from each ear, that is laid on the lips and under the eyes, that is shaved from the legs, that is brushed on the teeth, that is fixed on the thighs, that is slipped on the foot.

square which becomes blobby

Mel Ramos

Interview by Dan Tooker, *Art International*, 20 December 1973, pp. 24–5.

I got my M.A. in 1958, and I was doing figure paintings – one single isolated figure not too much unlike Nathan Oliveira, in those days. It stayed that way for about two years, until 1960, when I really sort of said fuck art, I'm not going to do that shit any more. I'm just going to do what I want to do, so I painted some pictures of Batman. They were similar to the early figures, in that they were paintings of a single figure locked into a gray background. By 'locked into' I mean that the edges of the background came right up and locked together with the figure rather than existing behind the figure. It was all on the same plane. I did the painting of Batman the same way, and then Superman and Wonderwoman, and all of the comic heroes that meant a lot to me when I was a kid. Before I knew it, I had about forty paintings like that, and I didn't know quite what to do with them, so I sent some slides to a guy that was recommended to me in New York. He started selling a few, and when he started selling paintings that you never really thought you could sell, it really does something to you. Pretty soon I ran out of comic heroes, so I started doing comic queens – Tiger Girls and Sheena and Wonderwoman and Glory Forbes and Senorita Rio the crime fighter.

Was anyone else in Sacramento interested in comic imagery when you were painting Batman?
No, not really.

Were you in touch with people back east who were?
No. The only person that I knew about in those days was Roy Lichtenstein, whom I really didn't know anything about until I saw a picture of his one day in *Newsweek* or *Time* – a reproduction of one of his paintings of a comic strip, a girl holding a ball over her head. And Leo Castelli had just given him a show, and there was a big artist in one of the magazines saying how bad he was. All the press said it was the worst art ever made, copying the comics. Of course he was copying comics – that's what he was trying to do. And I wrote Roy in care of the gallery and I said I was very sympathetic with his work, I really dug it, mainly because I had been doing a similar thing. I wasn't painting in a comic strip style like he was, but I was using the comic book as a vehicle for expression. The paintings themselves were still my thick, gooey kind of San Francisco style. They kind of looked like Oliveira's, but with comic characters. But no one else around was doing that. Wayne was painting hot dogs.

Robert Rauschenberg

Statement by Robert Rauschenberg, *Sixteen Americans*, exhibition catalogue, Museum of Modern Art, New York, 1959, p. 58.

Any incentive to paint is as good as any other. There is no poor subject.

Painting is always strongest when in spite of composition, color, etc. it appears as a fact, or an inevitability, as opposed to a souvenir or arrangement.

Painting relates to both art and life. Neither can be made. (I try to act in that gap between the two.)

A pair of socks is no less suitable to make a painting with than wood, nails, turpentine, oil and fabric.

A canvas is never empty.

Robert Rauschenberg

Dorothy Seckler, 'The Artist speaks: Robert Rauschenberg', *Art in America*, 54, May–June 1966, pp. 73–4, 81.

As he discovered how quickly the disreputable castoffs were estheticized (the beauty of a rusting license plate, for example, became apparent to everyone), he abandoned his combines and began to compose with images daily disgorged by the press: the split-second action that takes place on a baseball diamond, in a parachute, in a traffic clover-leaf, at a Fourth of July parade or among the swinging clubs of riot police. Photograph sections were transferred to canvas by a silk-screen process. But last year as he went off on tour with the Merce Cunningham Dance Company (designing sets and costumes, occasionally directing and taking part in dance performances), he decided that the silk-screened images no longer held the requisite element of surprise for him. He then had one hundred and fifty of the prepared silk-screen panels removed from his studio so that he would be forced to turn to new materials on his return.

...

Part of the reward of working with street discards and other found objects in his combines was, he felt, in the possibility this offered him to act simply 'as a collaborator with objects.' Actually this fantasy that the objects are active while he is passive, which he knows is not literally true, is acted out in his role in 'Map Room II,' where he makes his body a conductor of electricity. Objects such as battered umbrellas were also useful because they brought to the canvas a sense of experience undergone – the wear and tear of weather and of human usage – while permitting the artist to remain dead-pan and out of sight emotionally. Rauschenberg said that such castoffs served strong, basic shapes, also that they served to throw up a barrier against his 'esthetic' taste.

...

Because of his aversion to colors that could be read as emotionally loaded, he developed his 'all colors, no color,' approach, in which no single color stands out ... He seems to feel that in his own work he is most successful when he has discovered and then revealed qualities in things that are objectively real and never preconceived or imposed in a reflection of his own prejudices. Thus his *Combines* offered not only objects and fragments that are really present in New York but also a succession of surprising contracts that are everywhere evident to him in the city.

He has consistently favored images of public reference over those of private association. In his combines he used umbrellas, tires, Coca-Cola bottles, electric fans and street signs. A notable exception, *Bed*, with its paint-spattered bed covers, was the product of necessity; on a day when neither canvas nor funds was available, he pressed into service his previously functional quilt. In his subsequent, silk-screened images, public references are even more pointed; *Barge* is a notable example.

...

He was asked to clarify his own position vis-a-vis pop art.

R.R. The word 'pop' is more Hollywoodian than historian. Pop art decontaminated our art of stream-of-consciousness. We have a frontier country – the means have to be direct. Today in New York we have masters and matters of all sorts. Their voluntary cooperation indicates a certain amount of communication, tolerance and pleasure in each others' ideas. At the same time, I think that one of the aspects of my work that I criticize myself for the most is that so many people recognized it as a way of working, as an end in itself, so that the influence that the work has had on other artists who work in what they would call the same direction, is really a weakness of my concept. The reason: even the socially interesting misleads directly to the embalming of the work.

Larry Rivers

Interview by Frank O'Hara, 'Why I paint as I do', *Horizon,* September–October 1959, pp. 95–6, 98, 100.

I am a native New Yorker. I grew up in the streets of what was much less inhabited in those days – the Bronx. From about the age of six to ten I went to the zoo four or five times a week. I loved the big cats more than any other animal. I used to trail behind men until they dropped cigarettes and then I'd pick them up and smoke them. The only things in our house resembling art were a cheap tapestry, a cross between a Fragonard and a Minsky popular in many dining rooms in the twenties, and a five-and-ten-cent store 8 by 10 reproduction of a Spanish *señorita* holding a flower just above an exposed breast, a painting which, to make matters worse, followed us from one apartment to another. Mind you, when I took my mother to her first exhibition of paintings – she having had such a profound dining room education in art – she told me which were good paintings and which were bad in a *very* strong voice. But if I've inherited natural bad taste I'd praise my parents for passing on to me their strength, their natural physical endurance and animal concentration.

...

The famous George Washington Crossing the Delaware *was painted soon after your return from Europe, wasn't it? Was it influenced in any way by what was going on in New York art circles?*

Luckily for me I didn't give a crap about what was going on at the time in New York painting, which was obviously interested in chopping down other forests. In fact, I was energetic and egomaniacal and what is even more: important, cocky, and angry enough to want to do something no one in the New York art world could doubt was *disgusting, dead,* and *absurd.* So, what could be dopier than a painting dedicated to a national cliché – Washington Crossing the Delaware. The last painting that dealt with George and the rebels is hanging in the Met and was painted by a coarse German nineteenth-century academician who really loved Napoleon more than anyone and thought crossing a river on a late December afternoon was just another excuse for a general to assume a heroic, slightly tragic pose. He practically put you in the rowboat with George. What could have inspired him I'll never know. What *I* saw in the crossing was quite different. I saw the moment as nerve-racking and uncomfortable. I couldn't picture anyone getting into a chilly river around Christmas time with anything resembling hand-on-chest heroics.

...

Isn't idea or subject matter important?

Only for the primitive and the semantically misinformed can enthusiasm for subject matter be the inspiration for painting. The roundness of a bright yellow grapefruit may make me happy for a few moments. Its juice may satisfy my thirst. I may find its genetic history engrossing, but as an artist what has meaning for me is the color I'm going to choose and where I'm going to put it on the surface and the way I put it there. What to choose and where to put it and how.

...

How does this [accident] apply in painting?

In painting something happens – paint falls on your canvas – and you can use it. Or reject it by rubbing it out. When Jackson Pollock decided the brush inhibited him and he began to shake paint off a stick onto canvases laid out on the floor, he couldn't *predict* his paintings, but he could *direct* them. Canvases that look the same (and anyone can tell a Pollock) must have direction. I've often heard modern works condemned on the ground that a five-year-old child could do them as well. Of course, there *are* paintings a child could do – but not *repeat.* She'll do something, but then something else that'll show you she's someone's granddaughter.

Have you ever invented *a shape in your paintings?*

As far as I'm concerned *nothing* makes an invented shape more moving or interesting than a recognizable one. I can't put down on canvas what I can't see. I think of a picture as a smorgasbord of the recognizable.

Could you illustrate what you mean?
I may see something – a ribbon, say, and I'll use it to enliven a three-inch area of the canvas. Eventually it may turn into a milk container, a snake or a rectangle.

So it's unlikely the ribbon has any meaning?
I may have a private association with that piece of ribbon, but I don't want to *interpret* that association, it's impossible, it doesn't interest me. Some painters think that associations with real images are terribly strong, and that people in general identify the same meaning with them as they themselves do. I don't think so. The associations which arise from objects or events are hardly *ever* the same. Therefore, I feel free to use the appearance of a thing – that piece of ribbon – without assigning any specific meaning to it as an object.And besides, the only qualities you can take from an object for use in a painting – at least as far as I'm concerned – are its shape and color. You can't use the actual texture or the function.

Larry Rivers

Larry Rivers, statement read to the International Association of Plastic Arts at the Museum of Modern Art Symposium on 'Mass Culture & The Artist', New York, 8 October 1963, printed in *Larry Rivers,* exhibition catalogue, Gimpel Fils, London 1964.

Because I move into some of my work things you recognize as portions of Camel Cigarette packs, the front grill of a 1960 Buick, French Money, Rembrandt's Syndics of the Drapery Guild from Dutchmasters Cigars, Vocabulary Lessons, A Menu, Playing Cards etc it doesn't mean I love what they look like in the original or that as an artist I'm agitated to introduce these images of Mass Production as some socially significant statement. I have a bad arm and am not interested in the art of holding up mirrors. Perhaps you will see Camel Cigarettes or French Money differently after looking at my paintings. But what's so marvelous about that. I hope you feel a thrill and think about something different and then maybe think about Art and Me. I find the energy and invention and organization and the scale of industry that produces these things thrilling enough. The business section of the N.Y. Times is much more exciting to me than all the opinions on this & that show or dance or whatever. But unlike a great many snobs who spend their time educating I don't think there is some super visual strength and mystery in the products of Mass Culture: That Mass Culture = Vulgarity which somehow equals the Good & The Beautiful. This slumming is really just a dopey extension of 18th Century sentimentality about the Noble Savage. Remember todays Noble Savages who sit down to create the images for these products went to art schools, traditional & bohemian & were exposed to everything that tends to civilize. They admired the Old Masters & still tell you all about Picasso or perhaps Klee & they made lots of drawings. They really tried. When you meet them you are not in the presence of a brute. I'm not original when I tell you what adorns these products is the remnants of a form 'Tried & True' watered down further by 55 committee meetings. It's not vulgar. It's just inoffensive and clear. I'm not calling for quality or what I think is quality. The world is beautiful enough & of course ugly enough to service the range of human imagination. After all if everyone were as full of quality as you & I there would be no one to serve us a frankfurter at Needicks. So I don't hate the Camel rendered on the cigarette pack. It doesn't matter. I like a lot of things I see that I never use. I used to see Mass Products in a more relaxed way. Their use in 'Art' has made them a bit of a problem. But that's Life. If I am moved to work from these products it's for what I can take from them for my ideas of a work of Art. Excuse the tone. In order to paint I must look at something & I must think that in some way it is about the thing I'm looking at. I think what I choose to look at is based primarily on, 'what out there will allow me to use what's in my bag of tricks'. I'm quite a one eyed face maker and probably think my drawing is greater than anyone's around. Letters of the alphabet & home made stencils found there in great abundance, because of their manufactured look, set off the artiness of my rendering. There are smudges. The right amount of laziness etc. Outside of these personal conventions, bulging and changing in my bag, a combination of factors influence my choosing objects from Mass Production. At least they pass through my mind. Availability . . . a cheap easily gotten model, any store almost any time. Flatness . . . the reduced conflict between what you are looking at and what you end up with on your canvas. 10 years of abstract art adoration leading to neglect and then hunger for something you delude yourself into thinking you can call your own. In certain instances the way in which you want to go down in history. Embarrassment with seriousness, quote 'straight painting'. Perhaps accident, innocence and of course fun & the various reliefs experienced in the presence of absurdity. It is these things I think which account for much more in my choosing portions of Mass Culture than the obvious everyday humanistic or politically responsible overtones. Thank you . . .

James Rosenquist

Interviews by G.R. Swenson, 'What is Pop Art?', part II, *ARTnews*, LXII, 10, February 1964, pp. 41,62–4.

I think critics are hot blooded. They don't take very much time to analyse what's in the painting ...

O.K., the critics can say [that Pop artists accept the mechanization of the soul]. I think it's very enlightening that *if* we do, we realize it instead of protesting too much. It hasn't been my reason. I have some reasons for using commercial images that these people probably haven't thought about. If I use anonymous images – it's true my images have not been hot blooded images – they've been anonymous images of recent history. In 1960 and 1961 I painted the front of a 1950 Ford. I felt it was an anonymous image. I wasn't angry about that, and it wasn't a nostalgic image either. Just an image. I use images from old magazines – when I say old, I mean 1945 to 1955 – a time we haven't started to ferret out as history yet. If it was the front end of a new car there would be people who would be passionate about it, and the front end of an old car might make some people nostalgic. The images are like no-images. There is a freedom there. If it were abstract, people might make it into something. If you paint Franco-American spaghetti, they won't make a crucifixion out of it, and also who could be nostalgic about canned spaghetti? They'll bring their reactions but, probably, they won't have as many irrelevant ones ...

The images are now, already, on the canvas and the time I painted it is on the canvas. That will always be seen. That time span, people will look at it and say, 'why did he paint a '50 Ford in 1960, why didn't he paint a '60 Ford?' That relationship is one of the important things we have as painters. The immediacy may be lost in a hundred years, but don't forget that by that time it will be like collecting a stamp; this thing might have ivy growing around it. If it bothers to stand up – I don't know – it will belong to a stamp collector, it will have nostalgia then. But still that time reference will mean something ...

I have a feeling, as soon as I do something, or as I do something, nature comes along and lays some dust on it. There's a relationship between nature – nature's nature – and time, the day and the hour and the minute. If you do an iron sculpture, in time it becomes rusty, it gains a patina and that patina can only get to be beautiful. A painter searches for a brutality that hasn't been assimilated by nature. I believe there is a heavy hand of nature on the artist. My studio floor could be, some people would say that is part of me and part of my painting because that is the way I arranged it, the way things are. But it's not, because it's an accidental arrangement; it *is* nature, like flowers or other things ...

[Paint and paint quality] are natural things before you touch them, before they're arranged. As time goes by the brutality of what art is, the idea of what art can be, changes; different feelings about things become at home, become accepted, natural ... [Brutality is] a new vision or method to express something, its value geared right to the present time ...

When I was a student, I explored paint quality. Then I started working, doing commercial painting and I got all of the paint quality I ever wanted. I had paint running down my armpits. I kept looking at everything I was doing – a wall, a gasoline tank, I kept looking to see what happened, looking at a rusty surface, at the nature, at changing color. I've seen a lot of different ways paint takes form and what it does, and what excited me and what didn't. After some Abstract-Expressionism painting I did then, I felt I had to slice through all that, because I had a lot of residue, things I didn't want. I thought that I would be a stronger painter if I made most of my decisions before I approached the canvas; that way I hoped for a vision that would be more simple and direct. I don't know what the rules for Abstract-Expressionism are, but I think one is that you make a connection with the canvas and then you discover; that's what you paint – and eliminate what you don't want. I felt my canvases were jammed with stuff I didn't want ...

I'm amazed and excited and fascinated about the way things are thrust at us, the way this invisible screen that's a couple of feet in front of our mind and our senses is attacked by radio and television and visual communications, through things larger than life, the impact of things thrown at us, at such a speed and with such a force that painting and the attitudes toward painting and communication through doing a painting now seem very old-fashioned ...

I think we have a free society, and the action that goes on in this free society allows encroachments, as a commercial society. So I geared myself, like an advertiser or a large company, to this visual inflation – in commercial advertising which is one of the foundations of our society. I'm living in it, and it has such impact and excitement in its means of imagery. Painting is probably more exciting than advertising – so why shouldn't it be done with that power and gusto, with that impact. I see very few paintings with the impact that I've felt, that I feel and try to do in my work ... My metaphor, if that is what you can call it, is my relations to the power of commercial advertising which is in turn related to our free society, the visual inflation which accompanies the money that produces box tops and space cadets ...

When I use a combination of fragments of things, the fragments or objects or real things are caustic to one another, and the title is also caustic to the fragments ... The images are expendable, and the images are in the painting and therefore the painting is also expendable. I only hope for a colorful shoe-horn to get the person off, to turn him on to his own feelings ...

The more we explore, the more we dig through, the more we learn the more mystery there is. For instance, how can I justify myself, how can I make my mark, my 'X' on the wall in my studio, or in my experience, when somebody is jumping in a rocket ship and exploring outer space? Like, he begins to explore space, the deeper he goes in space the more there is of nature, the more mystery there is. You may make a discovery, but you get to a certain point and that point opens up a whole new area that's never even been touched ...

I treat the billboard image as it is, so apart from nature. I paint it as a reproduction of other things; I try to get as far away from the nature as possible ...

An empty canvas is full, as Bob [Rauschenberg] said. Things are always gorgeous and juicy – an empty canvas is – so I put something in to dry it up. Just the canvas and paint – that would be nature. I see all this stuff [pointing to the texture of a canvas] – that's a whole other school of painting. All that very beautiful canvas can be wonderful, but it's another thing. The image – certainly it's juicy, too – but it throws your mind to something else, into art. From having an empty canvas, you have a painted canvas. It may have more action; but the action is like a confrontation, like a blow that cancels out a lot of other stuff, numbing your appreciation for a lot of juicy things. Then, too, somebody will ask, why do I want that image there? I don't want that image, but it's there. To put an image in, or a combination of images, is an attempt to make it at least not nature, cancel it from nature, wrest it away. Look at that fabric, there, the canvas, and the paint – those are like nature ...

I learned a lot more about painting paint when I painted signs. I painted things from photos and I had quite a bit of freedom in the interpretation, but still, after I did it, it felt cold to me, it felt like I hadn't done it, that it had been done by a machine. The photograph was a machine-produced image. I threw myself at it. I reproduced it as photographically and stark as I could. They're still done the same way; I like to paint them as stark as I can ...

I thought for a while I would like to use machine-made images, silk-screens, maybe. But by the time I could get them – I have specifics in my mind – it would take longer or as long, and it would be in a limited size, than if I did them as detached as I could by hand, in the detached method I learned as a commercial painter . . .

When I first started thinking like this, feeling like this, from my outdoor painting, painting commercial advertising, I would bring home colors that I liked, associations that I liked using in my abstract painting, and I would remember specifics by saying this was a dirty bacon tan, this was a yellow T-shirt yellow, this was a Man-Tan suntan orange. I remember these like I was remembering an alphabet, a specific color. So then I started painting Man-Tan orange and – I always remember Franco-American spaghetti orange, I can't forget it – so I felt it as a remembrance of things, like a color chart, like learning an alphabet. Other people talk about painting nothing. You just can't do it. I paint something as detached as I can and as well as I can; then I have one image, that's it. But in a sense the image is expendable; I have to keep the image so that the thing doesn't become an attempt at a grand illusion, an elegance . . .

If I use a lamp or a chair, that isn't the subject, it isn't the subject matter. The relationships may be the subject matter, the relationships of the fragments I do. The content will be something more, gained from the relationships. If I have three things, their relationship will be the subject matter; but the content will, hopefully, be fatter, balloon to more than the subject matter. One thing, though, the subject matter isn't popular images, it isn't that at all.

James Rosenquist

G. R. Swenson, 'Social Realism in Blue: An Interview with James Rosenquist', *Studio International*, CLXXV, 897, February 1968, pp. 76, 79–80, 83,

My grandfather in North Dakota used to do wood carvings in the wintertime. He had a lathe made out of an old sewing machine. He did jokes. He would secretly make nice eggs out of wood, and paint them white. He'd put them under the chickens, and my grandmother would go out and collect the eggs and come to this one. It would be hard like a rock; she'd look at it and try to break it.

. . .

. . . Here, in this other picture, this is another exploration called *Circles of confusion*. This is about identity. I became interested in the paradox between the eye and the camera. Things occur in the eye – after-images from seeing a light bulb . . . the identity is a General Electric symbol from a light bulb . . . It could be something other than General Electric. I didn't like the company very much. . . . They made me mad. I was down in Texas at a plastics company that was making canopies for jet planes. I was trying to get a plastic thing made there and was waiting around. A typical young salesman was standing there; and they had a small laminated plastic American flag lying on the desk. I said, 'Take that flat plastic flag, for instance, that's typical of a novelty item, a dime store item that doesn't sell too well.' The salesman said, 'What do you mean won't sell? General Electric just bought ten thousand of them.' And I said, 'What do you mean, General Electric bought ten thousand?' And he said, 'Well, probably to see which of their employees are American or not'. He said the employees would put them on their car aerials. So it was very interesting, and I started putting G.E.s on my paintings of *Circles of confusion*.

. . .

I have this idea about solid appreciation – realizing things but not really being attached, like renting everything I'm involved with, and so depersonalizing things. Solid appreciation would be: a mass of things around you, a mass that you've been involved with that passes you by . . .

I'm not a realistic painter. I'm a realist. I don't think in terms of fantasy. Like, I'm fixed on the floor and I'm really here with you. That's the way I feel.

O, I am poetically involved, partially. Part of my reality has been dented by being taught to appreciate objects, material things, a progression of appreciation of material things: Blue Socialism, I call it. It's like U-Rent-It, an analogy of everyone being filed into a huge hall, and someone with a great ledger in a vast giveaway contest saying, 'Now, which one of these things do you want?' It's marked in the ledger and you have a sense of owning it, but you never use it.

James Rosenquist

Jeanne Siegel, 'An Interview with James Rosenquist', *Artforum*, 10, June 1972, pp. 30–2.

It's so funny that the people have gotten into Pop art . . . In my case it wasn't meant to be present, passionate imagery – it was meant to be no image, nothing image, nowhere.

. . .

I've often wished in the past that I could bring people to the back of the Astor Theater and have them look out the window of the sign into Times Square to let them see the color and the feeling. So the simplest and the cheapest thing I could do would be to make an oil painting of the illusion on canvas and try to give the feeling of this numbness that I felt when being immersed in painting large imagery. The imagery was expendable to me but it was the color and texture that I was interested in, for instance, if I thought I felt like painting red I might have painted a great big tomato.

. . . certain images are recurrent, for example, body fragments, particularly hands, automobiles, and food. Why did you choose them?

Hands for me have always been sort of an offering, a suggestion saying 2 cents off, buy this, try a new steam-iron. They had to do with advertising, and advertising, as I said before, was like the power on the street that a lot of money was poured into, to make something bright and flashy, to make something go. And that was a powerful gesture that people would recognize, so if I put them in a painting, they would see them and they couldn't mistake them for a crucifix because it would be a hand offering something. I used that imagery so it wouldn't be mistaken for something else.

As for automobiles and car parts, I was brought up with automobiles in the Midwest and I used to know the names of all of them and I came here and spent some time in New York and I didn't know anything that was stylish, and I didn't have any affiliation with anything that was stylish, and I found myself standing on the corner, and things going by, and I couldn't recognize anything and that wasn't only automobiles. There were a lot of other things and I began to feel that what was precious to my thing was what I could remember.

...

Things, billboard signs, everything thrust at me, and when I came to New York I used to live on Columbus Circle on 59th Street in rooming houses and there was spit in the hallway and tobacco juice and dirty and brown looking things. I couldn't stand it. And I thought the only way I could stand it was by saying 'Oh, doesn't that hallway have a beautiful green patina.' And so with all kinds of advertisements, in the numbness that occurred, I thought that something could be done in that numbness, that power ... I began to think there was more power and more massive things in advertising than there was in the intellect of a person making a painting in a studio. ... I thought there's more visual things worked out there than there is in an artist's studio working singularly, so I thought of imagery spilling from my billboard experience – imagery spilling off the picture plane – and then after you see that imagery, what's behind it. It's like a thought or a feeling.

Wayne Thiebaud

John Coplans, 'Wayne Thiebaud: An Interview', *Wayne Thiebaud,* exhibition catalogue, Pasadena Art Museum, 1968.

If you take the notion of mass production, the thing that interests me about it is if you paint with or without mechanical aids of any kind you can only make your image superficially like the original. The concept of close discriminations combined with the notion of how much alike yet how different an image can be is a fascinating proposal.

...

I paint those foods which have mostly undergone some kind of a change or metamorphosis. For example, even if it is something as simple as a cantelope melon, the edges of the halves of the melon have been cut in a decorative fashion. It is obviously American food and there are certain characteristic kinds of ways this food is handled, particularly in the texture, color and shape. Also most of it is low grade or mass-produced foodstuff. There are a lot of foods I haven't painted, such as pizza or spaghetti. I have no interest in painting them. It is mostly the food every American child has been brought up on. It is the kind of food that Allan Kaprow has referred to as 'italicized nostalgia.'

...

... then there is another aspect of foodstuffs, one which interests me a great deal. Food as a ritualistic offering – that is – making food seem like it is something more than it is – dressing it up and making it very special. It has something to do with our preoccupation for wanting more than we have. Or a little something more than we know.

...

Only when food is used obscenely is it banal. But cakes, they are glorious, they are like toys.

...

But why the obsessive repetition of cut pies?

You see them on display that way all the time, but it is a dual thing. The serial aspect is very interesting, but everything is stacked against an imagery of this kind because the logical progression is too predictable. In spite of the fact that every pie appears to be similar, it was interesting to take all the spaces in between and make each shape dissimilar. Also all the pies are painted at a slightly different angle and they vary in size and area displacement. It is a play on the closeness of similarities and dissimilarities. At first glance, the pies look mechanical and have a sameness. At least, most people think they do until they study them closely.

Edward Ruscha

John Coplans, 'Edward Ruscha discusses his perplexing publications', *Artforum,* III, 5, February 1965, p. 25.

... I am interested in unusual kinds of publications. The first book came out of a play with words. The title came before I even thought about the pictures. I like the word 'gasoline' and I like the specific quality of 'twenty-six.' If you look at the book you will see how well the typography works – I worked on all that before I took the photographs. Not that I had an important message about photographs or gasoline, or anything like that – I merely wanted a cohesive thing. Above all, the photographs I use are not 'arty' in any sense of the word. I think photography is dead as a fine art; its only place is in the commercial world, for technical or information purposes. I don't mean cinema photography, but still photography, that is, limited edition, individual, hand-processed photos. Mine are simply reproductions of photos. Thus, it is not a book to house a collection of art photographs – they are technical data like industrial photography. To me, they are nothing more than snapshots.

George Segal

George Segal, Excerpts from an unpublished interview by Marco Livingstone, New Jersey, 15 March 1988 (slightly amended by the artist).

Over the years I've had my philosophic disagreements with some of the critics who have written about Pop Art. For instance both Rauschenberg and Johns are *always* mentioned as progenitors of Pop. Both Rauschenberg and Johns were heavily influenced by John Cage's ideas, for instance. My own early art school days involved a rush of attraction on my part towards this brand-new Abstract Expressionist movement. I transferred from Pratt to N.Y.U. because the Abstract Expressionists were teaching there. Much as I loved those paintings,

I was distressed that I was being asked to shut out what I could see with my eyes and touch with my hands. I was asked to throw away images of the real world. My teacher was Tony Smith, and he spoke glowingly of the then brand-new very realistic post-war Italian movies. So you could be realistic in film. He also spoke very enthusiastically of James Joyce's writing as an equivalent of Cubism. I'd looked at Cubism and I'd read Joyce, and everything was based upon the real world. There were images that shuttled back and forth between memory and direct observation, and near and far, and images where you were moving through space. But it was interior, internal movement plus *external* movement. It seemed to me a contradiction. I thought, 'On what basis do I throw away the real world?' And I said, 'What do I paint?'

At that point I met Kaprow. It was Kaprow who introduced me to Rauschenberg and Johns in the late fifties, and Kaprow at that moment was entranced with Cage, taking a class with Cage, and invited me to attend one of the classes. So I knew about Cage's philosophic underpinning in dealing with the real world: four minutes of silence and the music composed of the accidental sounds that you heard. I also had heard about Duchamp . . . growing out of Futurist ideas into his characteristic baffling reality plus internal imagination. The definitions of Pop Art always sounded bright, cheerful, bouncy, witty, dispassionate, embracing the materialism of a prosperous America with its vulgarity and kitsch. And that's supposed to be a description of both Lichtenstein and Warhol, and I don't think it's anywhere near accurate in describing their work.

All of us, our entire generation, were looking for a new basis to deal with the real world. No one was about to throw away the complexity of internal response or the validity of abstract forms. I think there was a new sense of reality, of synthesis, in the air. And Kaprow was writing articles about extending the logic of Jackson Pollock, making very large paintings that became total environments that filled your entire field of vision. So you could look at a Pollock that was, say, 7 feet high and 20 feet wide and the scale could envelop you, and implicit in that was the idea of environment. I saw a retrospective at the Museum of Modern Art by Rothko, *designed* by Rothko, where he had a series of small rooms made and put his paintings in very close together, and I thought that people never looked more marvellous than they were in front of these lovely bands of colour.

So all these ideas were implicit, and I couldn't care less about being witty, detached and ironic. We came equipped with our own temperament, our own nature. My sculpture represented a totality, architecture loaded with emotional freight.

Andy Warhol

Interviews by G. R. Swenson, 'What is Pop Art?', part I, *ARTnews*, LXII, November 1963, pp. 26, 60–61.

Someone said that Brecht wanted everybody to think alike. I want everybody to think alike. But Brecht wanted to do it through Communism, in a way. Russia is doing it under government. It's happening here all by itself without being under a strict government; so if it's working without trying, why can't it work without being Communist? Everybody looks alike and acts alike, and we're getting more and more that way.

I think everybody should be a machine.

I think everybody should like everybody.

Is that what Pop Art is all about?
Yes. It's liking things.

And liking things is like being a machine?
Yes, because you do the same thing every time. You do it over and over again.

And you approve of that?
Yes, because it's all fantasy. It's hard to be creative and it's also hard not to think what you do is creative or hard not to be called creative because everybody is always talking about that and individuality. Everybody's always being creative. And it's so funny when you say things aren't, like the shoe I would draw for an advertisement was called a 'creation' but the drawing of it was not. But I guess I believe in both ways. All these people who aren't very good should be really good. Everybody is too good now, really. Like, how many actors are there? There are millions of actors. They're all pretty good. And how many painters are there? Millions of painters and all pretty good. How can you say one style is better than another? You ought to be able to be an Abstract-Expressionist next week, or a Pop artist, or a realist, without feeling you've given up something. I think the artists who aren't very good should become like everybody else so that people would like things that aren't very good. It's already happening. All you have to do is read the magazines and the catalogues. It's this style or that style, this or that image of man – but that really doesn't make any difference. Some artists get left out that way, and why should they?

Is Pop Art a fad?
Yes, it's a fad, but I don't see what difference it makes. I just heard a rumor that G. quit working, that she's given up art altogether. And everyone is saying how awful it is that A. gave up his style and is doing it in a different way. I don't think so at all. If an artist can't do any more, then he should just quit; and an artist ought to be able to change his style without feeling bad. I heard that Lichtenstein said he might not be painting comic strips a year or two from now – I think that would be so great to be able to change styles. And I think that's what's going to happen, that's going to be the whole new scene. That's probably one reason I'm using silk screens now. I think somebody should be able to do all my paintings for me. I haven't been able to make every image clear and simple and the same as the first one. I think it would be so great if more people took up silk screens so that no one would know whether my picture was mine or somebody else's.

It would turn art history upside down?
Yes.

Is that your aim?
No. The reason I'm painting this way is that I want to be a machine, and I feel that whatever I do and do machine-like is what I want to do.

Was commercial art more machine-like?
No, it wasn't. I was getting paid for it and did anything they told me to do. If they told me to draw a shoe, I'd do it, and if they told me to correct it, I would – I'd do anything they told me to

do, correct it and do it right. I'd have to invent and now I don't; after all that 'correction,' those commercial drawings would have feelings, they would have a style. The attitude of those who hired me had feeling or something to it; they knew what they wanted, they insisted; sometimes they got very emotional. The process of doing work in commercial art was machine-like, but the attitude had feeling to it.

Why did you start painting soup cans?
Because I used to drink it. I used to have the same lunch every day, for twenty years, I guess, the same thing over and over again. Someone said my life has dominated me; I liked that idea. I used to want to live at the Waldorf Towers and have soup and a sandwich, like that scene in the restaurant in *Naked Lunch* . . .

. . .

We went to see *Dr No* at Forty-second Street. It's a fantastic movie, so cool. We walked outside and somebody threw a cherry bomb right in front of us, in this big crowd. And there was blood, I saw blood on people and all over. I felt like I was bleeding all over. I saw in the paper last week that there are more people throwing them – it's just part of the scene – and hurting people. My show in Paris is going to be called 'Death in America'. I'll show the electric chair pictures and the dogs in Birmingham and car wrecks and some suicide pictures.

Why did you start these 'Death' pictures?
I believe in it. Did you see the *Enquirer* this week? It had 'The Wreck that Made Cops Cry' – a head cut in half, the arms and hands just lying there. It's sick, but I'm sure it happens all the time. I've met a lot of cops recently. They take pictures of everything, only it's almost impossible to get pictures from them.

When did you start with the 'Death' series?
I guess it was the big plane crash picture, the front page of a newspaper: 129 DIE. I was also painting the *Marilyns*. I realized that everything I was doing must have been Death. It was Christmas or Labor Day – a holiday – and every time you turned on the radio they said something like, '4 million are going to die.' That started it. But when you see a gruesome picture over and over again, it doesn't really have any effect.

But you're still doing 'Elizabeth Taylor' pictures.
I started those a long time ago, when she was so sick and everybody said she was going to die. Now I'm doing them all over, putting bright colors on her lips and eyes.

My next series will be pornographic pictures, they will look blank; when you turn on the black lights, then you see them – big breasts and . . . If a cop came in, you could just flick out the lights or turn on the regular lights – how could you say that was pornography? But I'm still just practising with these yet. Segal did a sculpture of two people making love, but he cut it all up, I guess because he thought it was too pornographic to be art. Actually it was very beautiful, perhaps a little too good, or he may feel a little protective about art. When you read Genêt you get all hot, and that makes some people say this is not art. The thing I like about it is that it makes you forget about style and that sort of thing; style isn't really important.

Is 'Pop' a bad name?
The name sounds so awful. Dada must have something to do with Pop – it's so funny, the names are really synonyms. Does anyone know what they're supposed to mean or have to do with, those names? Johns and Rauschenberg – Neo-Dada for all these years, and everyone calling them derivative and unable to transform the things they use – are now called progenitors of Pop. It's funny the way things change. I think John Cage has been very influential, and Merce Cunningham, too, maybe. Did you see that article in the *Hudson Review* ['The End of the Renaissance?', Summer, 1963]? It was about Cage and that whole crowd, but with a lot of big words like radical empiricism and teleology. Who knows? Maybe Jap and Bob were Neo-Dada and aren't any more. History books are being re-written all the time. It doesn't matter what you do. Everybody just goes on thinking the same thing, and every year it gets more and more alike. Those who talk about individuality the most are the ones who most object to deviation, and in a few years it may be the other way around. Some day everybody will think just what they want to think, and then everybody will probably be thinking alike; that seems to be what is happening.

Andy Warhol

Andy Warhol, *POPism: The Warhol '60s*, New York, 1980, p. 3.

If I'd gone ahead and died ten years ago, I'd probably be a cult figure today. By 1960, when Pop Art first came out in New York, the art scene here had so much going for it that even all the stiff European types had to finally admit we were a part of world culture . . .

The Pop artists did images that anybody walking down Broadway could recognize in a split second – comics, picnic tables, men's trousers, celebrities, shower curtains, refrigerators, Coke bottles – all the great modern things that the Abstract Expressionists tried so hard not to notice at all.

One of the phenomenal things about the Pop painters is that they were already painting alike when they met. My friend Henry Geldzahler, curator of twentieth-century art at the Metropolitan Museum before he was appointed official culture czar of New York once described the beginnings of Pop this way: 'It was like a science fiction movie – you Pop artists in different parts of the city, unknown to each other, rising up out of the muck and staggering forward with your paintings in front of you.'

Andy Warhol

Gerald Malanga, 'A Conversation with Andy Warhol', *The Print Collector's Newsletter*, I, 6, January–February 1971, p. 125.

I scrutinized Andy's photograph collection . . . The photos were an odd assortment of car crashes, people being tortured, candid and posed movie stars, and nature lovers. I realized that the photos were the actual subject matter Andy reproduced in his silk-screens. From these photos, Andy was taking what he wanted stylistically from the media and from commercial art, elaborating and commenting on a technique and vision that was to begin with second-hand. He was a Social Realist in reverse; he was satirizing the methods of commercial art as well as the American Scene. But instead of satirizing the products themselves, he had satirized the 'artful' way they were presented.

Tom Wesselmann

Interviews by G. R. Swenson, 'What is Pop Art?' part II, *ARTnews*, LXII, 10 February 1964, pp. 41, 64, 65.

What is Pop Art?
I dislike labels in general and Pop in particular, especially because it over-emphasizes the material used. There does seem to be a tendency to use similar materials and images, but the different ways they are used denies any kind of group intention.

When I first came to painting there was only de Kooning – that was what I wanted to be, with all its self-dramatization. But it didn't work for me. I did one sort of non-objective collage that I liked, but when I tried to do it again I had a kind of artistic nervous breakdown. I didn't know where I was. I couldn't stand the insecurity and frustration involved in trying to come to grips with something that just wasn't right, that wasn't me at any rate.

Have you banished the brushstroke from your work?
I'm painting now more than I used to because I'm working so big; there's a shortage of collage material. So brushstrokes can occur, but they are often present as a collage element; for example, in one big still-life I just did there's a tablecloth section painted as if it were a fragment from an Abstract-Expressionist painting inserted into my picture. I use de Kooning's brush knowing it is his brush.

One thing I like about collage is that you can use anything, which gives you that kind of variety; it sets up reverberations in a picture from one kind of reality to another. I don't attach any kind of value to brushstrokes, I just use them as another thing from the world of existence. My first interest is the painting which is the whole, final product. I'm interested in assembling a situation resembling painting, rather than painting; I like the use of painting because it has a constant resemblance to painting.

What is the purpose of juxtaposing different kinds of representations?
If there was any single aspect of my work that excited me, it was that possibility – not just the differences between what they were, but the aura each had with it. They each had such a fulfilled reality: the reverberations seemed a way of making the picture more intense. A painted pack of cigarettes next to a painted apple wasn't enough for me. They are both the same kind of thing. But if one is from a cigarette ad and the other a painted apple, they are two different realities and they trade on each other; lots of things – bright strong colors, the qualities of materials, images from art history or advertising – trade on each other. This kind of relationship helps establish a momentum throughout the picture – all the elements are in some way very intense. Therefore throughout the picture all the elements compete with each other. At first glance, my pictures seem well-behaved, as if – that is a still-life, O.K. But these things have such crazy gives and takes that I feel they get really very wild.

What does esthetics mean to you and your work?
Esthetics is very important to me, but it doesn't deal with beauty or ugliness – they aren't values in painting for me, they're beside the point. Painting relates to both beauty and ugliness. Neither can be made. (I try to work in the gap between the two.) I've been thinking about that, as you can see. Perhaps 'intensity' would be a better emphasis. I always liked Marsicano's quote – from ARTnews – 'Truth can be defined as the intensity with which a picture forces one to participate in its illusion.'

Some of the worst things I've read about Pop Art have come from its admirers. They begin to sound like some nostalgia cult – they really worship Marilyn Monroe or Coca-Cola. The importance people attach to things the artist uses is irrelevant. My use of elements from advertising came about gradually. One day I used a tiny bottle picture on a table in one of my little nude collages. It was a logical extension of what I was doing. I use a billboard picture because it is a real, special representation of something, not because it is from a billboard. Advertising images excite me mainly because of what I can make from them. Also I use real objects because I need to use objects, not because objects need to be used. But the objects remain part of a painting because I don't make environments. My rug is not to be walked on.

Tom Wesselmann

Slim Stealingworth, *Tom Wesselmann*, New York 1980, p. 31.

So this period of dimensional and other experiments found him exuberantly indifferent to his earlier restrictions of form, and totally caught up in the problems of trying to make his paintings work with all these competing elements . . . And since his use of the real object was so different from Rauschenberg or Johns, it seemed unrelated to them. They would use a clock for example, as a clock, but in an abstract environment totally alien to the normal function and presence of a clock; Wesselmann used a clock in the normal, literal environment where a clock plays an integral role with other objects associated with it. And, he uses the real clock to intensify an image that could have been merely flat or painted. He put things together in such a way that they were not transformed but were simply heightened. Dine and Johns softened the elements with poetic or changed circumstances – this is not a criticism, it is just the difference. In a way, an object, such as a clock, is not just a clock but also a context – its identity is quite incomplete until it functions in the fullest sense of a clock, with other related objects and in the context established by all of them. The context heightens the impact and sense of what the object is.

Wesselmann didn't choose certain objects or images because they were significant or crucial to our times or because others found them an integral part of our lives – his choices were purely personal: he found them visually exciting or pertinent to a possible painting.

Is Pop Art a counter-revolution?
I don't think so. As for me, I got my subject matter from Hans Memling (I started with 'Portrait Collages') and de Kooning gave me content and motivation. My work evolves from that.

What influences have you felt in your work from, say, Dada?
When I first came across it, I respected it and thought it was pretty good; but it didn't have anything to do with me. As my work began to evolve I realized – not consciously, it was like a surprise – that maybe it had something to do with my work.

It was the same with Rauschenberg. When I saw his painting with the radios in it I thought it was fine, O.K., but it had no effect on me. It ceased to exist for me except in Rauschenberg's world. Much later I got interested in the addition of movement to painting, so a part of the painting was attached to a motor. An interest in using light and sound followed – I put in a television. But not only for the television image – who cares about television images? – but because I cared about the dimension it gave to painting, something that moved, and gave off light and sound. I used a radio and when I did I felt as if I were the first who'd ever used a radio. It's not that I think of that as an accomplishment – it's just that Rauschenberg didn't seem an immediate factor in it. He was, of course; his use of objects in paintings made it somehow legitimate; but I used a radio for my own reasons . . .

I've been painting more, lately, in these big works. I'm more and more aware of how audacious the act of painting is. One of the reasons I got started making collages was that I lacked involvement with the thing I was painting; I didn't have enough interest in a rose to paint it. Some of this, I think, comes from the painting of the 'fifties – I mean, for a painter the love of flowers was gone. I don't love roses or bottles or anything like that enough to want to sit down and paint them lovingly and patiently. Now with these big pictures, well, there aren't enough billboards around and I have to paint a bowl – and I don't have any feelings about bowls or how a bowl should be. I only know I have to have a bowl in that painting. Here in this picture I'm working on, I made this plain blue bowl and then I realized it had to have something on it. I had to invent, a bowl and – god! – I couldn't believe how audacious it was. And it's threatening too – painting something without any conviction about what it should be.

Do you mean that collage materials permit you to use an image and still be neutral toward the object represented?
I think painting is essentially the same as it has always been. It confuses me that people expect Pop Art to make a comment or say that its adherents merely accept their environment. I've viewed most of the paintings I've loved – Mondrians, Matisses, Pollocks – as being rather dead-pan in that sense. All painting is fact, and that is enough; the paintings are charged with their very presence. The situation, physical ideas, physical presence – I feel that is the comment.

H. C. Westermann

Dennis Adrian, 'Some Notes on H. C. Westermann', *Art International*, 7, February 1963, p. 55.

There is the vexed question of Pop Art. Westermann has of course used images and articles of popular culture for nearly ten years, and their effect today is undoubtedly Pop. This is not likely to be so much the case once Dame Fashion directs her fickle favour elsewhere. This is because Westermann's use of popular images and items is invariably within the context of a larger metaphorical statement. And, his elevation of craft and technique to a level of interest in their own right is far from the anonymous (however careful) or spontaneous techniques typical of main Pop Art currents. In this sense Westermann is a very traditional artist: his stated aim is 'to make art'.

1 **Jasper Johns** Flag above White 1954 (cat 120)

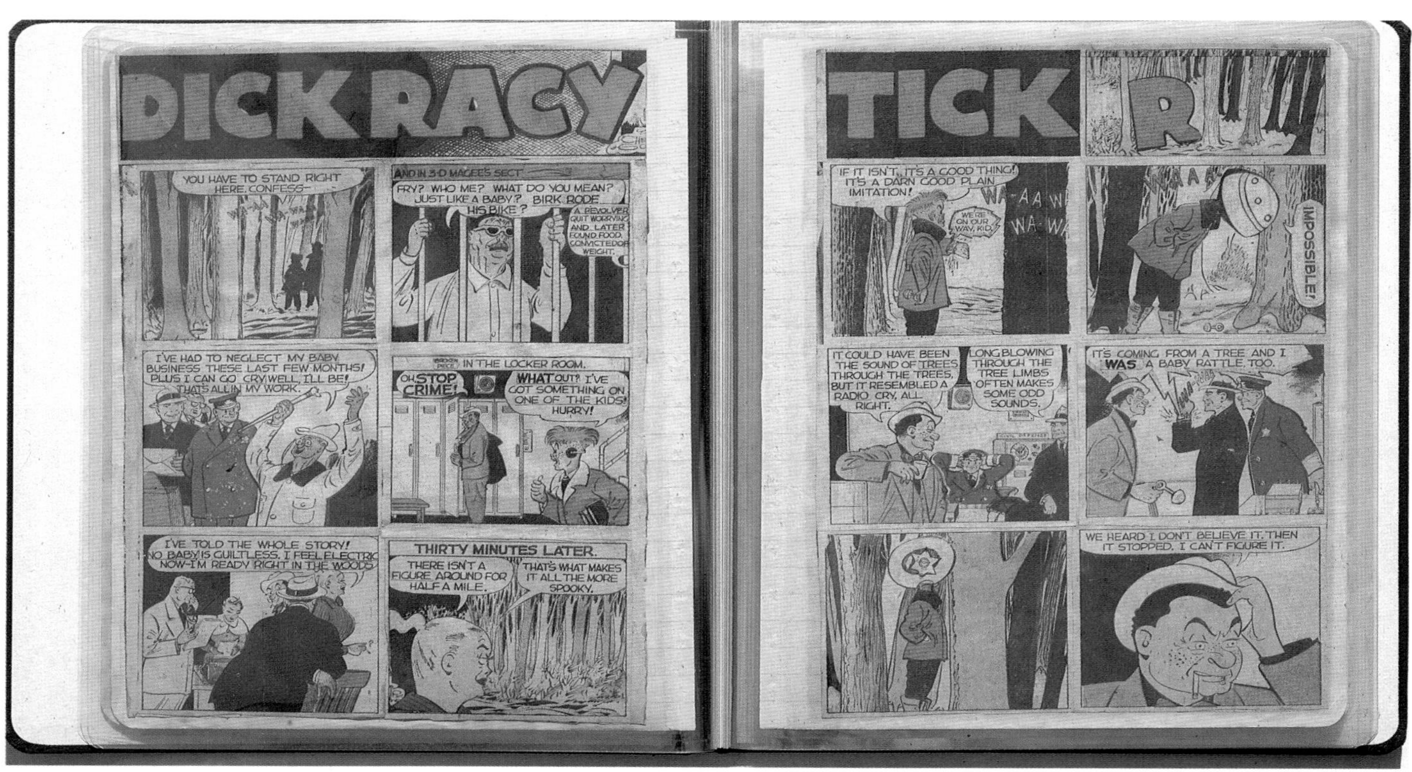

2 **Jess** Tricky Cad – Case 1 1954 (cat 118)

3 **Jess** Tricky Cad – Case IV 1957 (cat 119)

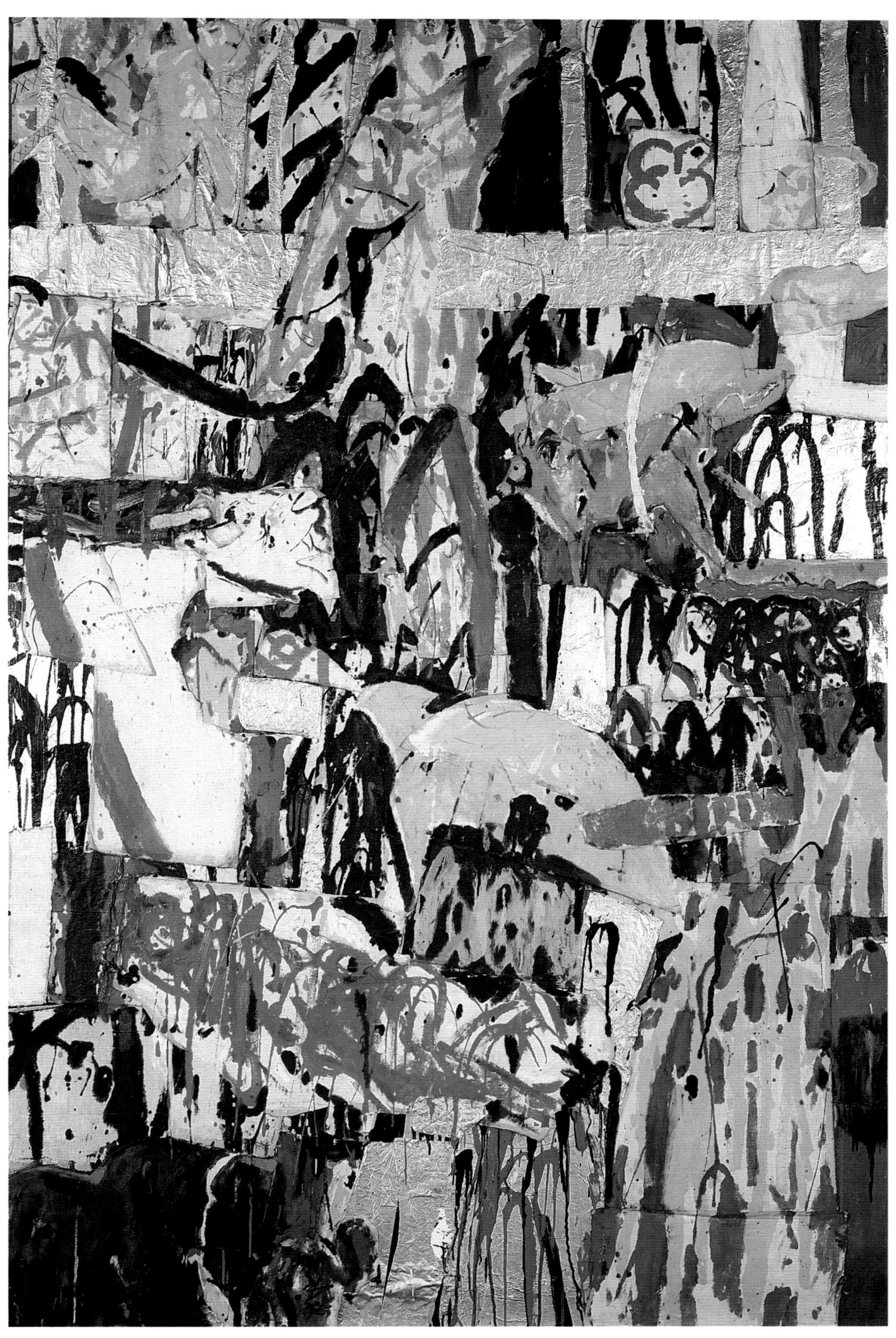

4 **Allan Kaprow** Stained Glass Window 1956 (cat 138)

5 **Ray Johnson** Untitled (Gymnastics) 1958 (cat 131)

6 **Ray Johnson** Shirley Temple 1958 (cat 130)

7 **Ray Johnson** Elvis Presley 2 1955 (cat 128)

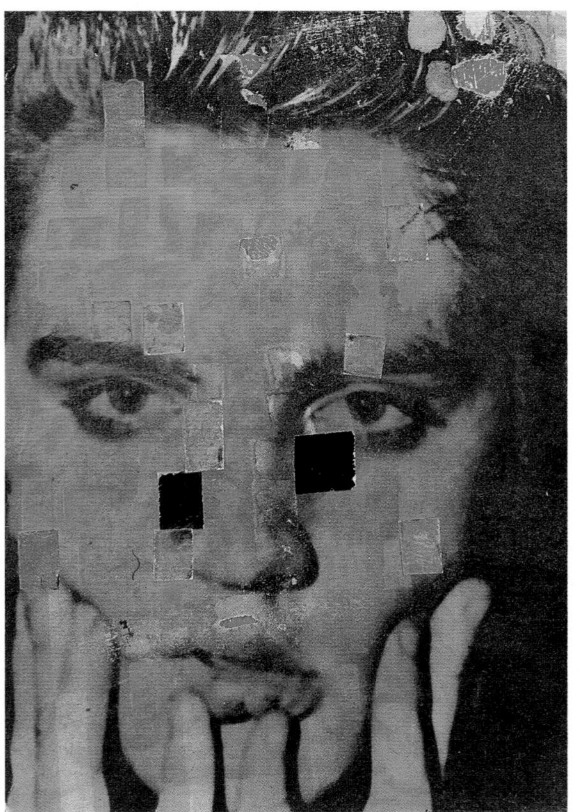

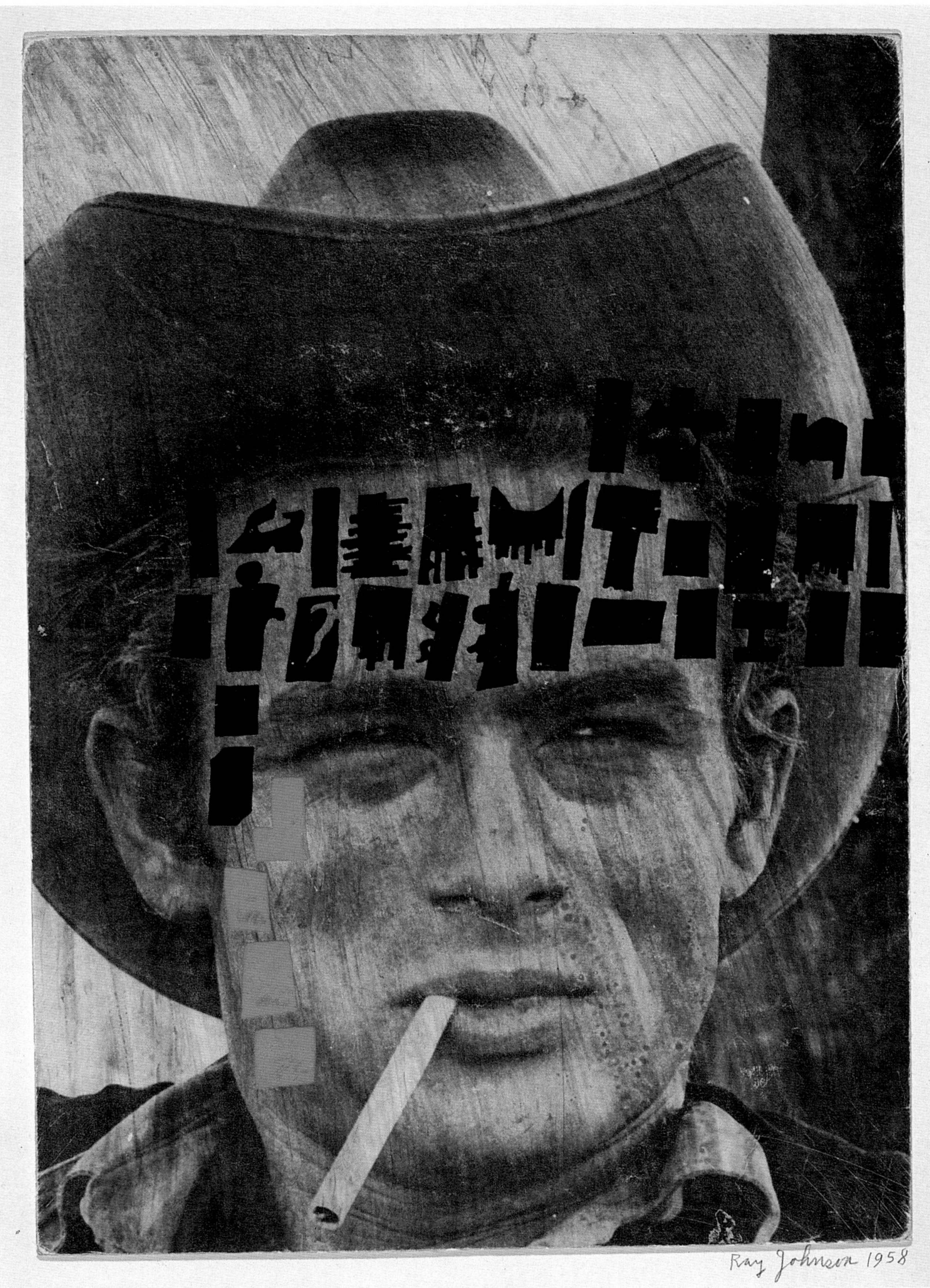

8 **Ray Johnson** James Dean 1958 (cat 129)

9 **Jim Dine** Car Crash 1959–60 (cat 34)

10 **Jim Dine** Green Suit 1959 (cat 33)

11 **Robert Rauschenberg** Gift for Apollo 1959 (cat 189)

12 **Robert Rauschenberg** Pilgrim 1960 (cat 190)

13 **Jasper Johns** Map 1960 (cat 122)

14 **Jasper Johns** Painted Bronze (Savarin Can) 1960 (cat 124)

15 **Jasper Johns** Gray Target 1958 (cat 121)

16 **Jasper Johns** Painted Bronze (Ale Cans) 1960 (cat 123)

17 **Edward Kienholz** George Warshington in Drag 1957 (cat 139)

18 **Edward Kienholz** Walter Hopps, Hopps, Hopps 1959 (cat 141)

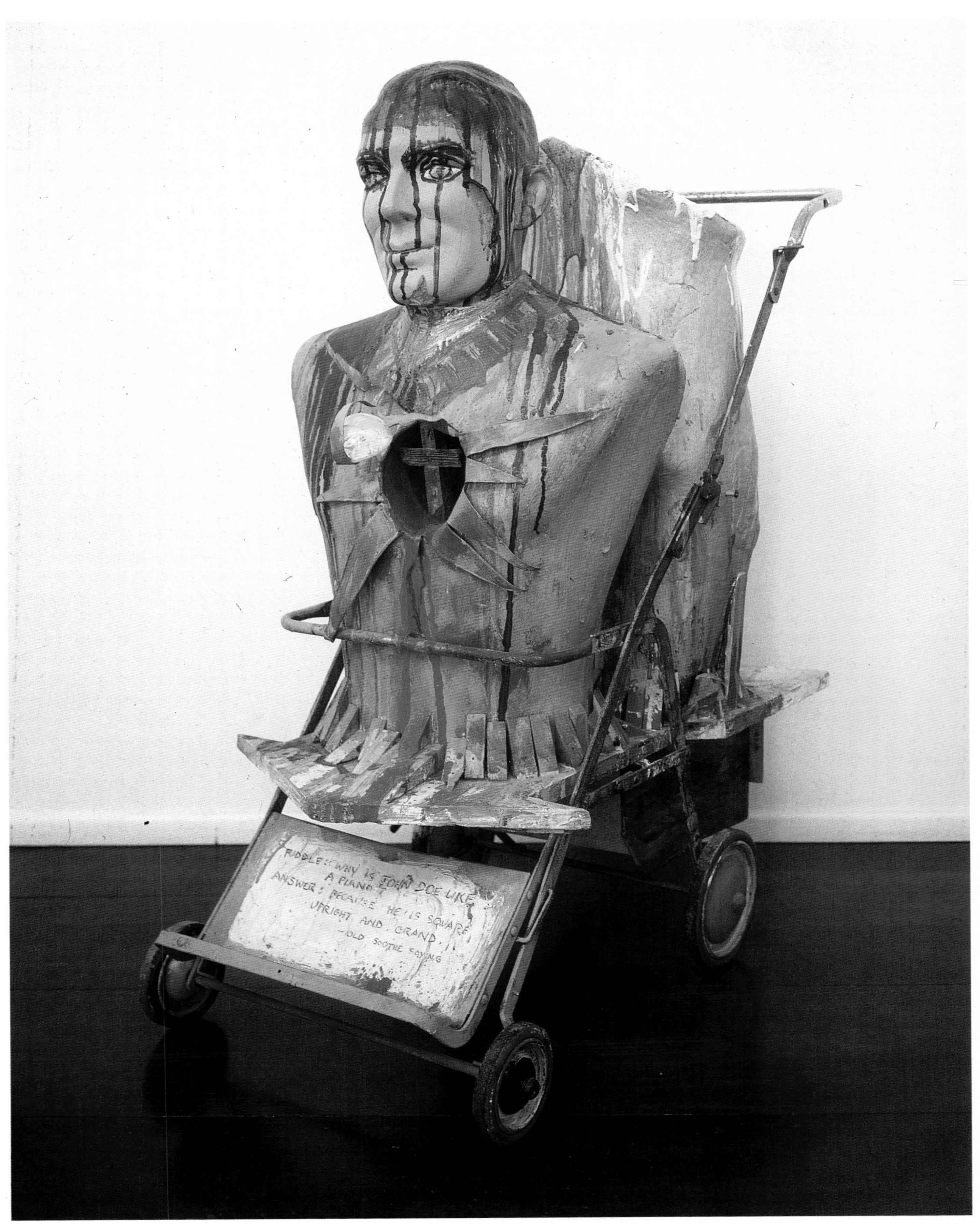

19 **Edward Kienholz** John Doe 1959 (cat 140)

20 **Larry Rivers and Jean Tinguely** Turning Friendship of America and France 1961 (cat 202)

21 **Larry Rivers** Final Veteran: The Last Civil War Veteran in the Coffin 1961 (cat 201)

22 **Larry Rivers** Kings 1960 (cat 200)

23 **Roy Lichtenstein** Popeye 1961 (cat 147)

24 **Andy Warhol** Saturday's Popeye 1960 (cat 236)

25 **Roy Lichtenstein** Washing Machine 1961 (cat 148)

26 **Robert Indiana** Zig 1960 (cat 114)

27 **H. C. Westermann** Swingin' Red King and Silver Queen 1960 (cat 255)

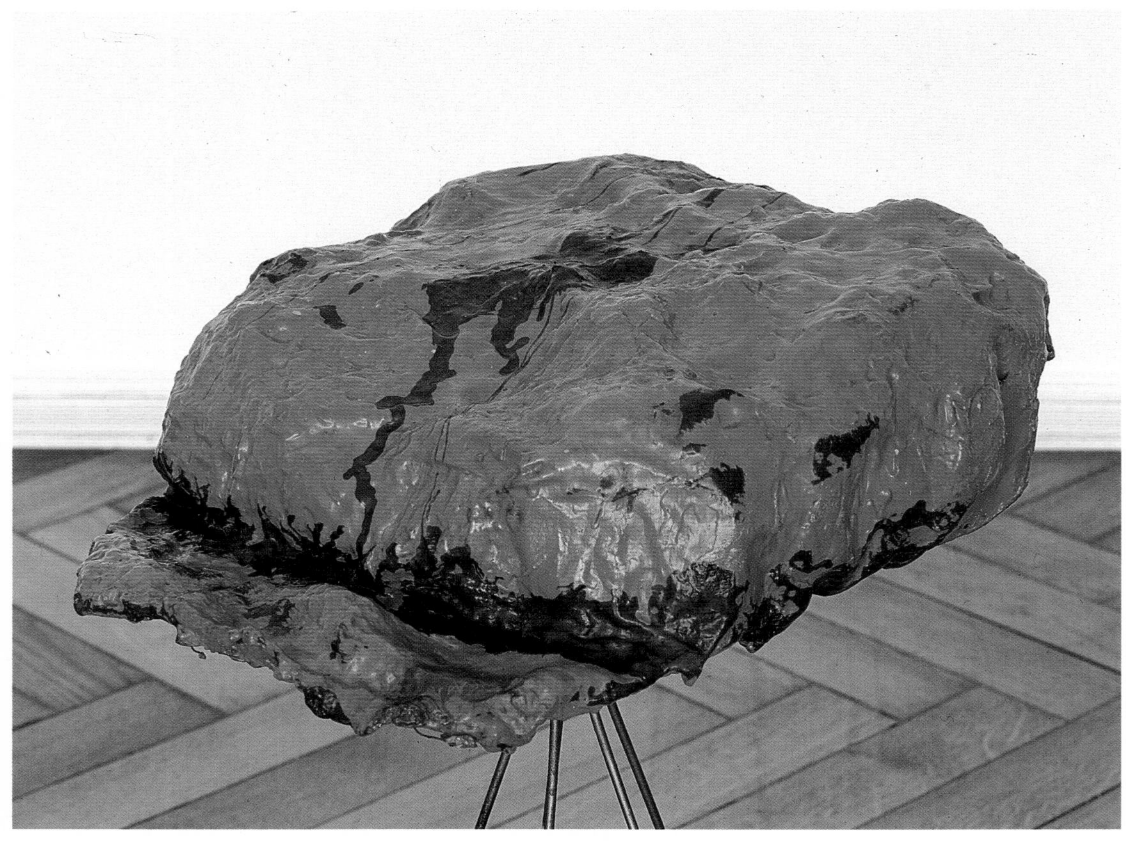

28 **Claes Oldenburg** Cap 1961 (cat 158)

29 **Claes Oldenburg** Plate of Meat 1961 (cat 160)

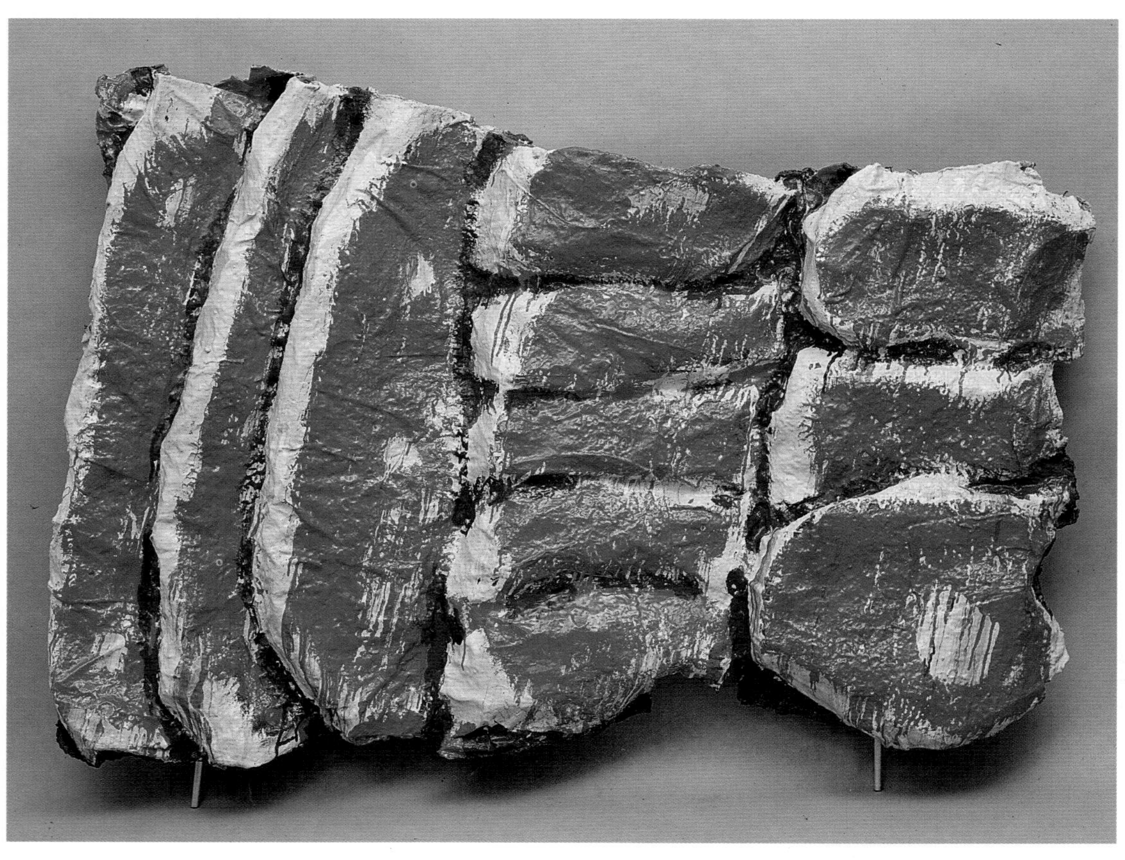

30 **Claes Oldenburg** Sewing Machine 1961 (cat 161)

31 **Claes Oldenburg** U.S. Flag Fragment 1961 (cat 162)

32 **Claes Oldenburg** Green Ladies' Shoes 1962 (cat 159)

33 **Jasper Johns** Good Time Charley 1961 (cat 126)

34 **Jasper Johns** 0 Through 9 1961 (cat 125)

35 **James Rosenquist** Hey, Let's Go for a Ride 1961 (cat 203)

36 **James Rosenquist** Look Alive (Blue Feet, Look Alive) 1961 (cat 205)

37 **Billy Al Bengston** Clint 1961 (cat 13)

38 **Billy Al Bengston** Carburetor Floatbowl 1961 (cat 12)

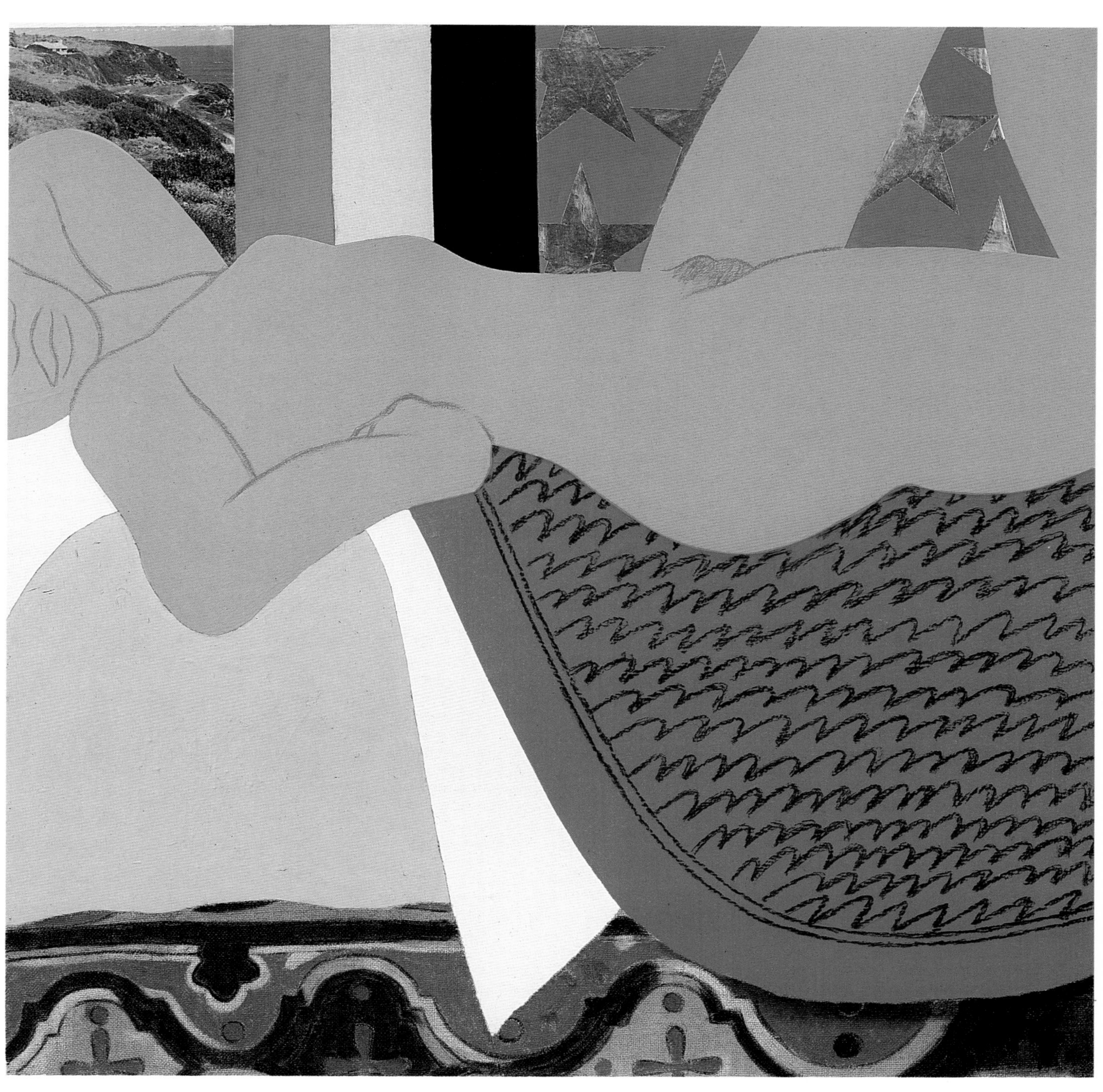

39 **Tom Wesselmann** Great American Nude #1 1961 (cat 251)

40 **Wayne Thiebaud** Five Hot Dogs 1961 (cat 226)

41 **Mel Ramos** Batmobile 1962 (cat 187)

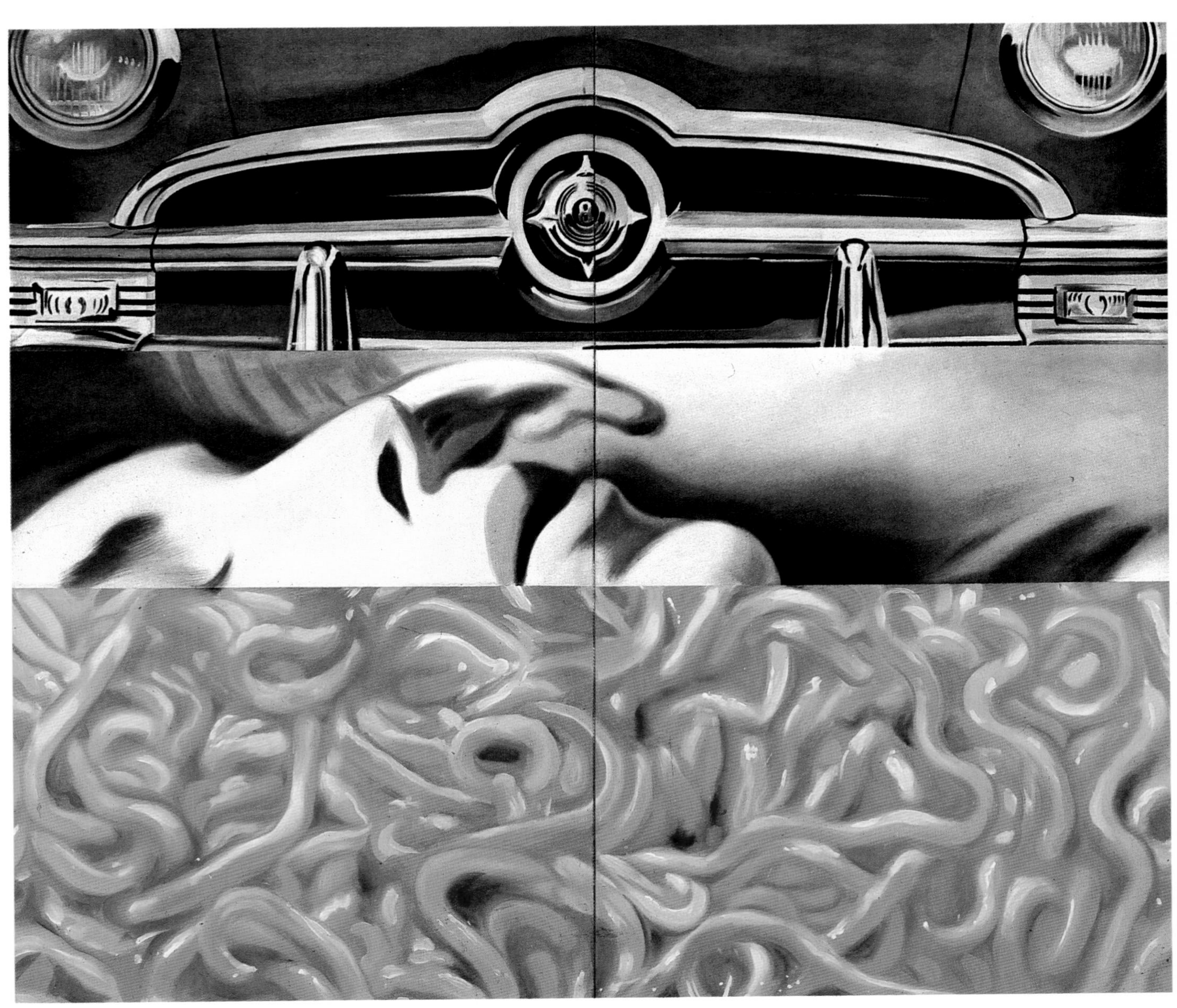

42 **James Rosenquist** I Love You with My Ford 1961 (cat 204)

43 **Jim Dine** Summer Tools 1962 (cat 35)

44 **Jim Dine** Tennis Shoe 1962 (cat 36)

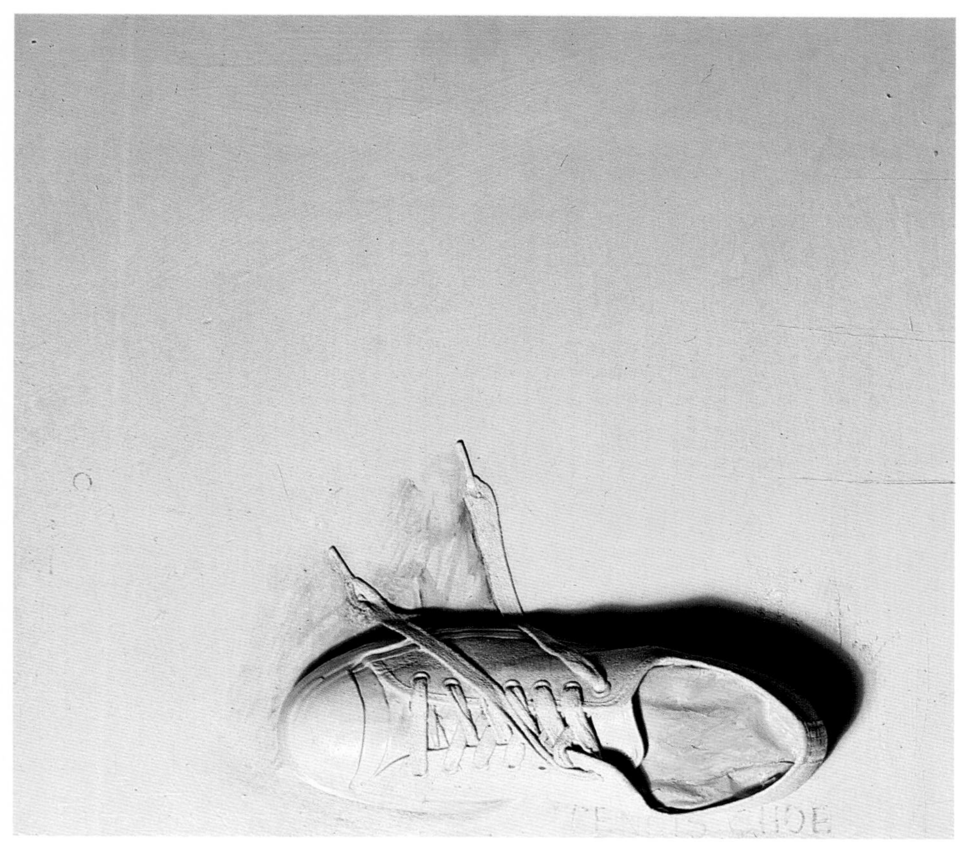

45 **Robert Rauschenberg** Dylaby 1962 (cat 191)

46 **Roy Lichtenstein** Blam 1962 (cat 149)

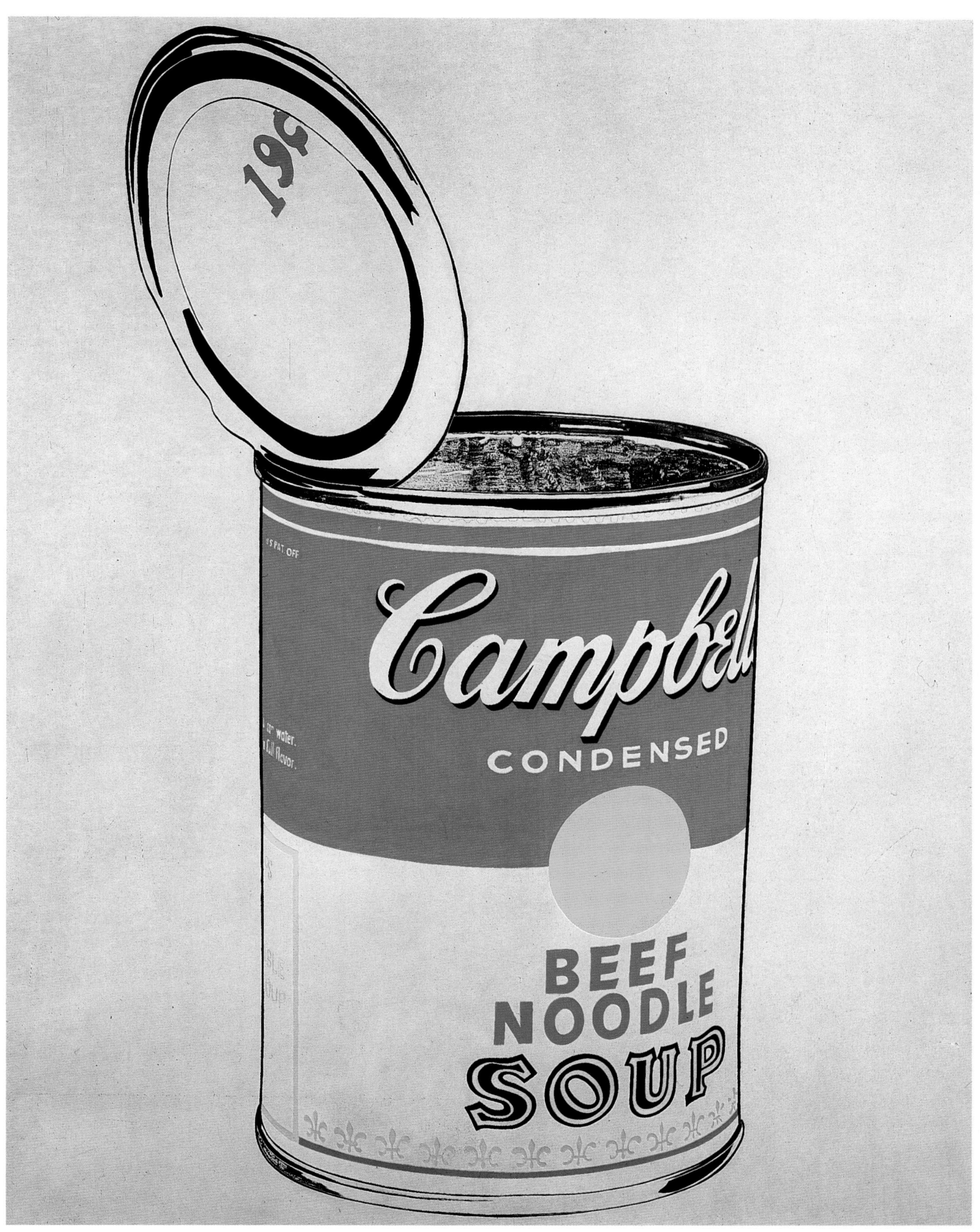

47 **Andy Warhol** Big Campbell's Soup Can (19¢) 1962 (cat 238)

48 **Andy Warhol** Do It Yourself: Landscape 1962 (cat 239)

49 **Roy Lichtenstein** Masterpiece 1962 (cat 150)

50 **Robert Indiana** American Gas Works 1962 (cat 115)

51 **Richard Artschwager** Portrait 1 1962 (cat 5)

52 **Andy Warhol** 80 2-Dollar Bills, Front and Rear 1962 (cat 237)

53 **Jasper Johns** Double Flag 1962 (cat 127)

54 **John Wesley** Olympic Field Hockey Officials 1962 (cat 250)

55 **Allan d'Arcangelo** The Wedding (Unfinished) 1962 (cat 32)

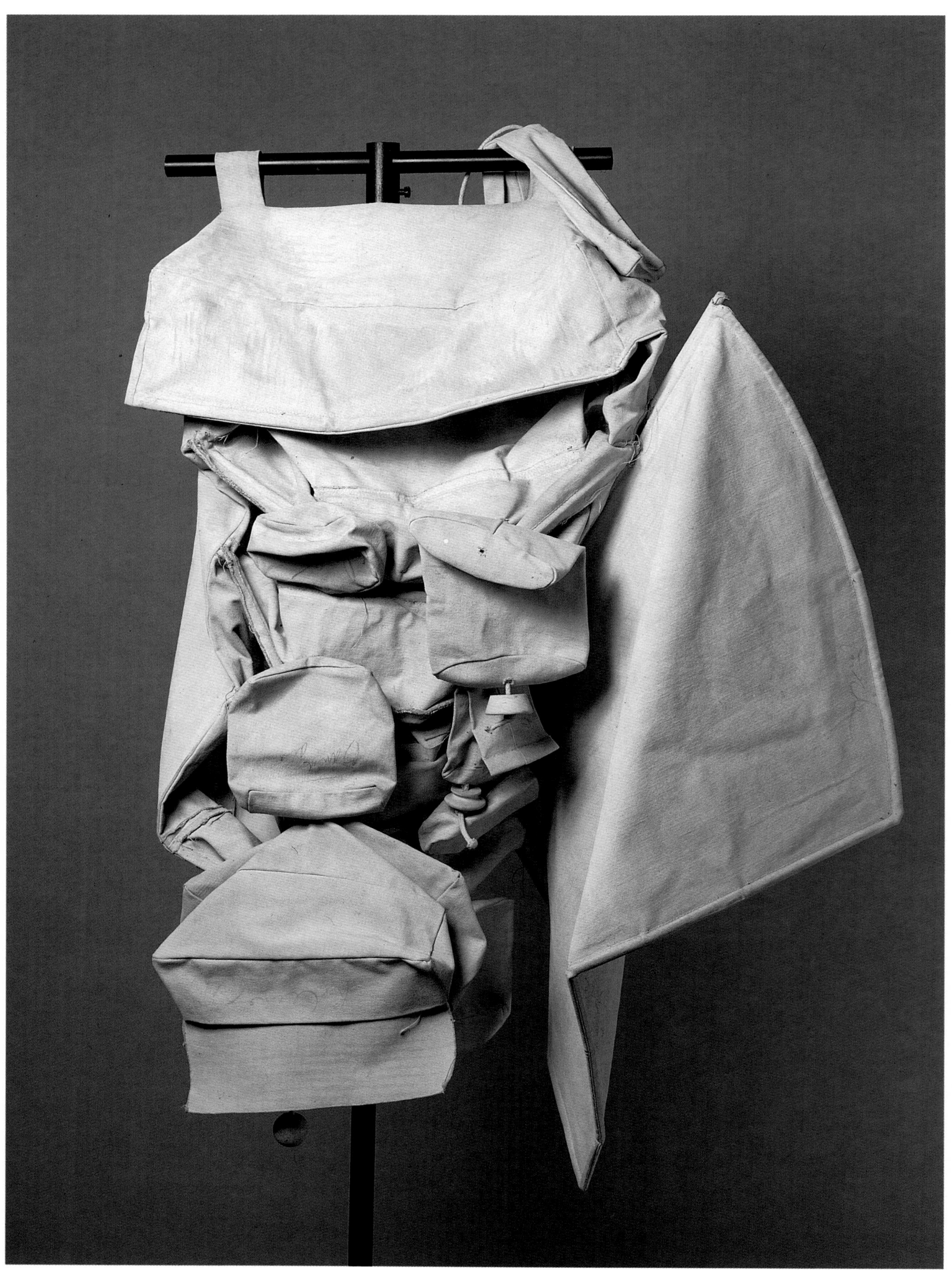

56 **Claes Oldenburg** Model (Ghost) Medicine Cabinet 1966 (cat 165)

57 **Claes Oldenburg** Soft Medicine Cabinet 1966 (cat 166)

58 **George Segal** Woman Standing in a Bathtub 1964 (cat 215)

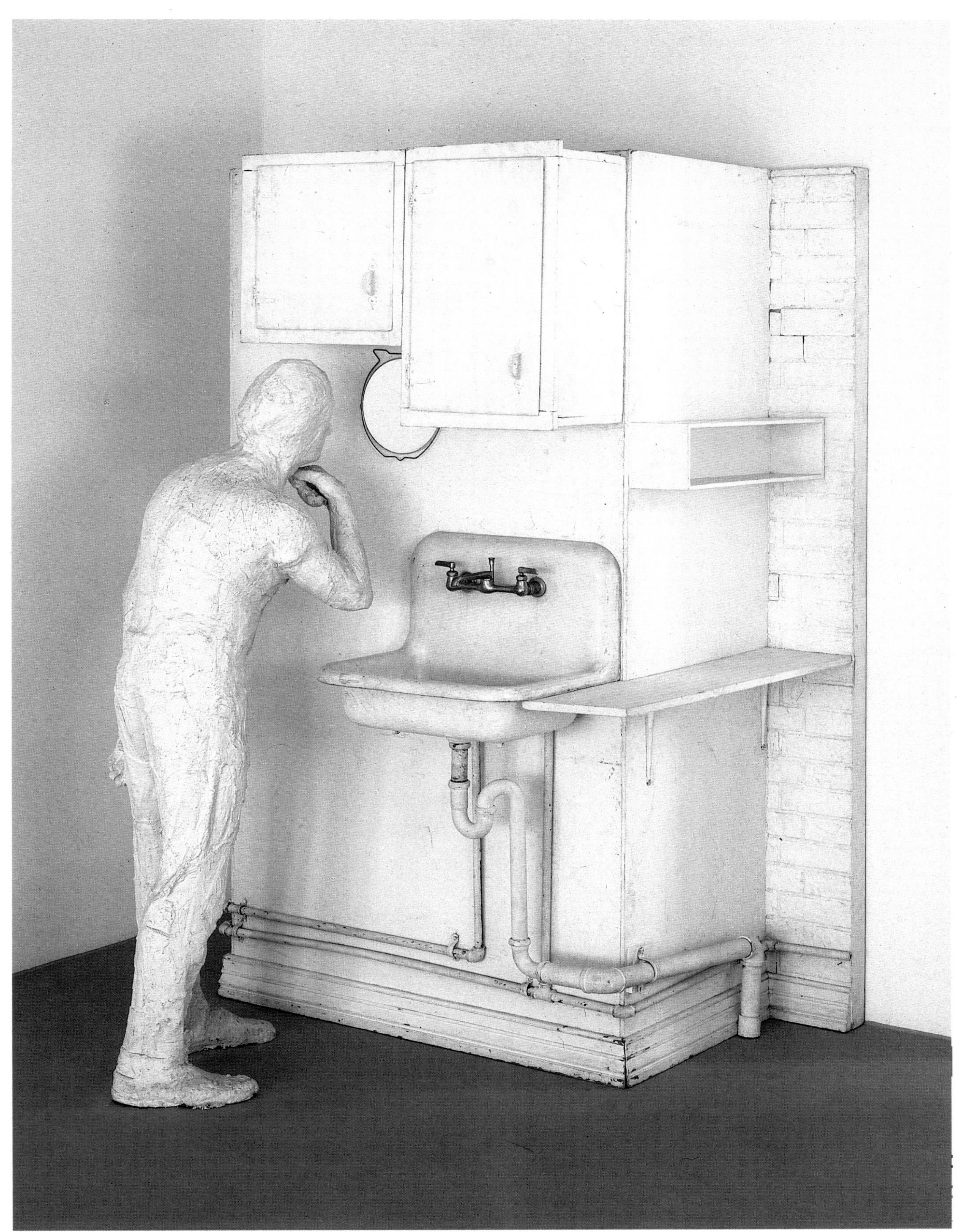

59 **George Segal** Artist in His Loft 1969 (cat 216)

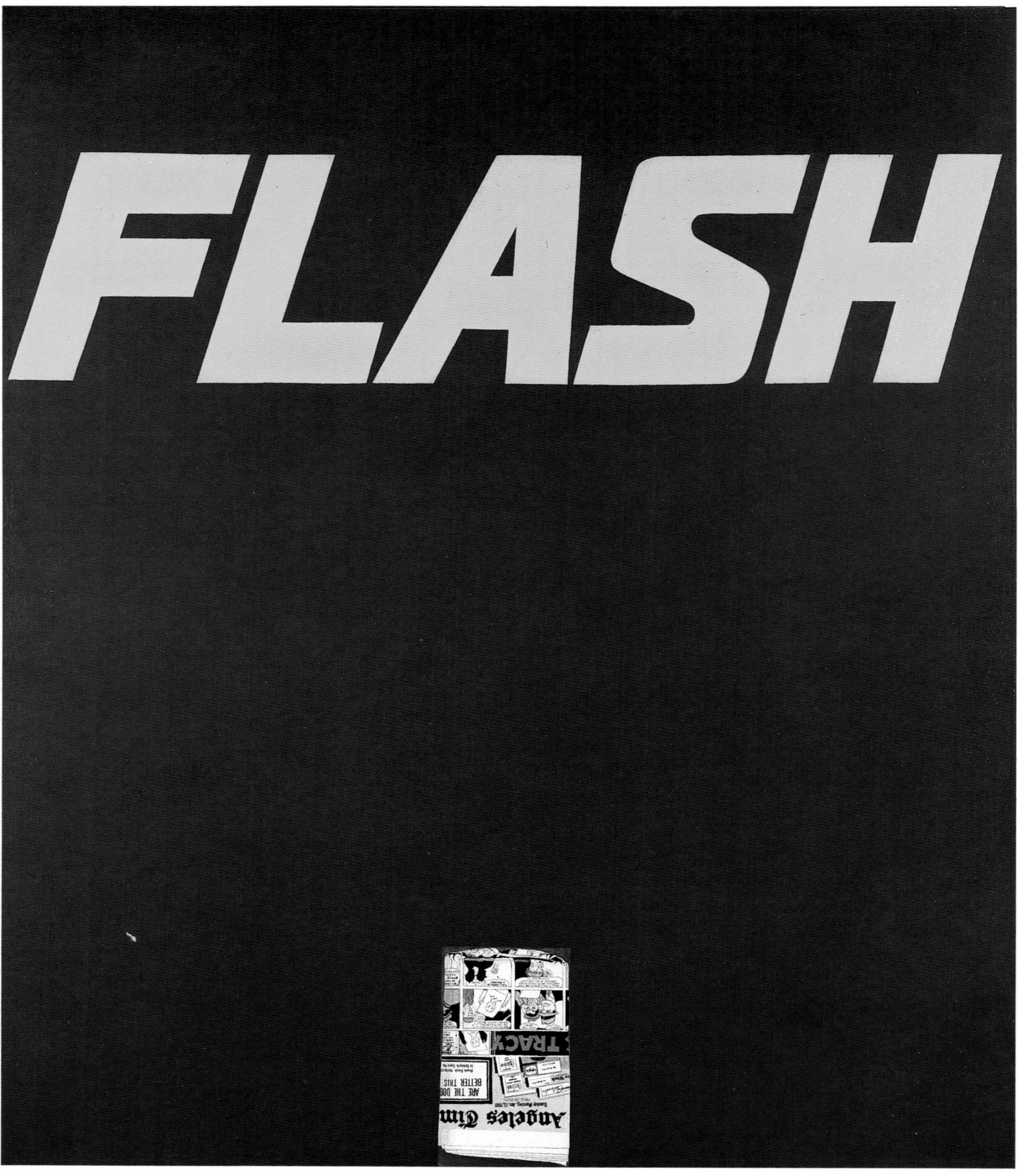

60 **Ed Ruscha** Flash, L.A. Times 1963 (cat 209)

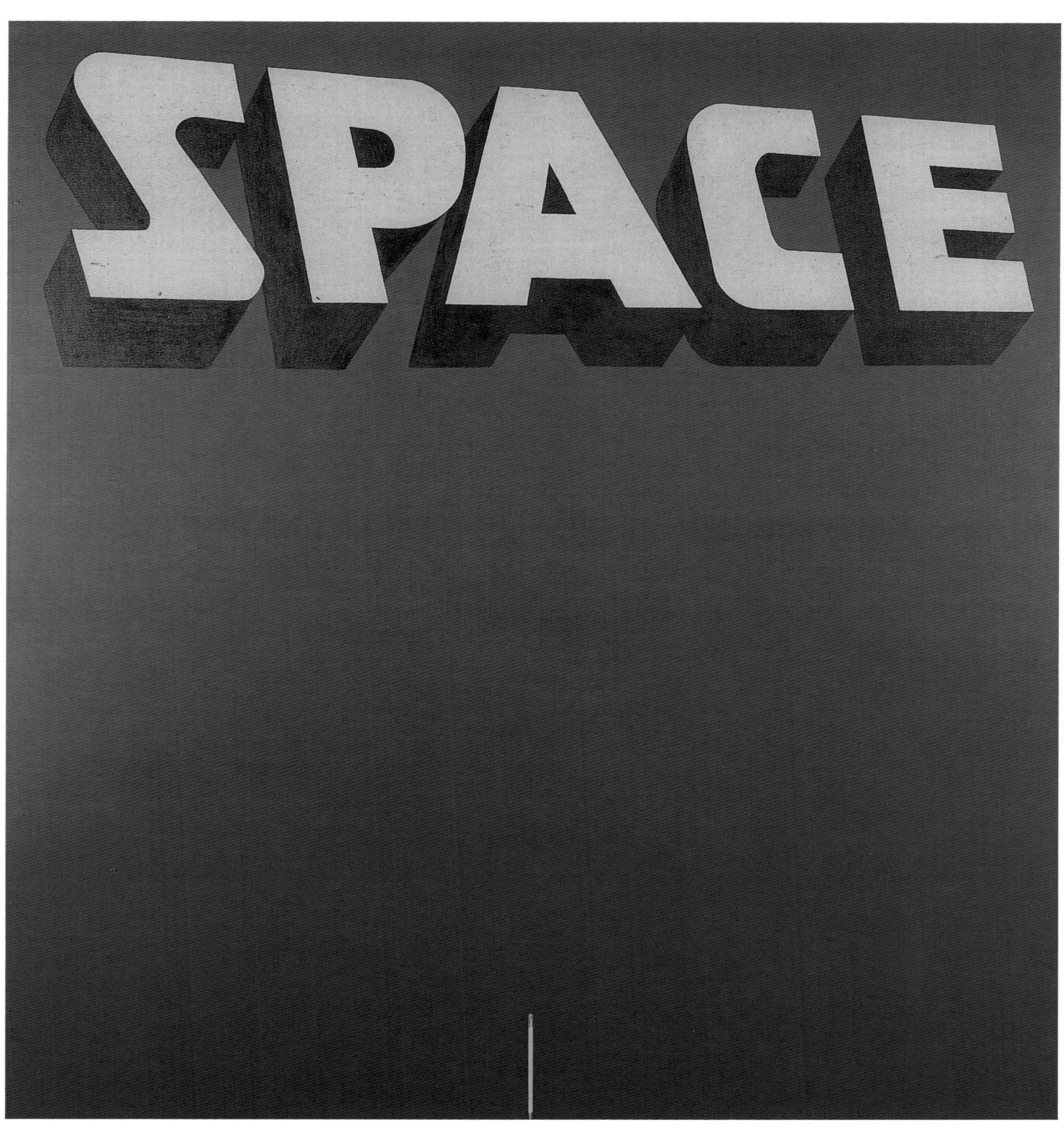

61 **Ed Ruscha** Talk about Space 1963 (cat 210)

62 **Roy Lichtenstein** Torpedo . . . los! 1963 (cat 152)

63 **Roy Lichtenstein** I Know ... Brad 1963 (cat 151)

64 **Andy Warhol** Early Colored Liz 1963 (cat 241)

65 **Andy Warhol** Marilyn 1964 (cat 244)

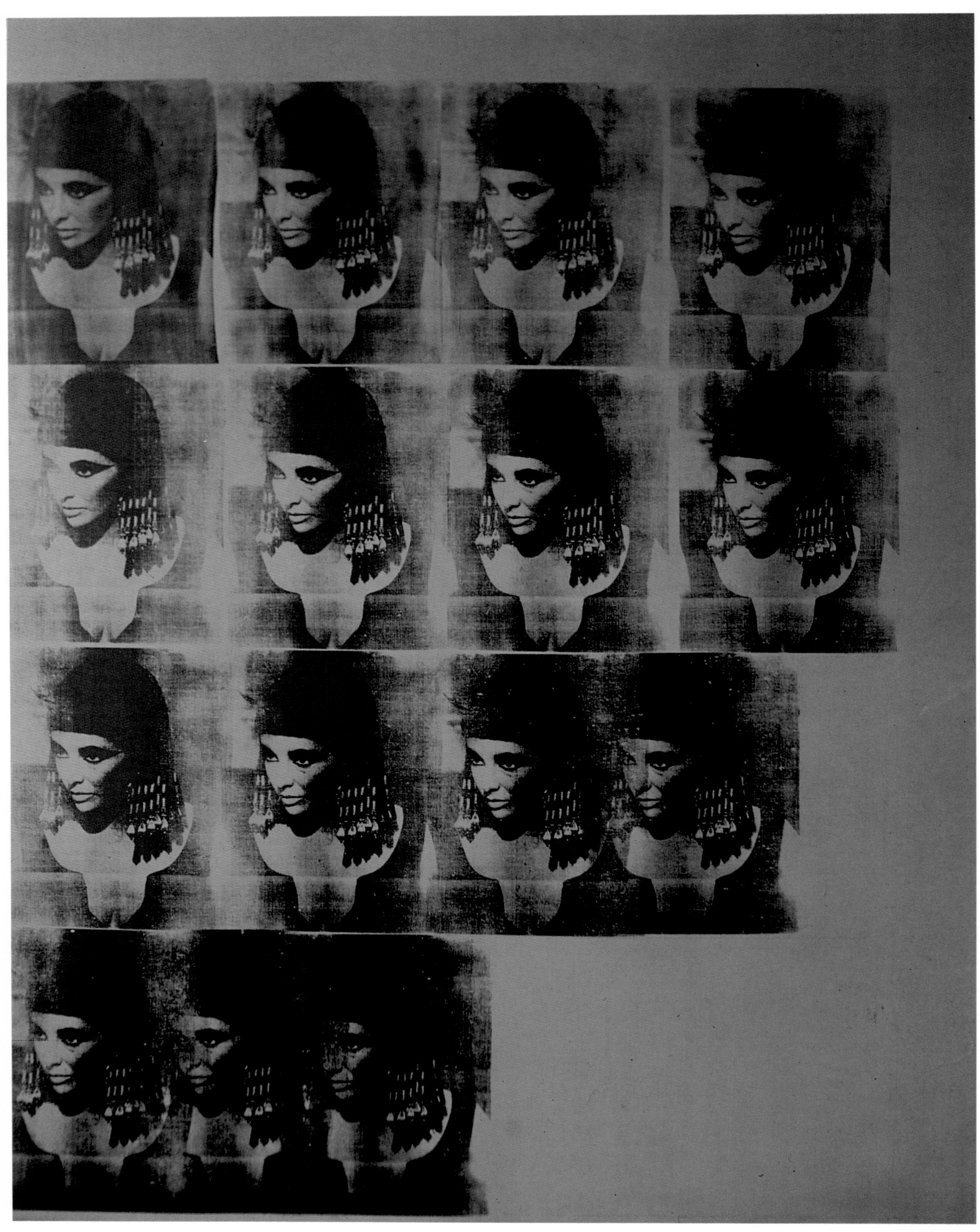

66 **Andy Warhol** Blue Liz as Cleopatra 1963 (cat 240)

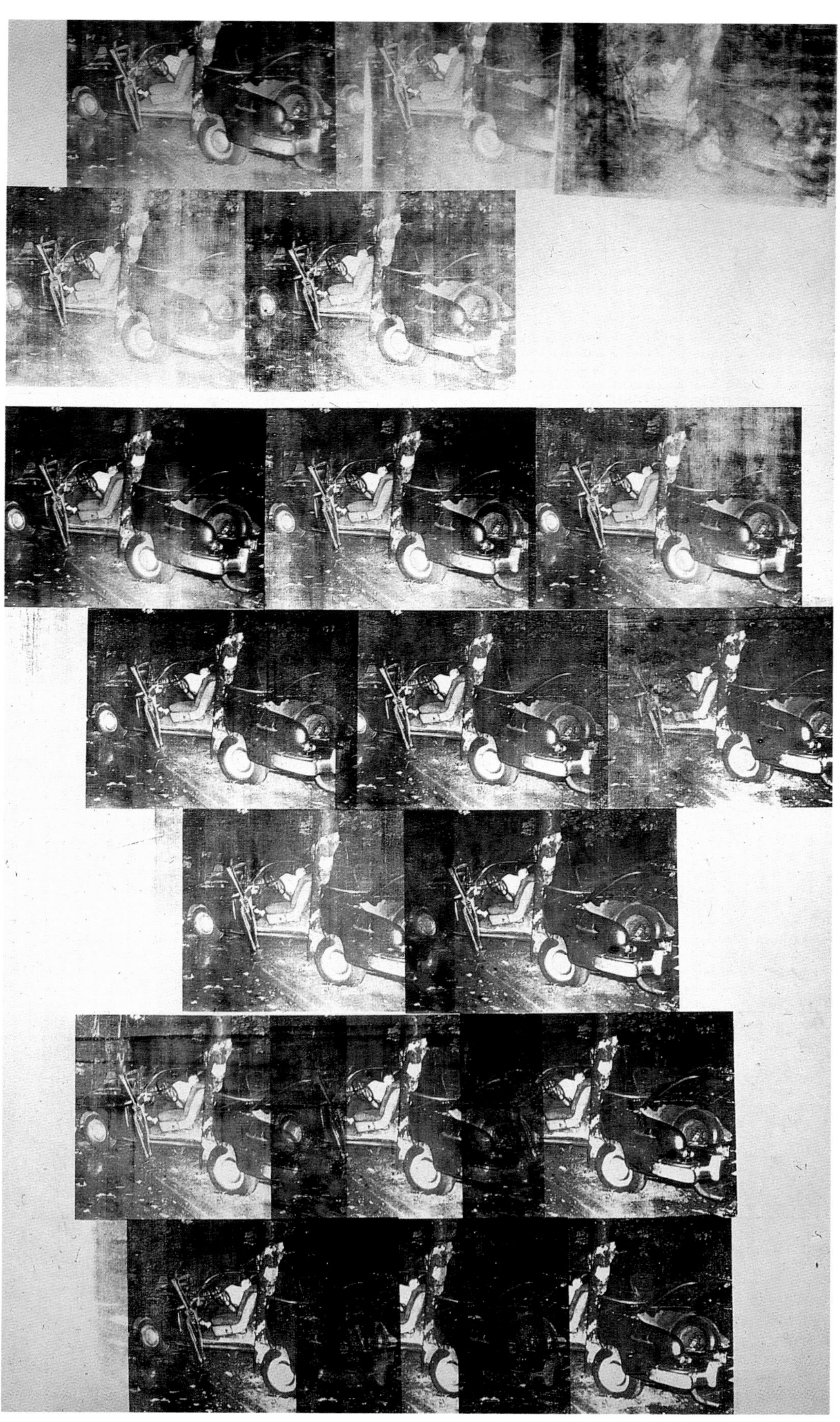

67 **Andy Warhol** White Car Crash 19 times 1963 (cat 242)

68 **Andy Warhol** Boxes 1964 (cat 243)

69 **Robert Rauschenberg** Spot 1963 (cat 192)

70 **Tom Wesselmann** Bathtub Collage #2 1963 (cat 252)

71 **Tom Wesselmann** Interior #1 1964 (cat 253)

72 **Wayne Thiebaud** Cake Counter 1963 (cat 227)

73 **Wayne Thiebaud** Jawbreaker Machine (Bubble Gum Machine) 1963 (cat 228)

74 **Claes Oldenburg** Banana Splits and Glaces en Dégustation 1964 (cat 163)

75 **Claes Oldenburg** Giant Soft Toothpaste 1964 (cat 164)

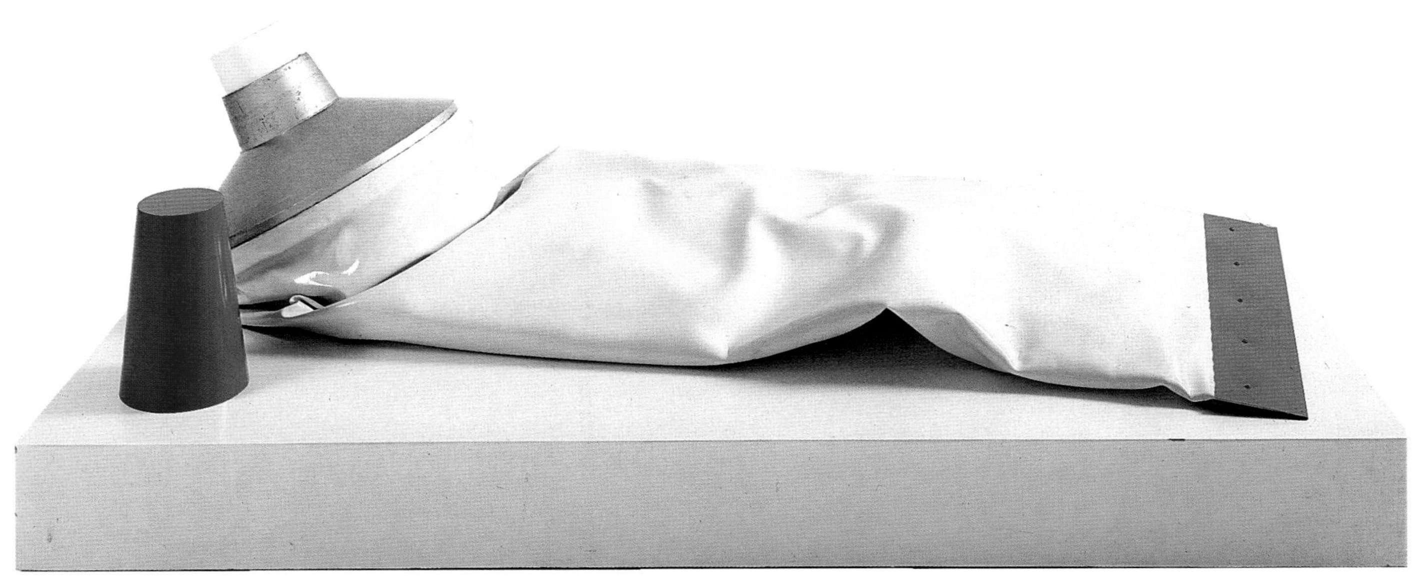

76 **Joe Goode** Small Space 1963 (cat 96)

77 **Joe Goode** Untitled (Staircase) *c* 1966 (cat 97)

78 **H. C. Westermann** Bowling Trophy 1967 (cat 257)

79 **H. C. Westermann** A Little Black Cage 1965 (cat 256)

80 **Richard Artschwager** Apartment House 1964 (cat 6)

81 **Richard Artschwager** Piano 1965 (cat 7)

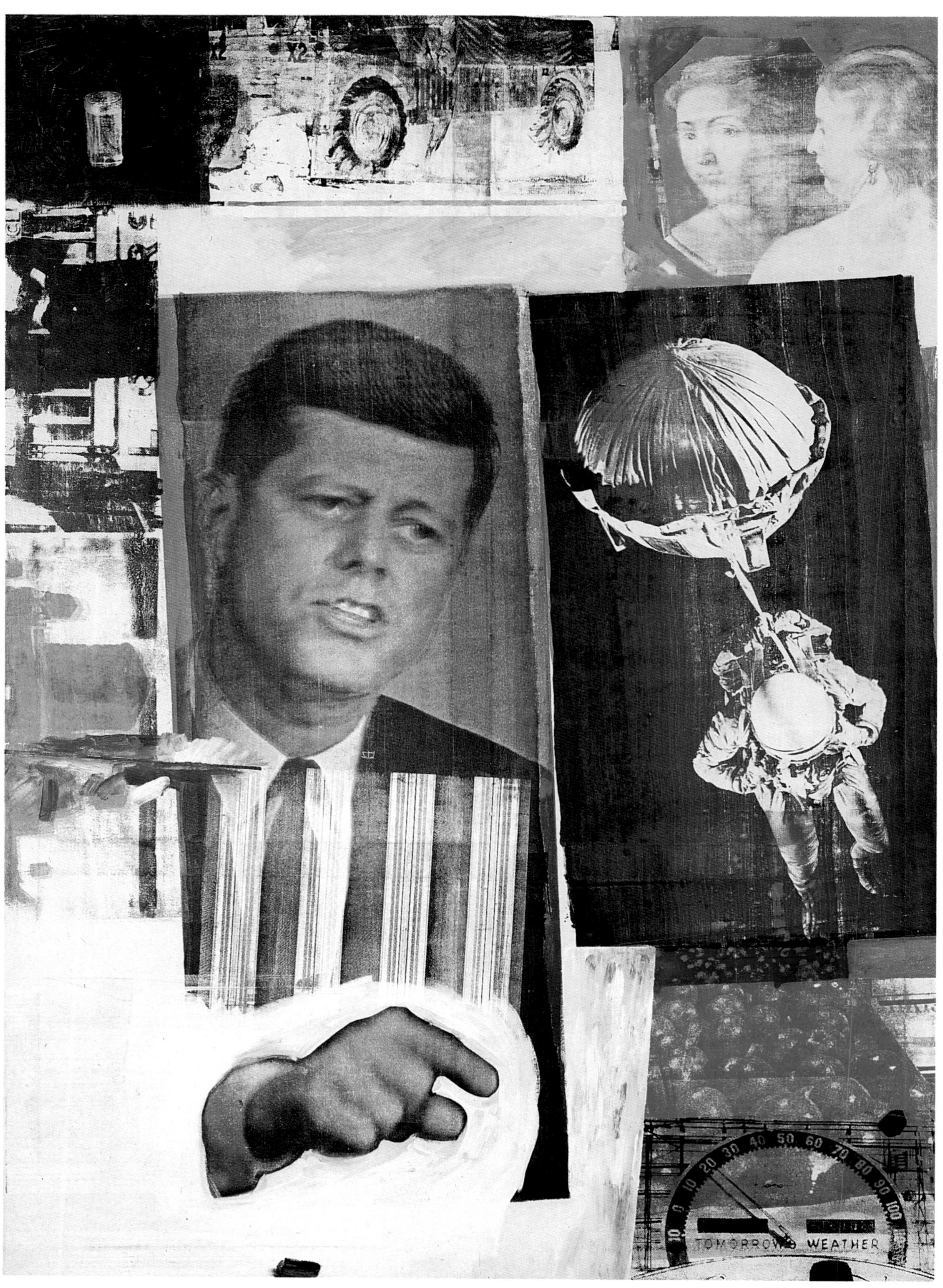

82 **Robert Rauschenberg** Retroactive II 1964 (cat 193)

83 **Andy Warhol** Flowers 1966 (cat 245)

84 **Roy Lichtenstein** White Brushstroke #1 1965 (cat 153)

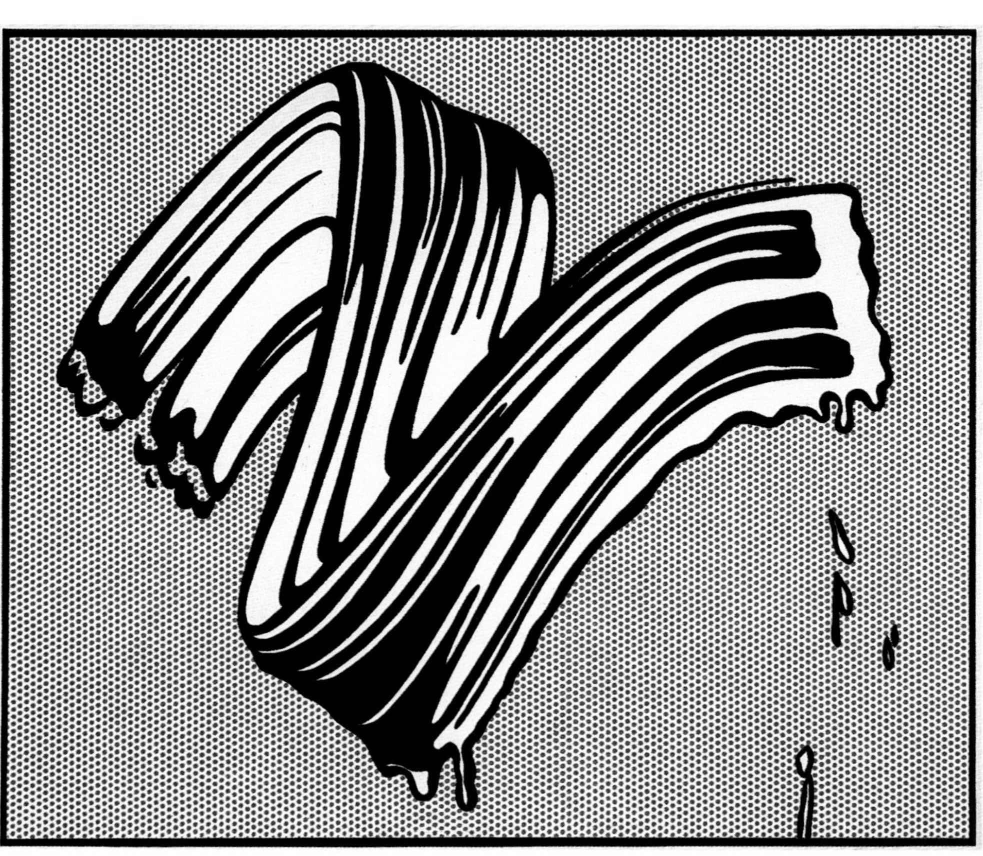

85 **Mel Ramos** Miss Cushion Air (Miss Firestone) 1965 (cat 188)

86 **Ed Ruscha** The Los Angeles County Museum of Art on Fire 1965–68 (cat 211)

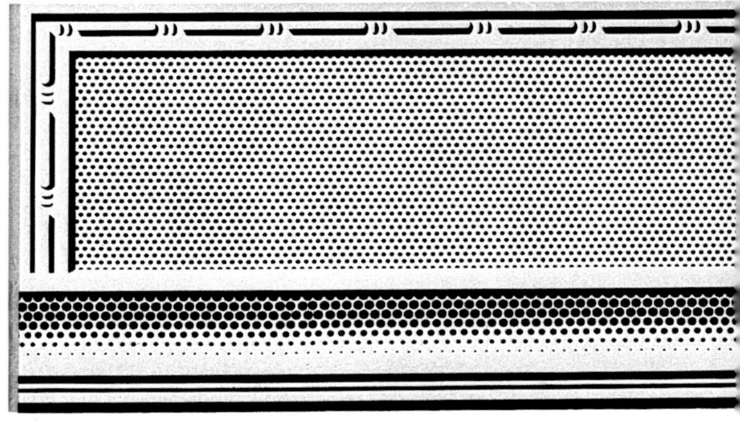

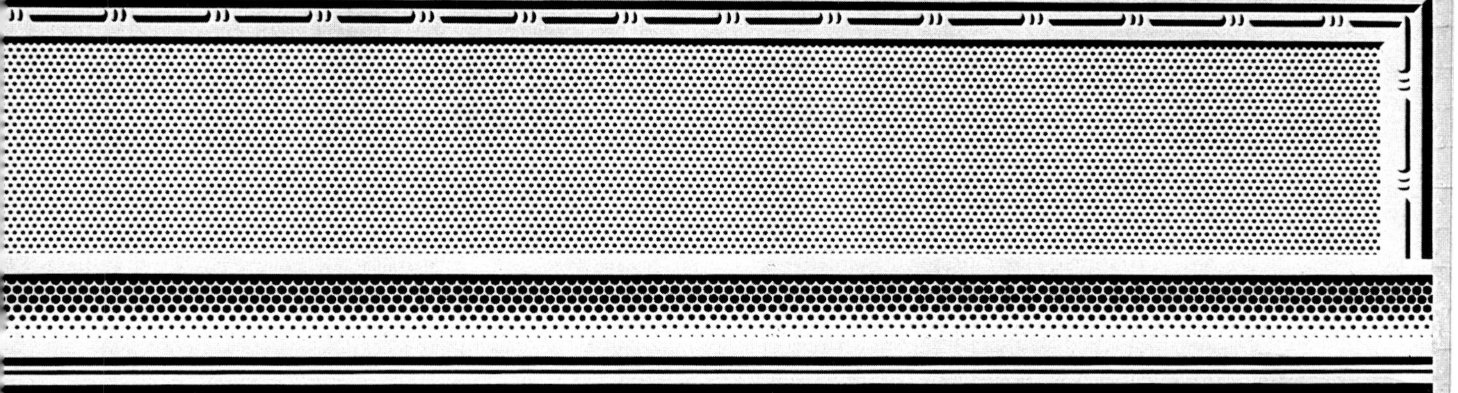

87 **Roy Lichtenstein** Entablature 1971 (cat 155)

88 **Roy Lichtenstein** Rouen Cathedral II (seen at three different times of day) 1969 (cat 154)

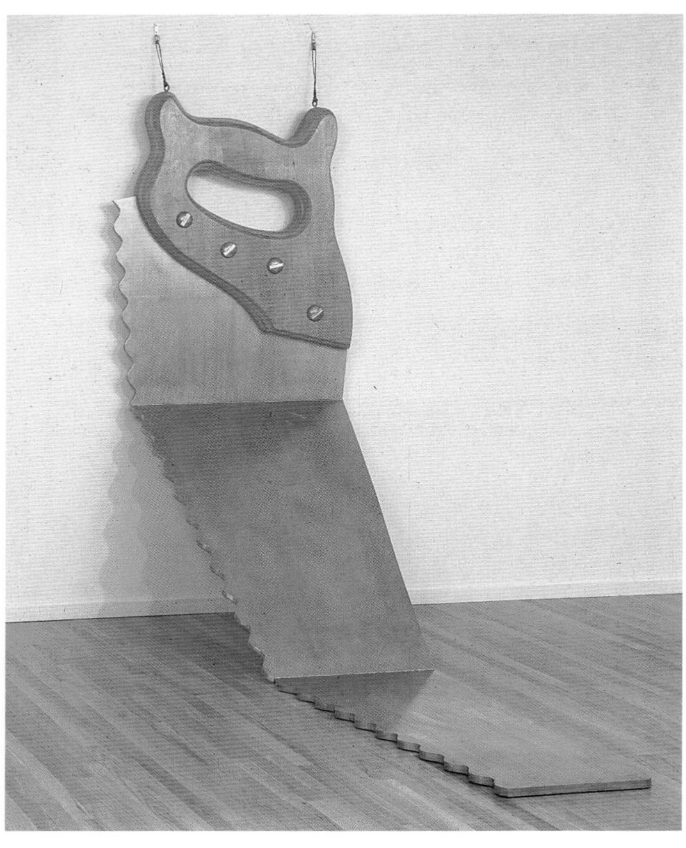

89 **Claes Oldenburg** Giant Saw – Hard Version 1969 (cat 167)

90 **Claes Oldenburg** Geometric Mouse – scale A 1973 (cat 168)

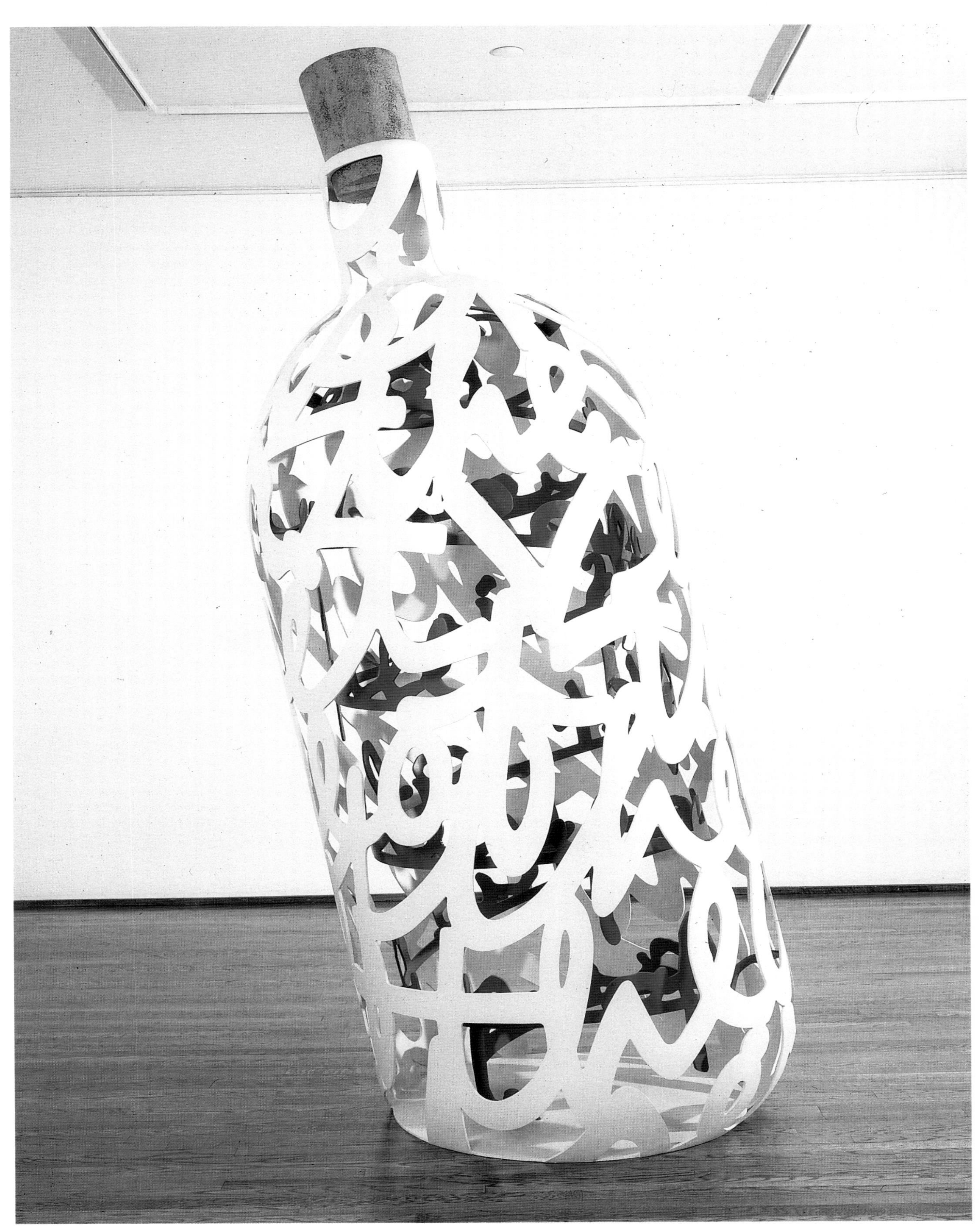

91 **Claes Oldenburg and Coosje van Bruggen** Bottle of Notes (Model) 1989–90 (cat 169)

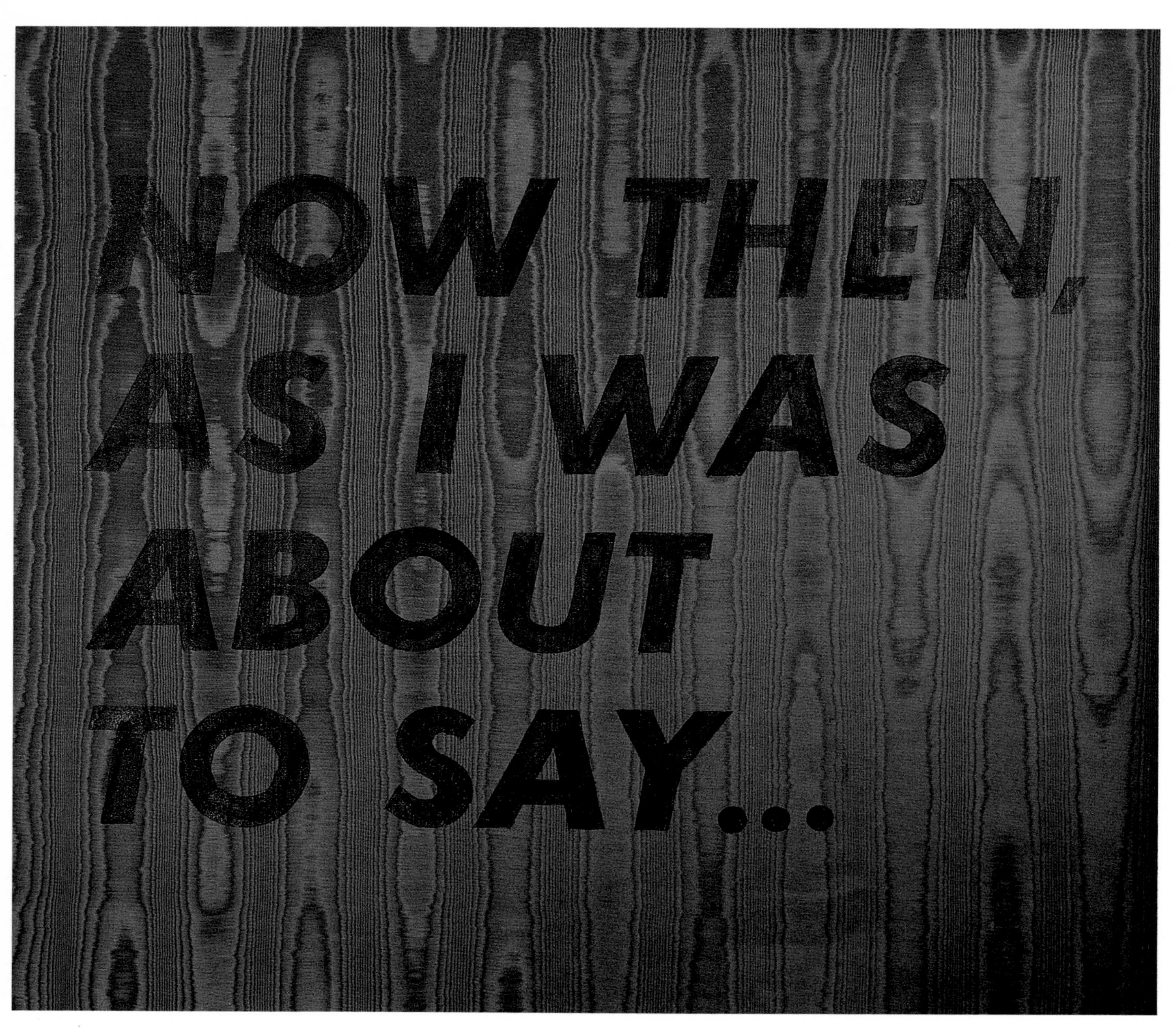

92 **Ed Ruscha** Now Then, As I Was About To Say 1973 (cat 212)

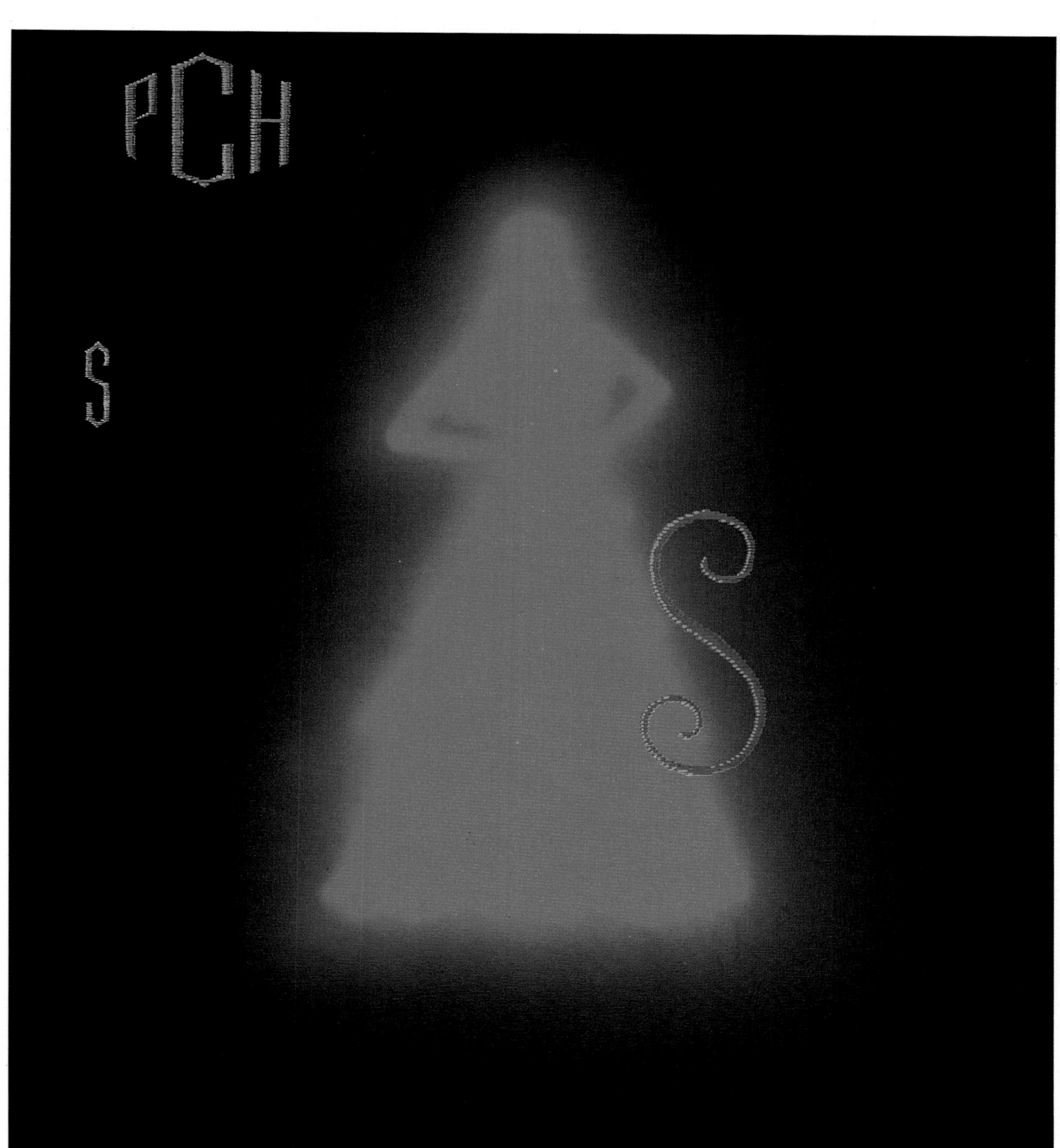

93 **Ed Ruscha** Pacific Coast Highway 1987 (cat 213)

94 **Andy Warhol** Mao 1973 (cat 246)

95 **Andy Warhol** Dollar Signs 1981 (cat 247)

96 **James Rosenquist** Star Thief 1980 (cat 206)

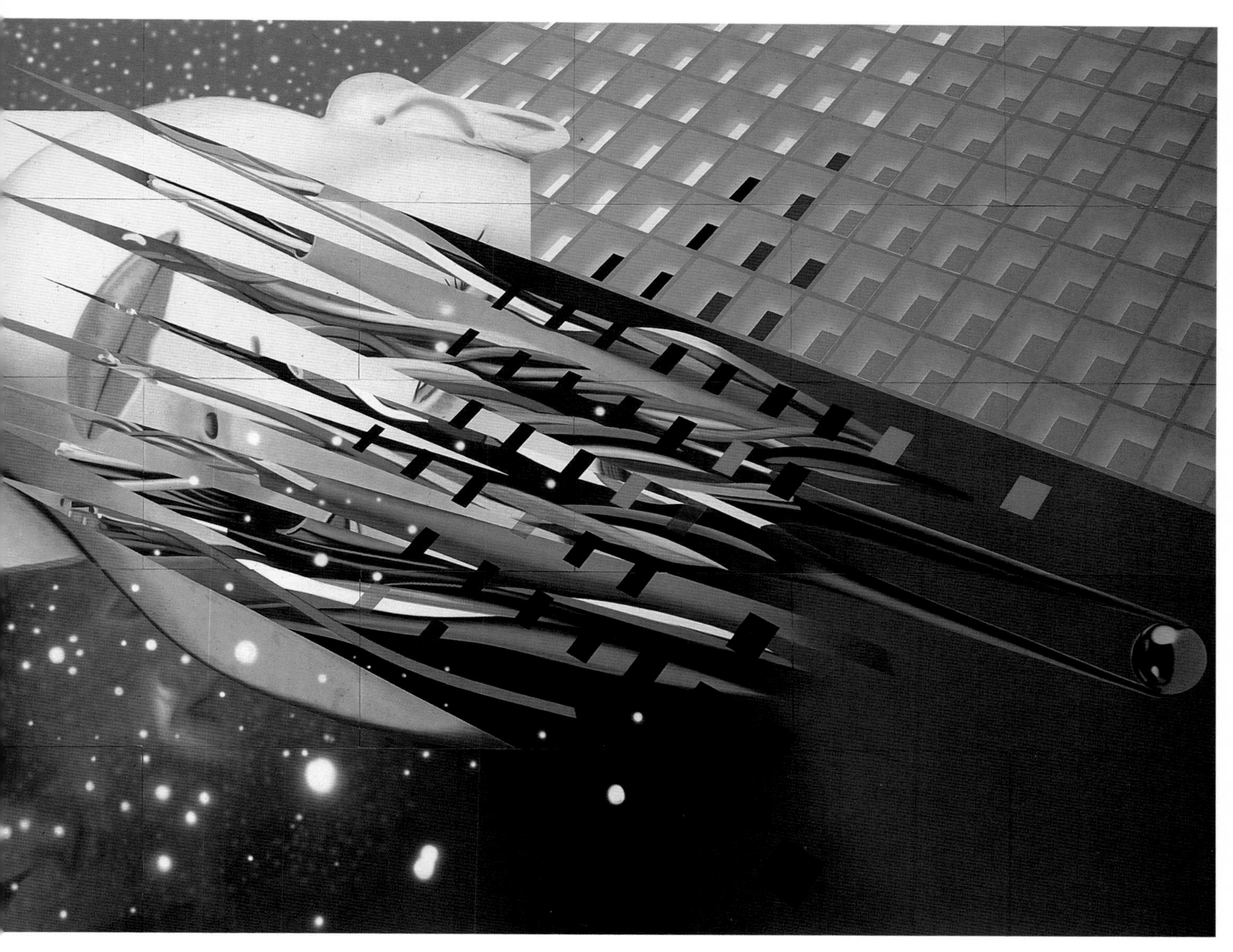

97 **Robert Rauschenberg** Courtyard (Urban Bourbon Series) 1989 (cat 194)

98 **Roy Lichtenstein** Interior with Built-in Bar 1991 (cat 156)

99 **Tom Wesselmann** Big Blonde #2 1988 (cat 254)

100 **Richard Artschwager** Running Man 1991 (cat 8)

101 **Andy Warhol** Raphael 1 – $6.99 1985 (cat 248)

uk pop

a big sensation

PEOPLE TRY TO PUT US DOWN
JUST BECAUSE WE GET AROUND
I'M NOT TRYING TO CAUSE A BIG SENSATION
I'M JUST TALKIN' 'BOUT MY GENERATION

PETE TOWNSHEND *(1965)*

MARCO LIVINGSTONE

Pop Art in Britain was created largely by very young men both as a direct reflection of their viewpoint on culture and as a rebellion against the art establishment. It erupted first in the early 1950s through a small band of artists, architects and critics known as the Independent Group, notably Eduardo Paolozzi and Richard Hamilton, and in Peter Blake's student work at the Royal College of Art, a post-graduate institution. Later in the 1950s and early 1960s a more cohesive movement was created by younger painters at the Royal College together with Blake's former colleagues, Richard Smith and Joe Tilson. They were followed in the early 1960s by the sculptor Clive Barker, by the painter Gerald Laing and at the Slade School of Fine Art by Colin Self, Jann Haworth and Anthony Donaldson, who presented less of a united front than their counterparts at the Royal College but who nevertheless made important contributions to the spread of the movement.

Pop artists in Britain, as in the United States, sought to inflict deliberate destruction on the elaborate preconceptions constructed by artists of the generation immediately before them. While the Americans were intent both on rivalling the visual presence and energy of Abstract Expressionism and on debunking its lofty ideals, the British were fighting against what they felt to be the insularity, cosiness and sense of decorum of the art that was most admired in their country during the 1950s, as exemplified particularly by the abstract and landscape-based painting associated with the artists' colony at St Ives in Cornwall. An appreciation of nature was expected of the English; one was also meant to know one's place, which by and large meant respecting a hierarchy of values formulated by the upper classes.

Pop artists in Britain proposed an aggressively urban and contemporary art as a counter to the worship of the timelessness of nature that they were due to inherit, and they made their points in a plain-speaking language born of a democratic impulse stirring in their society at large. For the most part these were artists born just before the outbreak of World War II, often to working-class families. Their earliest experiences would thus date from one of the rare periods during which people pulled together for the common good in spite of class differences, followed by a prolonged period of austerity, with a fairly limited range of consumer products and food rationing in force until the early 1950s. They were also among the first to benefit from changes in regulations that made art school more accessible to those without an academic background, a situation that proved short-lived with the reintroduction of O level and A level requirements during the 1960s.

I make these observations here only to recall the climate in which Pop emerged and the particular circumstances that led to its rapid public appreciation. I have no intention, however, of proposing a sociological interpretation of British Pop, given that this art is only marginally and sporadically concerned with such aspects of subject-matter or with semiological decodings of the social, political or economic sub-texts of particular imagery. In this sense the Independent Group's detached observations of popular culture during the 1950s, while helping to create the basis of an iconography of Pop, remained the exception rather than the rule, wielding no direct influence on the younger artists at the Royal College whose first Pop works followed a few years later. For a painter such as Peter Phillips, only 21 years old when he produced pictures such as *Purple Flag* (1960; cat. 178), such material could be used unceremoniously and placed to purely visual ends. As he wrote in 1964:

> *My awareness of machines, advertising, and mass communication is not probably in the same sense as an older generation . . . I've been conditioned by them and grew up with it all and use it without a second thought. I wouldn't analyse these images in a way that an artist of an older generation might. I've lived with them ever since I can remember and so it's natural to use them without thinking. I'm basically interested in painting and not just a presentation of imagery.*[1]

The divergence of approach in British Pop is evident from the inception of the movement, especially in the contrast between the celebration of popular culture in Blake's work and the intellectual, analytical approach adopted by Hamilton and the Independent Group. While studying art and graphic design during the late 1940s and early 1950s in Gravesend, Kent, just outside London, Blake became interested in folk art, recognising direct links with the popular entertainments with which he became involved as a teenager, such as wrestling matches, fairgrounds and live jazz. By the time he began to train as a painter at the Royal College in 1953, his vocation and his pastimes were so seamlessly united that it seemed obvious for the two activities to interact, although there was no clear fine art precedent for his interest in comic books as a form of narrative imagery (as in *Children Reading Comics,* cat. 15) nor for his presentation of his paintings in the guise of weatherbeaten fairground art in a naive style. The tone of much of this work is frankly nostalgic, with a pathos rooted in a longing for the lost innocence of childhood.

The Independent Group, which first met in London at the Institute of Contemporary Arts on Dover Street in 1952, was basically a discussion group. In its ranks were Hamilton, Paolozzi, the sculptor and painter William Turnbull, the collagist John McHale, the Hungarian-born painter Magda Cordell, the photographer Nigel Henderson and the Constructivist painter Victor Pasmore. Membership also included the architects Alison and Peter Smithson, the architectural historian Reyner Banham and the critics Lawrence Alloway and Toni del Renzio. They met on a regular basis at the ICA until 1955. Their importance to the later history of Pop Art, however, lay not so much in the work they produced during that time – which on the whole was more closely related to the figurative idiom of Jean Dubuffet's Art Brut – as in the notion they developed of a spectrum running from popular art to fine art as an entire field of visual production open to analysis. Their meetings over the first two years were on a wide variety of topics.[2] They included a presentation in April 1952 of material culled from magazines by Eduardo Paolozzi, closely related to his *Bunk* collages (cat. 170–3), which he projected on an epidiascope; a talk on aircraft design in the same month by employees of the De Havilland company; lectures at various meetings from August 1952 to September 1953 on helicopter design, the machine aesthetic and pioneers of the modern movement; and a lecture in November 1953 on proportion and symmetry by the architect Colin St John Wilson, who in the 1960s became one of the leading collectors of British Pop Art. In 1955, after the IG had been reconvened by

1 Quoted in *The New Generation: 1964,* exhibition catalogue, Whitechapel Gallery, London, March–May 1964, p. 72.

2 See the detailed chronology by Graham Whitham in David Robbins, ed., *The Independent Group: Postwar Britain and the Aesthetics of Plenty,* Cambridge, MA, and London, 1990, pp. 12–48.

Alloway and McHale, meetings were devoted to a number of topics related to the mass media and related areas: advertising,[3] fashion and fashion magazines, Italian product design.

The explorations of the Independent Group into popular culture, culminating in the first published use of the term 'pop art',[4] was made public not so much in the work of individual members as in the thematic exhibitions organised by them, such as 'Parallel of Life and Art' (1953) and 'Man, Machine and Motion' (1955), the installations for which were conceived as three-dimensional collages of photographs and other found material.[5] The sense they conveyed of a kaleidoscopic view of culture, which became such a central element of Paolozzi's collages and of his screenprints of the 1960s, was one of their prime legacies to Pop Art. Direct reference to popular culture was made only, however, in the installation produced by Hamilton in collaboration with McHale and John Voelcker for the Whitechapel Gallery exhibition 'This is Tomorrow' in 1956 (fig. 1); among the elements in their display were an operative jukebox stacked with popular records, a life-sized photographic still of Marilyn Monroe as seen in Billy Wilder's film *The Seven Year Itch* (released a year earlier), and a portrait 5 m (16 ft) high of Robbie the Robot, hero of the science fiction film *Forbidden Planet,* borrowed from the London Pavilion cinema at Piccadilly Circus. It was for this exhibition that Hamilton created a small collage for reproduction as a poster and in the catalogue, *Just what is it that makes today's homes so different, so appealing?* (cat. 99), which has since assumed status as one of the most prophetic images in the early history of Pop Art. Here, in a nutshell, Hamilton has presented a wide range of the source material later taken up by him and his colleagues: photography, the cinema, television, advertising, comic-strips, pin-up and muscle-men magazines, pre-packed convenience foods, consumer products and brand names. Here, too, are some of the themes that proved of lasting interest to Pop artists – sex, technology, entertainment and the mass media – conveyed with a wit and humour that were to give Pop Art its special appeal.

It was only after formulating a definition of Pop Art in January 1957, however, that Hamilton began to apply its principles to his own paintings. In *Hommage à Chrysler Corp* (1957; cat. 100), for instance, he pictured the front of a glamorously chromed American car in a voluptuously feminine way as a knowing paraphrase of the seductive language of advertising. Other works of this period, such as *$he* (1958–61; fig. 2), make even more sophisticated reference to the conventions of current advertising and product design, with an analysis of the implicit messages about social conditioning worthy of the most acute semiologist. The references, however, remain in inverted commas, as if they were detachable from the concise post-Cubist rendering of space that continued to provide Hamilton with his basic grammar of form. It was not until 1962, by which time Pop Art was fully recognised as an international movement, that Hamilton adopted a language that resembled more closely that of his popular sources, but even since that moment he has maintained a greater aloofness from this material than any other major Pop artist.

Like Hamilton, Paolozzi initially found his way into Pop Art through an examination of the iconography of popular culture. By the late 1940s, when he was living in Paris, he was collecting cuttings from American magazines, some of which found their way into collages that served as a kind of scrapbook account of his interests. Printed ephemera, cheap toys and other mass-produced objects, which he amassed equally voraciously, became the basis of his Krazy Kat Archive, which he deposited in the 1970s at the University of St Andrews and later transferred to the Victoria and Albert Museum in London. By the mid-1950s he was using objets trouvés to make imprints in his wax

fig 1 Installation by **Richard Hamilton John McHale John Voelcker** for 'This is Tomorrow' at the Whitechapel Art Gallery, London 1956

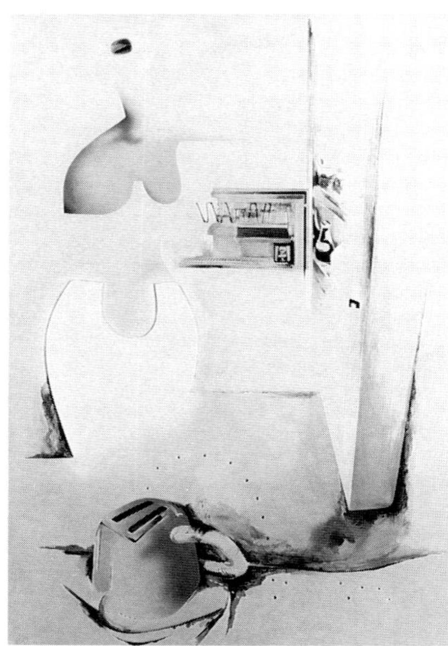

fig 2 **Richard Hamilton** $he 1958–61 Tate Gallery, London

3 Advertising was also the subject of an article by the Smithsons published in the Royal College's magazine, *Ark,* in 1956 and reprinted in this volume (see p. 162).

4 See introduction, note 5.

5 See Graham Whitham, 'Exhibitions', in Robbins, op. cit., pp. 123–61, for a comprehensive analysis of these and other Independent Group exhibitions.

fig 3 **Eduardo Paolozzi** The Philosopher 1957
British Council Collection

maquettes so that, once they were cast in bronze, they would leave their ghost-like traces in the encrusted surface. The scarred and mutilated figures which resulted, such as *The Philosopher* (1957; fig. 3), deliberately echoed the grotesque appearance of the monsters featured in the shoddy science fiction films so beloved of the Independent Group. These popular connections, while having a direct bearing both on the imagery and methods employed by Paolozzi, at this stage functioned more on a conceptual than a purely visual level, since the overall effect was of an anxious brutalism with Surrealist overtones. It was only in 1962, when he began to produce robot-like sculptures with a machine-made look, that he made the complete transition into Pop Art.

The mainstream American Pop Art practised by painters such as Warhol, Lichtenstein, Rosenquist and Wesselmann did not begin to be seen in New York until 1961 and 1962, and there was a slight time lag before any of these pictures began to be seen in England even in photographic form. In the late 1950s, however, British artists saw their first reproductions of the incipient Pop Art of Americans such as Johns, Rauschenberg, Rivers and Westermann, which affected even those like Peter Blake who were already working on similar lines. The sharp shift that took place in Blake's art in 1959, when he began to incorporate photographs, postcards and found or store-bought things into painted constructions that bore no obvious trace of his handwork, was directly inspired by their example. The object quality and bold designs of Johns's flags and targets or Westermann's quirky sculptures, which he liked also for their humour and intimacy, and the play of actual objects against the painted surface of Rauschenberg's 'combines' all left a particular mark.

Richard Smith and Joe Tilson, with whom Blake had studied at the Royal College in the mid-1950s, also transformed themselves into Pop artists at least in part as a result of their contact with recent American art. Supported by a Harkness Fellowship, Smith lived in New York from 1959 to 1961, during the period that American Pop Art was beginning to emerge, and he was visibly inspired both by the general atmosphere of possibilities and by the brash allure of uptown Manhattan. Having undergone the influence of Rothko and other American Abstract Expressionist painters while still living in London, he now adapted their brushwork and colour fields to a sensibility attuned to the luscious colour of glossy magazines and the bold scale and striking imagery of billboards and Hollywood movies. The paintings that he featured in 1961 at his first one-man show at the Green Gallery, New York, such as *Formal Giant* (1960; cat. 223), attest to the beauty and subtlety of his rare marriage of abstract form and Pop imagery. Smith's work remained conspicuously apart from the image-conscious and hard-edged art generally seen to typify Pop Art both in the United States and Britain, even though the shaped canvases he produced in 1962–3, such as *Alpine* (cat. 224), had impeccable sources in mass production and the mass media, taking their form from cigarette packets and emulating the grandeur of scale and presentation techniques of billboard advertising. By the end of the 1960s the links with popular culture were far more tenuous, and abstract form was again the dominant aspect of his paintings. Nevertheless his importance to the development of Pop Art in England was acknowledged not only by old friends such as Blake but also by younger artists with whom he came into contact on his return; Clive Barker, Derek Boshier and later Stephen Buckley (who trained under Hamilton at the University of Newcastle-upon-Tyne) all even worked for brief spells as his assistant.

The painted wooden constructions that established Tilson's credentials as a Pop artist in the early 1960s were also indebted in certain respects to the American influences that had helped Blake reformulate his approach in the late 1950s, but he appears to have been even more affected by his sense of a common purpose with a group of younger painters who entered the Royal College in 1959: Derek Boshier, David Hockney, Allen Jones, R. B. Kitaj and Peter Phillips, joined a year later by Patrick Caulfield. By February 1961, when they made a united showing in London at the 'Young Contemporaries' exhibition of student work, it was apparent that there were sufficient shared concerns to qualify as a movement. Although Hockney, Kitaj and Caulfield were all at pains to dissociate themselves from the term Pop Art almost as soon as it was applied to them, it was at this time, and in large part in response to their work, that the label came into general currency in Britain. The exuberance of their discoveries and a sense of their conjoined identities are vividly captured in the collaborative work orchestrated by Tilson, *A–Z Box of Friends and Family* (1963; cat. 229), to which most of the prime movers of British Pop Art made contributions under their respective initials.[6] In this and related works Tilson created a 'user-friendly' variety of Pop Art by suggesting that the object-picture is a game to be played, substituting traditional fine art techniques with do-it-yourself carpentry skills and creating a vocabulary of emblematic images endowed with the immediacy of a child's pictorial alphabet.

Kitaj and Hockney, in spite of their antipathy to the word 'Pop', were influential in formulating the idea of a Royal College style that had as its main feature a freewheeling approach to images and pictorial idioms as discrete entities that could be called into action at will. In contrast to the Pop Art that was beginning to emerge at the same time on the other side of the Atlantic, they sought to relate personal experiences and enthusiasms in a consciously intimate tone, laying great stress on their subject-matter. Kitaj's pictures often had their origins in written sources (from literature, history and politics) and in second-hand images taken from photographs or reproductions from the history of art, their conjunctions giving rise to a complex composite view that reflected a sense of his own identity as a cosmopolitan American romantically inclined to the idea of the bookish intellectual. He had arrived in England only at the beginning of 1958 as a student under the terms of the American G.I. Bill and had first attended the Ruskin School of Drawing in Oxford; his greater maturity (he was five years older than the others in his year) and his knowledge of the work of Rauschenberg and other recent American artists gave him a particular authority among his fellow students. He had only a passing interest in popular culture as such, however, shunning pop music and other attributes of teenage life as anathema. He came closest to a true Pop identity in his references to the cinema, hinted at both in the structure of a painting such as *Junta* (1962; cat. 144), which has been compared to the use of jump cuts in experimental films of the period such as *L'Année dernière à Marienbad,* and in his derivation of particular images from film stills; *Good News for Incunabulists* (1962; cat. 143), for example, is from a photograph by Edward Steichen of the stage version of Lewis Milestone's 1931 film *The Front Page.*

The urgency of Hockney's student pictures, such as *Adhesiveness* (1960; cat. 108) – titled after Walt Whitman's term for closely bonded friendships between men – and *I'm in the Mood for Love* (1961; cat. 110), is inextricably linked to the image they convey of his own identity as a young homosexual. Although he clearly set out in these pictures to promote a life style still considered rather shocking, referring to the series as 'propaganda pictures', it is as much for their visual wit and cheeky humour as for their sex that we now remember them. In making reference to the most humble and familiar material to hand, including such things as a wall calendar, boxes of Alka Seltzer or packets of Ty-Phoo Tea (fig. 4), he more or less stumbled his way into Pop Art. It was not just in such specifics, however, nor only in their riposte to the painting-as-

6 The Pop artists featured are: Peter Blake [B], Clive Barker [C], David Hockney [D], Eduardo Paolozzi [E], Allen Jones [J], R. B. Kitaj [K], Peter Phillips [P], Richard Hamilton [R] and Richard Smith [S]. Tilson himself is represented with a miniature version of his Ziggurat motif [Z], and there are contributions, too, from his wife Jos [J] and by his young children Anna [A] and Jake [J], now established as a Pop-influenced artist in his own right. The F box features the photographer Robert Freeman, whose Pop Art credentials include the photograph used on the front cover of the LP *Meet the Beatles.* The other artist friends are Frank Auerbach [A], Bernard Cohen [C], Harold Cohen [H], John Latham [L], Tony Messenger [M], Tony Caro [T], Brian Wall [W] and Brian Young [X].

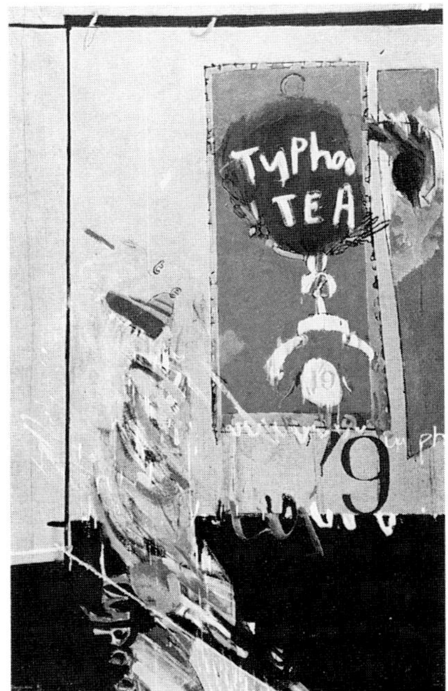

fig 4 **David Hockney** The Second Tea Painting 1961 Private Collection

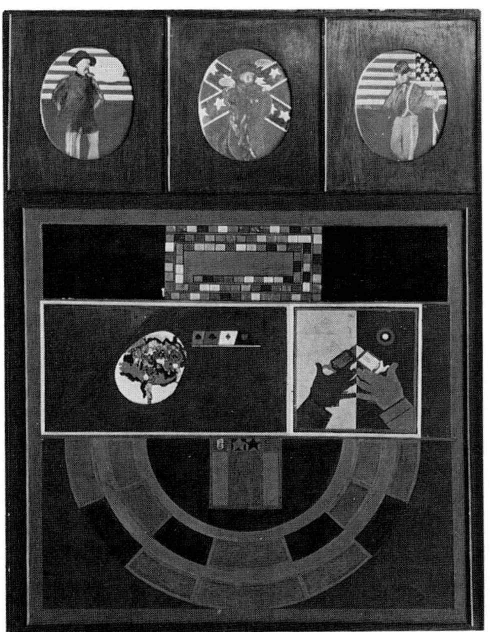

fig 5 **Peter Phillips** War/Game 1961 Albright-Knox Art Gallery, New York

object idea proposed in Johns's flags and targets, that they helped open the way to a peculiarly British strain of the movement. The tone of the work produced by Hockney and his colleagues, with its insolent and cheerful plundering of styles and images, conveyed an exuberant sense of the opening up of possibilities. In rejecting the constraints of tradition exemplified by art school education, they also captured the libertarian mood of the moment.

While Hockney and Kitaj did much to set the terms for the Royal College approach, it was Phillips, Jones, Boshier and Caulfield who constituted its Pop Art core. As early as 1960, in *Purple Flag* (cat. 178), Phillips responded to the first reports of Johns's work in a confidently British accent, bringing into play not only the Union Jack but also references to the amusement arcades where his rock'n'roll identity was lived out. His embrace of youth culture, then a relatively new phenomenon, was unapologetic, even aggressive, with explicit references to motorcycles and other attributes of his generation's energy, disdain of authority and commitment to the fast pace of city life. His flaunting of sex, fun and entertainment, however, masked the serious and calculated way in which he planned and executed his pictures; working on a larger scale than any of his British colleagues and seeking a finish as polished and professional as that of a well-made manufactured item, he produced barely half a dozen major paintings in 1960–61 (fig. 5). Speed and casualness were only illusions with which to confront his audience, and in compositional terms his pictures owed at least as much to Italian pre-Renaissance art as they did to the formats of game boards or pinball machines to which they made more obvious reference.

Formal concerns were paramount, too, for Jones, in his case revolving on the relationship between clearly defined shape and strong flat colour. The artists that most interested him as a student, and who continued to define the terms of his art in later years, were early twentieth-century pioneers of abstraction such as Delaunay and Kandinsky. Yet to make more accessible a resolution of form that might otherwise seem rather esoteric, he clothed his shapes in recognisable imagery drawn from the world around him and introduced erotic themes as a counterpart to the conceptual act of making art. In *Thinking about Women* (1961; cat. 132) thoughts of a sexual nature are shown hovering over his schematised head as if in the 'thinks' balloon of a comic strip, while his *Bus* paintings of 1962 (cat. 134) – one of the earliest and most sustained explorations of the shaped canvas – induce a sense of movement and momentum through the contours of the lozenge-like stretcher itself, presented as if plunging forward into space. These early works contributed to the language of Pop through their brilliance of colour and through their allusions to the mundane circumstances of everyday life. In the context of Jones's own development, however, they seem mild when compared to the much more forceful sexual statements of the paintings and sculptures that he began to produce after living in New York in 1964–65, when he discovered a rich fund of imagery in fetish magazines and other kinds of illustration that defied the sense of propriety of fine art. It was at that stage, properly speaking, that Jones became one of the most aggressive purveyors of Pop Art in England.

Of all the Royal College painters, Boshier was the only one involved with a decoding of advertising and contemporary political events, sometimes bordering on satire, close in spirit to certain strains in continental European Pop Art. His first contributions to the language of Pop Art were highly formalised paintings such as *Airmail Letter* (1961; cat. 21), a grossly enlarged image closer to Smith than to Johns. Soon, however, he developed a narrative mode through which he made allusion to such matters as the Americanisation of Europe, the race into space between the United States and the Soviet Union, political crises such as the Bay of Pigs invasion in Cuba, and capital punishment. While most Pop Art in Britain, as in the United States, adopted a provocatively ambiguous stance with regard to its subject-matter, Boshier was rare in his unconditional declaration of his point of view. A number of his pictures of this period, notably the series of toothpaste paintings initiated in 1961 (cat. 22), took a critical look at the exploitative ruses employed in advertising and market research, with their attendant dehumanisation and reduction of the consumer to a cipher. Taking his cue from the writings of authors such as Marshall McLuhan, John Kenneth Galbraith and Vance Packard, Boshier pictured modern man as uniform, faceless and lacking in personality, swallowed up by consumerism or so deformed by bogus promises that he becomes a mere piece of a jigsaw puzzle, an *Epitaph for Somewhere over the Rainbow* (fig. 6).[7] Boshier had too restless a personality to capitalise on his early Pop work after leaving the Royal College, abandoning painting for many years in favour of sculpture, photography, collage and film. When he did return to the medium, however, shortly before his move to Texas in 1980, it was from the spirit of this period that he made his fresh start.

fig 6 **Derek Boshier** Epitaph for Somewhere over the Rainbow 1962

Caulfield was the last of the Pop painters to arrive at the Royal College, and one of the most reluctant to have the term used in relation to his work, which from the beginning was contemplative, introspective and somewhat outside of its time in its frame of reference. His resistance to being categorised notwithstanding, his adoption in pictures such as *Engagement Ring* (1963; cat. 26) of the materials and pictorial language of the sign-painter made for some of the most memorable and lasting icons of the movement to be produced in Britain. Sophisticated in its apparent artlessness, teetering precariously on the edge of banality, toying with bad taste, corny jokes and old-fashioned presentation techniques and processes, Caulfield's art somehow transcends all the obstacles set up by the artist himself against a success that might seem too easily achieved. Who but Caulfield would have responded to a choice between two set subjects – 'Christ at Emmaus' and 'Figures in a High Wind' – by combining the two to produce an image that he describes as 'Christ at Emmaus slightly in the wind' (cat. 25)? And who but he would engineer a picture by synthesising sources from high art and the most trivial ephemera, taking the equestrian figure from Delacroix and the decorative border from a packet of dates? Through the wistful lure of the exotic Caulfield found his way into a variation on Pop Art that remained exclusively his own. Even at his most apparently cheerful and escapist, as in the Mediterranean picture-postcard tranquillity of *View of the Bay* (1964; fig. 7), with its reminiscences of Dufy and the Fauves, a melancholic atmosphere descends – just as it does when our romantic reveries are broken when we turn from the travel poster back to our cluttered desks. In spite of the ways in which his art acknowledges those moments of snatched peace and fulfilment, exemplified by a weekend retreat or the feeling of well-being induced by a convivial meal and a glass of wine, the eventual effect is the opposite of escapism or celebration. Caulfield is right to deny that he is a Pop artist, if one interprets the term in its narrowest sense; in my view, however, it is sufficiently neutral in itself to encompass even his oblique rejection of contemporary values.

fig 7 **Patrick Caulfield** View of the Bay 1964
Calouste Gulbenkian Foundation, Lisbon

The activities of painters studying at the Royal College in the early 1960s provide the central episode in the story of British Pop, but important and original contributions to the movement continued to be made by other painters and sculptors including Gerald Laing (fig. 8), Anthony Donaldson, Nicholas Monro, the American-born Jann Haworth (Blake's first wife) and David Oxtoby.[8] Each artist brought an individual perspective to the terms of the movement, a remarkable achievement given the shared set of references from popular culture and the drive in much Pop Art towards an apparent anonymity or

7 Boshier's reading included McLuhan's *The Mechanical Bride: Folklore of Industrial Man*, New York, 1951, a much-cited text of the period, as well as D. J. Boorstin's *The Image: or, What Happened to the American Dream*, London, 1962, Galbraith's *The Affluent Society*, Boston and London, 1958, and Packard's *The Hidden Persuaders*, London, 1957, and *The Status Seekers*, London, 1960.

8 For a discussion of their work, see my *Pop Art: A Continuing History*, London, 1990, chapter 8.

fig 8 **Gerald Laing** Skydiver 1964 Tate Gallery, London

depersonalisation. Clive Barker, for instance, working pretty much on his own although on close terms with Blake, made direct allusion in his first sculptures in 1962 to his experience of working in a car factory. The materials he employed in works such as *Two Palettes for Jim Dine* (1964; cat. 9) were those with which he was already most familiar from the automobile industry: leather and chrome-plated metal. By 1964 he was using neon, sending off drawings of the lettering he wanted to be fabricated to the same size. The practice of having his conceptions realised by specialists adept at particular processes was itself suggested to him by assembly-line methods. Everything in Barker's work is mediated, in terms both of process and image, notably in a sequence of sculptures based on familiar motifs from the history of art, such as *Van Gogh's Chair* (1966; cat. 10). In this and in his cool, detached approach he comes close to the most extreme forms of American Pop Art.

No British artist displays more adeptly than Colin Self the diverse ends to which a Pop language can be placed. His most characteristic early works – intensely worked pencil and collage drawings – are also among the smallest in size to have been produced by any Pop artist. The often sinister overtones of the images, however, and the sense of their physical presence engendered by his remarkable technique, endow them with an incomparable vividness and psychological charge. In his hands the most banal or innocuous motif, such as a girl sitting on a sofa or the disembodied image projected onto a screen in a darkened cinema, can take on the quality of a revelation. The way a girl contemplates a popsicle transforms this everyday act into one of voracious sexuality (cat. 218). That most humble of junk foods, the hot dog, takes on the appearance of an ecstatic female nude in the act of being penetrated by a man whose animal nature has made him all penis (cat. 221). This metamorphic quality, taken further, turns into nightmarish mutation: an aeroplane the size of a model fitted together by a child is shown as half machine, half predatory animal (cat. 217). A symbol for a nuclear shelter, as seen during a visit to the United States, becomes the nexus for anxieties about the imminent destruction of the planet; its conjunction with an overweight woman oblivious to her own potential oblivion exaggerates its repercussions to a point just short of hysteria (cat. 222). The cumulative effect of the outpourings of Self's imagination in several thousand drawings over nearly 30 years can only be hinted at in such a survey. Even in small doses, however, his art makes no effort to suppress his strongly felt, at times violent, opposition to what he sees as the inequities and tendencies to self-destruction of his society (fig. 9).

fig 9 **Colin Self** Guard Dog on a Missile Base No.1 1965 Tate Gallery, London

The immense variety of approach among British Pop artists detailed so far – ranging from tiny drawings to large-scale paintings and machine-made sculpture, and from an open celebration of popular culture to unforgiving attacks on its shortcomings, with all points in between – covers only its origins from the mid-1950s to the mid-1960s. Since then it has undergone further permutations that have exaggerated its scope and extended its iconographic repertory to include, among other things, Hockney's California poolside idylls, Jones's stylised and sexually provocative images of women, Caulfield's downmarket restaurant interiors, Tilson's screenprinted news flashes, Paolozzi's recycled popular motifs and the assault on the senses of Phillips's collages of found images on a billboard scale. Each in its way asserts itself without taking heed of the limits imposed by any one definition of Pop Art, which is as it should be, given the subversive character of the movement's origins and its emphasis on widening the range of choice. The one thing they all have in common, unlike the rebellious teenager in Pete Townshend's mid-'60s anthem, is a desire to create a big sensation in the very act of talking about their generation.

pop art in britain
an anthology of sources

Lawrence Alloway

'The arts and the mass media', *Architectural Design*, 28, February 1958, pp. 84–5.

As Ortega pointed out in *The Revolt of the Masses*: 'the masses are to-day exercising functions in social life which coincide with those which hitherto seemed reserved to minorities.' As a result the élite, accustomed to set aesthetic standards, has found that it no longer possesses the power to dominate all aspects of art. It is in this situation that we need to consider the arts of the mass media. It is impossible to see them clearly within a code of aesthetics associated with minorities with pastoral and upper-class ideas because mass art is urban and democratic.

...

The Western movie, for example, often quoted as timeless and ritualistic, has since the end of World War II been highly flexible. There have been cycles of psychological Westerns (complicated characters, both the heroes and the villains), anthropological Westerns (attentive to Indian rights and rites), weapon Westerns (colt revolvers and repeating Winchesters as analogues of the present armament race). The protagonist has changed greatly, too: the typical hero of the American depression who married the boss's daughter and so entered the bright archaic world of the gentleman has vanished. The ideal of the gentleman has expired, too, and with it evening dress which is no longer part of the typical hero-garb.

If justice is to be done to the mass arts which are, after all, one of the most remarkable, and characteristic achievements of industrial society, some of the common objections to it need to be faced. A summary of the opposition to mass popular art is in *Avant Garde and Kitsch* (*Partisan Review,* 1939, *Horizon,* 1940), by Clement Greenberg, an art critic and a good one, but fatally prejudiced when he leaves modern fine art. By kitsch he means 'popular, commercial art and literature, with their chromeotypes, magazine covers, illustrations, advertisements, slick and pulp fiction, comics, Tin Pan Alley music, tap dancing, Hollywood movies, etc.' All these activities to Greenberg and the minority he speaks for are 'ersatz culture . . . destined for those who are insensible to the value of *genuine* culture . . . Kitsch, using for raw material the debased and academic semulacra of *genuine* culture welcomes and cultivates this insensibility' (my italics). Greenberg insists that 'all kitsch is academic', but only some of it is, such as Cecil B. De Mille-type historical epics which use nineteenth-century history-picture material. In fact, stylistically, technically, and iconographically the mass arts are anti-academic. Topicality and a rapid rate of change are not academic in any usual sense of the word, which means a system is static, rigid, self-perpetuating. Sensitiveness to the variables of our life and economy enable the mass arts to accompany the changes in our life far more closely than the fine arts which are a repository of time-binding values.

...

An important factor in communication in the mass arts is high redundancy. TV plays, radio serials, entertainers, tend to resemble each other (though there are important and clearly visible differences for the expert consumer). You can go into the movies at any point, leave your seat, eat an ice-cream, and still follow the action on the screen pretty well.

...

There is in popular art a continuum from data to fantasy. Fantasy resides in, to sample a few examples, film stars, perfume ads, beauty and the beast situations, terrible deaths, sexy women. This is the aspect of popular art which is most easily accepted by art minorities who see it as a vital substratum of the folk, as something primitive. This notion has a history since Herder in the eighteenth-century, who emphasized national folk arts in opposition to international classicism. Now, however, mass-produced folk art is international: Kim Novak, *Galaxy Science Fiction*, Mickey Spillane, are available wherever you go in the West.

Clive Barker

Unpublished catalogue introduction, *c.* 1976.

Anything that feeds back is of interest to me. It's the feedback that concerns me, that I like. A thousand different people may see one of my things, and have a thousand different ideas about it. That is what is important, not what I have to say about a specific thing. It's rather like chrome itself. It isn't chrome, as such, that interests me, but what it reflects. Chrome is nothing unless it reflects something. If it doesn't, it's dead.

...

A lot of my works begin with what are just very fleeting ideas: sometimes they get lost, sometimes they end up as works. For example, I once got an idea from a lady who was a waitress in a restaurant. She had just cleared up all the cutlery. She had this sort of tray, with all the knives and forks piled up on it. A big mound of them. That sort of thing can just create an idea for me. I can get ideas of this kind walking down the street, and I'm not necessarily conscious of any meaning beyond what I see . . . And incidents, too. I might open the door and see someone turn on a light across the road. And thinking about the fact that I opened the door at that specific time, just when the light went on, or when something else happened, that can interest me too, and lead to an idea for a work.

...

In England, I have always been dragged into Pop Art, but I have never felt myself to be part of a school, or a movement. It's just a matter of convenience, this sticking of labels on people. It's strange because in Germany, I have always been talked about as a Surrealist. But I don't look on myself as a Surrealist either, any more than I think I am a Pop artist. It just so happened that my work could be fitted into these different things . . .

Clive Barker

Excerpts from an unpublished interview by Marco Livingstone, London, 10 July 1989.

In using other craftsmen in making your sculptures, did you conceive of your work in relation to Duchamp's ready-mades or to Moholy-Nagy's idea of making works by telephone, if necessary, or by instructing the factory?
It wasn't a question of ready-mades because I very rarely used anything that was already made. I would see something and remake it.

But there were things like the bucket.
The bucket was maybe the only real piece that I've used.

But how were the Coke bottles done, for example?
The Coke bottles I cast *from* them, but I think that's OK.

But it's still in a way related to the ready-made idea, isn't it?
Well, no, because you're remaking it.

You're remaking it, but from the original object rather than reinventing it with your own hands.
Yes, but I think the actual idea of a ready-made is that you can just go in, buy something, pick it up, and there it is, and it's done, and all you do is sign it, like the urinal. The fact of remaking the bottle from glass into bronze, you *change* that image, it's no longer a ready-made, it's something else.

So what would have been the process involved in making, for example, Three Coke Bottles?
I think I went to the foundry with one Coke bottle and we made a mould from that. I think we made a plaster mould from that. We poured three waxes and cast them. I think the base we just cut out, I don't think that was cast. Two weeks later the casts were done and finished, and I took them to the chromium plater. He had them for another day and polished them.

I think that's one of the things that people probably found shocking about your work, that you weren't physically *remaking it.*
I think so. I wasn't a true artist in a lot of people's eyes. It wasn't the fact that they didn't like the end result, it's that they couldn't understand . . . I mean now you can do anything. But I think I did have a lot of trouble, especially with the *Bucket of Raindrops*.

After leaving art school at Luton you worked for eighteen months on the shop floor at Vauxhall Motors. By the time you had begun to make objects using a division of labour, was this something you could consciously relate to the factory experience?
I remember thinking when I worked on the track, 'Wouldn't it be nice if you could make art like this?' I didn't think of making sculpture or anything like that, I was just thinking of art . . . Every day we made hundreds of cars, and I liked seeing the shiny new cars in the parking lot.

Your sculptures of the 1960s had those qualities of being shiny and glamorous. Was it important to you that they should look perfect?
Yes, I was looking for a perfect finish, in a way. Maybe that *was* something to do with Vauxhall Motors, but I think I'm a perfectionist anyway.

Peter Blake

Mervyn Levy, 'Peter Blake: Pop Art for Admass: The Artist at Work: 23', *Studio International*, CLXVI, 847, November 1963, pp. 184–9.

'I started to become a pop artist from my interest in English folk art,' he said. 'Especially my interest in the visual art of the fairground, and barge painting too. It all originated while I was still a student at the Royal College. Now I want to recapture and bring to life again something of this old-time popular art. For instance, I'm working at the moment on a small picture of a boxer called Kid McCoy. He was fighting around 1910. I read all the boxing and wrestling magazines, by the way. So that this picture will have an authentic old-time feel about it. I'm making the wooden surface look old. I feel that if I bore artificial wood-worm holes in it, it will acquire the quality of age. This is essential to my purpose. For me, pop art is often rooted in nostalgia: the nostalgia of old, popular things. And although I'm also continually trying to establish a *new* pop art, one which stems directly from our own time, I'm always looking back at the sources of the idiom and trying to find the technical forms that will best recapture the authentic feel of folk pop.'

As we talked he punched wood-worm holes in *Kid McCoy* with hammer and nail. The title was laid on in newsprint. Blake went on to explain that his work flowed in two channels, according to the requirements of each piece. 'Sometimes, as in that well-known self-portrait of mine, I work in normal, 3-D space, in the first person, and as any traditional portraitist does, from Rembrandt to John. But when I'm using images that have become part of the folk art stream of things, I work in a second person, 2-D space, because such imagery already exists in the flat. Folk art is flat; its spirit is flat. My *Kid McCoy* is a flat, 2-D folk image type portrait. But I'm also experimenting with the conversion of contemporary folk imagery into 3-D as for example in my series of "Windows". In these I involve another aspect of communal folk art; the sort that's represented by coronation mugs and plastic flowers.'

We discussed one of these windows, which included a pin-up type photograph of the Queen. 'She's there,' said Blake, 'not because I *don't* like the Queen, but because I do like her.' . . . For Peter Blake, pop art, like pop music, is fundamentally an illusion. Both are concerned with states of illusion that spring, respectively, from popular sounds and popular images. Illusionistic moods are the essence of pop music and pop art, and in the *recherché* sense it is not difficult to imagine the kind of pop music that should accompany the portrait of Kid McCoy, and other backward looking and nostalgic items of pop. Like the sentimental postcard pictures Peter Blake was producing a short while ago.

Of his contemporary pop he says: 'I like to think my pictures can be enjoyed by young people who like pop music. At the moment I'm working on a large conversation piece of the Liverpool song group, *The Beatles*. Each of these chaps is closely associated with the city and I hope that the local Beatle fans will find in this picture a visual significance that will somehow match the mood of Beatle music.' I asked Blake why it was that today so many young artists so readily identify themselves, and their inspiration, with the idols of pop music and films: the idols of the masses, in fact. Blake, by the way, is addicted to rhythm and blues – not 'trad' – which he likes listening to while he works. He replied: 'Partly, of course, as a normal reaction against the orthodox, so-called cultural things – you know, Beethoven and D. H. Lawrence, the whole culture-monger concept of foreign films and such-like. But also, of course, because Elvis and Bridget, *The Beatles* and *The Lettermen* and *The Four Preps,* really do symbolize the vast popular culture from which pop art so largely derives its sources of inspiration.'

Jazz, vocal groups, films and advertising, are all part of the fairground of modern life, in which the side-shows are the dance halls and strip clubs, lit by the star names of the teeming anti-culture that is the age in which we live. These are the fertilizing agents from which pop art emanates.

In one corner of the artist's studio was a large, protoplasmic canvas evolving around the name and image of Elvis Presley. This, explained Blake, was one of the three major projects he envisaged as absorbing his painting life during the next two or three years ... 'I want to re-establish the idea of myself as a *painter*; as an artist who uses *paint*. I'm not just a collagist. I've always painted. Many people have forgotten this – or don't know. Anyway, the projects I've lined up for the future consist of a major work on the life and times of Elvis Presley, another based on my wife Jann, her two little sisters, April and Hollies, and a pixie called *Pipola,* and a third subject also in my mind, which is evolving around pin-up girls. I'll probably call this *The pin-up girls in my garden,* and I'll have them all over the place; hanging on the trees, lurking in the background – everywhere. The thing about pop is that you've got to get *inside* the popular culture of the time whether you're doing the thing historically, or working in the present tense. I've got to get right in with the pin-ups and Elvis, with *The Beatles* and *The Lettermen.* And inside every house that has plastic flowers and curtains.'

And here, I think, lies the real strength and significance of pop art: in an age of amateurs it provides a professional bridge between the mass obsessions of society and their rationalization in the patterns of a truly popular art form. This is the age of the masses and it is they, more than we think, who shape the destiny of contemporary art. The work of Peter Blake is a crystallization of the obsessions, nostalgias, and the sex-dreamy, sometimes muscle-flexing illusions of admass. Pin-ups and boxers are only emblems, and in this sense, pop is a genuine art of the proletariat ...

Derek Boshier

Richard Smith, 'New readers start here ...', *Ark,* 32, Summer 1962, p. 40.

Boshier's paintings are, in part, social statements that can be as anonymous as an editorial ... Events are out of the headlines before the paint dries. All the elements in the paintings are taken from material in a printed format, nothing 'from life'. This reflects the method by which we acquire facts in these post information-explosion days. The paintings sometimes take the form of something else – an envelope, a jigsaw puzzle, a snooker table – so that the paint area is basically an object.

...

Some of the themes are recurring like Americanization. Stars and stripes eat into an 'England's Glory' matchbox, or a Cuban flag; the Union Jack is cornered by two Pepsi-Cola bottle tops. Whether this Americanization is welcomed, deplored or just accepted is left in the air. Also in the air are the space subjects he tackles. The interest is not, it appears, to glorify modern technology. The fact that there is a space race is shown some concern: the space heroes are important but other heroes get equal billing in the cosmos.

Patrick Caulfield

Marco Livingstone, 'An interview with Patrick Caulfield', *Aspects,* 15, Summer 1981

Christopher Finch remarks in his monograph that you expected at one time to become a commercial artist rather than a painter. In the '60s you began using the language of contemporary design, mail order catalogue illustration and so forth in your paintings. Do you think you were unconsciously reminding yourself of what might have been, daring yourself to use that as source material yet to make paintings out of them?

No, it was a reaction which I shared with other people against academic work, the idea of English painting in muted tones where marks were never quite finished. It seemed a reason to use very crisp black lines.

You wanted to make very assertive statements?

Yes. In advertising you have to project or you don't make a sale, and I used that. It seemed worth doing to try to project, and not to expect the spectator to make all the effort. Dick Smith, for instance, made paintings that literally project. I imagine that it was very much in the atmosphere at the time.

...

The imagery you have used since the early 1960s has been consistently ordinary and familiar, rooted either in daily experience – the objects and places which we use all the time – or in images which are equally familiar to us through postcards, advertisements, travel brochures, or the work of other artists. Did you decide early on to limit yourself to mundane imagery as a way of guaranteeing accessibility in at least that respect?

In a way it's not mundane for me. You say it's day to day imagery. In some cases it is, but in some it isn't. Some things are slightly exotic, which is not so everyday. I think it's not so much mundane as familiar, in any sense that it might be seen.

...

In 1964 you painted your first Mediterranean pictures, a theme to which you have returned on later occasions. Did you see that as being tied to the image of the twentieth century artist, the Frenchman living in that type of environment and leading the type of life associated with that area? An ordinary person who is not involved with art would be more likely still to think of the south of France, rather than New York or London, as an artistic locale. The Mediterranean view, in a way, is like a textbook idea of the twentieth-century picture.
I think that's the reason I chose the Mediterranean, because, as you're suggesting, artists would now think of going to New York. It's a contrary attitude to looking at an amusing New York Pop imagery.

But you're playing along with another tradition, an older tradition. You could have chosen to paint Tibet or something, but it wouldn't have had the right sort of resonance.
No, that would have been more New York somehow, the 'Mystic East' . . .

There's something very corny about the idea of painting a coastal resort on the Mediterranean.
Oh, yes. It's a postcard sort of world. That's why I used it. It gives one a jumping-off point to make a painting.

Richard Hamilton

'For the Finest Art try – POP', *Richard Hamilton, Collected Words,* London, 1982, pp. 42–3.

It is the *Playboy* 'Playmate of the month' pull-out pin-up which provides us with the closest contemporary equivalent of the odalisque in painting. Automobile body stylists have absorbed the symbolism of the space age more successfully than any artist. Social comment is left to TV and comic strip. Epic has become synonymous with a certain kind of film and the heroic archetype is now buried deep in movie lore. If the artist is not to lose much of his ancient purpose he may have to plunder the popular arts to recover the imagery which is his rightful inheritance.

. . .

. . . The history of art is that of a long series of attacks upon social and aesthetic values held to be dead and moribund, although the avant-garde position is frequently nostalgic and absolute. The Pop-Fine-Art standpoint, on the other hand – the expression of popular culture in fine art terms – is, like Futurism, fundamentally a statement of belief in the changing values of society. Pop-Fine-Art is a profession of approbation of mass culture, therefore also antiartistic. It is positive Dada, creative where Dada was destructive. Perhaps it is Mama – a cross-fertilization of Futurism and Dada which upholds a respect for the culture of the masses and a conviction that the artist in 20th century urban life is inevitably a consumer of mass culture and potentially a contributor to it.

Richard Hamilton

Letter to Peter and Alison Smithson, *Richard Hamilton, Collected Words,* London, 1982, p. 28.

16th January 1957

Dear Peter and Alison

I have been thinking about our conversation of the other evening and thought that it might be a good idea to get something on paper, as much to sort it out for myself as to put a point of view to you.

. . .

Suppose we were to start with the objective of providing a unique solution to the specific requirements of a domestic environment e.g. some kind of shelter, some kind of equipment, some kind of art. This solution could then be formulated and rated on the basis of compliance with a table of characteristics of Pop Art.

Pop Art is:

Popular (designed for a mass audience)
Transient (short-term solution)
Expendable (easily forgotten)
Low cost
Mass produced
Young (aimed at youth)
Witty
Sexy
Gimmicky
Glamorous
Big business

. . .

Yours,

[*The letter was written to propose an exhibition of Pop Art, although at the time there was no such thing as it is known today, and the term referred solely to art manufactured for a mass audience.*]

David Hockney

Note by David Hockney, *Image in Progress,* exhibition catalogue, Grabowski Gallery, London, 1962.

I paint what I like, when I like, and where I like, with occasional nostalgic journeys.
When asked to write on 'the strange possibilities of inspiration' it did occur to me that my own sources of inspiration were wide, – but acceptable. In fact, I am sure my own sources are classic, or even epic themes. Landscapes of foreign lands, beautiful people, love, propaganda, and major incidents (of my own life). These seem to me to be reasonably traditional.

David Hockney

Richard Smith, 'New readers start here ...', *Ark*, 32, Summer 1962, p. 38.

In Hockney a monster Typhoo Tea or Alka-Seltzer packet is a souvenir which could take its place in the Lost and Found columns along with other things of sentimental value. The scale makes an object take its correct place in the memory-pattern of his mainly autobiographic paintings – like ribbon-tied letters or 'the tinkling piano in the next apartment'. Hockney's cartoon technique is a legitimate use of a known, readily readable convention. The figures, spindle-legged and beetle-bodied, have many cousins in contemporary graphics but they serve his purpose, for within the conventions is enough room for him to move.

Hockney's paintings have the look of an ad-man's Sunday painting. This is not a criticism for it demonstrates that there is now the possibility of a two-way exchange between the selling-arts and the fine ... Written messages play an important part in Hockney's paintings. Sometimes they are no more than a title but on occasion the painting is covered with words overloading the image like screen credits. Hockney as a personality is bound up with his paintings. The paintings can serve as letters, or diary-jottings or mementoes: the figures are portraits; events portrayed *did* happen; someone *did* dance the cha-cha at three in the morning. A curtain of fantasy is drawn between the spectator and the painter but the curtain is part of the structure which is as essential as Bardot's towel.

David Hockney

'The Tea Paintings', *David Hockney by David Hockney*, edited by N. Stangos, London, 1976, p. 64.

The tea packets piled up with the cans and tubes of paint and they were lying around all the time and I just thought, in a way it's like still-life paintings for me; I'd like to paint something, take something different as a subject. There were postcards, Cliff Richard, cheap reproductions and newspaper photographs pinned up on the wall. I thought, there must be other things lying around, something I could use. There was a packet of Typhoo tea, a very ordinary popular brand of tea, so I used it as a motif. This is as close to pop art as I ever came. But I didn't use it because I was interested in the design of the packet or anything; it was just that it was a very common design, a very common packet, lying around, and I thought it could be used in some way. And again, it's not used in an ordinary still-life way at all ... To make a painting of a packet of tea more illusionistic, I hit on the idea of 'drawing' it with the shape of the canvas. The stretcher is made up from sections and I made the stretchers myself. It was quite difficult stretching them all up – the back is almost as complicated as the front; it took me five days. I don't think anybody had done shapes before. It meant that the blank canvas was itself already illusionistic and I could ignore the concept of illusionistic space and paint merrily in a flat style – people were always talking about flatness in painting in those days.

Allen Jones

Note by Allen Jones, *Image in Progress*, exhibition catalogue, Grabowski Gallery, London, 1962.

It is not my intention to create a picture consisting of merely literal references to things outside the area of the canvas. This is like reading a sign which instructs you not to look at it. The notice EXIT only has value because it refers to something else, once we have read it, we look elsewhere.

I don't mind a picture having a story as long as the beginning and the end exist within the four edges of the canvas.
A picture is only finished when it is self-sufficient.
The title should not be a synopsis.

Allen Jones

'Allen Jones: Some statements', edited by Marco Livingstone, *Aspects*, 6, Spring 1979.

'Non-art' material
If pin-ups make you want to paint more than the life model upstairs, then rush round to the magazine store. If your stimulations come from unartistic or untasteful sources and not from Bach, don't worry; if as a result you produce work, then it's justified ...

I don't know where inspiration comes from, or what form it may take, so I keep my eyelids wide open in case I miss something. (1963)

The figure–eroticism–social concerns
The 'stiletto' is archetypal and timeless representing SHOE. To use any other would have been to suggest a descriptive interest in the environment – Mary Quant etc. – the picture would have had a chic connotation and become dated with the shoe style, and thus need a generation to pass before the viewer would just perceive 'SHOE' and all its attendant implications ... Vogue now referring to St Laurent's last collection mentioned girls in Allen Jones shoes. 'Fashion' catches up with my work but the current interest in the '40s is not part of my aesthetic. To me in the mid '60s the important thing was that shoes were out of style. (c. 1971)

An interview with a drawing

You appear to be a woman of character, what is it that upsets you like this?

Well, it's not much really. Some women get upset when they see me, feeling that I cater to the chauvinist male.

Isn't there some truth in that? Speaking as a male, I certainly find you attractive.

That is neither here nor there. My values are not their values. I might understand their hostility if I were a woman, but I am not, I am a sign for one – call it Art if you like.

Can you elaborate on that theme?

Well we are quite different from each other, unlike them I cannot be abused, unless someone uses a rubber.

Ahem! I realise that you are only a drawing, but do excuse me crossing my legs.

I am not flesh and blood. I was conceived by a man after hours of labour. Aesthetics rather than Genetics decided the shape of my anatomy.

Yes, but like a real woman you can be seen; people go a lot on appearances.

Yes, and they usually make snap decisions, recognising those things that support their own opinions and prejudices. I call it defensive viewing. People do not give themselves enough to Art.

Well, to return to the point. I understand that social comment is not your reason for existence, but do you offer anything in this direction?

As a drawing I am quite passive, but with a disciplined audience I think I can do some good.

What! Discipline emotion?

Well, if my appearance arouses political/social discontent that is good so long as the emotions are directed to the real problem, but alas, a few have thought better to defile me and all I want is to give pleasure.

These few, what else could they do?

Direct their energies to the inequalities that exist in real life, through the educational system and the Labour Exchange. But I must point out that even for a woman with long hair, sensuous mouth and strong legs it is the same fight.

Noble sentiments, but aren't you part of life?

Now don't try and trick me, I'm only a drawing.

Thank you for your time.

(Interview conducted by I. Seymour-Legge, London, for *Le Petit Journal de Vogue,* 1974)

R. B. Kitaj

Maurice Tuchman, 'Interview with R. B. Kitaj', *R. B. Kitaj: Paintings and Prints,* exhibition catalogue, Los Angeles County Museum of Art, 1965.

What do you think is your relationship to Pop art – English or American?

I still balk at the word Pop ... Real Pop (not art) bores hell out of me but often when High Camp insinuates itself into recent art, the results are engaging (given the quality, intrinsic and relative of the art-piece at hand). I guess I've decided on occasion in favor of certain Camp themes or passages but not often enough to get pinned down.

...

You wrote, 'Some books have pictures and some pictures have books' – a marvellous evocation of your work. The look and feel of books as material things, as well as their value as containers of ideas, obviously fascinates you in your work. But filmic *kinds of association and transmutation are also apparent in the organization and tone of your work. Do movies interest you for painterly reasons?*

Yes, movies are great ... I love them ... but I haven't seen more than ten this last year. I would rather see a movie than a play. Movies *must* be a prime animating factor for me ... as you say – FILMIC – that sounds like a goodish word. I wouldn't mind achieving the *scope* of films like Lost Horizon or Seven Samurai or any number of others in pictures ... *Plural* energies engage my hopes for picture-making rather than *Less* is More and Film Sense moves me.

Eduardo Paolozzi

Edouard Roditi, 'Interview with Eduardo Paolozzi: The artist sketches "an aesthetic of the *objet trouvé*" based on a conscious metamorphosis of the derelict,' *Arts,* May 1959, p. 44.

... I seek to stress all that is wonderful or ambiguous in the most ordinary objects, in fact often in objects that nobody stops to look at or to admire. Besides, I try to subject these objects, which are the basic materials of my sculptures, to more than one metamorphosis. Generally I am conscious, as I work, of seeking to achieve two or at most three such changes in my materials, but sometimes I then discover that I have unconsciously achieved a fourth or even a fifth metamorphosis too. That is why I believe that an artist who works with *objets trouvés* must avoid being dominated by his materials. Wonderful as these may be, they are not endowed with a mind and cannot, as the artist often does, change their mind as they are being transformed. On the contrary, the artist must dominate his materials completely, so as to transform or transmute them fully. You have probably seen, in New York and in Paris, a lot of work by younger sculptors who, like Stankiewicz, Cesar and me, work mainly with *objets trouvés.* Well, I often feel that if one of us chances to find a particularly nice and spooky-looking piece of junk like an old discarded boiler, he can scarcely avoid using it as the trunk or body of a figure, if only because its shape suggests a body to anyone who sets out to do this kind of assembly work. Then one only needs to weld something smaller onto the top to suggest a head, and four limblike bits and pieces onto the sides and the bottom to suggest arms and legs, and there you have the whole figure, which has come to life like a traditional golem or robot ...

Eduardo Paolozzi

'Speculative illustrations', Eduardo Paolozzi in conversation with J. G. Ballard and Frank Whitford, *Studio International,* CLXXXIII, 937, October 1971, p. 136.

Whitford: ... I began by putting it to Ballard that both he and Paolozzi are working within a surrealist tradition, a tradition which, especially in this country, has never been taken very seriously. ...

Paolozzi: I wouldn't quarrel with the use of the word Surrealism in my case because, after all, it's the reason I went to Paris, to see the Surrealists. Any book on Surrealism excites me still. I don't mind trying to extend the tradition. It's easier for me to identify with that tradition than to allow myself to be described by some term, invented by others, called 'Pop', which immediately means that you dive into a barrel of Coca-Cola bottles. What I like to think I'm doing is an extension of radical Surrealism.

Peter Phillips

Peter Phillips, Extracts from unpublished interviews by Marco Livingstone, 2 February 1982.

In the end we just carried on making collages of American-type images, women from the German magazines, all these sort of things that young guys do. I was 20, 21 years old. You can't really expect some profound intellectual: it was again just an emotional response to various things that young guys would like, and an attempt to find another type of imagery to present on a painting. Jasper Johns's targets gave the clue ...

It was trying to discover another way of using imagery and trying to put it together ... One just had a peculiar feeling and tried to get this into the painting, using imagery that responded to this feeling. Certain types of fairground activity somehow came in with this feeling, rather like Orson Welles would often use these halls of mirrors or something in his movies. One got a particular response from the nature of this funfair imagery. It's a place of fun, but somehow it has an undercurrent of menace the whole time ...

Everything is worked out totally intuitively. This is all the way through my work. It's to do with placement and balance of these often very dissimilar elements against each other ... I really think the same thing applies now, and I think always did ...

You can make your interpretation, but you're never certain ... I would prefer that it remain in that state of tension. I would prefer that there is a game which can constantly be played with the painting which is never resolved. You can't win, you can't lose. It's better that way, because then the painting is self-generative because each individual can interpret it in his own way.

Peter Phillips

Statement by Peter Phillips, *The New Generation,* exhibition catalogue, Whitechapel Art Gallery, London, 1964.

'In pre-Renaissance painting you get a complex visual situation with a central image, and other things related to the central image – but they are also a story or a presence in themselves. My attitude to painting hasn't been motivated by this, but it's something you can tie it to. I look on what I am trying to do now as a multi-assemblage of ideas inside one format, and I'm not restricted by one type of space, or by anything else. The different parts are arbitrary to each other but related because of their format. My paintings now are multi-assemblages of spatial, iconographical and technical factors which combine to make one object.

'My awareness of machines, advertising, and mass communication is not probably in the same sense as an older generation that's been without these factors; I've been conditioned by them and grew up with it all and use it without a second thought. I wouldn't analyse these images in a way that an artist of an older generation might. I've lived with them ever since I can remember and so it's natural to use them without thinking. I'm basically interested in painting and not just a presentation of imagery.'

Colin Self

Colin Self, Excerpts from an unpublished letter to Marco Livingstone, 1 December 1987.

Mention might be made of the Left Wing standing of British Art Schools after World War II to keep up student numbers. They opened their doors to the Working Classes (the *War Babies*) and Pop Art was, within a generation, what happened ... Sociologically, there is something of a point here to make. Art Schools as 'Working Class' hotbeds of 'anarchy' & *unbridled* centres of creative expression. Pop came out of that. Now, it couldn't ...

I think many Pop Artists imagined for themselves a different kind of role (to the traditional artist) and, I think, *were* nearer in spirit to what they imagined Rock stars to be, or the spirit of Rock'n'Roll to be, e.g. Hamilton, Blake, Oxtoby. It was even one of my private fantasies ... Personally for me, Pop Art represented being 'understood', being 'open'. The antithesis of all that abstract, pseudo, complex 'arty-farty art', dribble art. Tachism etc. Swamped by all that crap at Art School, I eventually rebelled and worked in the opposing sphere to the abstractionism & jargonism. Pop Art was the pendulum swing back *to* rationality. *Away* from deliberate nurtured *'obscurantism'.* Thinking its 'refined' obscurity 'super intellectual'.

Pop Art was the first art movement for goodness knows how long, to *accept* and reflect the world in which it lives. As opposed to being escapist 'classical', 'romantic', reactionary, elitist, 'scientific', anthropological, analytical & cold. Art still seemed to be hoping cars and aeroplanes 'went away' – and horses made a comeback so they could re-do 'The Hay Wain'. In other words, there is a conspicuous *absence* of 20th century iconography in 20th century art – *until* Pop Art. Before POP all ART *hid* behind being 'ARTY'. Art had reached such a state of insincerity and pretentiousness, POP was a *real* revelation.

Richard Smith

Richard Smith, 'That Pink', *Gazette*, 2, 1961

The place of mass media and other artefacts of mass culture in the esthetic canons, practical, spiritual, and social of some painters, has been quite firmly demonstrated over the last few years, a phenomena that seems to be gaining momentum. Most acceptable have been the products of the most popular level, as if the widest dissemination gave the product a particular worth. This could be because wide acceptance as part of the everyday scene tends to make certain objects invisible, till put in a different context: a Woodbine packet on a Riviera beach, or a Pepsi bottle in a painting. The most sophisticated media, however, have been neglected.

For New York painters working popular culture elements the accent is always on the below-14th Street ambiance (which includes discount stores, street markets, junk shops, and 10th St). Midtown (Bergdorf Goodman, Brooks Brothers, Park Avenue), except for Times Square, just does not figure. In London where topographical divisions are impossible, there is an emphasis on Americana which is slightly exotic. The choice of elements is more specialised; publications and products which are out and out non-fine art (cereal box premimums, for instance) are in, whereas non-fine art with pretensions (Primavera, About Town) is out.

I would like to consider colour photography as it appears in 'Harper's Bazaar', 'Vogue', and other sophisticated products of the mass media. Colour photography has made a very complex world. It is a fantasy world, for the colour is heightened and the view highly edited, but what is left makes a whole. It is impossible to get an image of Revlon, Bermuda, IBM, and Smirnoff Vodka, except in terms of colour photography and colour links them in the same fantasy.

Richard Smith

Bruce Glaser, '3 British Artists in New York', *Studio International*, CLXX, November 1965, pp. 181–2.

Glaser: To get back to the influence of the ICA, would you say that the imagery of pop art had its roots in the ideas and exhibitions of this group? Is there anything to the claim that British artists invented pop art?
Jones: I think the ICA was responsible for some of the pop imagery but whenever there is a movement or a manifestation of any sort going on there will always be someone who will be looking around to find the father of it, and he usually turns out to be somebody who was working in obscurity. Although an artist may work in obscurity and then find his point of view confirmed in the emergence of some current movement. I also think such an artist improves his position because of the impact of the people who come after him, even if his work does not deserve the extra attention. So I don't think chronology is as important to the current style as it is to the artist who wasn't known until some idea he employed came into wide usage. And I don't believe that an older painting is made any better because it has fragments of something which is happening now.
Glaser: Why is pop art so strong in England, in any case? In relation to this I was struck by a comment of Annette Michelson's that appeared in one of her articles in *Art International*, where she said that she felt pop art comes only from affluent societies, where there are signs of satiety and waste, and she specifically cited the fact that there is no pop art coming from Spain, where there is clearly nothing like the affluence of England. Is there a link between the situation in post-war Britain and the manifestations of pop art?
Smith: I think pop art is most likely to come from an urban environment and Britain is a very urban country. Although we may have spent our lives in the towns, and there is where one would be exposed to the raw material of pop art, and then, more inclined to use it.
Jones: One reason for the prevalence of popular imagery in England is that it may be related to her closeness to America that comes from the sharing of a common language and our traditional alliance. And I think the lack of a language barrier shouldn't be underrated. It's natural that something happening in one place would be communicated all the more rapidly if the exchange were easier, so that it is quite probable that many of the forces that produced popular imagery in American art were similarly felt in the air in England.
Smith: It's interesting to see how language barriers and therefore greater cultural barriers affect the transportation of ordinary things such as American movies when they are seen, say, in France. They become so exotic according to the way French movie critics interpret them. I remember having a French book on monster movies that included everything from ladies with unicorns on medieval tapestries to Fay Wray and King Kong and presumed to see a connection throughout. Comparing that with a British movie magazine like *Movie*, you could see that American movies were not exotic to us. You take them straight, and this is mostly due to language. I think that's probably why the French can't produce the same kind of pop art that the English speaking people do. And also, the best commercial art, from which pop art comes, is American.

Richard Smith

Richard Smith, 'Trailer: Notes additional to a film', *Living Arts*, 1, 1963, pp. 29–30.

I paint about communication.

The communication media are a large part of my landscape. My interest is not in the message so much as in the method. There is a multiplicity of messages (smoke these, vote this, ban that), fewer methods. Can how something is communicated be divorced from what is being communicated, and can it be divorced from who it is being communicated to?

...

... I am aware that the message might be trivial, the form banal, but this places me and the spectator in a different, more open relationship to the work than to forms and messages of recognized validity and seriousness. It is not quite a question of bringing painting to the people but of bringing more of the spectator to art. Where the work stops being an advertisement and becomes a painting is not only the fact that it is painted. My painting does not have the same function as the 'subject'; whether the original subject-message was a hard or soft sell my concern may be more with a hard or soft edge, the emphasis is readjusted between the product and the production.

Alison and Peter Smithson

'But Today we collect Ads', *Ark,* 18, November 1956, pp. 49–50.

Traditionally the fine arts depend on the popular arts for their vitality, and the popular arts depend on the fine arts for their respectability. It has been said that things hardly 'exist' before the fine artist has made use of them, they are simply part of the unclassified background material against which we pass our lives. The transformation from everyday object to fine art manifestation happens in many ways, the object can be discovered – *objêt trouvé* or *l'art brut* – the object itself remaining the same; a literary or, the folk myth can arise and again the object itself remains unchanged; or, the object can be used as a jumping-off point and is itself transformed.

. . .

Why certain folk art objects, historical styles or industrial artifacts and methods become important at a particular moment cannot easily be explained.

> **Gropius wrote a book on grain silos,**
> **Le Corbusier one on aeroplanes,**
> **And Charlotte Perland brought a new object to the office every morning;**
> **But today we collect ads.**

Advertising has caused a revolution in the popular art field. Advertising has become respectable in its own right and is beating the fine arts at their old game. We cannot ignore the fact that one of the traditional functions of fine art, the definition of what is fine and desirable for the ruling class and therefore ultimately that which is desired by all society, has now been taken over by the ad-man.

. . .

The fine artist is often unaware that his patron, or more often his patron's wife who leafs through the magazines, is living in a different visual world to his own. The pop-art of today, the equivalent of the Dutch fruit and flower arrangement, the pictures of second rank of all Renaissance schools, and the plates that first presented to the public the Wonder of the Machine Age and the New Territories, is to be found in today's glossies – bound up with the throw-away object.

As far as architecture is concerned the influence on mass standards and mass aspirations of advertising is now infinitely stronger than the pace setting of *avant-garde* architects, and it is taking over the functions of social reformers and politicians. Already the mass production industries have revolutionized half the house – kitchen, bathroom, utility room, and garage – without the intervention of the architect, and the curtain wall and the modular prefabricated building are causing us to revise our attitude to the relationship between architect and industrial production.

. . .

Ordinary life is receiving powerful impulses from a new source. Where thirty years ago architects found in the field of the popular arts, techniques and formal stimuli, today we are being edged out of our traditional role by the new phenomenon of the popular arts – advertising.

Mass production advertising is establishing our whole pattern of life – principles, morals, aims, aspirations, and standard of living. We must somehow get the measure of this intervention if we are to match its powerful and exciting impulses with our own.

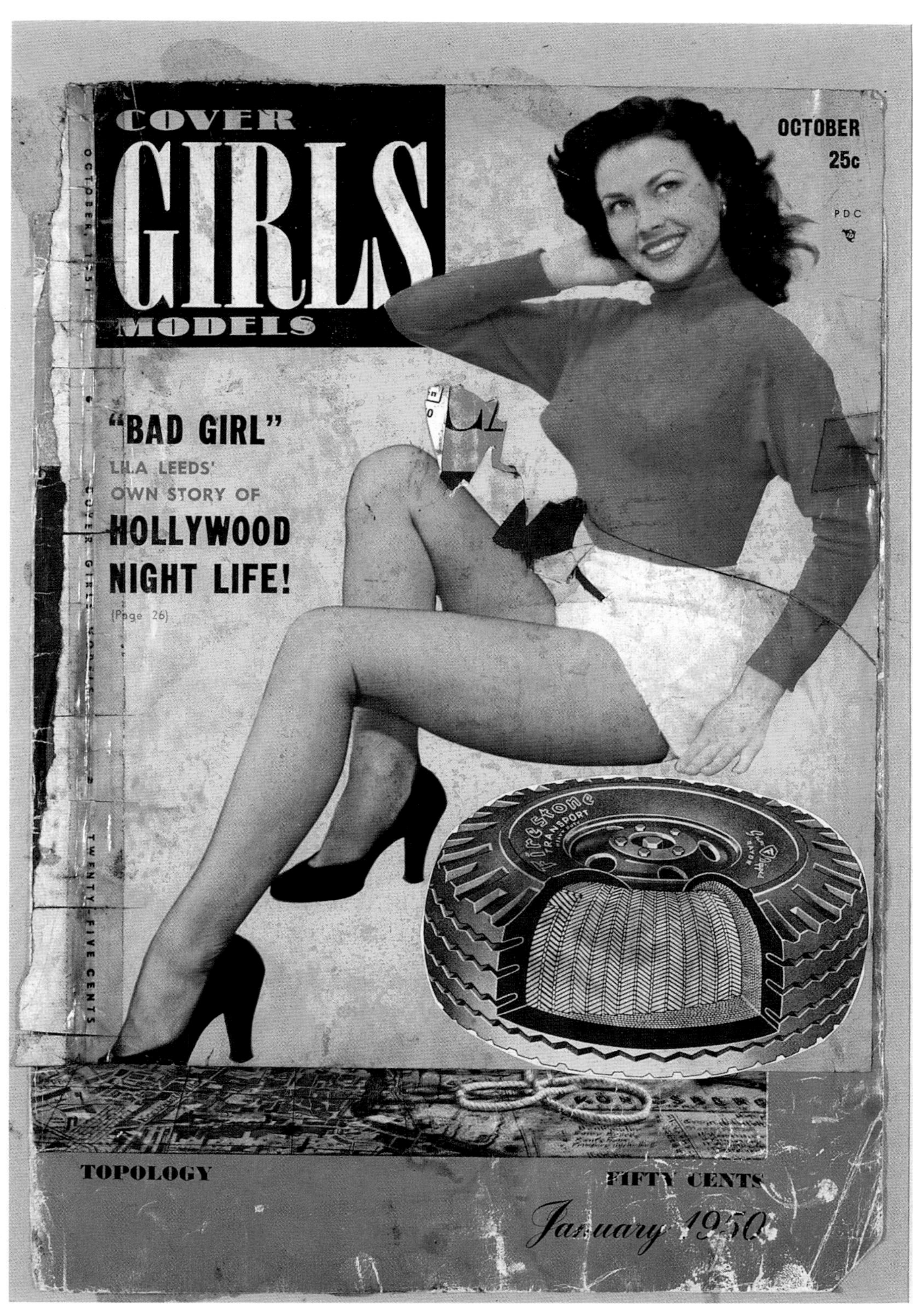

102 **Eduardo Paolozzi** You can't beat the Real Thing 1951 (cat 172)

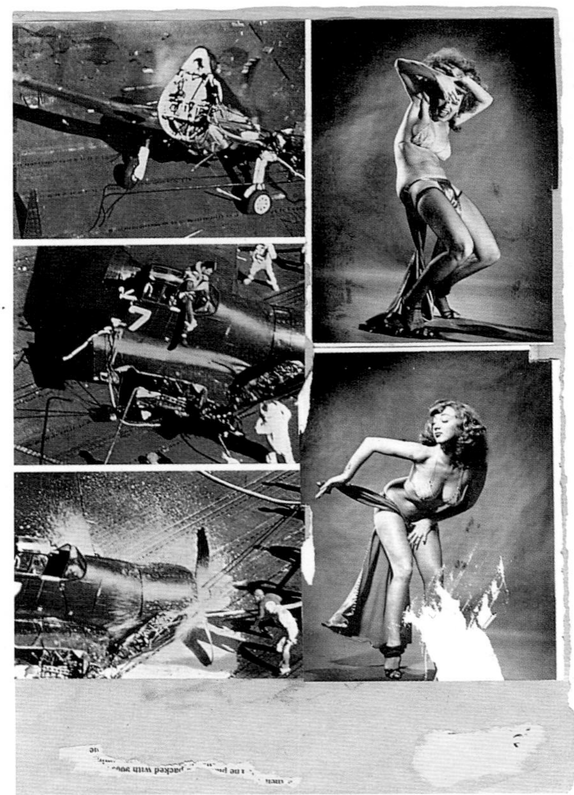

103 **Eduardo Paolozzi** Real Gold 1950 (cat 170)

104 **Eduardo Paolozzi** Yours Till the Boys Come Home 1951 (cat 173)

105 **Eduardo Paolozzi** Popular Mechanics 1951 (cat 171)

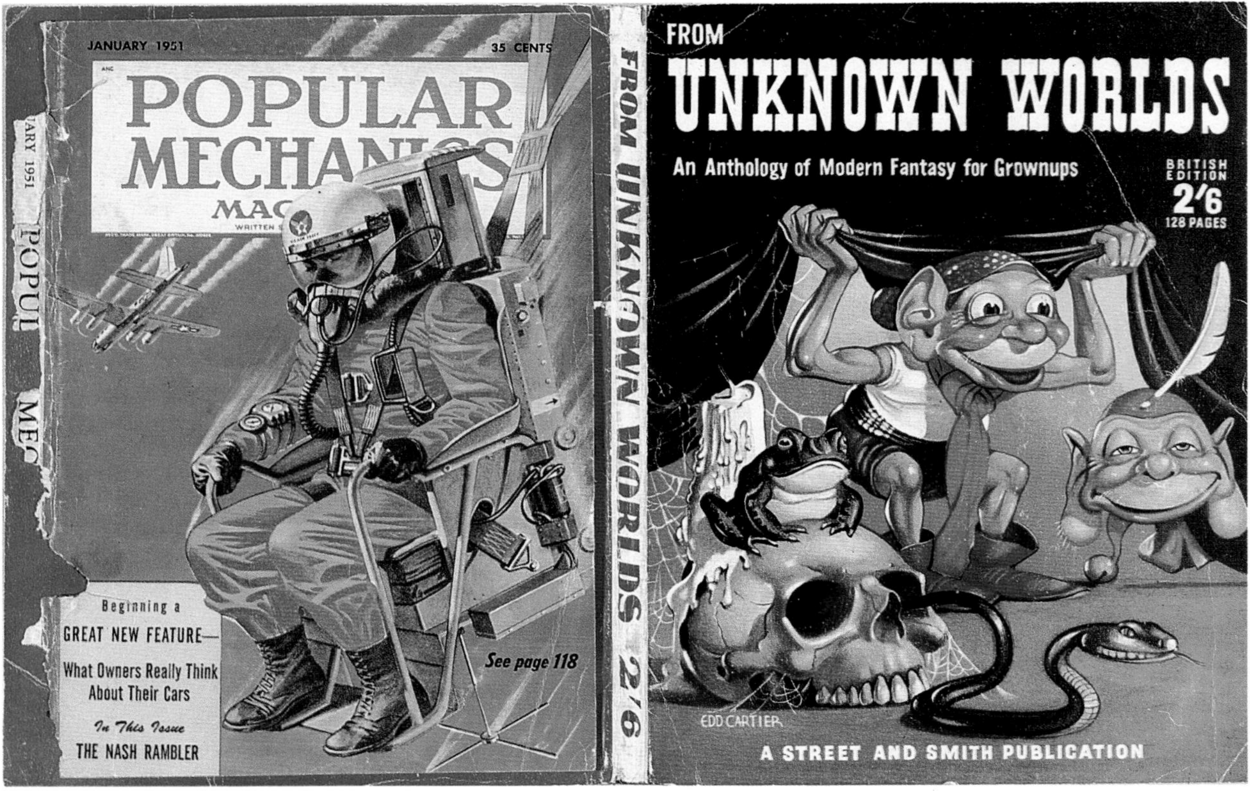

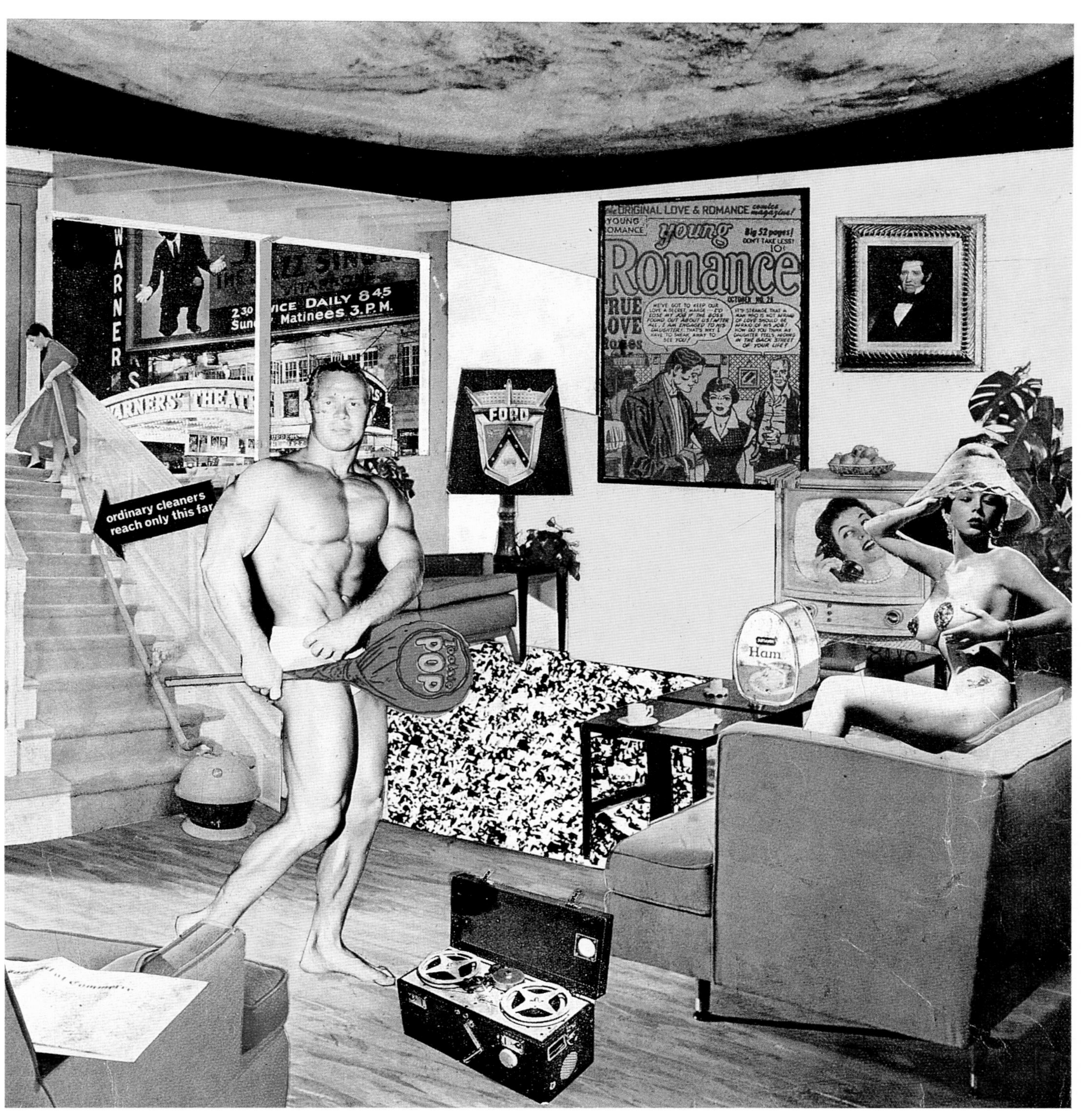

106 **Richard Hamilton** Just what is it that makes today's homes so different, so appealing? 1956 (cat 99)

107 **Peter Blake** Children Reading Comics 1956 (cat 15)

108 **Peter Blake** Siriol, She-Devil of Naked Madness 1957 (cat 16)

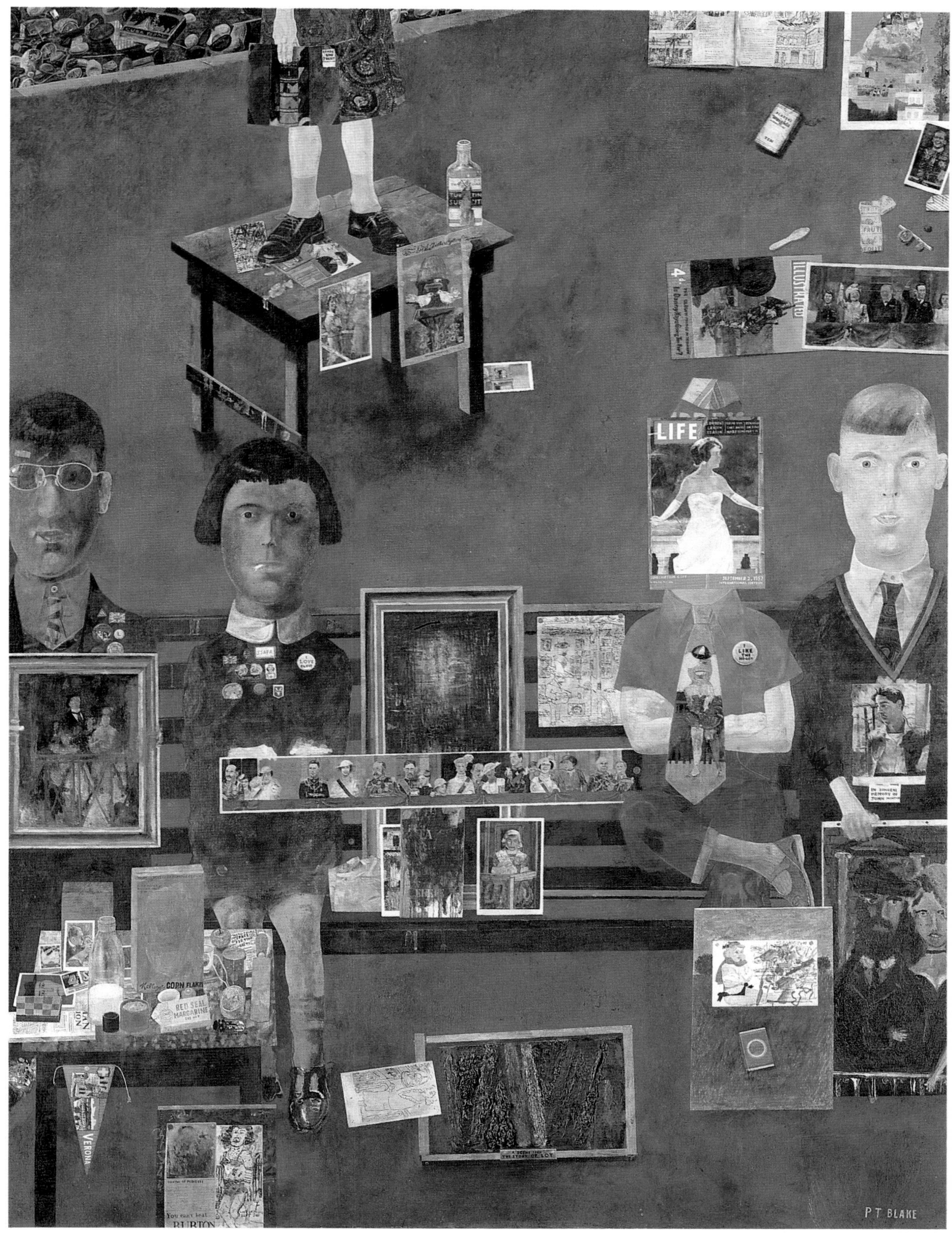

109 **Peter Blake** On the Balcony 1955–57 (cat 14)

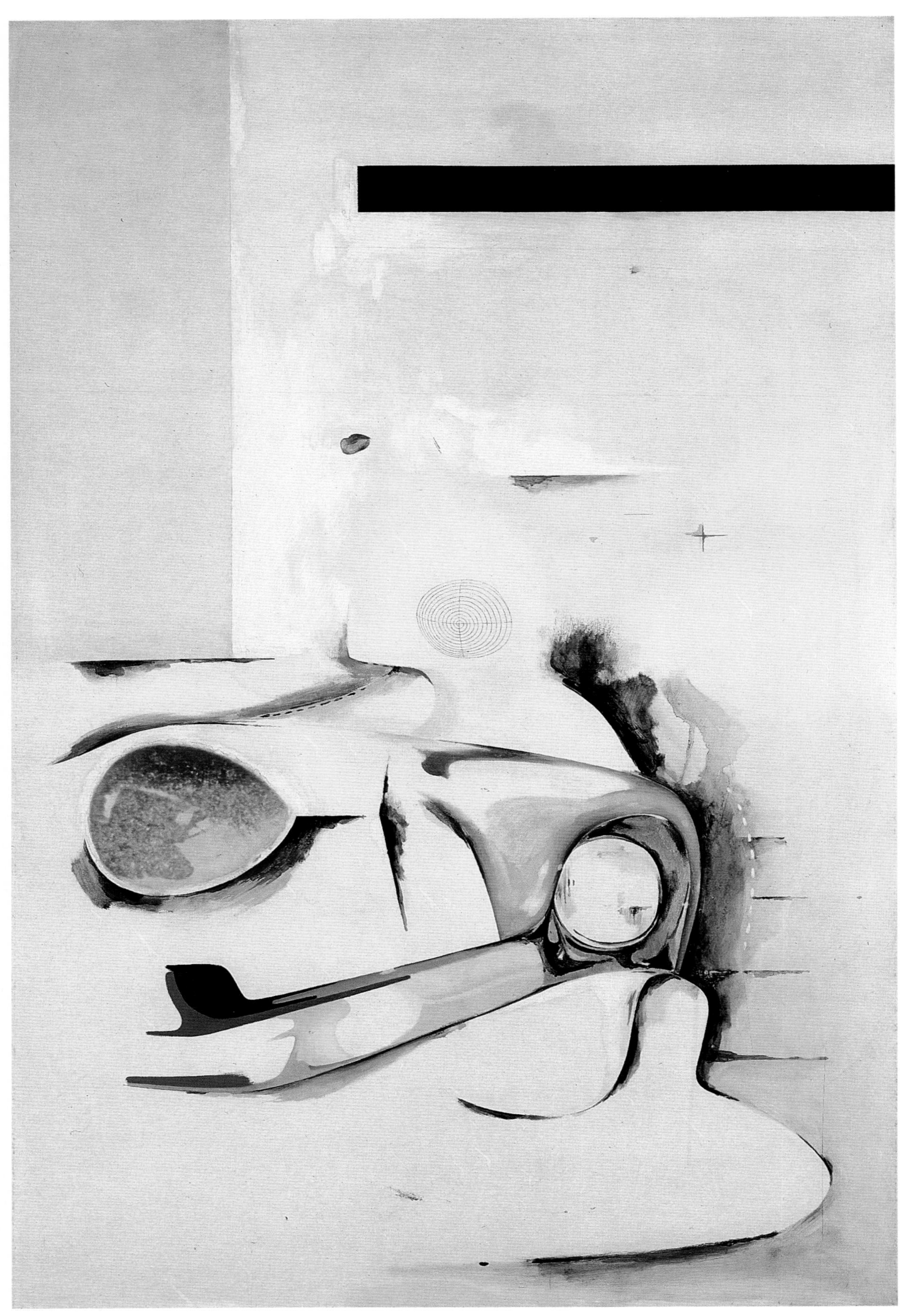

110 **Richard Hamilton** Hommage à Chrysler Corp 1957 (cat 100)

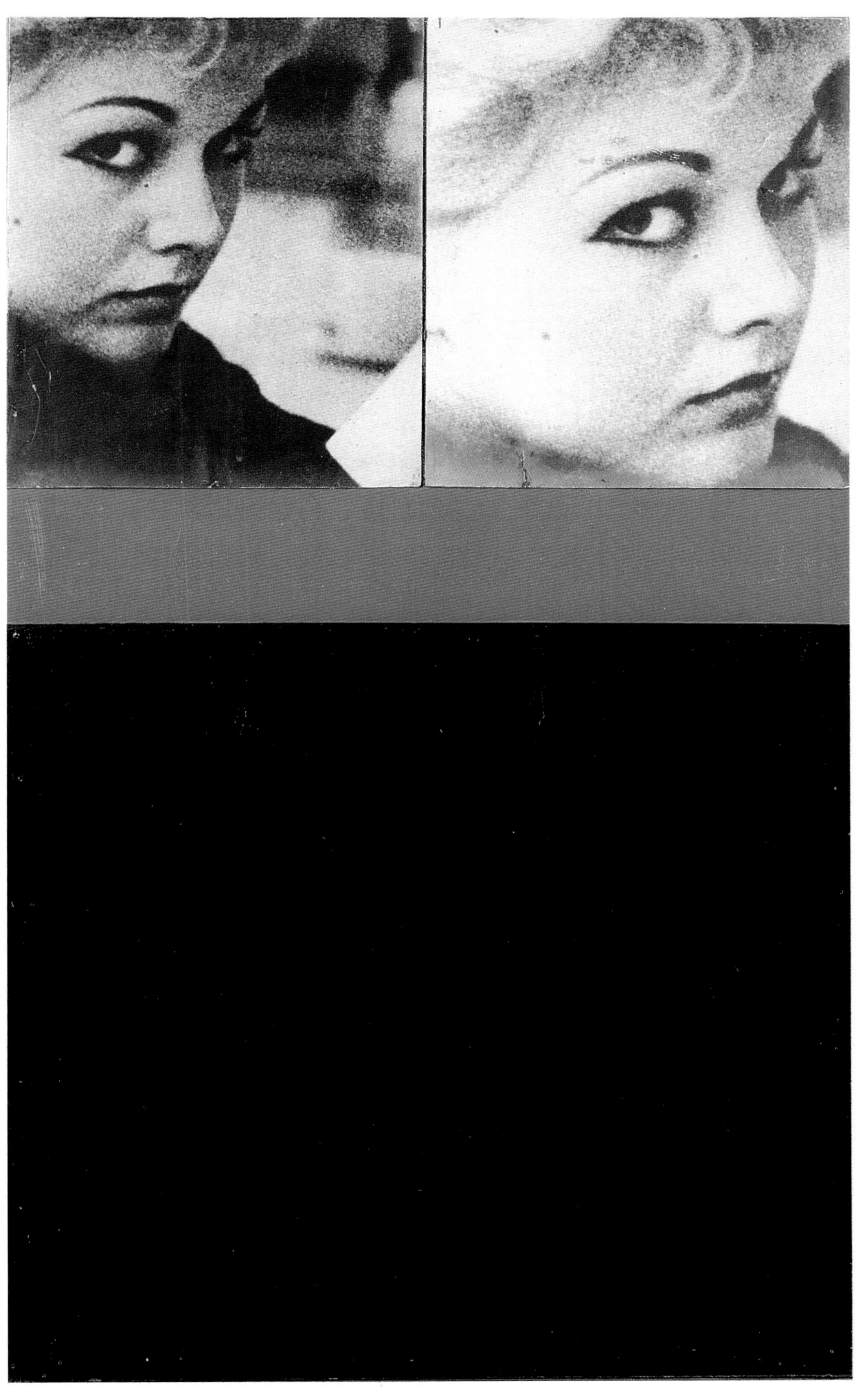

111 **Peter Blake** Kim Novak Wall 1959 (cat 17)

112 **Peter Phillips** Purple Flag 1960 (cat 178)

113 **Richard Smith** Formal Giant 1960 (cat 223)

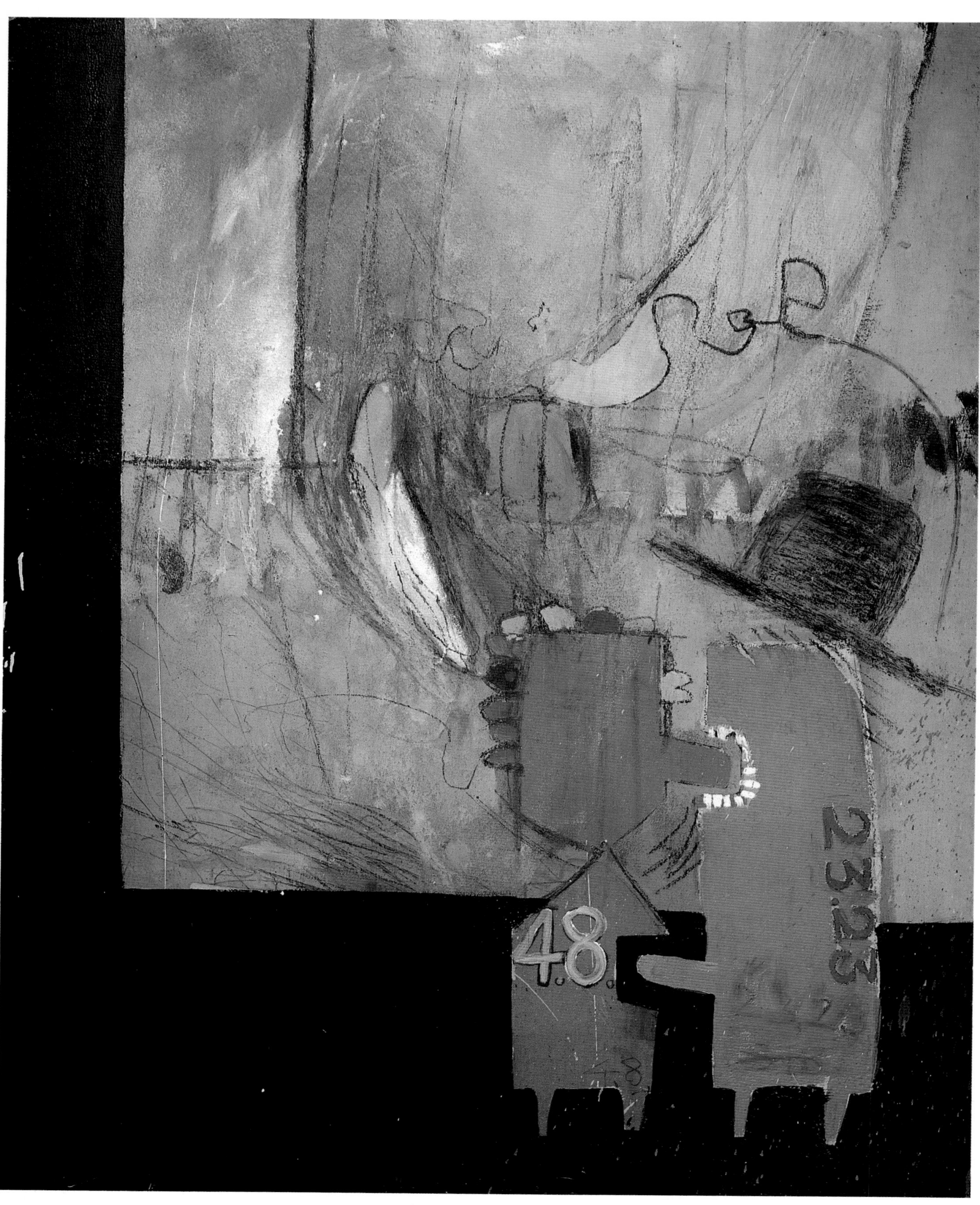

114 **David Hockney** Adhesiveness 1960 (cat 108)

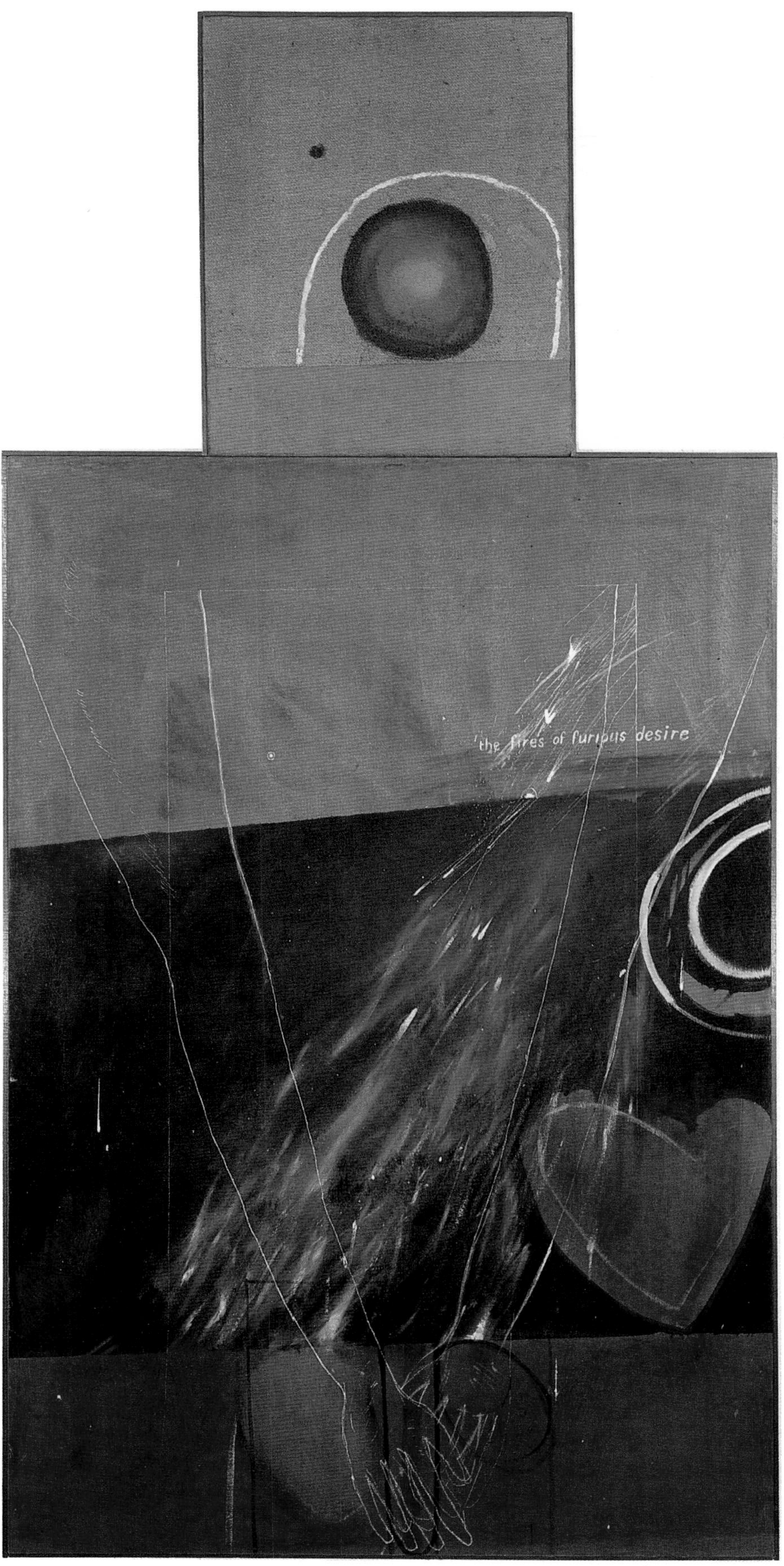

115 **David Hockney** Figure in a Flat Style 1961 (cat 109)

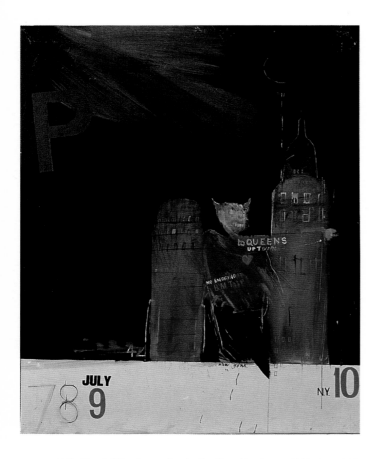

116 **David Hockney** I'm in the Mood for Love 1961 (cat 110)

117 **Derek Boshier** Airmail Letter 1961 (cat 21)

118 **Derek Boshier** First Toothpaste Painting 1962 (cat 22)

119 **Allen Jones** Thinking about Women 1961 (cat 132)

120 **Allen Jones** 2nd Bus 1962 (cat 134)

121 **Allen Jones** Bikini Baby 1962 (cat 133)

122 **Peter Phillips** Forces Sweetheart – Synchronised 1962 (cat 179)

123 **Peter Blake** Toy Shop 1962 (cat 18)

124 **R. B. Kitaj** Junta 1962 (cat 144)

125 **R. B. Kitaj** A Student of Vienna 1961–62 (cat 142)

126 **R. B. Kitaj** Good News for Incunabulists 1962 (cat 143)

127 **Eduardo Paolozzi** Solo 1962 (cat 175)

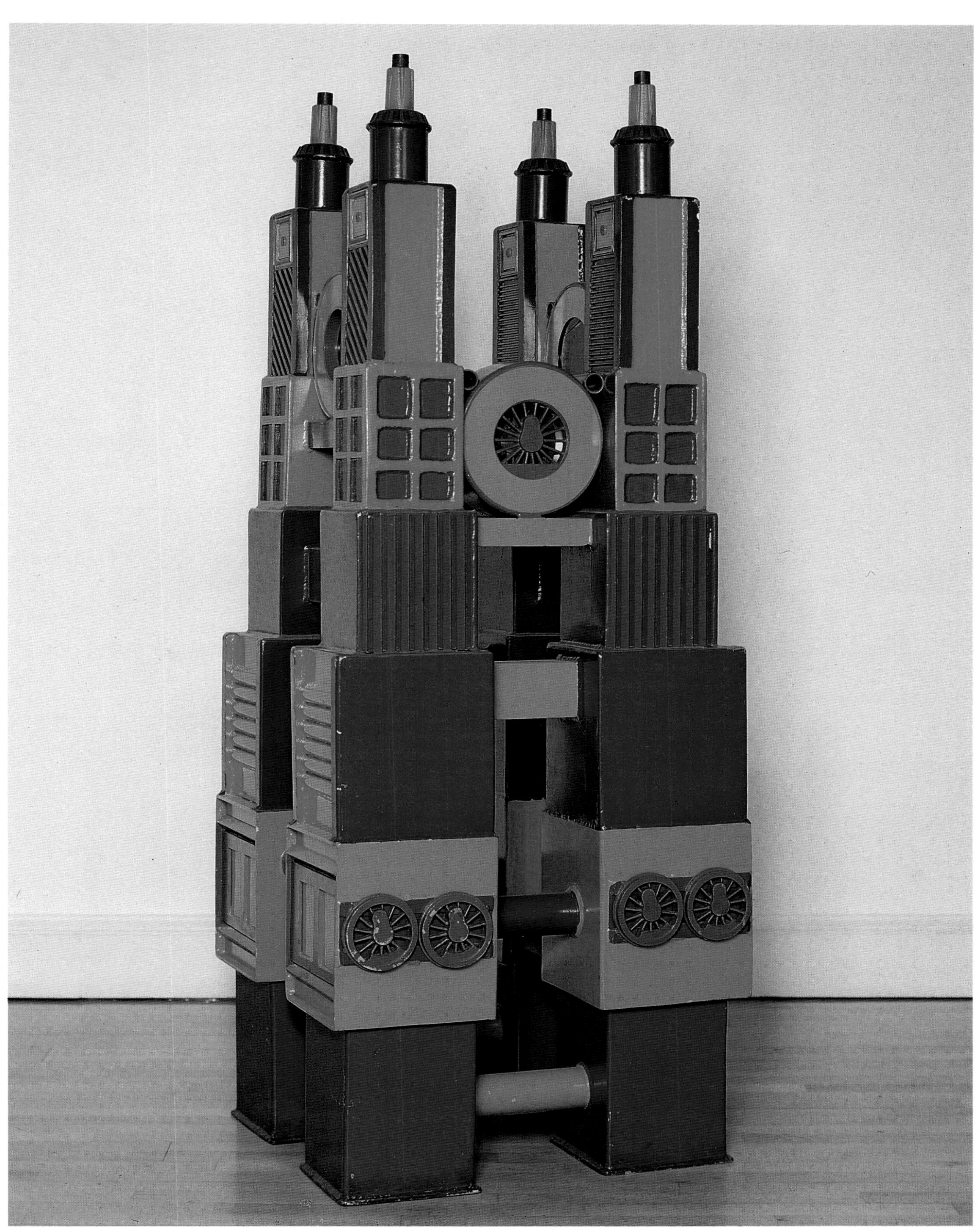

128 **Eduardo Paolozzi** Four Towers 1962 (cat 174)

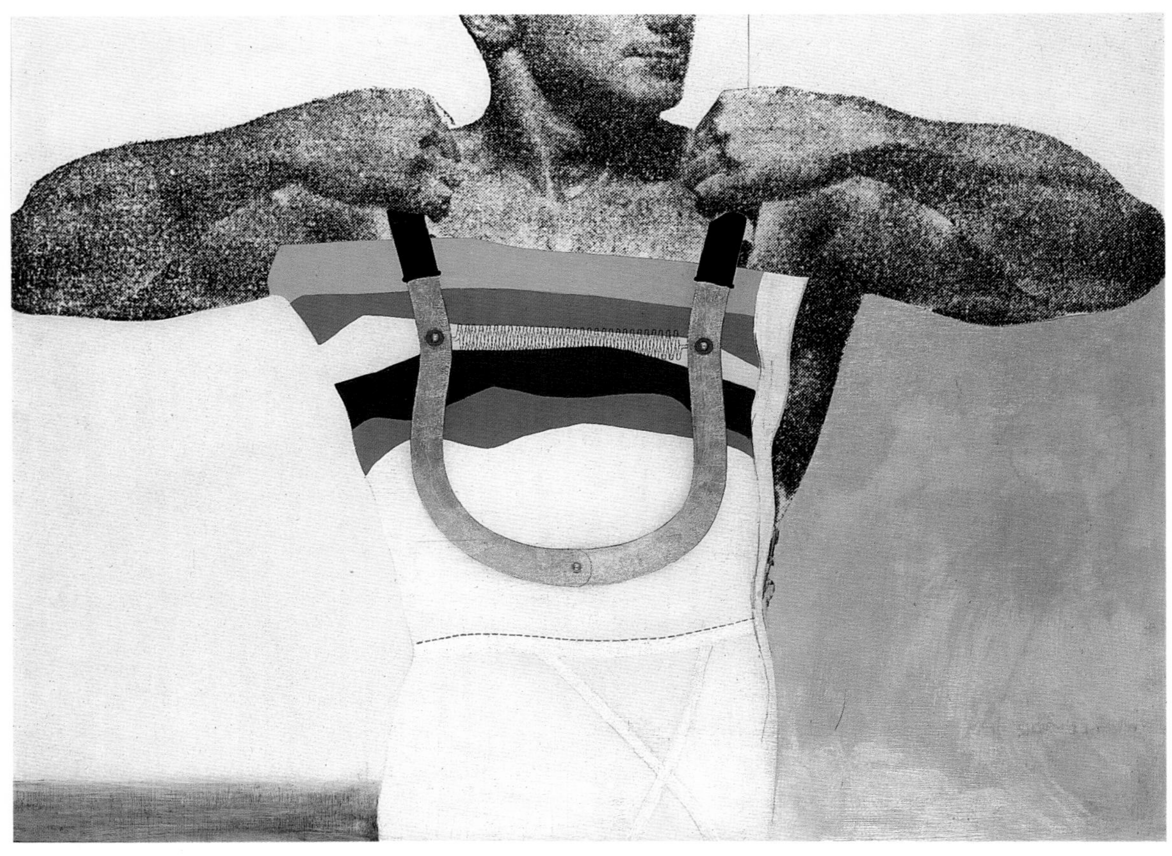

129 **Richard Hamilton** Towards a definitive statement on the coming trends in men's wear: Adonis in Y fronts 1962 (cat 102)

130 **Richard Hamilton** Glorious Techniculture 1961–64 (cat 101)

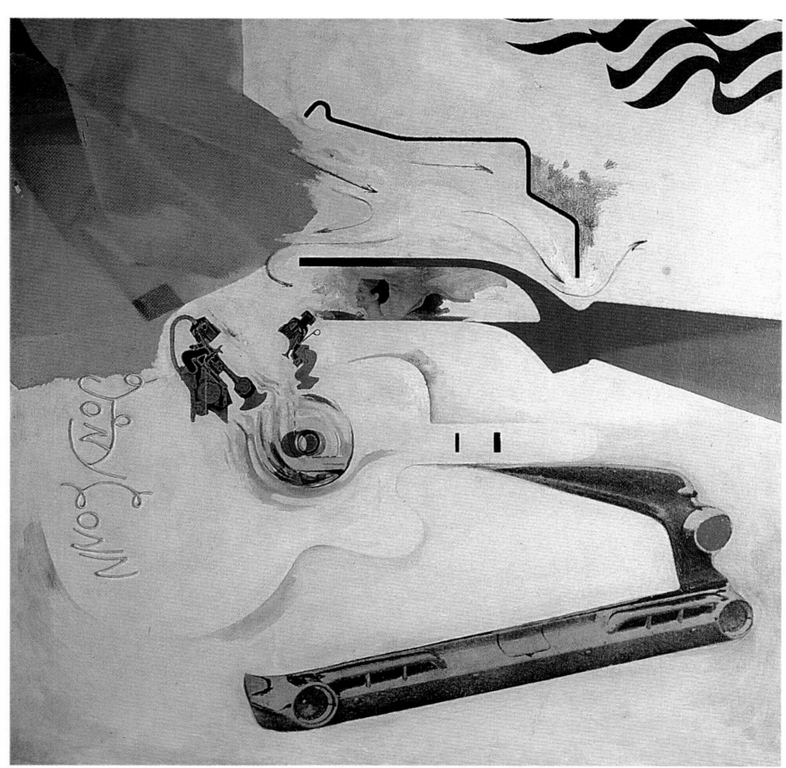

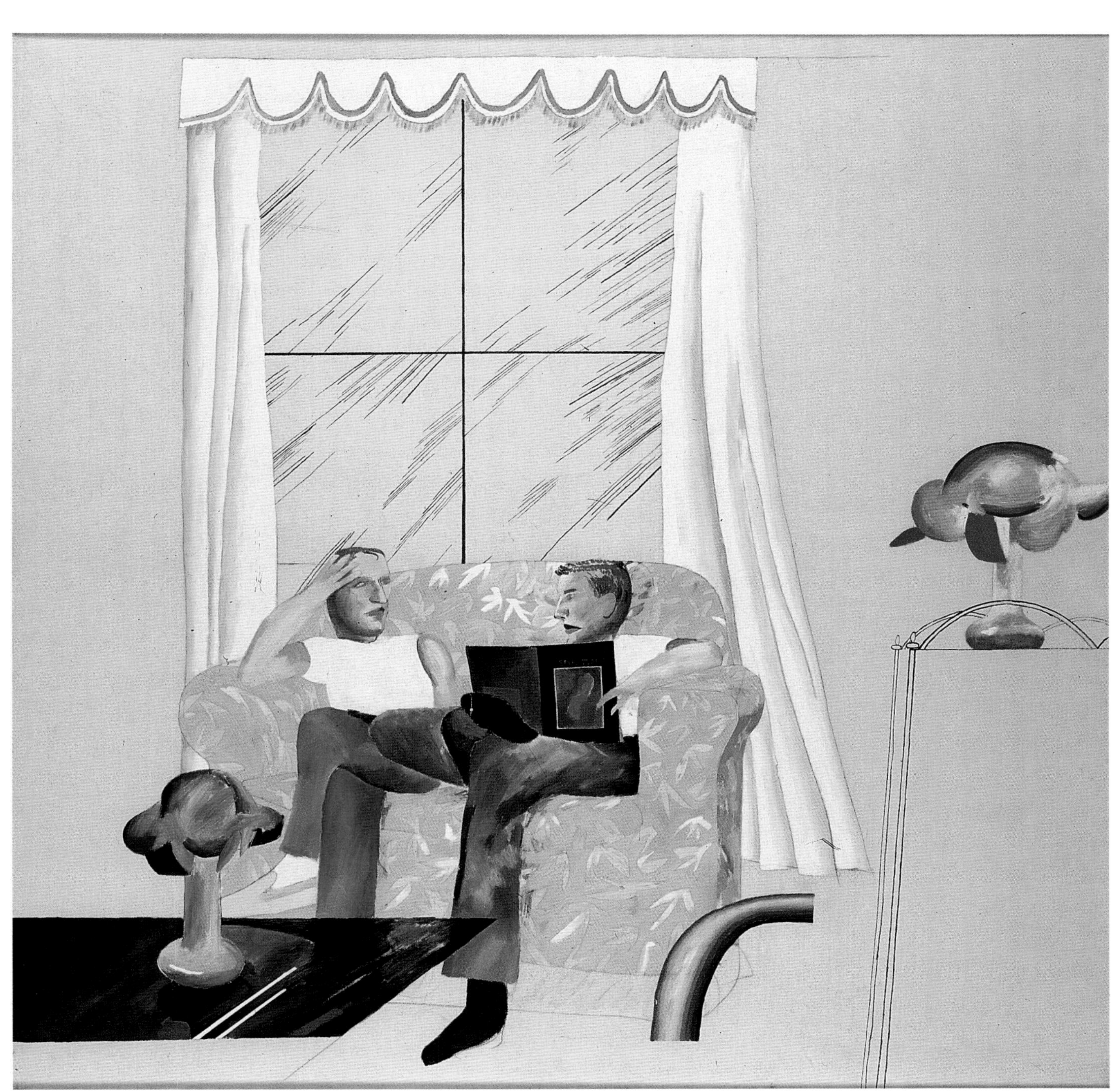

131 **David Hockney** Domestic Scene, Broadchalke, Wilts 1963 (cat 111)

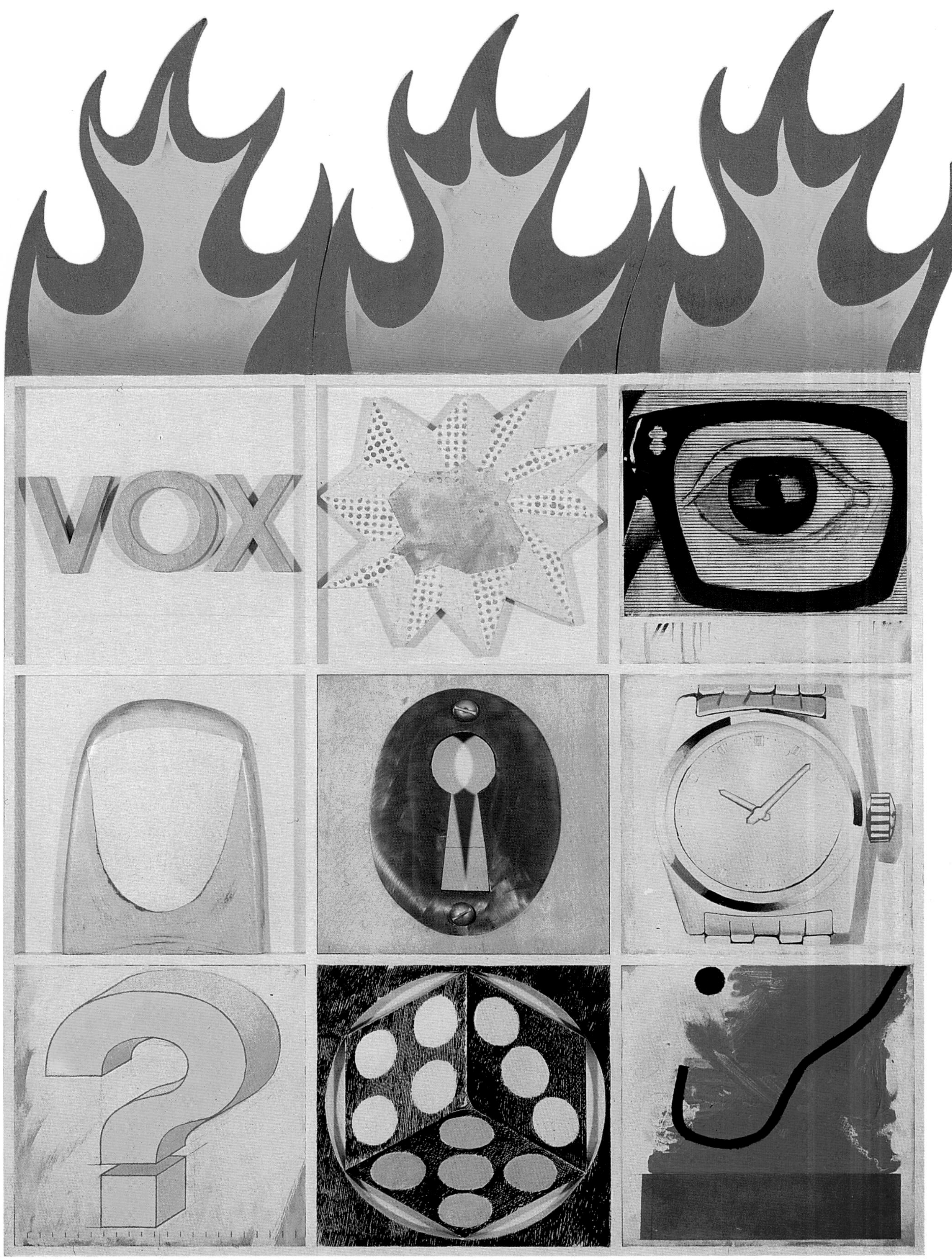

132 **Joe Tilson** Nine Elements 1963 (cat 230)

133 **Joe Tilson** A–Z Box of Friends and Family 1963 (cat 229)

134 **Richard Smith** Alpine 1963 (cat 224)

135 **Patrick Caulfield** Christ at Emmaus 1963 (cat 25)

136 **Patrick Caulfield** Engagement Ring 1963 (cat 26)

137 **Peter Blake** Bo Diddley 1963 (cat 19)

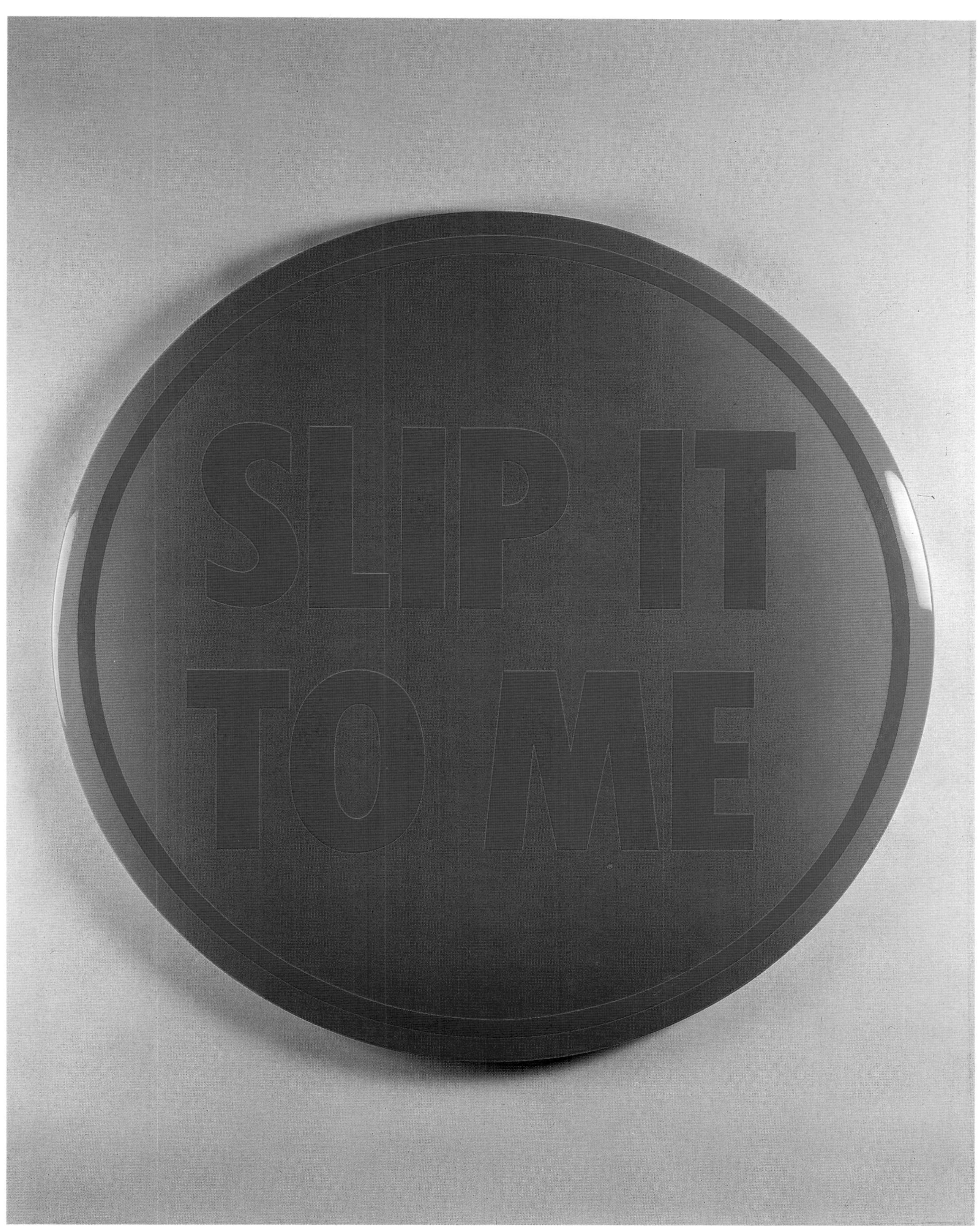

138 **Richard Hamilton** Epiphany 1964 (cat 103)

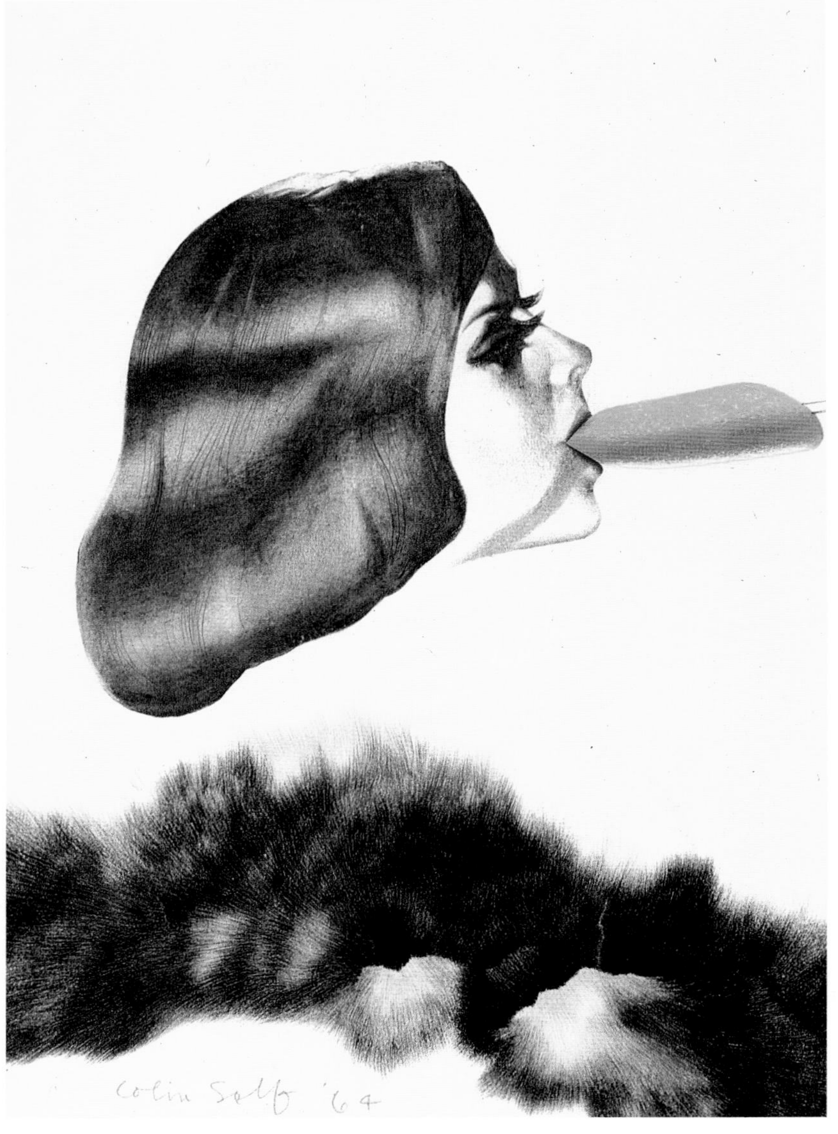

139 **Colin Self** Girl with a Popsicle 1964 (cat 218)

140 **Colin Self** Nuclear Bomber 1963 (cat 217)

141 **Colin Self** Hot Dog 3 (14.3.65) 1965 (cat 221)

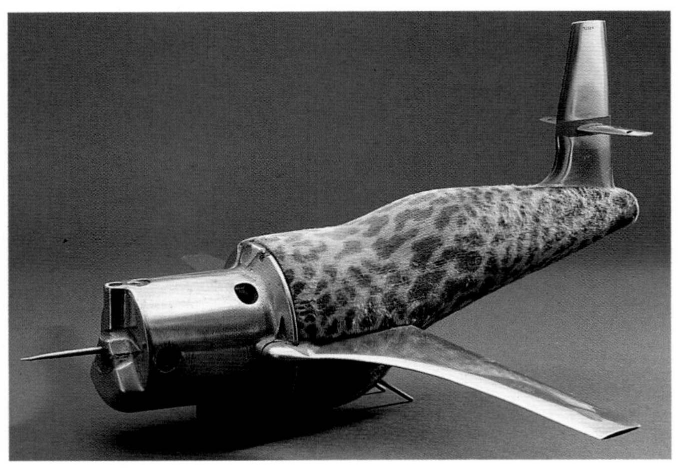

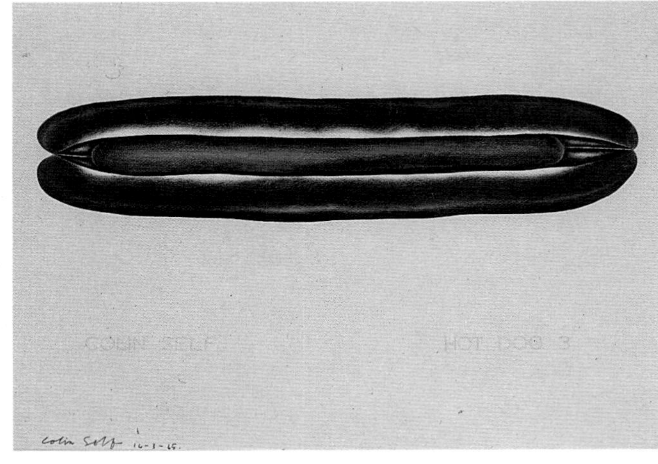

142 **Colin Self** Public Shelter 110 1965 (cat 222)

143 **Colin Self** Cinema 14 1965 (cat 220)

144 **Colin Self** Cinema 11 1965 (cat 219)

145 **Joe Tilson** P.C. from N.Y.C. 1965 (cat 231)

146 **Clive Barker** Two Palettes for Jim Dine 1964 (cat 9)

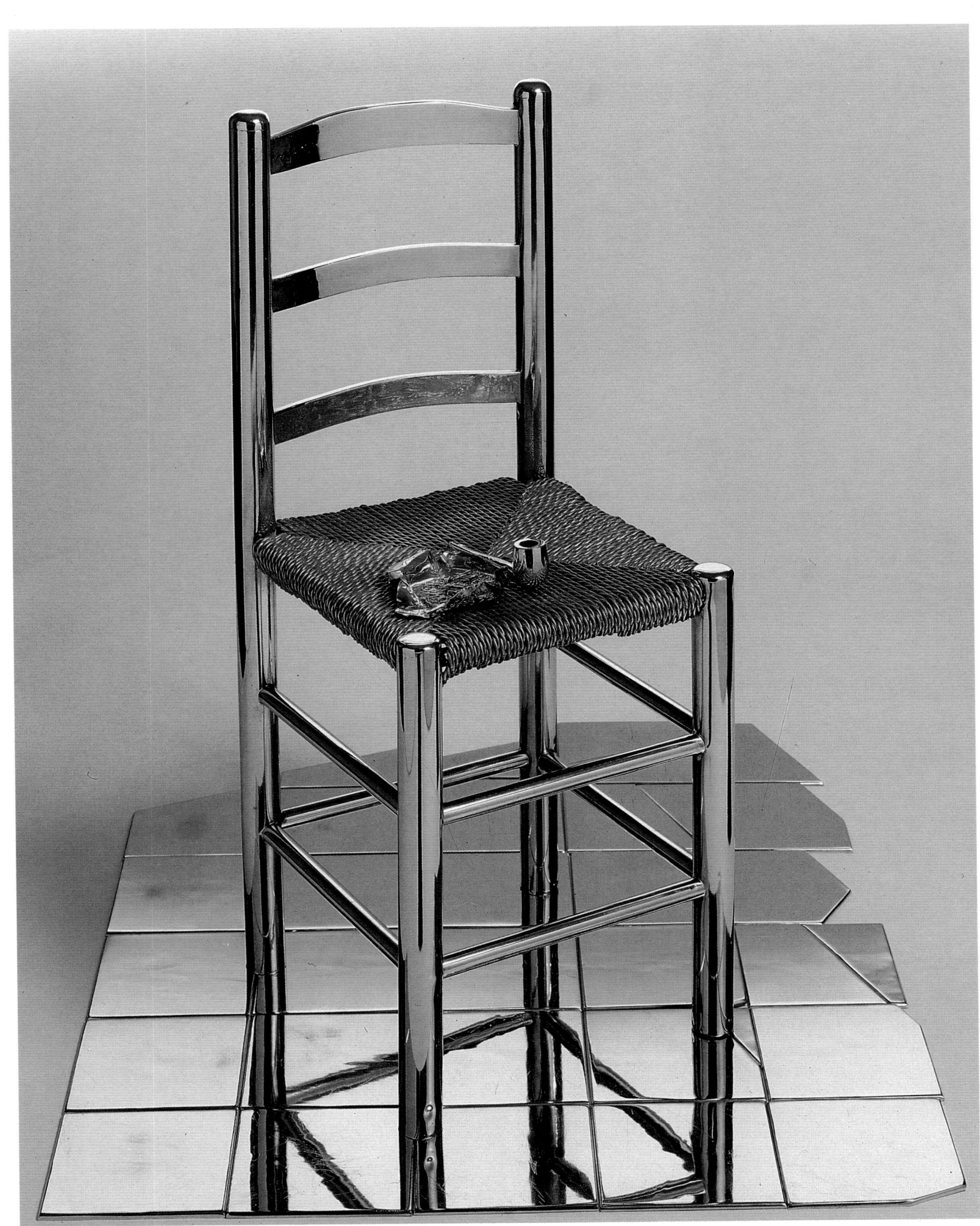

147 **Clive Barker** Van Gogh's Chair 1966 (cat 10)

148 **David Hockney** Rocky Mountains and Tired Indians 1965 (cat 112)

149 **David Hockney** A Bigger Splash 1967 (cat 113)

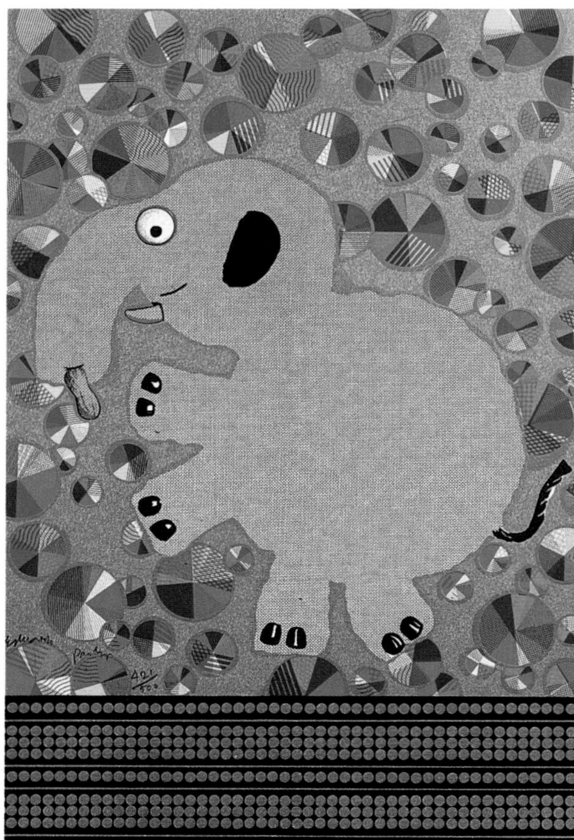

150 **Eduardo Paolozzi** Moonstrips Empire News 1967 (cat 176)

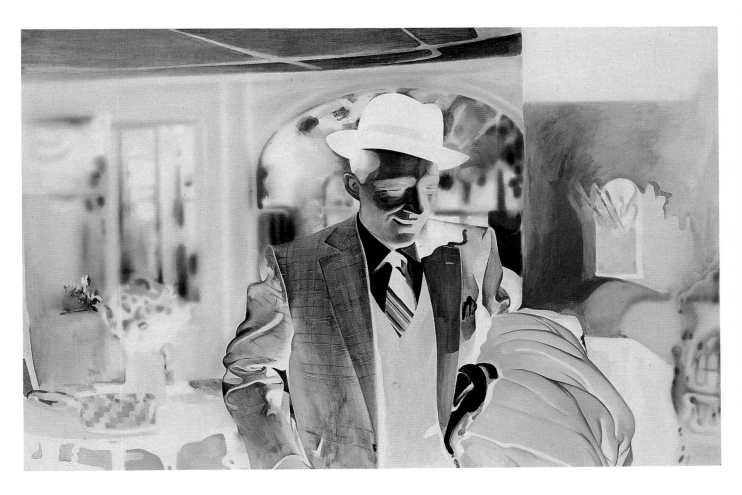

151 **Richard Hamilton** I'm dreaming of a white Christmas 1967–68 (cat 104)

152 **Richard Hamilton** Swingeing London 67 II 1968 (cat 105)

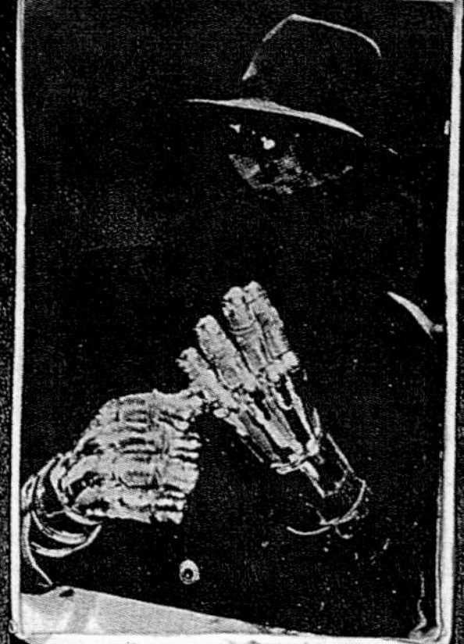

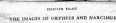

153 **Joe Tilson** Page 7, Snow White and the Black Dwarf 1969 (cat 232)

154 **Richard Hamilton** Soft Pink Landscape 1971–72 (cat 106)

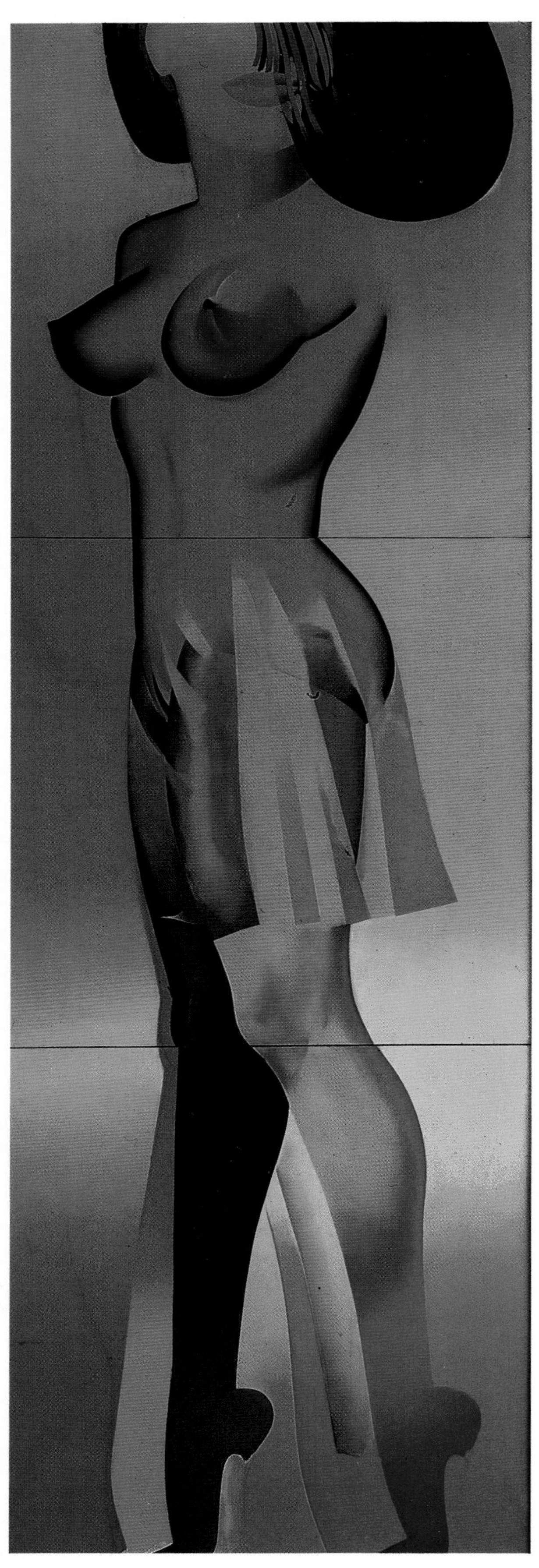

155 **Allen Jones** Perfect Match 1966–67 (cat 135)

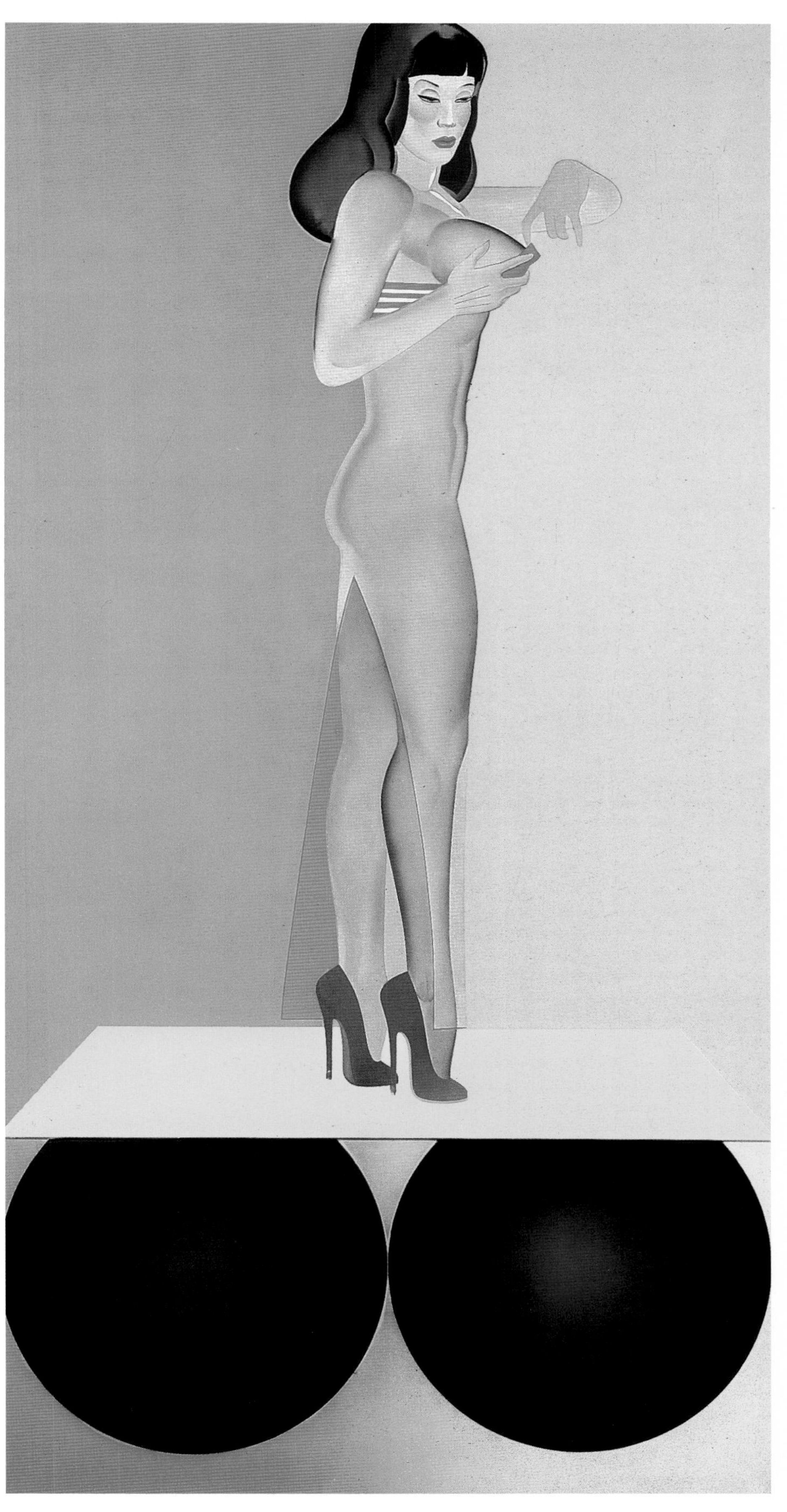

156 **Allen Jones** Bare Me 1972 (cat 137)

157 **Allen Jones** Table 1969 (cat 136)

Some observations about the table

1 With the care normally accorded to Works of Art, the table should last a lifetime - and more.

2 The sculpture is built to withstand the inevitable urge to use her as a table, but do not abuse this privilege with the use of very heavy objects.

3 She is painted with Rowney Cryla Colour and made of fibre-glass. A soft damp cloth may be used to wipe the figure, if necessary.

4 Her clothing has been custom made and is not strengthened in the normal manner for human usage.

5 The real-hair wig has been set and kiln dried. When the wig is removed from its box, brush out in the normal manner.

6 Reverse selo-tape is recommended for fixing the wig to the skull.

7 A key has been provided for screwing the glass onto the figure. Do not screw too tightly as refraction of light through the glass gives the impression of paint loss.

Allen Jones 1969

158 **Peter Phillips** Random Illusion No. 6 1969 (cat 180)

159 **Peter Phillips** Art-O-Matic Cudacutie 1972 (cat 181)

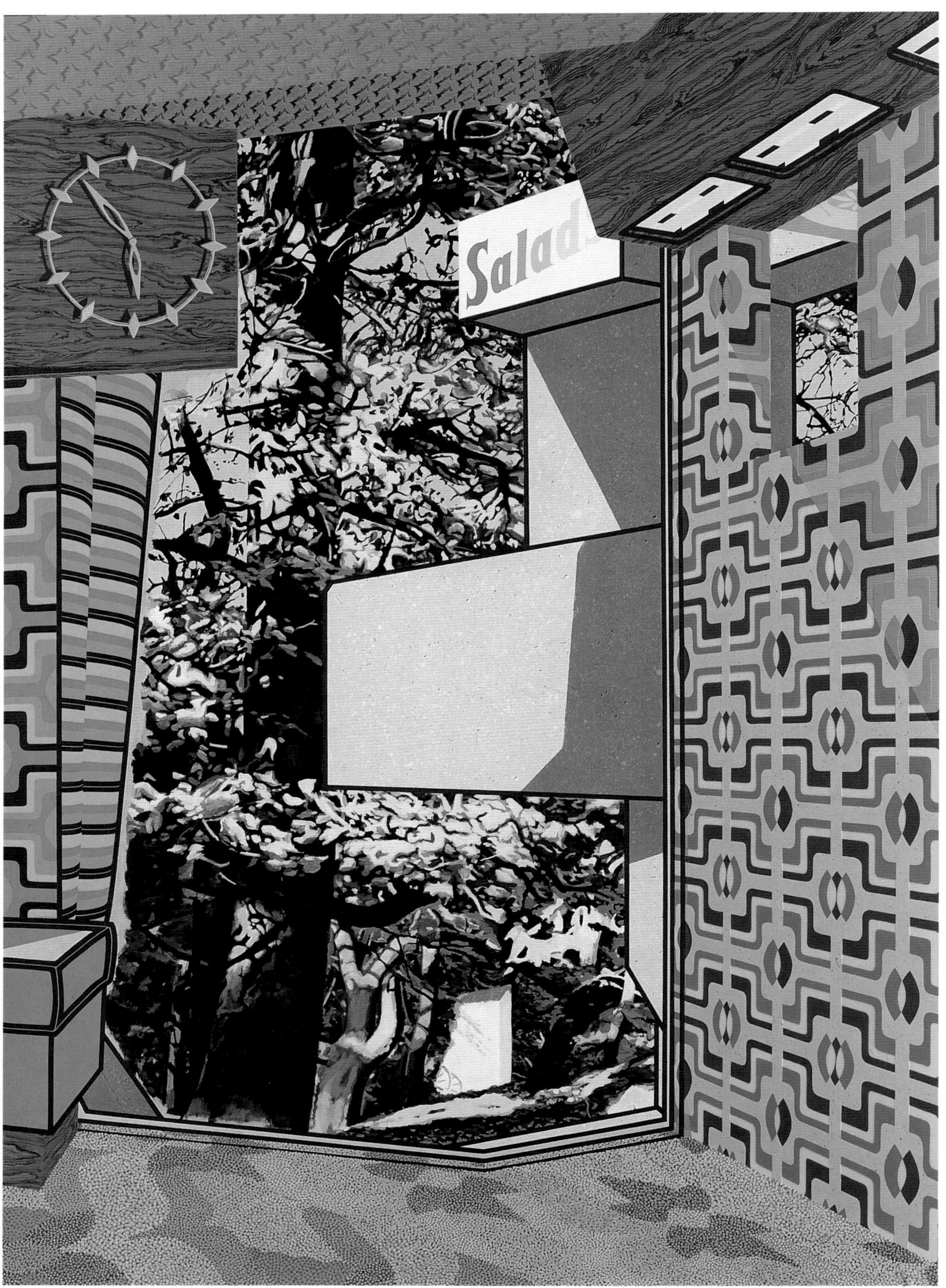

160 **Patrick Caulfield** Town and Country 1979 (cat 27)

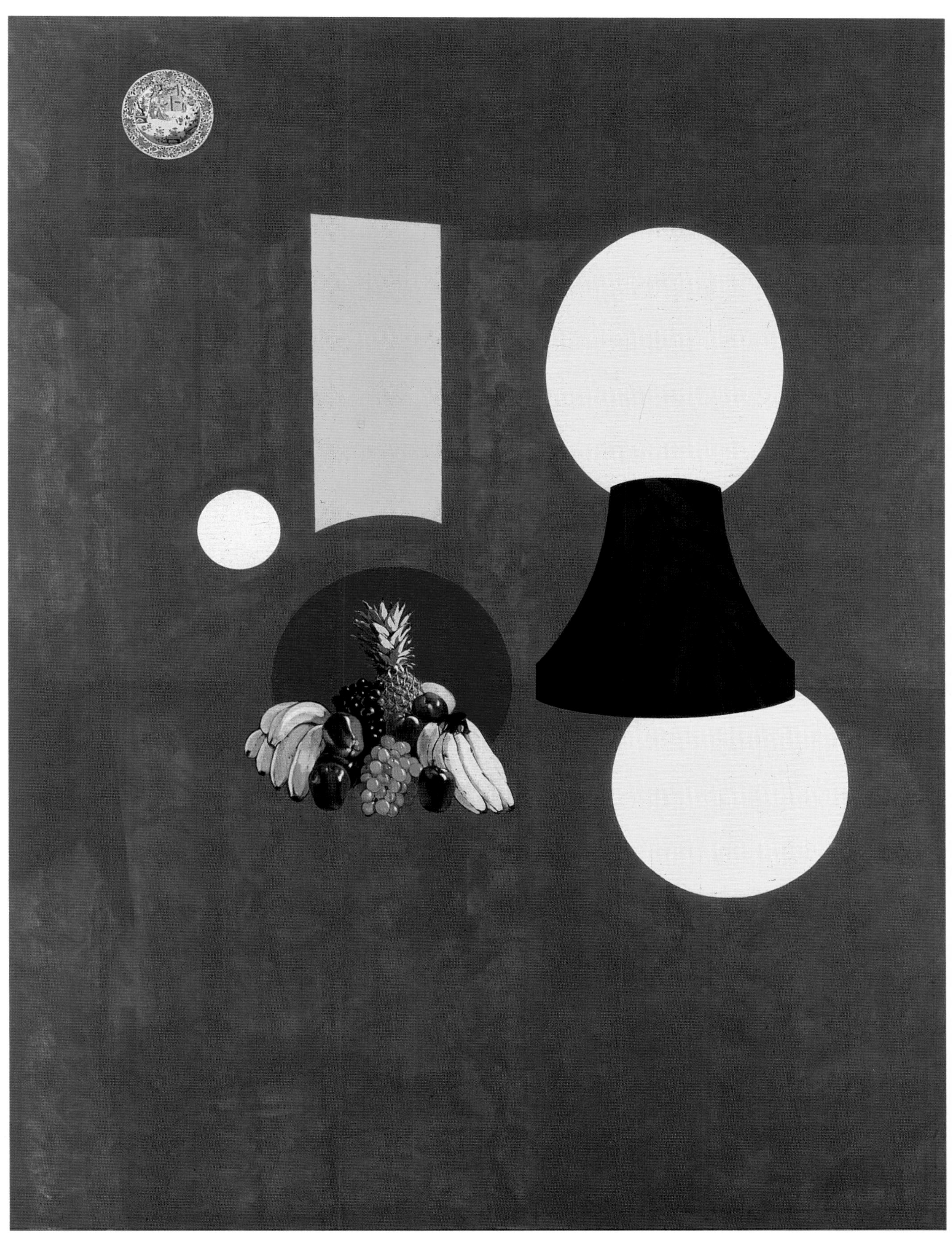

161 **Patrick Caulfield** Buffet 1987 (cat 28)

162 **Peter Blake** H.O.M.A.G.E. – JJ MM RR KS 1991 (cat 20)

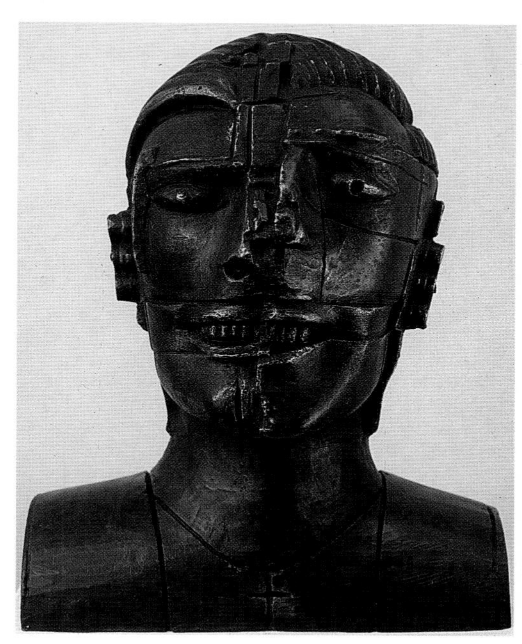

163 **Eduardo Paolozzi** Portrait of an Actor (for Luis Buñuel) 1984 (cat 177)

164 **Richard Hamilton** The Orangeman 1988–90 (cat 107)

euro pop

the nouveaux réalistes
the renewal of art in paris around 1960

ALFRED PACQUEMENT

Nouveau Réalisme is a gift to the art historian.[1] A perfectly structured movement, it has its critic-founder in the person of Pierre Restany; it has its 'Constitutive Declaration', signed by Restany and eight artists (they were shortly to number thirteen) on 27 October 1960 and summed up in a single lapidary formula, 'Nouveau Réalisme = New Perceptual Approaches to Reality' (fig. 1); it has a succession of exhibitions covering the period down to 1963, if not later, and affirming the group as a body of artists sharing similar aims; and it has not one but several manifestos, which define its scope in theoretical terms. Even today, more than thirty years after the foundation of the movement, and more than twenty years after its dissolution, the term 'Nouveau Réalisme' is still going strong. People still speak of the group as an historical phenomenon with a collective if not homogeneous identity, while at the same time recognising the marked diversity of the artists who composed it, and whose principal common feature (which no doubt explains their good press) is the undoubted influence exerted by their work in the course of the intervening decades.

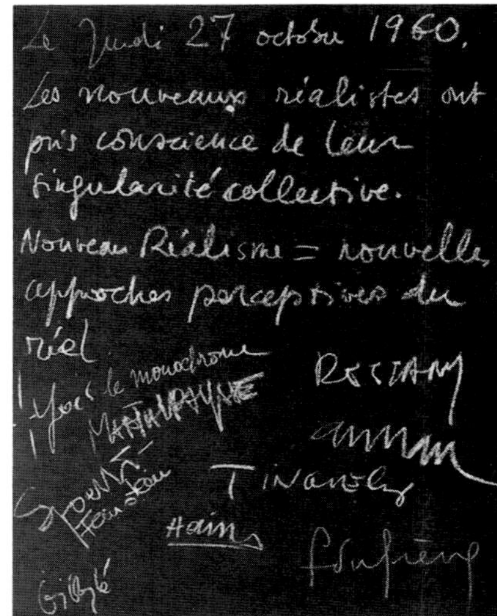
Le Jeudi 27 octobre 1960,
les nouveaux réalistes ont
pris conscience de leur
singularité collective.
Nouveau Réalisme = nouvelles
approches perceptives du
réel

fig 1 **Constitutive Declaration of Nouveau Réalisme** 1960 Collection Villeglé, Paris

French art in the 1950s was dominated by abstraction. The 'Cold' and 'Hot' factions – geometric or critical abstractionists versus lyrical, Art Informel or Tachist abstractionists – fought out their internecine battles by proxy: the proxies being the critics. Not surprisingly, the younger artists could hardly wait to get away from all this; and in this connection a number of crucial events took place between 1958 and 1960. The first was Yves Klein's exhibition 'Le Vide' (Emptiness) at the Galerie Iris Clert, Paris, in 1958.[2] While there was nothing actually 'realist' about this, it marked a turning point: as a sequel to the same artist's all-blue monochrome paintings, it challenged the hegemony of abstraction. Then, in 1959, came the first Paris Biennale,[3] which was meant to set the seal on the public recognition of abstract art, or so André Malraux announced at the opening. This was the moment when abstract art was shaken to its foundations by works such as those of Raymond Hains, for example *The Palissade of Reserved Spaces (La palissade des emplacements réservés),* and Jean Tinguely, whose drawing-machines, built from 1955 onwards, included one called *Meta-matic No. 17* that could turn out highly effective Art Informel works to order. Finally, at the Salon de Mai in 1960, the sculptor César, who had made his name in the 1950s with sculptures in welded metal, showed his *Compressions,* crushed motor cars that caused a sensation and were to mark his establishment as the doyen of the emergent Nouveau Réaliste group. As the only member with an established reputation, César brought the group to public attention at an early stage.

1 D. Abadie, 'Le Nouveau Réalisme' in *25 ans d'art en France 1960–1985,* Paris, 1986.
2 Private view, 28 April 1958. The actual title of the exhibition was *La Spécialisation de la sensibilité à l'état matière première en sensibilité picturale stabilisée* (The specialisation of sensibility in the raw state into stabilised pictorial sensibility).
3 Musée d'Art Moderne de la Ville de Paris, 2–25 October 1959.

The year 1960 will one day be acknowledged as an historical landmark. In that year a number of spectacular events and exhibitions took place, from Tinguely's *Hommage à New York* in the gardens of The Museum of Modern Art to Arman's 'Le Plein' (Fullness) in the same Galerie Iris Clert where Klein had presented 'Le Vide'. On both sides of the Atlantic there was a mood of cheerful rebellion; the dominant idea was that of the Happening, an ephemeral work of art linked to a playful and often aggressive and subversive action.

Nouveau Réalisme resolutely set its face against the prevalent aesthetic. Most of its members subscribed to radical principles that were perceived at the time as purely negative, even nihilist. These were an echo of the Dada movement, then still rather neglected, which the younger generation of Paris and New York artists were to do much to bring back into the picture. For some years a number of the Nouveaux Réalistes had been working, if not in a single direction, at least in unanimous opposition to the prevailing academicism of abstract art. Thus Raymond Hains, whose first *affiches lacérées* (torn posters) dating from 1949, and his friend Jacques de la Villeglé had in a way been caricaturing the emergent Art Informel by finding its equivalent in the urban landscape, though what these *affichistes,* and Hains especially, were doing was much more complex than a simple act of appropriation. Yves Klein, too, in his first studies in monochrome, which were rejected for the 1955 Salon des Réalités Nouvelles because he refused to turn them into abstracts by adding a black dot, had confronted the conformism of the established avant-garde. Through the extremism of his earliest works, and the sheer cosmic scope of his programme, Klein became a kind of ringleader of revolt. He was one of the founders of Nouveau Réalisme, although he was also the most atypical member of the group.

When Arman began work, he too set out to escape from a convention of pictorial space by revising it to suit himself. In his *Cachets* (Stamps) he subverted the concept of all-over composition by covering the surface with marks made by rubber stamps; later, in his *Allures d'objets* (Appearances of objects), the canvas was imprinted with objects soaked in paint. Similarly, Gérard Deschamps's first assemblages of rags or of corsets seem half-way between accumulation and abstract *matière.*

There was something provocative about the very word 'Réalisme', for it was adopted by Restany during a highly politicised period, when the polar opposite of abstract art was called Socialist Realism, which was abominated in all avant-garde circles for its reactionary hostility to all the achievements of modern art. There were, of course, some great twentieth-century painters who had never denied that they were 'realists'; the term 'Nouveau Réalisme' had actually been coined in 1936 by one of the precursors of Pop imagery, Fernand Léger, who identified it with modern life, speed, mass-produced objects and social progress. A number of more or less firmly structured 'realist' avant-garde movements had taken place in the twentieth-century, notably Surrealism, another movement run by a spokesman, André Breton, who was also the author of its founding manifesto.

Manifestos were a part of Nouveau Réalisme, and it is wise to refer to them if we are to understand either the state of mind that brought these artists together or the group ideology that then prevailed. Restany wrote two of them. The first, dated 16 April 1960, and printed in May as the preface to a catalogue for an exhibition in Milan, anticipated the official inauguration of the group by several months.[4] The second, 'A quarante degrés au-dessus de Dada' (Forty degrees above Dada), appeared in May 1961, in the catalogue for the group's first collective exhibition, held at the Galerie J in Paris. These texts contain a

4 The initial exhibition, under the title of 'Les Nouveaux Réalistes', took place at the Galerie Apollinaire, Milan, in May 1960. It included Arman, Dufrêne, Hains, Klein, Tinguely and Villeglé. The same artists, with the addition of Raysse and Spoerri, signed the 'Déclaration constitutive' on 27 October 1960. César and Rotella, although invited, were not present on that occasion; however, they took part in the later activities of the group, as did Niki de Saint Phalle (from 1961) and Christo and Deschamps (from 1962). The group's collective activities came to an end in 1963 with the second Festival of Nouveau Réalisme in Munich and the fourth San Marino Biennale.

number of historical references: to the ready-mades of Marcel Duchamp and to the Dada spirit, but also to Camille Bryen's *Objets à fonctionnement* (Objects with a function; fig. 2). The latter, although best known in his subsequent guise as an Art Informel painter, had produced a work called *The Adventure of Objects* (*L'Aventure des objets*) in 1937 ('adventure' is a word much used by Restany), as well as a number of Dadaist-sounding statements that anticipated the Nouveau Réaliste idea of 'appropriating' the real. Bryen's other works included a motor-bus nameplate embossed with his own name and a 'street object' consisting of the imprint of a lorry tyre on a sheet of paper.

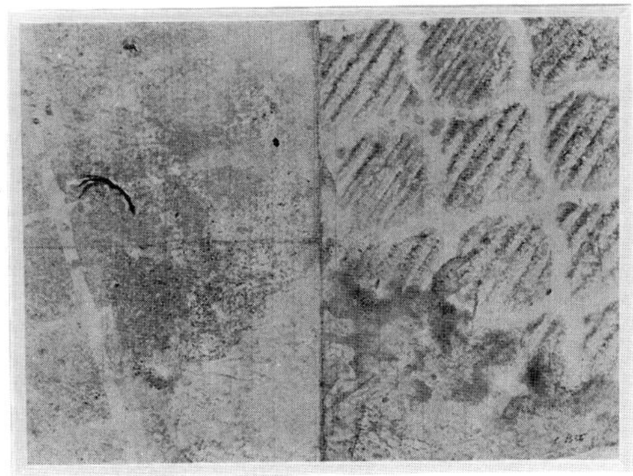

fig 2 **Camille Bryen** Objet de la Rue 1936 Musée National d'Art Moderne, Centre Georges Pompidou, Paris

Both manifestos stressed the common ground shared by all those artists in Europe and in the United States who were taking a stand against the hegemony of abstraction. Parallels are readily apparent between the Nouveaux Réalistes and the artists of the generation then known as Neo-Dada (including Rauschenberg, Johns and Dine). The two groups exhibited jointly as early as 1961, first in Paris[5] and shortly afterwards in New York, where the Pop artists joined forces with the Nouveaux Réalistes from Europe.[6] Friendships and affinities were reinforced when the Chelsea Hotel in New York came to serve as a temporary studio for most of the Nouveaux Réalistes, attracted by America and the dynamism of its art world. By the time Rauschenberg received the grand prize at the 1964 Venice Biennale – an event that scandalised Paris opinion – these young artists (or at least those with the strongest artistic affinities) had made their home in New York. Some, including Arman and Christo, settled there permanently, although rivalries soon emerged, and it was a long time before they were treated as equals. (The American reaction to Klein's exhibition at the Leo Castelli Gallery, New York, in 1961 had been uniformly negative, even on the part of the artists.)

In a nutshell, the manifestos proclaimed the bankruptcy of easel painting: a message corresponding to that of Klein's *Anthropométries,* in which the painter's traditional utensils were replaced by the 'living brush' of a woman's body applied to a canvas (fig. 3). When not dismissed out of hand, the picture survived as the debris of an act of 'rage' (Arman's *Colères*); or it took the form of an assemblage of rags (Gérard Deschamps); or of chain-store objects (Martial Raysse); or it was used to accommodate the visible residue of a random event, as with Daniel Spoerri's *tableaux-pièges* ('snare-pictures'); or it was shot at with a carbine loaded with bags of paint to produce a 'drip painting' calculated to debunk the aspirations of Tachism, in the case of Niki de Saint Phalle's *Shot-reliefs* (*Tirs*).

fig 3 **Yves Klein** Anthropométries de l'époque bleue performance at the Institut d'Art Contemporain, Paris 9 March 1960

Over and beyond the physical configuration of the work, which might take any shape, from an entire exhibition space to a single momentary action, Restany laid special stress in both his manifestos on its expressive nature: 'What is on offer? The exhilarating adventure of the real, perceived in itself, and not as refracted through some conceptual or imaginative transcription. What is the mark of this? The insertion of a sociological element into the essential stage of communication. Sociology comes to the rescue of consciousness and chance ... Here we are, neck-deep, soaked in expressiveness, and forty degrees above Dada Zero.' Although the initial point of reference remained the ready-made, this was not so much because the ready-made had upset the established order as because the Nouveaux Réalistes were seeking to identify themselves with one particular mode of appropriation of modern reality. It was a mode whose meaning they transformed: 'The anti-art gesture of Marcel Duchamp acquires a positive charge.'[7]

The *affichistes* had been the first to take over their own environment, by 'photographing' (as Hains called it) lacerated posters in the city. Hains's

5 'Le Nouveau Réalisme à Paris et à New York', Galerie Rive Droite, Paris, July 1961.
6 'The New Realists', Sidney Janis Gallery, New York, October–November 1962.
7 P. Restany, *Le Nouveau Réalisme*, Paris, 1978.

experiments with images distorted by fluted glass led him to make an experimental abstract film, his first collaboration with Villeglé. The association continued for a while, both artists sharing their collection of torn-down posters. Hains was interested in the juxtaposition of torn fragments of text; Villeglé concerned himself more with the visual effect. They were later joined by the poet François Dufrêne, who exhibited the reverse sides of torn posters. The Italian artist Mimmo Rotella had embarked on a similar line of work as early as 1954; his work was dominated by the Roman cinematic images of Cinecittà.

At the core of the Nouveau Réaliste vocabulary was the product *par excellence* of industrialised society, the mass-produced object, especially after it had been discarded and thus turned into a symbol of that society's excessive consumption. It was a period that harked back to the art of assemblage, in which the Surrealists had excelled;[8] but by now the object had acquired more autonomy. Whether drawing on its ready-made status for an ample supply of expressive and visual potential, as in the case of César's compressed cars, or piled up by Arman like surplus stock and even dumped in a bin, the object emerged from the process transformed, even poeticised, as the titles of the compositions reveal. The only artist to make deliberate use of the brand-new object, straight out of the shop window, was Martial Raysse, in pursuit of what he called his 'hygiene of vision'. This approach resembled, and anticipated, that of American Pop Art; but it remained resolutely personal, deploying colours and electric lights with great brio and relishing the references to classical painting that were to dominate his later work.

The last, but not the least essential, Nouveau Réaliste principle was the importance assigned to action in all its forms. Its natural champion was Tinguely, who introduced motion into sculpture, and with it sound, noise, spectator participation and the self-destruction of ingeniously purpose-built machines. But the impermanent work of art and the Happening were being practised in all manner of forms. Christo blocked off a Paris street with an 'Iron Curtain' of oil cans that anticipated his later environmental actions, such as *Valley Curtain*. Arman, in one of his *Colères,* smashed a grand piano; Tinguely dropped thousands of leaflets from an aeroplane. Tinguely's output also included numerous collaborative works; with Klein in 1958 he produced the experimental works entitled *Pure Speed and Monochrome Stability* (*Vitesse pure et Stabilité monochrome*), in which machines were used to drive rotating discs coloured I.K.B. (International Klein Blue).

Collaborations of this kind became more and more frequent, without depriving any participant artist of his identity. Examples are the 'Dylaby' exhibition of 1962,[9] in which Rauschenberg appeared in conjunction with several Nouveaux Réalistes, and the 'Hon' (She) exhibition of 1966 in Stockholm.[10] The death of Yves Klein in June 1962 curtailed the activities of the Nouveau Réaliste group,[11] which met officially for the last time to celebrate its tenth anniversary with a gigantic action-spectacle in Milan on 27 November 1970, in the course of which Tinguely exploded *Vittoria,* a gilded phallus 8 m (26 ft) high, in front of Milan Cathedral.

Nouveau Réalisme had an immediate impact on new generations of artists who were convinced that this presented a true alternative, and that the universe of objects offered them an endlessly rich vocabulary. There was also a genuine fascination with American art, from which young artists had long been cut off,[12] and which showed every sign of sharing the same preoccupations. This fascination also afforded a pretext for confusion with Pop Art, as the 'New Realists' exhibition in New York in 1962 showed. There

8 A big exhibition at The Museum of Modern Art, New York, in October 1961, bore the title 'The Art of Assemblage'. Its organiser, William Seitz, combined Dada and Surrealist works for the first time with American Neo-Dada constructions and those of the Nouveaux Réalistes.

9 Stedelijk Museum, Amsterdam, August–September 1962.

10 A collective work by Tinguely, Saint Phalle and Per-Olof Ultvedt at the Moderna Museet, Stockholm, 1966.

11 See note 4.

12 Johns and Rauschenberg nevertheless associated themselves with the 'Exposition internationale du Surréalisme' organised by André Breton and Marcel Duchamp at the Galerie Daniel Cordier, Paris, in December 1959. In April 1961 the same gallery showed Rauschenberg's 'combine' paintings.

then appeared a group of 'Objecteurs',[13] including Daniel Pommereulle and Jean-Pierre Raynaud, whose first assemblages, replete with personal references, might be described as psychoanalytical constructions (Raynaud called them *Psycho-Objets*; fig. 4). Alain Jacquet went on from the works known as *Camouflages* to rework famous paintings through the mechanically reproduced image, as seen on posters on city walls.

There were further obvious parallels: there was the work of Takis, with his theme of man in space and his retrieval of objets trouvés; there were the relations with Fluxus and the Happenings movement; there was Marcel Broodthaers's adoption of the idea of accumulation, replacing flea-market detritus with mussel shells. On every side, as the wave of Pop swept over Europe in its turn and provoked a variety of 'realist' responses, the Nouveaux Réalistes created new conditions for the existence of the work of art, bringing to the fore a new mentality that was to dominate the art of the 1960s, right through to Land Art, Arte Povera and Supports-Surfaces.

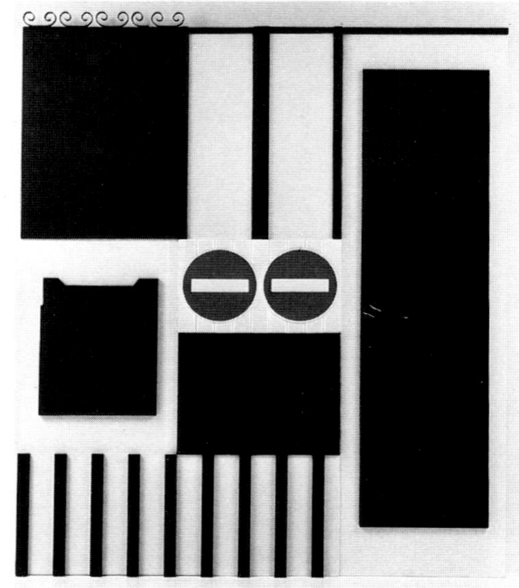

fig 4 **Jean-Pierre Raynaud** Sens + Sens 1962
Courtesy Archives Denyse Durand-Ruel

13 The name was coined by the critic Alain Jouffroy.

'Art = Life', was not very radically shaken by the rise of Pop Art, with its cult of the world of objects, its language of media and advertising, its icons of the mass consumer society. Nor did Fluxus treat Pop Art as a disruptive or hostile phenomenon. The fact is that by the later 1960s the most active phase of Fluxus in Germany was over, at precisely the moment when the response to American Pop Art and to its stars – Andy Warhol, Roy Lichtenstein, James Rosenquist and the others – was beginning to assume triumphal proportions.

The legacy of Fluxus was in an attitude that remained a living presence in Düsseldorf and Cologne until the mid-1970s. It was in this context, somewhere between Fluxus and Pop, that Sigmar Polke appeared. Always on the move, Polke presented his own existence as art (but never as a pose). Borrowings from Pop Art – often ironically transformed, often no more than hints – were overlaid by other pictorial forms. Polke created a 'Factory' of his own, but unlike Warhol he did so away from the big city, on a farm at Gaspelhof, near Düsseldorf. There he lived with a band of friends and hangers-on (his Family, as he called them), and there he produced pictures, often simply by throwing out an idea and sketching out the work, leaving the painting for his friends (notably Achim Duchow) to finish. At that time, however, unlike Warhol, Polke took no interest in the commercial exploitation of his art. Many paintings were simply piled up in his barn, and every artist who visited the farm left with a drawing or a gouache. Quite often, Polke did not even know how many people there were in his house. In the evenings everyone decamped to the bars frequented by artists and to exhibition openings, where Polke was always an impish presence with a camera that served as his tongue, his inspiration and his camouflage. Rooted in a European tradition personified by Francis Picabia, Polke presented himself as in a constant state of metamorphosis. His social comment is subliminal, subversive, and at first indecipherable for the onlooker. Polke loathes the specific and the unequivocal, and he is at pains to evade classification. His works of the 1960s and early 1970s make frequent and deliberate use of the iconographic motif of the puzzle picture in the sense that they look different, and convey a different message, according to the standpoint of the viewer. The comparative lateness of Polke's rise to fame was due to the way in which, for years on end, he resisted all attempts to market him or to absorb him into society. Unlike the American Pop artists, who ennobled the banal image by giving it the respectable appearance of art (Warhol and the Campbell's soup cans), Polke used the banal to deride, to shock and to debunk. He countered the reactionary arrogance of the German 'Economic Miracle' with images that were sometimes clownish and absurdist, sometimes highly suggestive and subtly poetic.

Polke worked collaboratively for a time with another artist living in Düsseldorf, Gerhard Richter, who in Paris in 1963 had declared himself a German Pop artist with his artist friend Konrad Lueg (alias Konrad Fischer, later one of the most important dealers in Düsseldorf). It was Richter and Lueg, too, who coined the celebrated term 'Capitalist Realism', regarded by some simply as a German variant of Pop Art. The label made its first appearance on 11 October 1963, at an event presented by a Düsseldorf furniture store, Möbelhaus Bergershaus, under the title of *Leben mit Pop* (*Living with Pop*). Small but telling modifications turned all the parts of the store into exhibition spaces. Papier-mâché visitors, including art dealer Alfred Schmela and President John F. Kennedy, stood in a waiting room. In the cloakroom hung the official Beuys uniform: hat, shirt, trousers, socks, shoes, all bearing tickets with brown crosses on them; beneath was a carton of margarine. A photograph of the event shows Richter and Lueg seated in a typical living-room, its furnishings displayed as sculptures on white plinths.[5] To understand the explosive force in Germany during the early 1960s of a phrase such as 'Capitalist Realism',

5 For an exact description see R. G. Dienst, *Pop Art*, Wiesbaden, 1965, p. 138 ff. Before the event at the Möbelhaus, Lueg, Richter, Polke and Manfred Kuttner had organised a show in an empty shop in Düsseldorf in May 1963 entitled 'Pop Art? Kapitalistischer Realismus? Nouveau Réalisme?' From Susanne Kuper, 'K. Lueg und G. Richter, Leben mit Pop – eine Demonstration für den Kapitalistischen Realismus 1963', unpublished manuscript, 1990.

with its overtones of Socialist Realism, it is necessary to know not only that Richter had moved from East Germany but that the words Socialism and Capitalism were perceived to be as irreconcilable as fire and water; the idea of an East-West dialogue was still a long way off. From today's viewpoint the name may well sound frivolous or comic, but its message then was one of bitter irony, and indeed of pain at the existence of an irremovable frontier; the Wall had been built only two years earlier.

Richter's early paintings, based on photographs and newspaper clippings, have frequently been mentioned in connection with Pop Art. But on closer analysis his intentions, apart from his choice of banal subject matter from the mass media and a sense of its mechanical replication, are very different. His primary interest is in the amateur photograph, with its camera shake and its loss of focus; the indirect statement, the schematic representation of a reality that is ultimately impossible to grasp: media language as medium of confusion. When a journalist asked Richter about his use of blurring, he answered:

> *I can say nothing about reality that is clearer than my relationship with reality; and this has to do with unsharpness, unsureness, evanescence ... That doesn't explain the pictures; at best, it explains what made me paint them. Pictures are something else. The blurred quality we see here is just the fact of being something else than the object depicted; but then pictures aren't made to be compared with reality.*[6]

Richter's whole mode of working, the level on which he deals with existing imagery, is based on this quality of otherness, of being 'something else'.

Questioning, sceptical, given to making fine distinctions, German artists seem more uncertain and less clearly defined than their American counterparts. The mechanical screen dots typical of Polke's work in the 1960s have often been likened by commentators to the Benday dots used by Lichtenstein, but Polke's own comments reveal that for him they are not a stylistic device or a design principle, but a disguise or hiding-place, a way of leading the viewer astray:

> *I love all dots. I am married to many of them. I would like all dots to be happy. Dots are my brothers. I too am a dot. Once we all played together; now each goes his separate way. We meet only at family celebrations, and then we ask each other 'How's it going?'*[7]

Though classified at an early stage as Pop artists, both Richter and Polke have remained true to a principle of their own. Chameleon-like, both have transformed their artistic strategies and turned them upside-down; both have avoided taking predictable steps forward but instead have sidestepped and dodged back and forth to produce groups of works that never reveal a clear artistic position at first sight. All this is very unlike Pop Art; and it may be the reason why both artists took twenty years to establish their reputations internationally.

If one maintains that the work of Polke and Richter is in some ways a critique of Pop Art, it may seem surprising to assert that a closer connection between the United States and Germany lies in the relationship between Warhol and Beuys. From very early on, Warhol was regarded as the superstar of Pop culture; and Beuys's pupil, collaborator and confidant, Johannes Stüttgen, wrote in the late 1960s:

> *With unexampled logic, Andy Warhol has steeped himself in the situation of America and the significance of its epoch-making achievement of having established large-*

6 Interview with R. Schön in *Deutsche Zeitung*, reproduced in *Biennale-Katalog*, Venedig, 1972, p. 23 ff.

7 *Graphik des Kapitalistischen Realismus: Werke von 1964 bis 1971*, exhibition catalogue, Gallery René Block, West Berlin, 1971, p. 43.

scale mass production worldwide, and with a uniquely sure instinct he has presented this achievement as the true cultural contribution of America to the world.[8]

Elsewhere in this little-known but highly interesting examination of Warhol's mode of working, there is an analysis of the famous statement, 'I want to be a machine'. The gist of this complex piece of argumentation by a Beuys disciple is that Warhol's sentence implies and proves the precise opposite of what it says. If Warhol had said 'I *don't* want to be a machine', then the unconscious message would have been 'but basically I am one'. The implicit message of 'I want to be a machine', on the other hand, is 'I am not a machine', or 'I am a human being'. Stüttgen remarked: 'The consciousness is confronted with itself and placed in a state of tension.' Stüttgen's commentary, which originated very close to Beuys himself, subsumes Warhol's work into the Beuysian doctrine of the 'expanded definition of art'. He ends on this surprising note:

Andy Warhol pointed his camera at the non-artistic, the art-killing area of life, the everyday world, the 'factory', the conveyor belt: i.e., at the end of art – the very region from which Joseph Beuys started out, and thus the beginning of art.[9]

In the emblematic figures of Warhol and Beuys, the antithetical principles of America and Europe were crystallised as two wholly different approaches to artistic creation; and it was because the difference was so clear and so unmistakable that friendship and mutual understanding existed between the two artists. One thing they shared was a perfect mastery of the media, which they deployed in different ways: Beuys the European, agitating and arguing in political and philosophical terms, driven by an inner sense of mission and aspiring to a utopian social order; Warhol the American, unmasking the brutality of the mass consumer society by indirect means through a kind of negative dialectic. Beuys perceived this with uncanny accuracy:

Even when Warhol talks a lot, he swamps his information content by setting up thousands of contradictions. Even when he talks, he is silent.

And so it seems entirely logical that when Warhol was asked 'Does your art have anything in common with that of Beuys?' he answered: 'We wear the same flying jacket'.

8 'Das Warhol-Ereignis', *Free International University*, Wangen, 2nd edition, 1979.

9 For quotations and further details on the relationship between Warhol and Beuys, see E. Weiss, 'Warhol und Deutschland', *Kölner Museumsbulletin*, 4, 1989, pp. 4–19.

fluxus
an addendum to pop?

THOMAS KELLEIN

'how the people of the 1960s lived, what they consumed, how they spent their time, what made up their life': that was the collector Peter Ludwig's stated reason for building up his Pop Art collection. Art, he said in 1972, contributes to the 'documentation' of an age.[1] If this task were to be entrusted to the Fluxus artists, and if George Maciunas, George Brecht, Robert Filliou, Nam June Paik, Ben Vautier (generally known as Ben), Robert Watts or Emmett Williams were to be asked for their response to the age that brought the shock of the first Sputnik and the beginnings of space travel, or to the 'Affluent Society', with its faith in the total automatisation of production, their answer would essentially consist of *Fluxkit*: the anthology of Fluxus pieces, in a box the size of a large briefcase, that was on sale between 1964 and 1970 for less than $200[2] (cat. 58).

With this variation on Duchamp's *Boîte-en-valise*, Fluxus was aiming neither at the museums nor at the major collectors. Its aim was to provide a zany gloss on the consumer society and to undermine the idea of art. 'Pop Art', wrote Lawrence Alloway in 1974 of Fluxus's far more official rival, 'is an iconographical art.'[3] Pop was open to interpretation, although it did not often take up a fixed position. ('I'm too high right now. Ask somebody else something else', said Andy Warhol in an early and important debate on the subject, in 1964, emphasising as he did so his indifference to the choice of subject matter.)[4] The aim of Fluxus, by contrast, was an 'entertainment and game environment' that would serve to clean up the art market and the history of art; in the eyes of its founder, Maciunas, it simulated 'a kind of Shoso-in warehouse of today'.[5]

Where the Pop artists analytically probed the aesthetics of mass media and the mass market, Fluxus aspired to be an accumulation of goods in its own right, distributed subversively through massive 'Headquarters' and 'Mail Order Houses'. What Fluxus wanted was not an artistic encapsulation of the consumer society but a direct sales strategy organised by artists themselves. Instead of the continuing high artistic culture of a Jasper Johns or a Roy Lichtenstein, it sought an alternative culture of anonymous 'non-fine-art-works'.[6] In 1964 Maciunas advised Ben, a colleague from the south of France, '(if you can) don't sign anything – don't attribute anything to yourself – depersonalize yourself'.[7]

There were virtually no direct personal links between Pop and Fluxus, although the exhibition 'The Art of Assemblage' at The Museum of Modern Art, New York, late in 1961, can be seen as the foundation of both movements. In June 1962, Claes Oldenburg received a letter from Dick Higgins inviting him to contribute to *An Anthology*, La Monte Young's 1960 and 1961 compilation of compositions, concepts, essays and pieces, which Maciunas was to publish.[8] However, the collaboration never went any further than the idea of a 'False

1 See catalogue of the Ludwig collection, Aachen, 1972.
2 Price lists in Jon Hendricks, *Fluxus Codex. The Gilbert and Lila Silverman Fluxus Collection*, Detroit and New York, 1988, pp. 73–6.
3 L. Alloway, *American Pop Art*, New York, 1974, p. 7.
4 B. Glaser, 'Oldenburg, Lichtenstein, Warhol: A Discussion', *Artforum*, IV, 6, February 1966, pp. 20–4.
5 Maciunas to Watts, 1962, referring to Brecht's collection of pieces *Water Yam*; quoted in Hendricks, op. cit., p. 217, note 2.
6 Maciunas to Tomas Schmit, 1964, referring to Brecht's *Exit*; quoted in Hendricks, op. cit., p. 193, note 2.
7 Quoted in Hendricks, op. cit., p. 133, note 2.
8 Original letter in the Sohm Archive, Staatsgalerie, Stuttgart.

Food Selection' and a number of prototypes made by Oldenburg in 1967.[9] In 1964, Watts, who had shown in 'The Art of Assemblage' alongside the Fluxus artist Brecht, had an idea that virtually stood Fluxus on its head, as Alloway later explained, 'to copyright the words *Pop Art*, thereby taking the term off the market and preventing its use'.[10]

If any Fluxus artist had ever succeeded in making good a claim to the label 'Pop Art', there is no doubt that he would have used it as a weapon against the artistic competition. For Fluxus, at least the way Maciunas and Watts saw it, was strictly opposed to the star system, the individual personality cult, the sensational innovation and the valuable unique piece. In a *Fluxus Newsletter* of the mid-1960s, Maciunas dismissed the individual in favour of the collective and proposed the following rule: 'Permission is granted to anyone, anywhere, anytime to perform any Fluxus piece at no cost whatever, provided publicity is given to the Fluxus group.'[11]

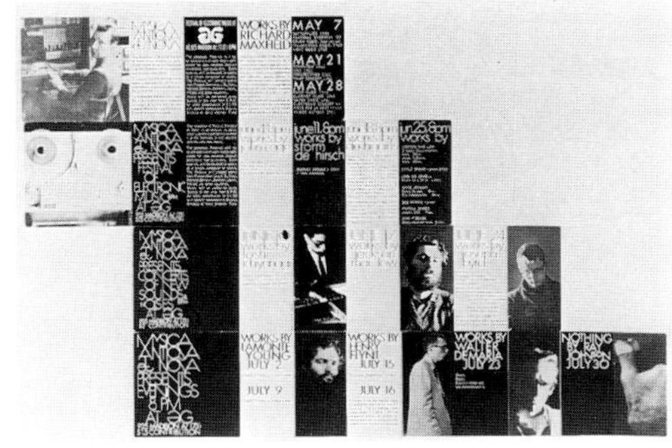

fig 1 **George Maciunas** Musica Antiqua et Nova 1961 Sohm Archive, Staatsgalerie Stuttgart

Like a political party or a record label, Fluxus had the function of protecting its members' rights in their work, and distributing – indeed monopolising – it in such a way as to maintain a common front against 'serious' culture. Maciunas found his artistic material in simple, terse, or paradoxical pieces such as those created by Brecht and Young from 1959 onwards under the influence of John Cage. In 1962 and 1963, for the duration of a few concerts, Fluxus afforded scope for development – and at times a sole means of support – to more than 50 artists, and thus operated as a movement. But soon the exclusive arrangement devised by 'Chairman Maciunas' began to give rise to intractable financial problems, and his political demands became ever more insistent. Even after a year, many musicians, writers and artists were already distancing themselves from the intended 'International'. Officially defining the Fluxus aesthetic for the first time, in 1965, Maciunas nevertheless stood his ground: 'It strives for the nonstructural and nontheatrical qualities of a simple natural event, a game or a gag. It is the fusion of Spike Jones, Vaudeville, gag, children's games and Duchamp.'[12] Single objects, such as a *Hand Tactile Box* by Ay-O; single sounds, such as Young's interval of a fifth, B to F sharp, with the title *Composition 1960 No. 7*; or single events, for example Brecht's *Exit*, which was repeated every time anyone walked out of any place, were necessary and highly appropriate aesthetic stimuli for the purpose of abolishing and transcending a bourgeois art system rooted in the Baroque and based on countless illusionistic stratagems.

Fluxus had its beginnings in New York in Cage's work as a teacher from 1956 at the New School for Social Research; in concerts held in Yoko Ono's loft on Chambers Street, between January and June 1961; and in the concerts at Maciunas's AG Gallery, under the title of *Musica Antiqua et Nova*, from March to July 1961 (fig. 1). Participants in these events included Richard Maxfield, Higgins, Toshi Ichiyanagi, Jackson Mac Low, Young, Henry Flynt, Walter De Maria and Ray Johnson. Having meanwhile conceived the idea of publishing a magazine under the title of *Fluxus*, Maciunas thereupon left New York, thus temporarily transplanting the activities of Fluxus to Europe.

The first artist to distance himself from Fluxus was Robert Morris. In 1963 Morris withdrew his contributions, *Traveling Sculpture*, *Blank Form* and *Project for Sculpture*, from *An Anthology*, and demanded the deletion of all mentions of his name. Then De Maria announced his own departure through a piece of direct criticism, his *Portrait of the School of Cage, Caged*, a drawing of a cage inside a cage, which was published in the second issue of the Fluxus magazine *ccVTRE* in 1964. When Karlheinz Stockhausen's *Originale*, successfully premiered in Cologne in 1960, was revived in New York in 1964

9 See T. Kellein, *Fröhliche Wissenschaft. Das Archiv Sohm*, Staatsgalerie, Stuttgart, 1986, p. 98 (No. 150); Hendricks, op. cit., p. 412 f.

10 Alloway, op. cit., p. 1; distributed by Watts in typescript form, with similar wording, as early as 1971.

11 Quoted in Hendricks, op. cit., p. 37, note 2.

12 See *Broadside Manifesto* in Hendricks, op. cit., p. 26, and *Fluxus Manifesto* (1966), p. 31.

with Allan Kaprow, Paik, Charlotte Moorman and others among the performers, the concerts were systematically disrupted by Maciunas and Flynt on the grounds that they were 'imperialistic'; and a rift opened up within the remaining membership of Fluxus. It was then that Maciunas embarked on the editorial and publishing activity that endowed Fluxus products with their characteristic, burlesque image; he went on with it until his death in 1978. His aim was a dictatorship of the artistic proletariat, although in financial and personal terms Fluxus was so dependent on him as to be virtually a one-man manufacturing business.

The first mention of Fluxus was on an invitation card to a concert at the AG Gallery in March 1961, in which Maciunas programmed compositions ranging from the Renaissance to the contemporary avant-garde, but deliberately excluding the whole of bourgeois musical culture from Johann Sebastian Bach to Arnold Schönberg. During the 1950s Maciunas had attended a variety of schools, evening classes and concerts and had made his own efforts to explore world culture, using charts, atlases and tabular aids of his own devising. In 1962 and subsequently, he took this personal odyssey of self-education out into the world with Fluxus concerts in Wiesbaden, Copenhagen, Paris and Düsseldorf, which were intended as the first stages in a global tour. The first Fluxus event in Germany was the *Internationale Festspiele Neuester Musik*, in the auditorium of the Städtisches Museum, Wiesbaden, from 1 to 23 September 1962 (figs 2 and 3). Maciunas had devoted every minute he could spare from his duties with the American Army to the preparation of these first fourteen Fluxus evenings. Publicity, props and programmes were subject to improvised last-minute changes, and there were often more musicians on the platform than there were members of the audience. The few spectators who stayed in their seats were put to the test by pieces of an entirely new kind. Emmett Williams counted the audience, pointing to each one in turn (*Counting Song*). Higgins climbed a ladder and poured water out of a can into a bowl on the floor (Brecht: *Drip Music*). A popular piece was Young's B to F sharp fifth (*Composition 1960 No. 7 'To Be Held for a Long Time'*), which could be played on a variety of instruments for hours at a time.

fig 2 **George Maciunas Dick Higgins Wolf Vostell Benjamin Patterson Emmett Williams** performing Philip Corner's *Piano Activities* at the Internationale Festspiele Neuester Musik, Wiesbaden September 1962

From 1964 onwards, after Maciunas's return to New York, Fluxus produced more anthologies, *Fluxus 1*, *Fluxkit* and finally, in 1968, *Fluxyearbox 2*. All three pursued the intention, embarked on with *An Anthology* and never successfully realised, of bypassing the art market through direct distribution of small objects and ready-mades. When Maciunas ran out of multiples or of packaging wood, he modified the product. If new artists came along, or if they changed their contributions, the production and ordering processes came to a halt. The assembling of the whole edition absorbed so much time and money that advertising and mailing became impossible. A new list was written every time there was a change; and each new list in its turn raised questions about the economics of the whole organisation, in which Maciunas gradually became more and more isolated. Almost every set of *Fluxkit*, the suitcase encyclopaedia of Fluxus art, was different. In 1964, while Pop artists such as Oldenburg, Rosenquist or Wesselmann alluded to an urban scale of public monuments and billboards Fluxus put the twentieth century on hold and withdrew into toyboxes and play-shops. *Fluxkit* neither reflected nor stimulated consumer culture; it was intended as a lexical art-substitute, and as a *memento mori* for the high culture that Fluxus believed to be moribund.

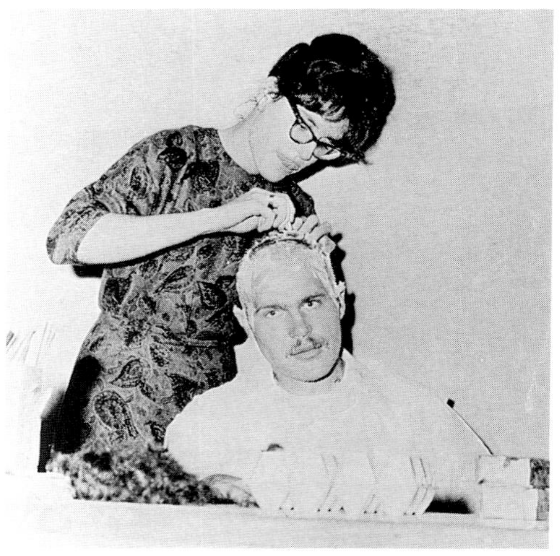

fig 3 **Alison Knowles Dick Higgins** performing *Danger Music No.2* at the Internationale Festspiele Neuester Musik, Wiesbaden September 1962

One early *Fluxkit* of 1964 contained 25 or so separate pieces by Ay-O, Brecht, Higgins, Joe Jones, Alison Knowles, Takehisa Kosugi, Maciunas himself, Benjamin Patterson, Paik, Mieko Shiomi, Watts and Young, as well as a copy of *An Anthology*, not mentioned in the prospectus. Later the number of items rose on occasion to 40, made by numerous new artists, including Eric Andersen, Ben, John Chick, Filliou, Albert Fine, Ken Friedman, the Japanese group Hi-Red-Center, Per Kirkeby, Milan Knizak, Shigeko Kubota, Serge Oldenbourg and James Riddle. Maciunas had a specially designed label for every individual Fluxus multiple and a special name-plate for every artist; every little wooden box was made to his detailed specifications.

Maciunas corresponded most intensively on the political goals of Fluxus with Watts, who had been making his toy-like, gently disruptive consumer goods since 1961. They included a *Stamp Machine*, designed to undermine the American postal system through the use of Fluxus stamps (fig. 4). In 1971 he published his volume, *An Addendum to Pop*, consisting of faint photocopies of American trade mark applications including the word 'Pop', again making manifest the disparity between the Pop and Fluxus approaches to the popular culture of industrialised nations. In an understated form of presentation, and without comment, Watts assembled telling pieces of information, for example that the Hubinger Company registered 'Pop's' as a 'trade mark for corn starch for food purposes' in 1932, and that Foodtown Kitchens used the same name in the same year 'for cereal breakfast foods'. In 1962 the Hobley Manufacturing Company laid claim to the name 'Super-Pop' for its 'toy rifles'. Commenting on Watts's book on the first page of *American Pop Art*, Alloway drily remarked: 'I used to wish that I had copyrighted it, not to restrict its use but to collect royalties.'

fig 4 **Robert Watts** Stamp Machine no.4 1961 Sohm Archive, Staatsgalerie Stuttgart

For the Fluxus artists, royalties and fees of any kind remained virtually out of reach, especially as they refused to have anything to do either with traditional media – drawing, painting and sculpture – or with the art exhibition system. For one moment, at the onset of the liaison between John Lennon and Yoko Ono, a gleam of hope shone on Maciunas's work: it seemed as if the pop musician's great wealth might support at least one of his objectives. And so, in 1970, Maciunas planned to set up a 'Flux Amusement Center' and organise a 'Fluxfest Presentation of John Lennon & Yoko Ono' in New York. But little came of it beyond a *Grapefruit Banquet* in belated tribute to Yoko Ono's 1963–64 collection of pieces. On the menu were grapefruit hors d'oeuvre, marinated grapefruit, grapefruit seed soup, grapefruit dumplings, grapefruit mashed potatoes, grapefruit pancakes and grapefruit wine.

pop art in europe
an anthology of sources

Arman

'Réalisme des accumulations', *Zero,* 3, July 1961

In search of new creations – a search made necessary by the shortcomings and the sheer exhaustion of all hedonistic and gestural forms of painting – I have deliberately explored the area of debris, refuse, discarded manufactured objects: in a word, the disused . . .

I affirm that discarded objects possess an expressive value of their own, in the absence of desire for any aesthetic modification that would obliterate them and reduce them to colours on a palette. In addition, I introduce the idea of a single, all-encompassing gesture, unremitting and remorseless.

With disused objects, one means of expression, in particular, attracts my attention and my efforts: and this is accumulation, by which I mean taking them in great numbers and packing them into a volume corresponding to the shape, number and dimensions of the manufactured objects in question.

Jacques de la Villeglé

'Des réalités collectives', *Grâmmes,* 2, 1958

The art of laceration comes at the end – and concludes the destruction – of the history of painting as transposition. By contrast with collage, which springs from the interplay of a range of possible attitudes, the lacerated poster is a spontaneous phenomenon; all intermediaries having withered away, it has been known for ten years now in all its vivid immediacy. Reeling from the impact, we have set out to collect these objects in all their 'otherness'. Keeping them free from contamination. As Camille Bryen has told us: 'Antipainting turns into the latest form of painting; for all its liberty, it forges new links with styles and refinements.' And that is another danger.

Roland Barthes

[Although Barthes had no official link with the Nouveaux Réalistes, some of his observations of popular culture in semiological texts provide a pertinent backdrop to their work.]

'The New Citroën', *Mythologies,* Paris, 1957, repr., London, 1972, p. 88

I think that cars today are almost the exact equivalent of the great Gothic cathedrals: I mean the supreme creation of an era, conceived with passion by unknown artists, and consumed in image if not in usage by a whole population which appropriates them as a purely magical object.

'Plastic', *Mythologies,* Paris, 1957, repr., London, 1972, p. 98

The fashion for plastic highlights an evolution in the myth of 'imitation' materials. It is well known that their use is historically bourgeois in origin (the first vestimentary postiches date back to the rise of capitalism). But until now imitation materials have always indicated pretension, they belonged to the world of appearances, not to that of actual use; they aimed at reproducing cheaply the rarest substances, diamonds, silk, feathers, furs, silver, all the luxurious brilliance of the world. Plastic has climbed down, it is a household material. It is the first magical substance which consents to be prosaic. But it is precisely because this prosaic character is a triumphant reason for its existence: for the first time, artifice aims at something common, not rare.

Pierre Restany

First manifesto, 'Les Nouveaux Réalistes', *Arman, Dufrêne, Hains, Yves le Monochrome, Tinguely, Villeglé,* exhibition catalogue preface, Galerie Apollinaire, Milan, 1960

At a more urgent and essential level, that of full emotional expression, in which the creative individual is beside himself, we see beyond the naturally baroque appearance of certain experimental phenomena and advance towards a *new realism* of pure sensibility. At the very least, this is one way forward. In Paris, with Yves Klein and Tinguely, Hains and Arman, Dufrêne and Villeglé, some widely varying points of departure are being adopted. This ferment will be a productive one; its overall effects remain unpredictable, but it is certain that they will be iconoclastic (for which blame the icons, and the idiocy of their worshippers). Here we are, neck-deep in direct expressiveness, and forty degrees above Dada zero, with no aggressive compulsions, no predefined polemical intention, and no itch for justification apart from our own realism. And all this is working in a positive direction. Whenever man succeeds in reintegrating himself into the Real, he identifies it with his own transcendent nature – which is emotion, feeling and, ultimately, poetry.

Pierre Restany

'La réalité dépasse la fiction', *Le Nouveau Réalisme à Paris et à New York,* exhibition catalogue preface, Galerie Rive Droite, Paris, 1961

This recognition of the expressive autonomy of the external object not only calls into question the concept of the work of art: it at once poses the issue of the interreaction of objects with the individual psyche. The resulting metaphysics of technology all too easily leads to a kind of meditative animism.

And here, in my view, is the essential distinction between Paris and New York. More rigorous in their logic, simpler and more precise in their presentation, appropriating objects more directly, the Europeans mostly remain 'New Realists' in every sense of the term.

Romantic in their hearts, Cubist in their heads and Baroque in their tone – and more susceptible to the temptations of Surrealism – those who are already being called the American 'Neo-Dadas' are busy creating a modern form of object fetishism . . .

The Parisian New Realists, for their part, turn to social reality for a breath of pure air, and not in order to inhale the incense of a new cult.

165 **Mimmo Rotella** Scotch Brand 1960 (cat 207)

166 **Jacques de la Villeglé** Boulevard St Martin 1959 (cat 234)

167 **Raymond Hains** Torn Poster (Affiche déchirée) 1961 (cat 98)

168 **Niki de Saint Phalle** St Sebastian or the Portrait of My Love (Saint-Sebastian ou le Portrait de mon amour) 1960 (cat 214)

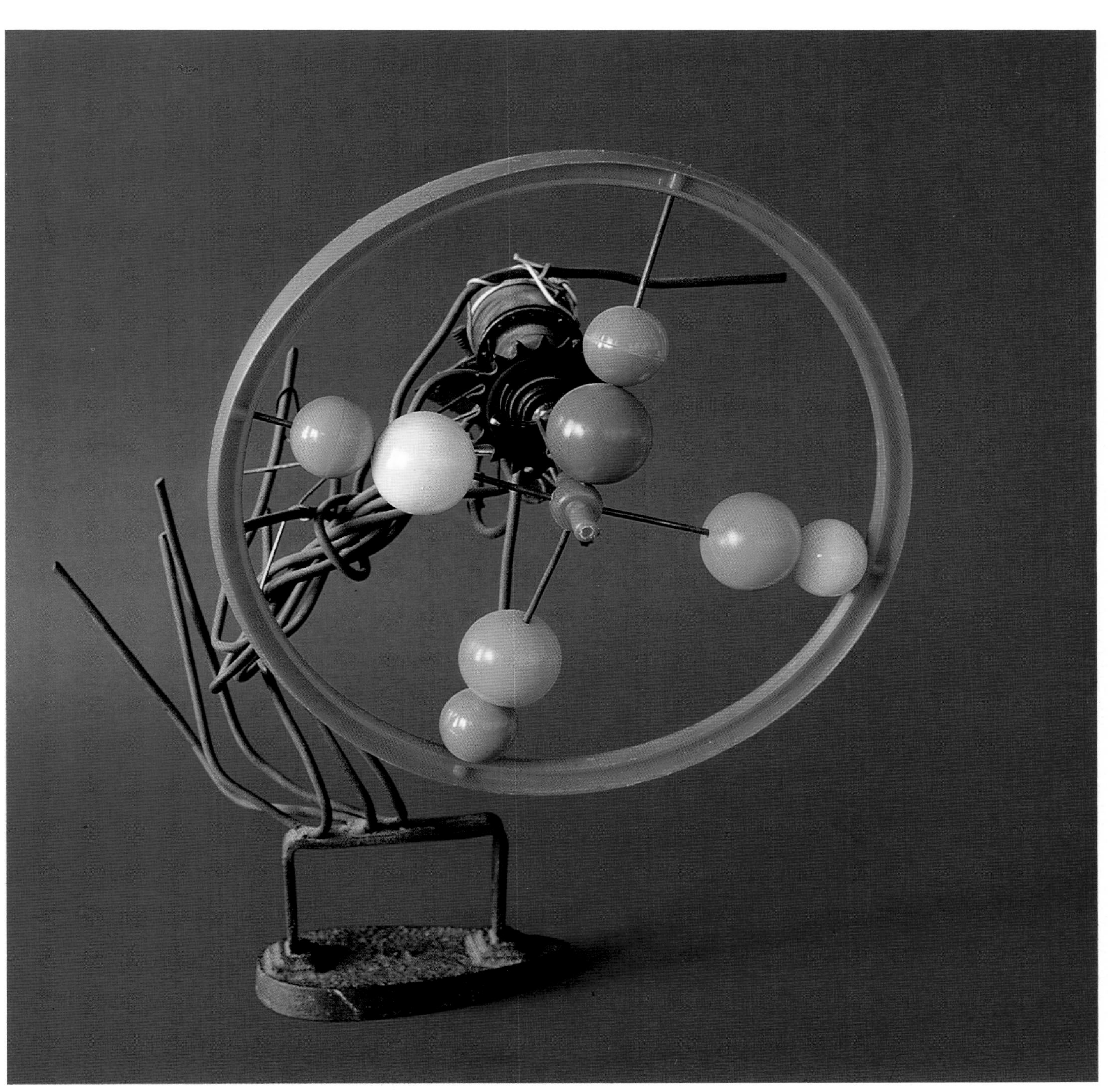

169 **Jean Tinguely** Flat Iron (Fer à repasser) 1962 (cat 233)

170 **Daniel Spoerri** The Playpen (Le Parc de bébé) 1961 (cat 225)

171 **César** Compression Sunbeam 1961 (cat 29)

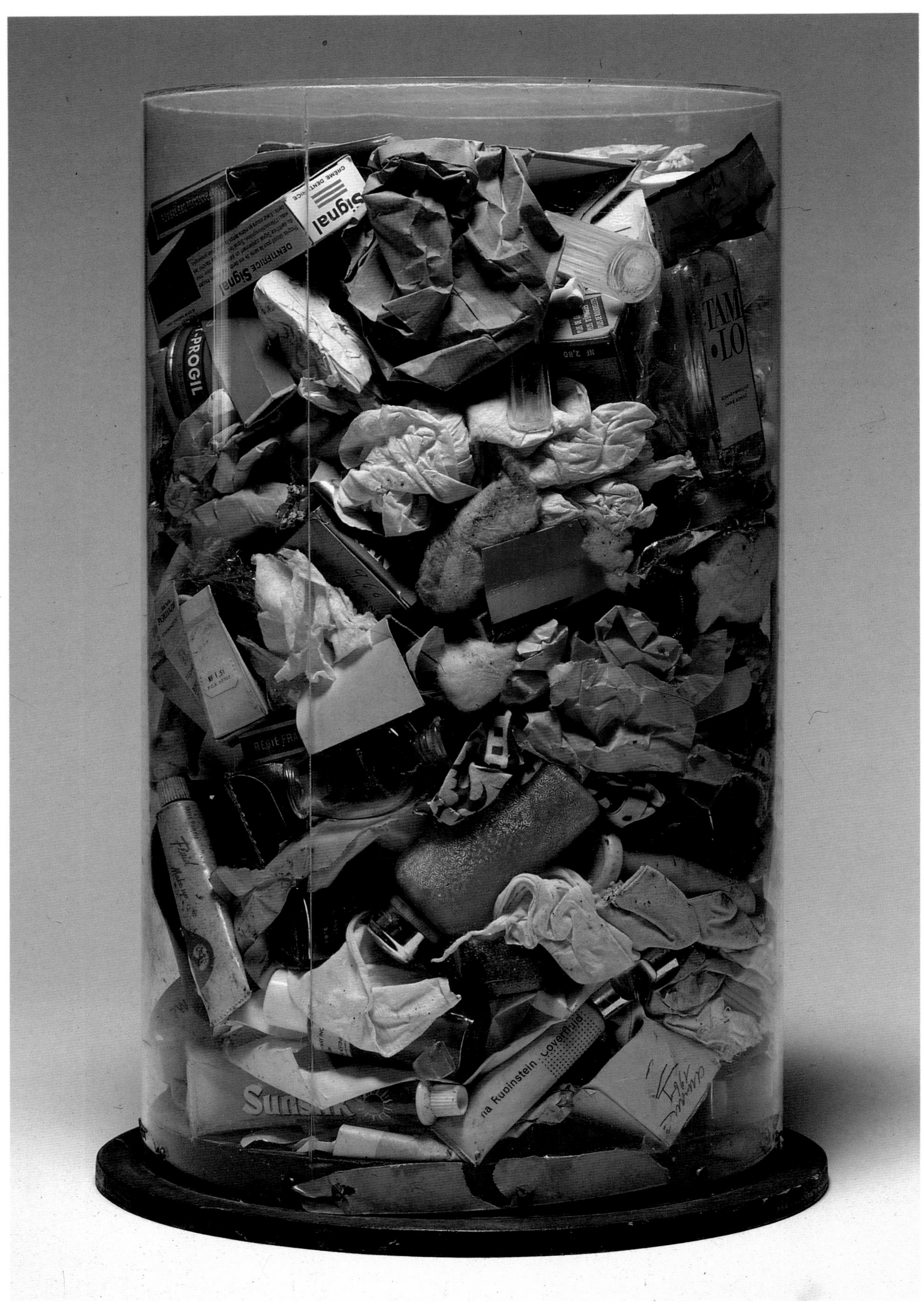

172 **Arman** Jim Dine's Dustbin (Poubelle) 1961 (cat 1)

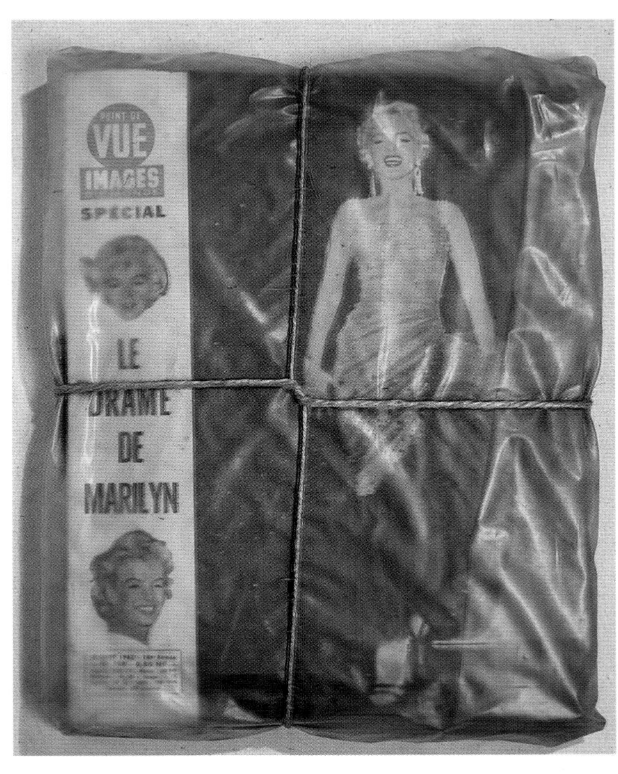

173 **Christo** Wrapped Magazines (Revues empaquetées) 1962 (cat 30)

174 **Arman** Madison Avenue 1962 (cat 2)

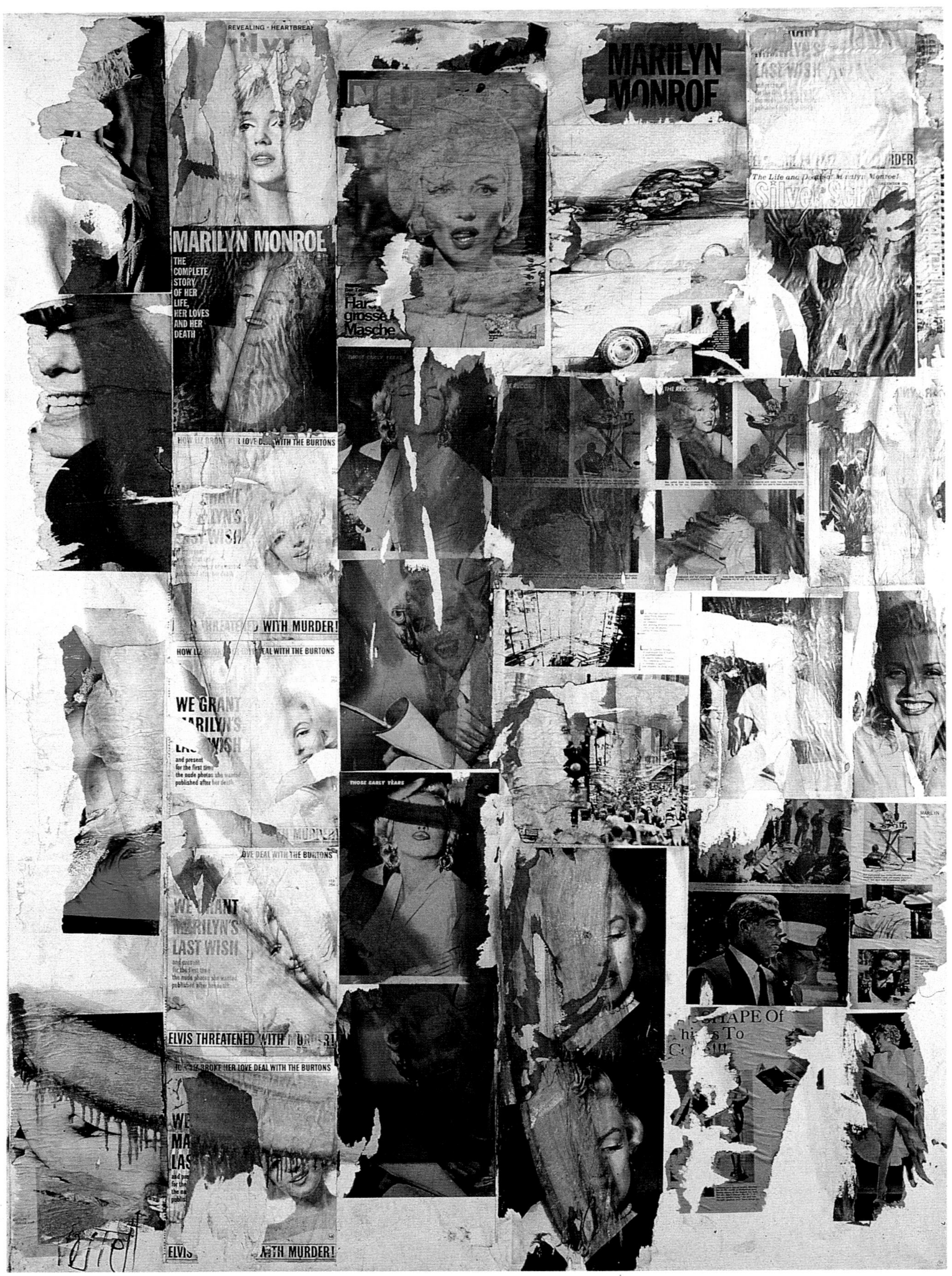

175 **Wolf Vostell** Marilyn Monroe (Marilyn Idolo) 1963 (cat 235)

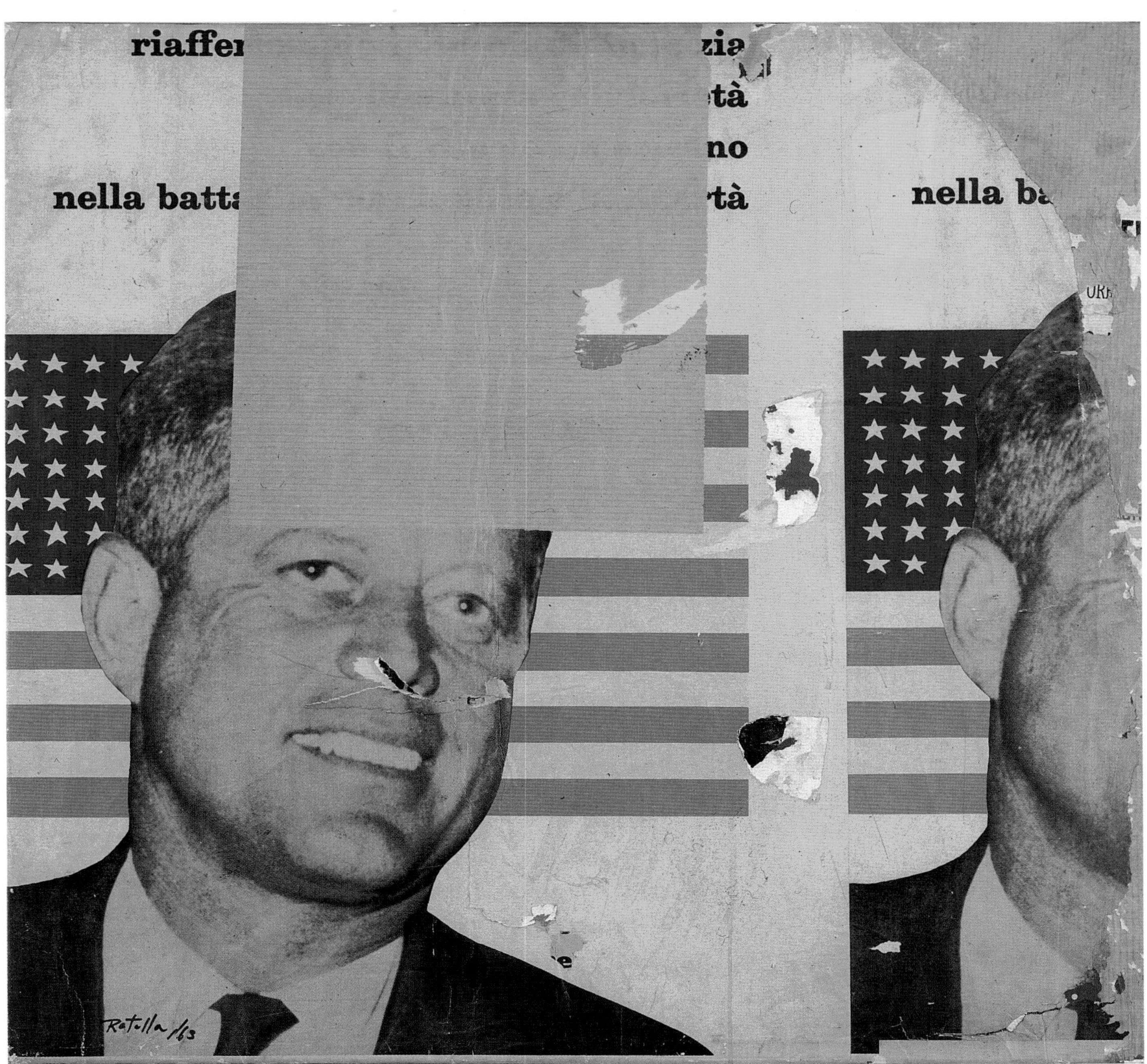

176 **Mimmo Rotella** Viva America 1963 (cat 208)

177 **Christo** Store Front 1964 (cat 31)

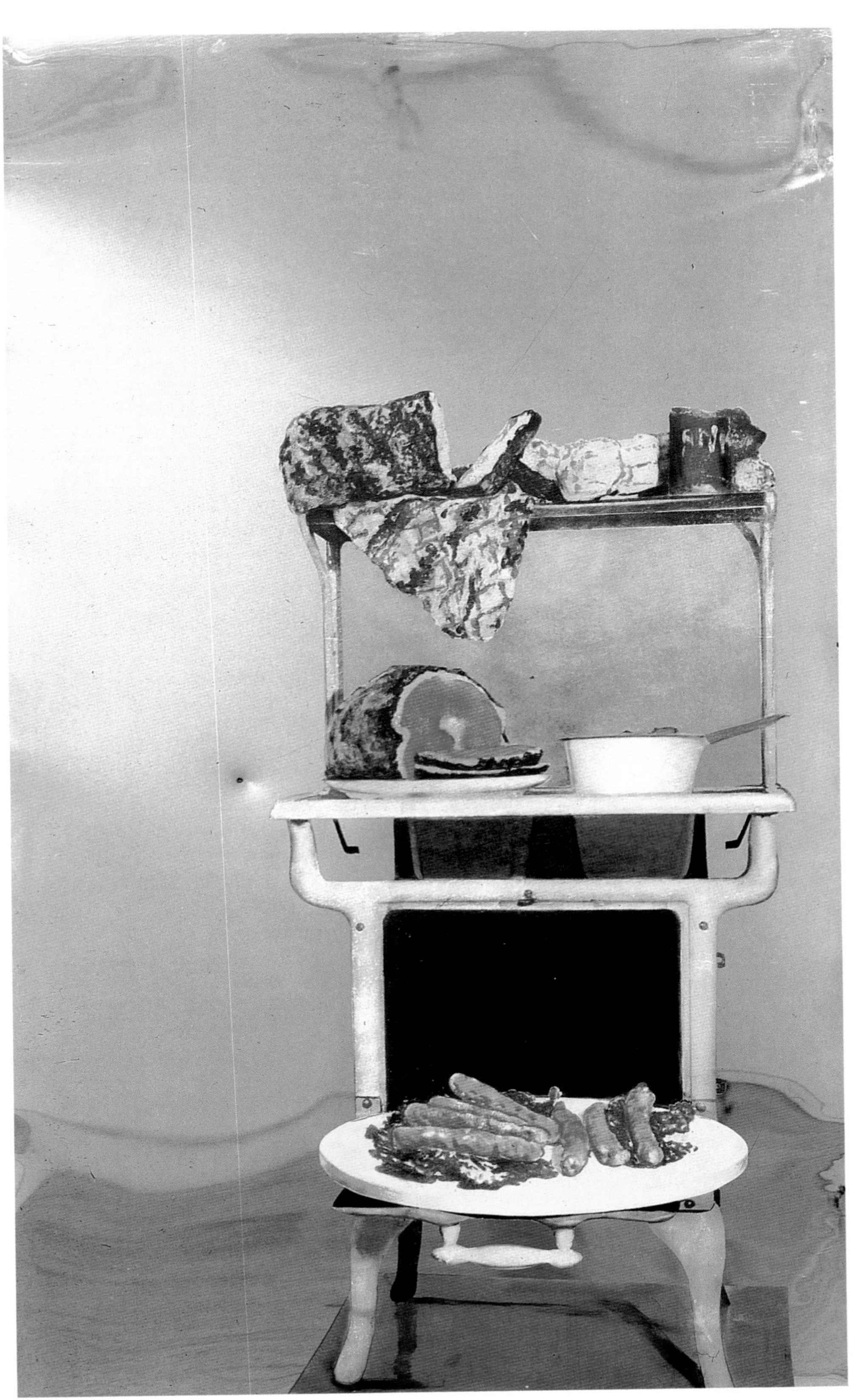

178 **Michelangelo Pistoletto** The Stove of Oldenburg (La Stufa di Oldenburg) 1965 (cat 182)

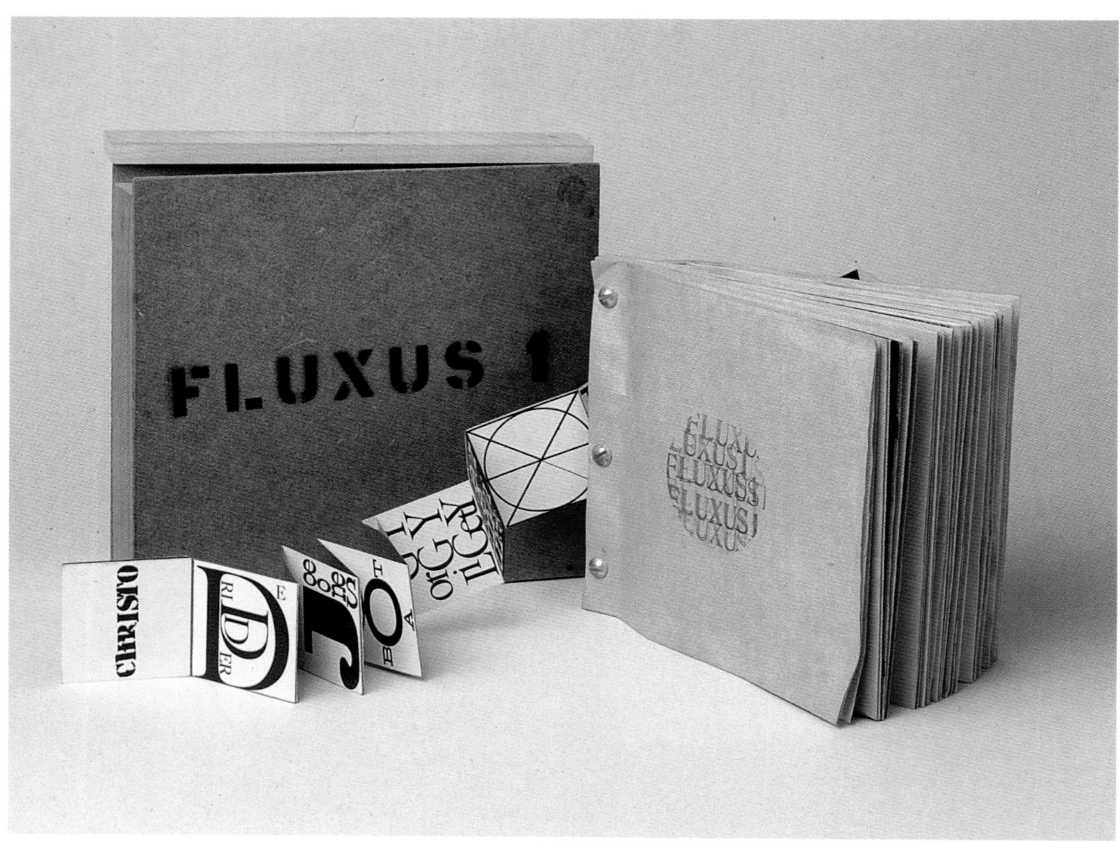

179 Fluxus I 1965 (cat 60)

180 **George Brecht (with Robert Watts and Alison Knowles)** Blink 1963 (cat 24)

181 Fluxkit 1964 (cat 58)

182 **George Brecht** Water Yam 1963–72 (cat 46)

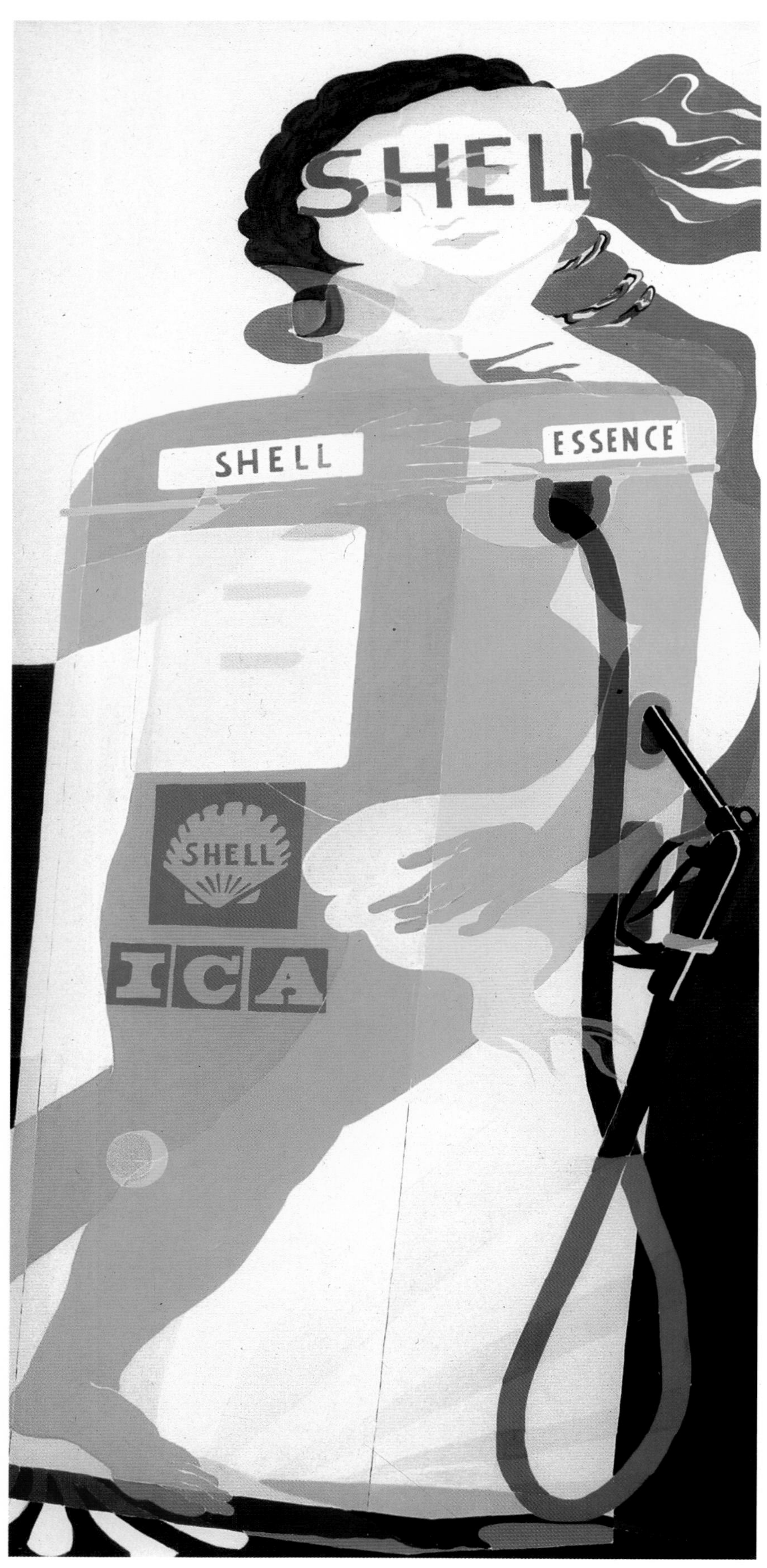

183 **Alain Jacquet** Birth of Venus 1963 (cat 116)

184 **Alain Jacquet** Déjeuner sur l'Herbe 1964–65 (cat 117)

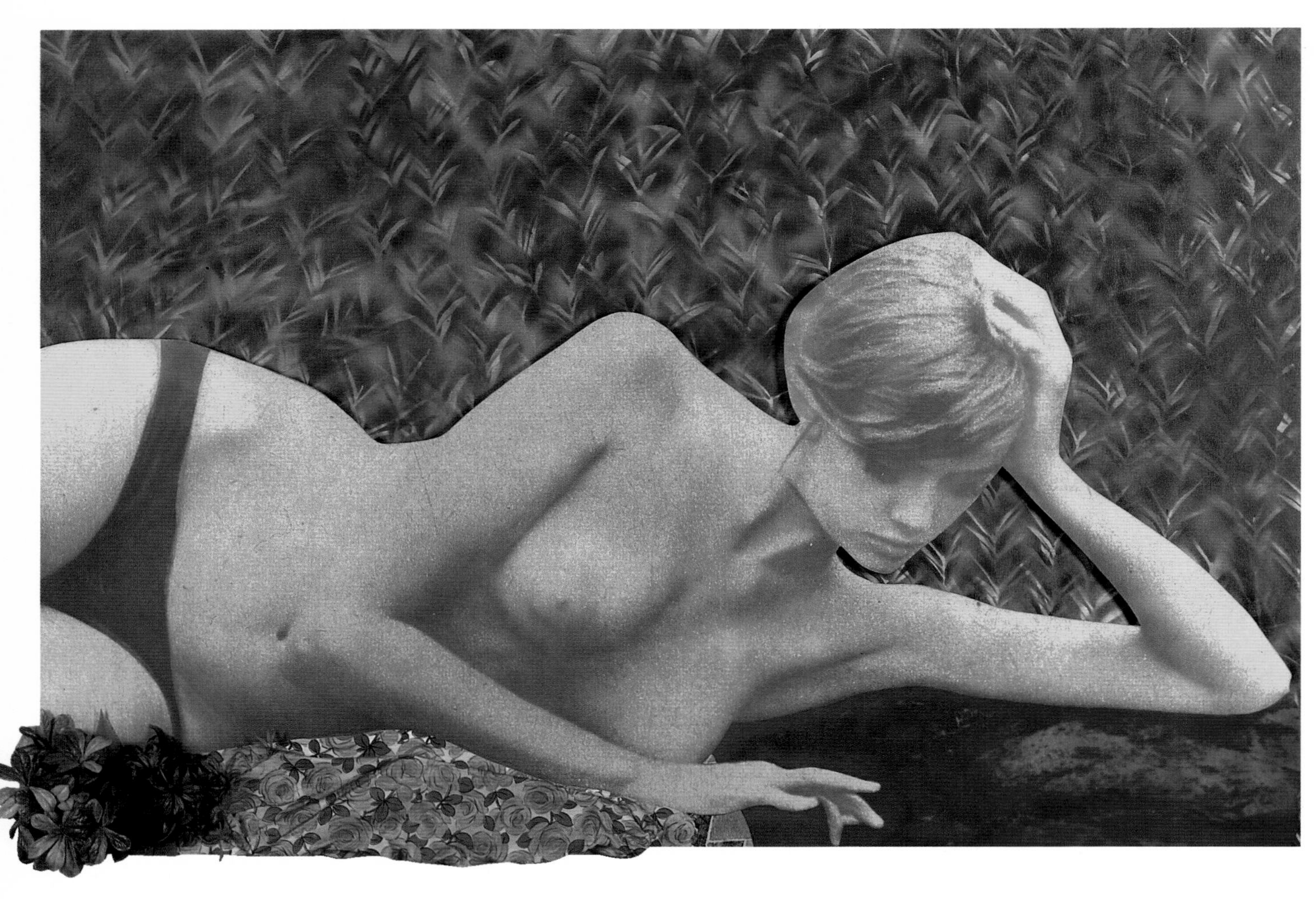

185 **Martial Raysse** Simple and Quiet Painting 1965 (cat 196)

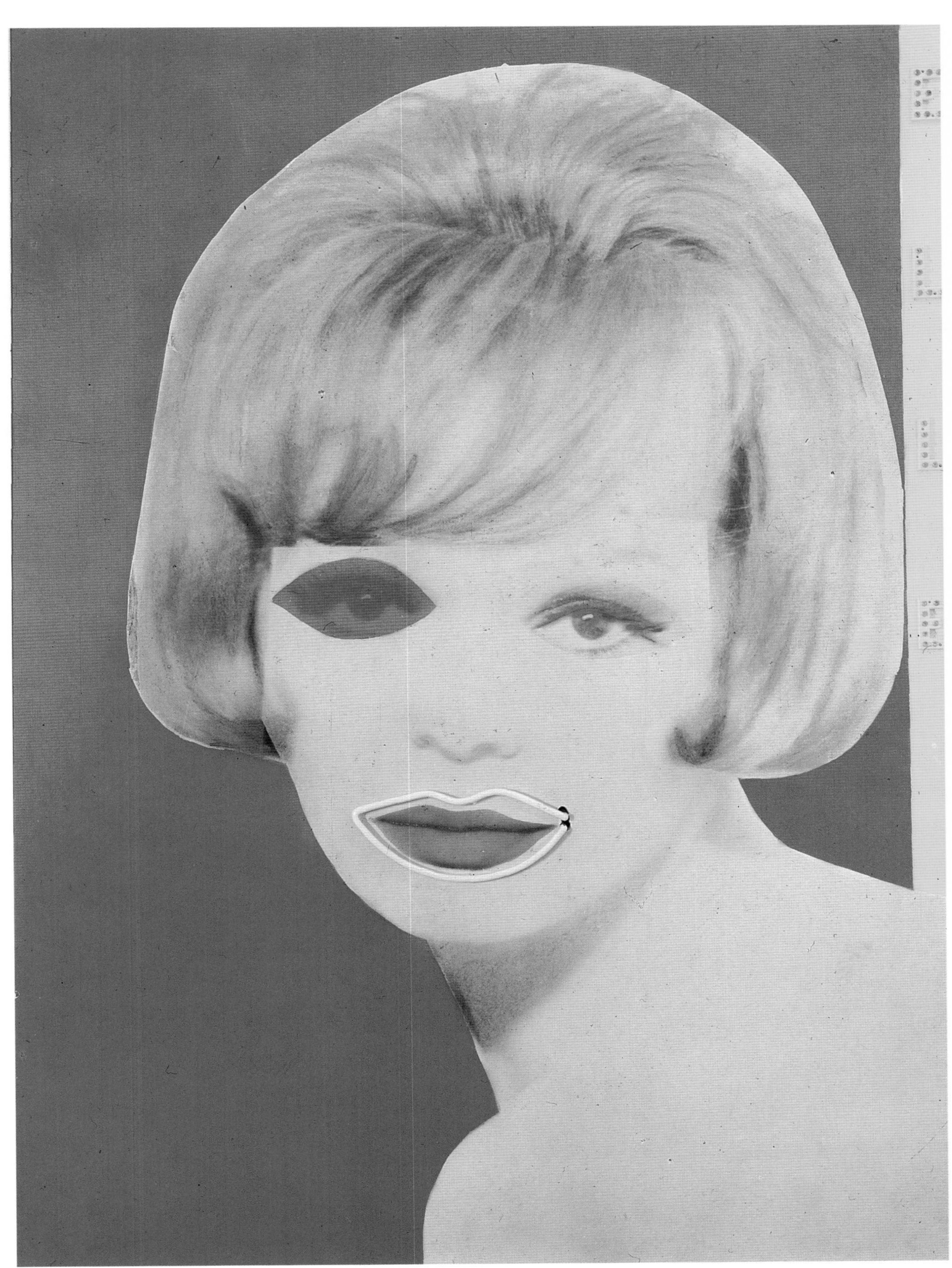

186 **Martial Raysse** Rose 1962 (cat 195)

187 **Sigmar Polke** Biscuits (Kekse) 1964 (cat 183)

188 **Sigmar Polke** Vase II 1965 (cat 184)

189 **Sigmar Polke** Woman at the Mirror (Frau vor Spiegel) 1966 (cat 185)

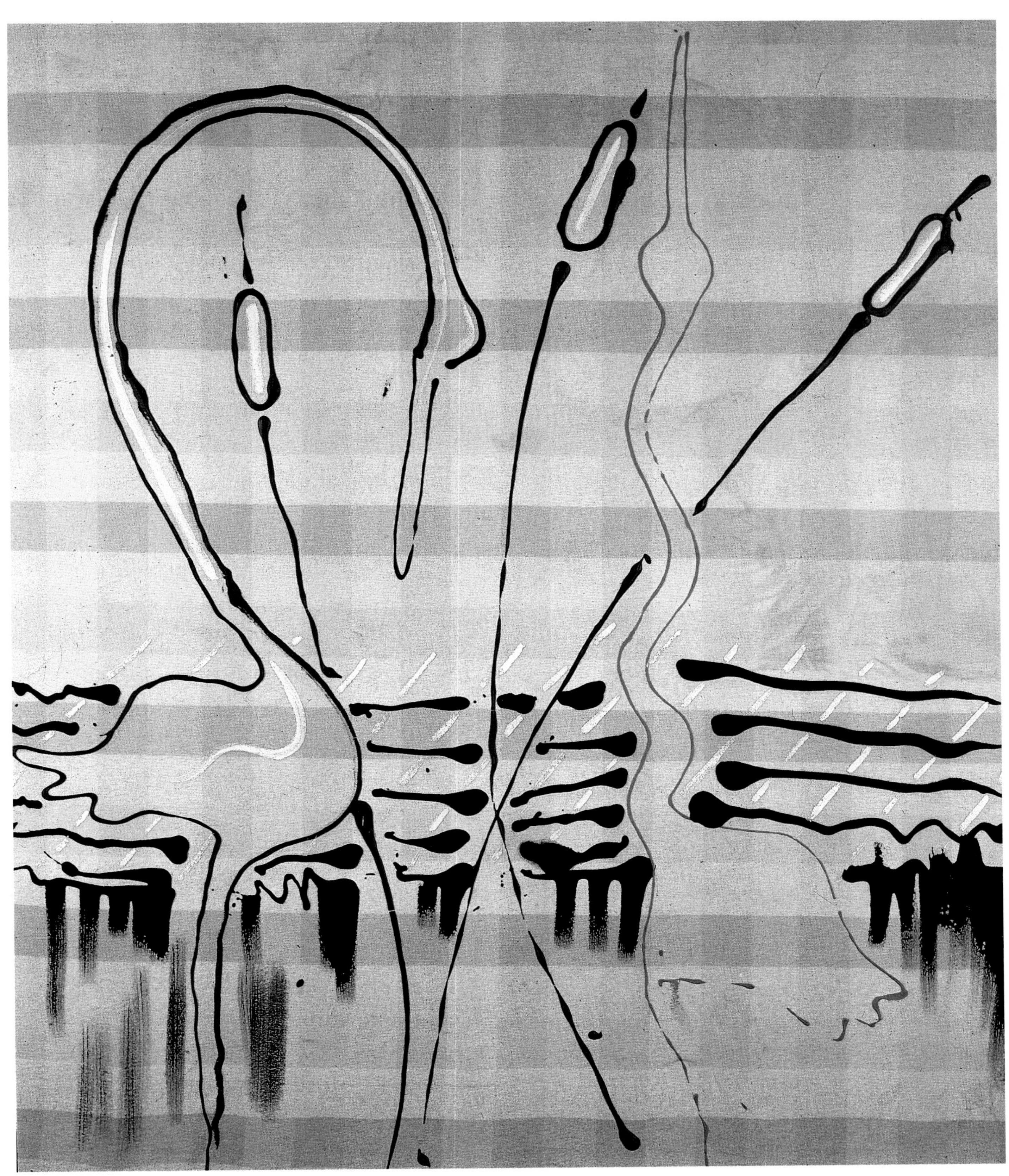

190 **Sigmar Polke** Heron Painting II (Reiherbild II) 1968 (cat 186)

191 **Gerhard Richter** Folding Clothes Horse (Faltbarer Trockner) 1962 (cat 197)

192 **Gerhard Richter** The Swimmers (Schwimmerinnen) 1965 (cat 199)

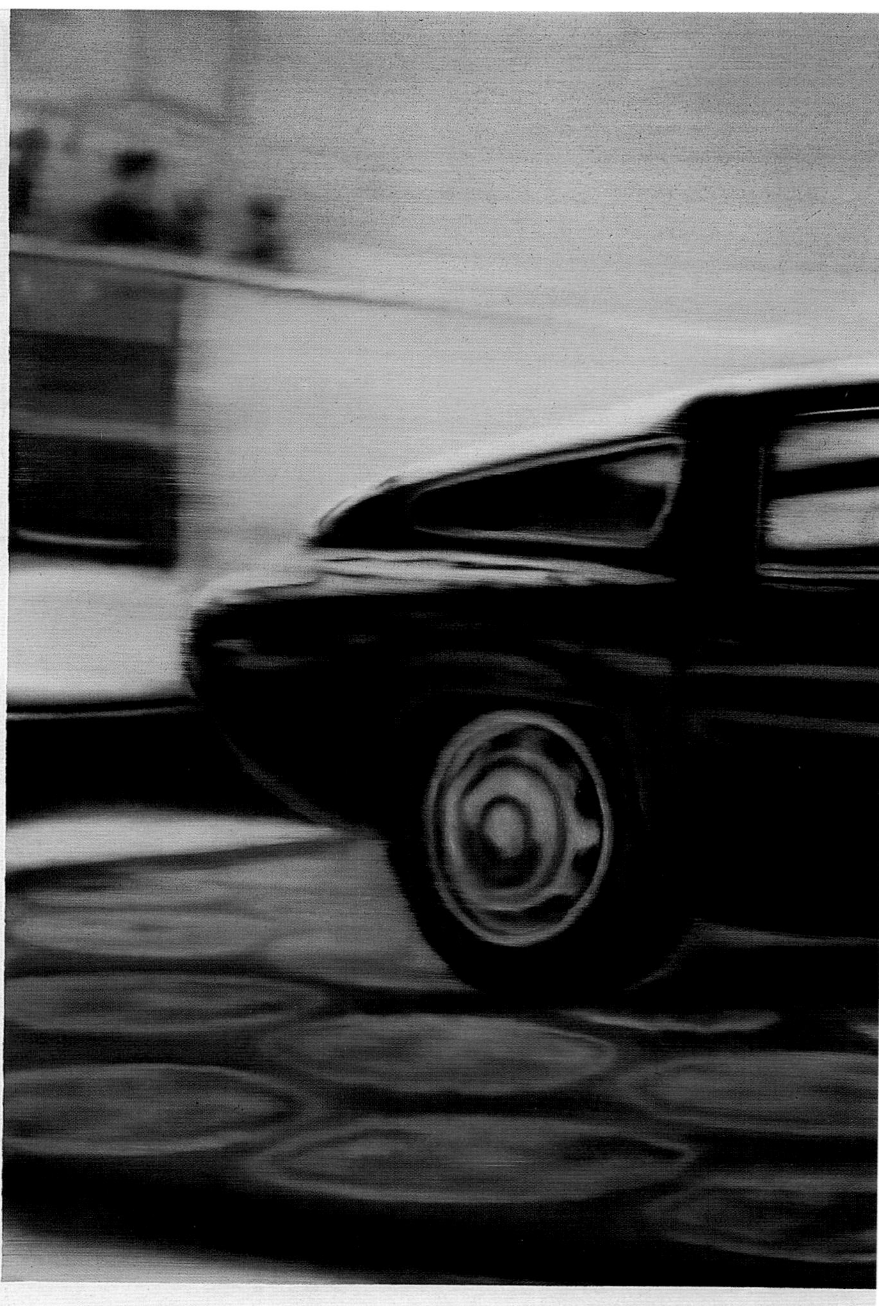

r als sein Vor-
n Stelle er ge-
iat die Zeichen
bis 1500 ccm
gesenkt, dabei
auf 12 Monate
m 1100 D der
England und
Einliter-Wagen
Cardinal, Mor-
M) begegnen.
für die Neu-
Fiat hat allen
n ausgereiftes,
laren zur Zu-
ufendes Auto-
generellen Ex-
orgesehen und

193 **Gerhard Richter** Alfa Romeo (with Text) (Alfa Romeo [mit Text]) 1965 (cat 198)

194 **Equipo Crónica** Concentration or Quantity becomes Quality (Concentración o La cantidad se transforma en calidad) 1966 (cat 37)

195 **Eduardo Arroyo** With Deference to Traditions 1965 (cat 3)

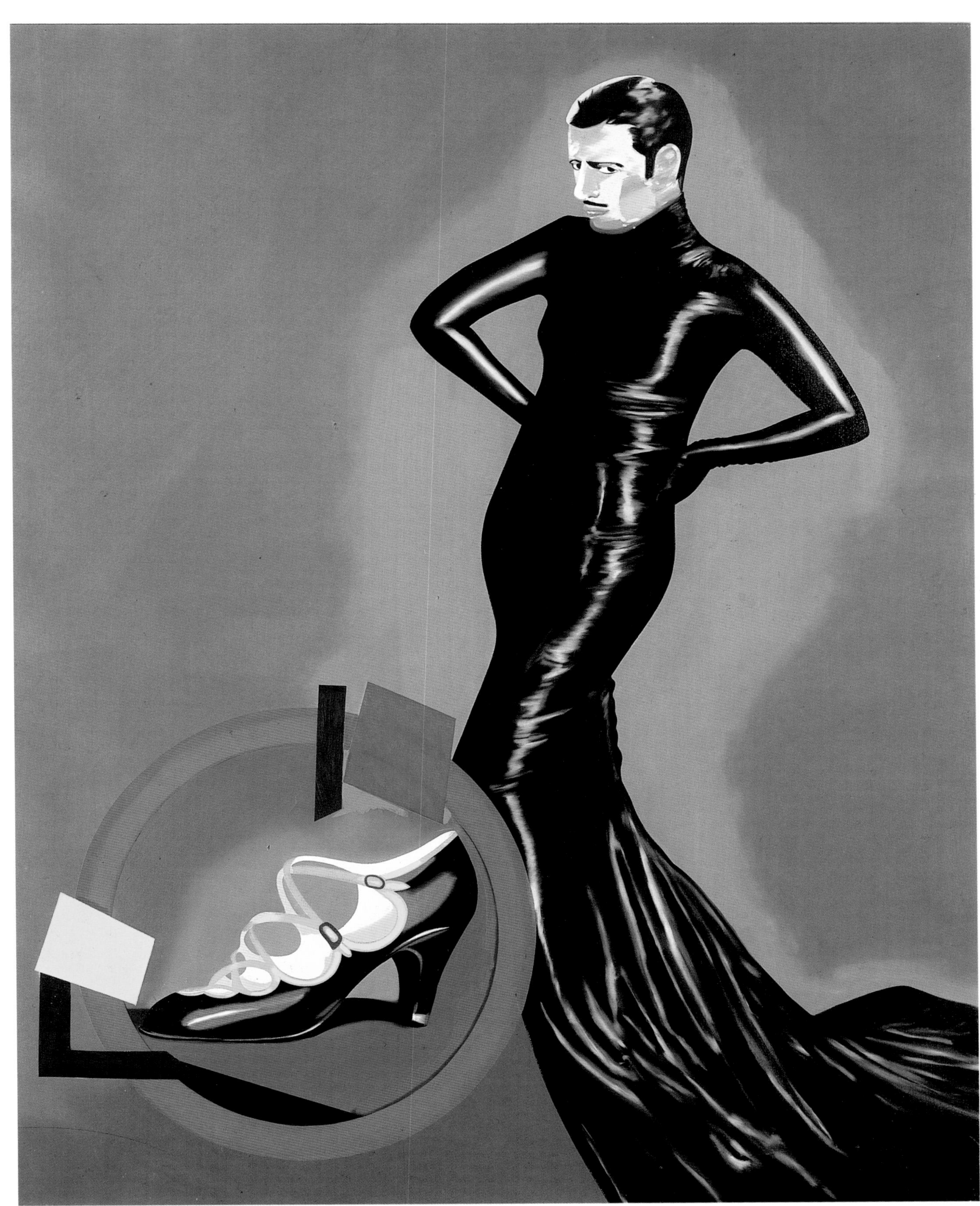

196 **Eduardo Arroyo** The Spanish Caballero 1970 (cat 4)

neo
pop

5

neo this, neo that
approaching pop art in the 1980s

DAN CAMERON

Before delving directly into the question of how Pop Art survived the wane of its influence in the 1970s, only to re-emerge as a seemingly limitless resource for artists throughout the 1980s, it is probably germane for us first to confront the more general issue of how a movement outlasts its time and in turn affects another. Certain germinal movements in modern art, such as Cubism or Surrealism, seem so closely connected to a specific time and place that any later effort to revive their forms and techniques is generally dismissed as a misguided attempt to live in the past. Expressionism, on the other hand, tends to be perceived more as the articulation of an attitude, or world view, than as a specific movement, in spite of being rooted in early twentieth-century Germany, so that it can and has been revived time and again.

It is common to speak of a Cubist or Surrealist influence on the formative years of Abstract Expressionism, a movement that is considered to have come into its own at the precise moment when it had succeeded in ridding itself of its early reliance on these existing models. In such a circumstance the revival of a prior movement is best spoken of in the past tense, as it were, when the new movement that it has influenced sheds its skin and assumes its own identity. A final category is the emergence of a second generation of a style or movement, as occurred with Cubism and Abstract Expressionism. In this case the new practitioners make no real attempt to capture faithfully the original impulse behind the movement, but rather gravitate towards a style previously regarded as having a fringe or avant-garde status but now widely accepted as the dominant movement of its time.

In the case of Pop, traces of the movement can be seen in the art of the 1970s, and they fall somewhere between the various states described above. Certainly there was no collective effort during that decade to perpetuate any of the original precepts of Pop, and the strategies of artists such as Warhol were largely appreciated for their influence on the 'system' aesthetics of Post-Minimalism and Conceptual Art. Neither can it be said that Pop Art produced a significant second generation during the early 1970s or that it overlapped noticeably with successive movements. In part, this conspicuous absence of Pop's enduring impact during this period can be explained both by its long germination through the late 1950s and early 1960s, and by its seemingly ubiquitous role throughout the latter decade. Therefore, if we think of Pop Art in the United States as the apotheosis of the vernacular, or even the profane, then it is not difficult to understand why as early as 1966 a younger generation began to emerge to reclaim art's formal and sacred terrain.

In retrospect Minimalism, with its severe, industrial edge, seems in close sympathy with Pop Art, complementing the latter's more frivolous inclinations in a mutually beneficial manner. The same cannot really be said of Conceptual Art, which developed later and in part as a response to or refutation of the two earlier movements. However, as with all periods of transition in recent history where the issues are still very real for many of the protagonists who are themselves still active, it is not easy to generalise about the relationship between Pop and Conceptual Art. In my opinion there are two approaches to the subject, those of the formalists and the regionalists. I would describe the formalists as those who see in Pop the seeds of Conceptual Art because of its elimination of subjectivity and the gradual replacement of the art object with language and event. The second approach to Pop, corresponding to the regionalist tendencies in twentieth-century American art rather than to the reductionism of the New York School, conceives of the movement as populist, seemingly naive, colourful and broadly humorous – in other words, in terms of the very qualities of Pop that had come to endear it to a wider audience. The connection I have implied in my use of the term 'regional' with the 'American scene' painters of the 1920s and '30s is intentional. Nevertheless groups such as Chicago's Hairy Who (a loosely-defined group that included Roger Brown, Ed Paschke, Karl Wirsum and Gladys Nilsson, among others) mixed folk art and Surrealist influences.

fig 1 **Richard Prince** *Untitled* 1983 Courtesy Barbara Gladstone Gallery, New York

The split over how to divide up the spoils of Pop Art's legacy continues to represent one of the most formidable struggles in late twentieth-century American art, with the formalist approach continuing in Richard Prince's media-based photographic art (fig. 1), Allan McCollum's 'surrogate' object-paintings or Jenny Holzer's high-tech, linguistic sculptures, and the regionalists' example surviving in the work of otherwise unrelated painters such as Kenny Scharf (fig. 2) or Elizabeth Murray. Ironically, considering that Pop is so often referred to as the quintessential American movement, it seems that the position one takes on the issue of how Pop has been assimilated by younger American artists tends also to define how one feels about the question of American Pop's interrelationship with European Pop. In other words the work of the American Pop regionalists of the late 1960s and '70s, as exemplified by Peter Saul, appears in retrospect to have much in common with European counterparts such as Sweden's Oyvind Fahlström or Spain's Equipo Crónica, as well as with the graffiti movement of the early 1980s and the recent Pop-influenced painters from Eastern Europe and the Soviet Union. On the other hand the formalist sensibility seems to have been more stereotypically American and to have had an influence on certain European artists only in the 1980s.

Instead of considering Pop as a finite movement, or even as the style that defined its age, here it will be treated instead as a loosely organised vocabulary of forms, a prefabricated tradition that never truly dispersed after its creation but served as a constant reference point even for those who did not succumb to its influence, as well as a rich source of ideas and strategies for those who did. Although there may not be an overwhelming historical precedent for discussing Pop in this manner, the methodological advantages are considerable, to the extent that it becomes easier to consider the Pop inflections in the work of non-American artists such as On Kawara and Gilbert & George, or to emphasise the integral relationship between Fluxus and Pop, without going through the fruitless exercise of dividing the world between Pop artists and non-Pop artists, or between European Pop and that which was 'Made in USA'.

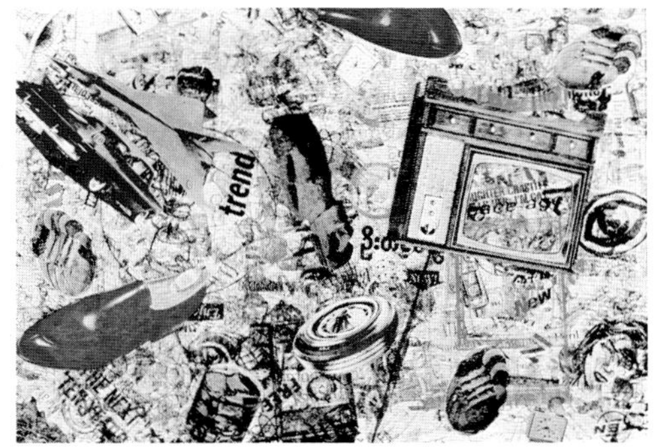

fig 2 **Kenny Scharf** *Staticontrol* 1990 Courtesy Tony Shafrazi Gallery

One significant outcome of the formalist/regionalist split is that it may now be somewhat easier to talk about certain aberrant strains of Pop, and the ways in which this kind of work sowed the seeds for a Pop-rooted explosion of styles and movements through the late 1970s and '80s. In particular, the examples of John Baldessari in California and Sigmar Polke in Germany serve to argue the point that the same artists who resisted being categorised as exclusively Pop or Conceptual tended to be the best equipped at showing a younger generation how to develop past the general tendency either to be intimidated by Pop, or to treat it as an empty vessel. While Baldessari's work was based on the use of artifacts gathered from popular culture and reassembled in an ostensibly critical fashion, Polke always used a Pop sensibility, together with other styles and techniques, to expand the limits of a picture's signifying capabilities.

Much has already been written on the California Institute of Arts in Valencia, better known as CalArts, and in particular on Baldessari's influence as a teacher there upon a range of young artists, including David Salle and Ashley Bickerton. Nevertheless, a facet often left unexplored is the degree to which the leading figures of this generation effectively became the illegitimate offspring of Pop and Conceptual Art, in the sense that they adapted the aloof, analytical premises of their anti-object predecessors while simultaneously immersing themselves in the complex maze of American popular culture. Accordingly, the late-1970s' and early 1980s' work of Salle, Jack Goldstein, Sherrie Levine, Eric Fischl, Matt Mullican and Barbara Bloom forms the first stages of American Pop's complete redefinition of itself in the wake of Conceptual Art, and as the first concise expression in American art of a new sensibility known as 'post-modernism'. Their use of photography to copy and reproduce history, rather than to perpetuate clichés of the myth of originality (as embodied, for example, by the art of Julian Schnabel), came to characterise their work as post-modern in the sense of being post-avant-garde; and their engagement with popular sources distinguishes their permutation of post-modernism from its European counterparts. By the time this new American work was shown alongside that of Cindy Sherman and Robert Longo in New York's Artists Space it was clear that a new generation had emerged, part formalist and part regionalist in outlook.

The post-modern position in contemporary culture was first formulated by architects in the United States and Britain, either to promote an extension of Robert Venturi's vernacular ideas into the 1970s or to formulate a vehemently neo-classical response to the last glimmerings of the International Style. By the time it was picked up by a handful of Italian art critics, however, post-modernism had already become something of a cliché. Many argued that the hyper-classicist look of Carlo Maria Mariani's painting, for example, was the quintessence of post-modern art, while others used a similar formula to promote the work of the young 'transavant-garde' artists such as Enzo Cucchi, Mimmo Paladino, Francesco Clemente and Sandro Chia. Regardless of who had the more convincing theory, the label 'post-modern' stuck more readily to the latter group, creating a common misconception that the new post-modernism consisted largely of a pastiche style, a slapping together of innumerable earlier genres to create a hybrid style which, while far from new in an historical sense, permitted artists to drop the earlier restrictions of syntax and forge a new type of expression from the remnants of modernist history.

As a result of this somewhat carefree application of the term 'post-modern' to anything that revealed a clear derivation from the past, the prefix 'neo-' became the most widely-used stylistic term of the late 1970s and '80s. By 1981 'Neo-Expressionism' had become the first test of the term, used by everyone except the Germans themselves to indicate the new, 'wild' painters of Berlin and Cologne. It soon became clear that the scavenging of the recent past was not a process confined to the regional history of Italy or Germany, but could in fact be applied to the work of any younger artists who explored an existing artistic vocabulary in an explicitly self-conscious manner. Although there is no theoretical position implicitly shared by artists working under the banner of 'neo', the most obvious result of this development was that it freed artists from the historical imperative of making art that was stylistically original. It unleashed an international wave of creativity by shifting the terms of aesthetic discourse from the shock of the unknown to the discomfort of the already-known. Probably the most consistent statement of the new American art could be found in the early 1980s in the work of the artists on the roster of the Metro Pictures Gallery in Soho, New York. Opened in 1981 to provide an outlet for the new conceptually-grounded photography, the gallery's emphasis has been on the recycling of popular culture through occasionally esoteric means. Sherman's early cinematic self-portraits and Longo's stark homages to *film noir* helped set the tone, but Jack Goldstein's dazzling atmospheric paintings, Laurie Simmons's ironic doll photographs, Sherrie Levine's appropriated photographs of well-known modernists' work (fig. 3) and Louise Lawler's spoofs on the art world's obsessions with ownership and taste, soon became recognised as icons of the 1980s. A few years later the gradual acceptance of Mike Kelley's ominous low-culture ramblings and John Miller's fecal obsessions proved that Metro Picture's interpretation of Pop was constantly closer to the mark than that of any other gallery of the period.

fig 3 **Sherrie Levine** *Untitled (After Giorgio Morandi)* 1985 Chase Manhattan Bank, New York Courtesy Mary Boone Gallery, New York

For most of the New York art establishment, however, painting was virtually the only game in town in the early 1980s, a development that required photographic artists such as Levine or Simmons to be pushed aside temporarily in favour of painters such as Salle, Schnabel or Fischl, whose work was heavily promoted in part as a response to the onslaught of new painters from Europe. The work of Salle and Schnabel was noteworthy because it transformed the New York art market from a respectable cottage industry into a hotbed of cutthroat speculation. While Salle's pictorial strategies had a considerable impact on artists of every stripe, the others were significant primarily for their return to the painterly excesses of the 1950s and early '60s, and to the prototype of the artist as a hero/celebrity/genius.

A still more unexpected development in the early 1980s was the sudden transformation of New York street art into an international phenomenon, and with it the emergence of the South Bronx and the East Village as part of the global art world. In retrospect, the short-lived graffiti movement can be credited with two things: it gave rise to solo shows of painters such as Daze, Crash and Rammellzee in established galleries such as Sidney Janis (who had organised the first Pop Art group show in New York); and it provided a launching-pad for the work of two artists only loosely connected with the movement: the charismatic neo-primitivist Jean-Michel Basquiat, who briefly scribbled on the sides of trains a couple of years before it became fashionable to do so, and Keith Haring, who first came to public attention with large crayon drawings in public sites, although these were far from the South Bronx. The clumsy promotion of graffiti as an urban-folk avant-garde art did not win it many long-term allies in the establishment, and as a movement it did not produce a single artist of note if one considers Basquiat and Haring as close cousins of graffiti, rather than as the real thing. Nevertheless it did start to make the New York art world more aware of the socio-cultural conditions of urban life, and it helped spawn a new group of mostly white artists – Haring, Scharf and Holzer, among others – whose work was initially directed more towards the street and club scene than it was to the more restricted world of the art galleries. Oddly, the most memorable aspect of graffiti's legacy, and its most natural connection with Pop Art, is probably the phenomenon of the East Village as a low-rent neighbourhood with an avant-garde identity. The new lease of life of this run-down part of Manhattan was initiated in 1983 by the Fun Gallery's efforts to show Haring, Scharf, Basquiat and others of their generation. Despite its impromptu origins the East Village was transformed within a matter of months into an intricate network of low-rent, storefront galleries and clubs, each with its own roster of funky, often expressionist-styled, but always Pop-based artists, very few of whom had anything to do with graffiti. The East Village has been explained as a grass-roots alternative to Soho's pricey art market and as New York's nostalgic attempt to re-live the bohemian utopia of the 1960s. Its most immediate result, however, was a rapidly-expanded art market, with new collectors, artists and dealers exchanging works for as little as $50 or $100 apiece and a sense of manic energy checked only by the feeling that it could not possibly last.

The East Village years roughly cover the period from 1983 to 1988, but even within such a short time the regionalist/formalist struggle had a chance to re-surface as one of the neighbourhood's main dramas. If we consider graffiti primarily as an expression of American Pop's regionalist sensibilities, a more conceptually-based movement was developing simultaneously, initially in the work of relatively established artists such as Lawler and Levine who showed at the tiny gallery Nature Morte, through the contacts they had forged with Metro Pictures. This new art was cool and reductivist, but also aggressively, unapologetically Pop, and it seemed to be completely in defiance of the rougher, informal art that had previously characterised the East Village. Eventually the careers of Haim Steinbach, Jeff Koons, Meyer Vaisman, Ashley Bickerton and Peter Halley came to eclipse those of their immediate predecessors, offering a complete about-turn from the dominant expressionist style of the times in favour of a more synthetic 'simulationist' aesthetic.

fig 4 **Jeff Koons** *Serpents* 1988 Courtesy Sonnabend Gallery, New York

Appropriation, the borrowing or scavenging of imagery from other sources in order to present it as part of one's own work, was for a few years the focus of debate in the East Village. Mike Bidlo's loosely executed paintings and sculptures, which were often 'performed' in clubs as part of the East Village's funkier side, became pitted against the drier, more brittle copies in watercolour and photography that Levine showed in the conceptually-based galleries. Levine's growing celebrity in the late 1980s was in some ways the most telling sign of a change in sensibility towards a more ironic, critical form of appropriation. It also led to the revival of certain Pop-era artists, such as Elaine Sturtevant and Richard Pettibone, who had practised appropriation when it was only thought of as a minor offshoot of Pop itself. The work of artists shown through such galleries as International with Monument and Nature Morte provides perhaps the most convincing argument for a full-fledged Pop revival in American art of the 1980s. Certainly Koons's sculpture, from the basketballs suspended in aquaria to his recent declaration of himself and La Cicciolina as the new Adam and Eve, provides a painstaking restatement of Pop Art's interest in banality, kitsch and commercial exploitation, as well as looking back to the absurdist stunts of Salvador Dalí and Yves Klein for some of its inspiration (fig. 4). In a similar vein Halley's hard-edge, day-glo abstractions and Steinbach's wedge-shaped shelves with arrangements of objects indicate a merger of styles between Pop and Minimal Art, with overtones, too, of Conceptual Art (figs 5 and 6). Yet if we also consider examples as broadly-based as Barbara Kruger's recent hard-hitting political billboards (fig. 7), Vaisman's fake historical tapestries with cartoon figures woven into them or Bickerton's high-tech meditations on global ecology, it becomes clear that the emergence of a Neo-Pop, Neo-Geo (as it was first dubbed by the critics)

fig 5 **Peter Halley** *Jane's Addiction* 1990 Courtesy Sonnabend Gallery, New York

fig 6 **Haim Steinbach** *stay with friends (Kellog's)* 1986 Courtesy Sonnabend Gallery, New York

or Neo-Conceptual aesthetic is a highly diversified proposition involving a myriad of historical hybrids. It is also evident that it has taken on the force of an imperative within American art, coming as it does a full quarter-century after the emergence of Pop, the one style that has probably defined a national viewpoint better than any other in the country's history.

fig 7 **Barbara Kruger** *Untitled (Your Body is a Battleground)* 1989 Edye and Eli Broad, Los Angeles Courtesy Mary Boone Gallery, New York

An entirely different perspective emerges when we consider European art of the late 1970s and early '80s. In general continental European Pop had been more politically oriented than the American variety; some of Gerhard Richter's work, in particular, skated a thin line between provocation and ambivalence. British Pop had tended towards a more literary world view. Both groups of artists were largely closed to each other as well as to the United States. Of course, one can hardly conceive of the existence of the Fluxus or Arte Povera movements without taking their Pop roots into account. But many of the artists shared the feeling that an alternative was needed to the unabashed consumerist orientation of American Pop, so that their art became a way of restoring Pop's links to the underground, which they believed formed its earliest critical justification.

At the same time that Pop Art began to be seen as a key reference in the work of Victor Burgin or Jörg Immendorff, for example, whose careers straddled both the 1970s and the 1980s, a number of international barriers were already being broken down by post-modern theory, in terms of the use of recognisable historic genres. Although the impact of Polke and Richter on the younger generation was considerable, very few of their students actually continued to work in a Pop-inflected vein, although the flamboyant public image of young painters in Berlin was reminiscent of Pop. As a result of this disconnectedness, it took the young emigré painters from Eastern Europe – Jiři Georg Dokoupil, Milan Kunc and Braco Dimitrijevic – to launch the more thorough reappraisal of Pop that occurred in relation to new European art in the early 1980s. By mixing modernist icons together with a glossy, illustrative painting style, these artists sought to undermine the angst-laden aesthetic of their time, while trying to point the way towards a new theory of pictorialism. The daredevil atmosphere created by them has since paved the way for quite different German artists, such as Rosemarie Trockel or Katharina Fritsch (fig. 8), who are also trying to develop a more ironic approach to imagery than their more expressionist forebears. Additionally, the second-hand impact of Pop Art on the latest artists to emerge from the Soviet Union since the mid-1980s has been considerable, with the work of more Westernised artists, such as Komar and Melamid, Alexander Kosolapov or Leonid Sokov, forming a unique repository of classic Pop images, updated to confront the paradoxes of contemporary Western life.

fig 8 **Katharina Fritsch** *Elephant* 1987 Courtesy Jablonka Galerie, Cologne

The most significant merger outside the United States of critical opinion and the new, Pop-influenced, artistic forms of the early 1980s can be felt in the one area where Pop's literal relationship to the work is actually the most tenuous, namely the loosely designated 'school' of British sculptors such as Tony Cragg, Bill Woodrow, Edward Allington, Richard Wentworth, David Mach and Julian Opie. Whereas Cragg and Woodrow, along with Richard Deacon, were largely responsible for the first important developments in sculpture at the beginning of the 1980s, the work of the others has served to broaden or refine the vocabulary. Although the important role played by the found object in these artists' work shows some indebtedness to Pop Art, it is not really British Pop that has been assimilated, but more the American or continental variety, with its shared fetish for the object as tactile sensation, implicitly removed from the system for which it stands. Even more apparent than its grounding in Pop, however, is the close relationship between much of this work and the constructivist tradition in modern British sculpture. In the art of

Cragg (fig. 9) and Woodrow the accumulation and transformation of object into sculpture reveals a metamorphic quality that substitutes philosophical concerns for mere formalist repetition; in the case of Allington or Mach, however, the cartoonish aspects of the work seem to increase as the artists' reliance on earlier gestures becomes more pronounced.

fig 9 **Tony Cragg** *Britain Seen from the North* 1981
Tate Gallery, London

Since the beginning of the 1980s, Paris has been host to a struggle between vying interpretations of Pop that could easily rival the regionalist/formalist split in the United States. As in New York, the first artists to raise the banner of Pop in Paris were the largely graffiti-inspired painters such as Jean-Charles Blais, Robert Combas and Hervé di Rosa, whose exuberant spirit and crudeness of execution were unfortunately not enough to conceal the more derivative aspects of their styles. Yet French art has maintained equally strong roots in Conceptual Art, as in the object-based sculptures of Bertrand Lavier, which in turn were influential on the work of emerging artists (fig. 10). On not quite the other end of the spectrum is a development that is exclusively, almost stereotypically, French, that of a highly stylised, photographic art exemplified by Philippe Cazal or Pierre et Gilles, which falls somewhere between the critical stance of Conceptual Art and the pure gloss of advertising.

Elsewhere in Europe the influence of Pop has come to seem almost ubiquitous, although its manifestations differ radically from one area to another. At first glance, the Swiss artist John Armleder's juxtapositions of found objects may seem to be practically interchangeable with the Belgian sculptor Guillaume Bijl's reconstructions of found tableaux, but whereas the one appears to have a great deal to do with the corporeality of the objects balanced against their symbolic weight, the other seems to be more of an exercise in the Surrealist principle of making the everyday into a discomforting unexperience. On the other hand, for European artists still in their 20s the question of whether or not to be Pop seems to have something of an historical ultimatum attached to it. Aware of the approaching millennium, these younger artists tend to view Pop not just as a symbol of mid-century optimism and naiveté, but as the most recent articulation of a sensibility that can probably be traced back to the earliest known debates on the issues of patronage and nature. Their example is vital to any examination of the influence of Pop beyond its formative years, because for them Pop is not only an apt metaphor for the spirit of classicism at the tail end of modernity, but also for the new populist, de-centred art that has already emerged and demanded to be taken seriously in the 1990s. In New York a related free-form adaptation of styles has resulted in a new assemblagist variation on Pop exemplified by sculptors such as Cady Noland. Today, in fact, the younger American and European artists seem much closer together in spirit and in achievement than ever before, perhaps because they are the first generation who cannot remember a time when Pop Art was not synonymous with art itself.

fig 10 **Bertrand Lavier** *Brandt/Fichet-Bauche* 1985
Collection of the Artist

list of **works**

ARMAN
1 *Jim Dine's Dustbin (Poubelle)* 1961
objects and plexiglass 51 × 30 × 30cm (20 × 12 × 12ins)
Sonnabend Collection
plate 172

ARMAN
2 *Madison Avenue* 1962
shoes, wooden box 60.5 × 100 × 15cm ($23\frac{3}{4}$ × $39\frac{3}{4}$ × 6ins)
Frank Stella Collection, New York
plate 174

ARROYO, Eduardo
3 *With Deference to Traditions* 1965
oil on canvas 142 × 184cm (56 × $72\frac{1}{2}$ins)
Collection of the Artist
plate 195

ARROYO, Eduardo
4 *The Spanish Caballero* 1970
oil on canvas 163 × 130cm ($64\frac{1}{2}$ × $51\frac{1}{8}$ins)
Musée National d'Art Moderne, Centre Georges Pompidou, Paris
plate 196

ARTSCHWAGER, Richard
5 *Portrait 1* 1962
acrylic on wood and celotex 188 × 66 × 30.5cm (74 × 26 × 12ins)
Kasper König, Frankfurt am Main
plate 51

ARTSCHWAGER, Richard
6 *Apartment House* 1964
liquitex on celotex with formica on wood panel 177.8 × 125.7 × 15.2cm (70 × $49\frac{1}{2}$ × 6ins)
Museum Ludwig, Ludwig Donation, Cologne
plate 80

ARTSCHWAGER, Richard
7 *Piano* 1965
formica on wood 81.3 × 121.9 × 48.3cm (32 × 48 × 19ins)
Leo Castelli
plate 81

ARTSCHWAGER, Richard
8 *Running Man* 1991
acrylic, fibre panel, formica, enamel, wood 188 × 147.3cm (74 × 58ins)
Courtesy Mary Boone Gallery, New York
plate 100

BARKER, Clive
9 *Two Palettes for Jim Dine* 1964
wood and metal 66 × 76 × 5cm (26 × 30 × 2ins)
Private Collection
plate 146

BARKER, Clive
10 *Van Gogh's Chair* 1966
chrome-plated steel 86.4cm high (34ins high)
Paul and Linda McCartney
plate 147

BEN (*see also Fluxus*)
11 *Drink to Forget Art* 1971
bottle on wooden board 34 × 58 × 38cm ($13\frac{3}{8}$ × $22\frac{7}{8}$ × 15ins)
Sohm Archive, Staatsgalerie Stuttgart

BENGSTON, Billy Al
12 *Carburetor Floatbowl* 1961
oil on canvas 106.7 × 101.6cm (42 × 40ins)
Collection of the Artist
plate 38

BENGSTON, Billy Al
13 *Clint* 1961
polymer and lacquer on masonite 121.9 × 118.1cm (48 × $46\frac{1}{2}$ins)
Collection of the Artist
plate 37

BLAKE, Peter
14 *On the Balcony* 1955–57
oil on canvas 121.3 × 90.8cm ($47\frac{3}{4}$ × $35\frac{3}{4}$ins)
Tate Gallery, Presented by the Contemporary Art Society 1963
plate 109

BLAKE, Peter
15 *Children Reading Comics* 1956
oil on canvas on hardboard 39.4 × 29.3cm ($15\frac{1}{2}$ × $11\frac{1}{2}$ins)
Royal College of Art Collection
plate 107

BLAKE, Peter
16 *Siriol, She-Devil of Naked Madness* 1957
oil and collage on panel 75 × 21.6cm ($29\frac{1}{2}$ × $8\frac{1}{2}$ins)
Private Collection
plate 108

BLAKE, Peter
17 *Kim Novak Wall* 1959
pigment and photo collage on masonite 76.2 × 48.3cm (30 × 19ins)
Pat Booth
plate 111

BLAKE, Peter
18 *Toy Shop* 1962
mixed media on wood 156.8 × 194 × 34cm ($61\frac{3}{4}$ × $76\frac{1}{2}$ × $13\frac{1}{8}$ins)
Tate Gallery, Purchased 1970
plate 123

BLAKE, Peter
19 *Bo Diddley* 1963
acrylic and sellotape on fibreboard 122.6 × 78.4cm ($48\frac{1}{4}$ × $30\frac{7}{8}$ins)
Museum Ludwig, Ludwig Donation, Cologne
plate 137

BLAKE, Peter
20 *H.O.M.A.G.E. – JJ MM RR KS* 1991
collage on Japanese screen 182.9 × 87.6cm (72 × $34\frac{1}{2}$ins) (before completion; May 1991)
The Peter and Chrissy Blake Collection
plate 162

BOSHIER, Derek
21 *Airmail Letter* 1961
oil on canvas 152.4 × 152.4cm (60 × 60ins)
The Peter and Chrissy Blake Collection
plate 117

BOSHIER, Derek
22 *First Toothpaste Painting* 1962
oil on canvas 137.4 × 76.5cm (54 × 30ins)
Sheffield City Art Galleries
plate 118

BRECHT, George
23 *Play Incident* 1961
assemblage 95 × 36 × 6cm ($37\frac{1}{2}$ × $14\frac{1}{4}$ × $2\frac{1}{2}$ins)
Hermann and Marietta Braun, Remscheid

BRECHT, George (with Watts, Robert and Knowles, Alison) (*see also Fluxus*)
24 *Blink* 1963
silkscreen on canvas 46 × 46cm (18 × 18ins)
Sohm Archive, Staatsgalerie Stuttgart
plate 180

CAULFIELD, Patrick
25 *Christ at Emmaus* 1963
household paint on hardboard 101.6 × 127cm (40 × 50ins)
Royal College of Art Collection
plate 135

CAULFIELD, Patrick
26 *Engagement Ring* 1963
oil on hardboard 122 × 122cm (48 × 48ins)
Central Selling Organisation's Contemporary Art Collection
plate 136

CAULFIELD, Patrick
27 *Town and Country* 1979
acrylic on canvas 231.1 × 165.1cm (91 × 65ins)
Michael D. Abrams
plate 160

CAULFIELD, Patrick
28 *Buffet* 1987
acrylic on canvas 274.3 × 205.7cm (108 × 81ins)
Waddington Galleries
plate 161

CESAR
29 *Compression Sunbeam* 1961
compressed metal 156 × 75 × 62cm ($61\frac{1}{2}$ × $29\frac{1}{2}$ × $24\frac{1}{2}$ins)
Galerie Beaubourg, Marianne and Pierre Nahon, Paris
plate 171

CHRISTO (*see also Fluxus*)
30 *Wrapped Magazines (Revues empaquetées)* 1962
paper, plastic and string 36 × 28 × 4cm ($14\frac{1}{4}$ × 11 × $1\frac{1}{2}$ins)
Sonnabend Collection
plate 173

CHRISTO
31 *Store Front* 1964
mixed media 235 × 220 × 35.5cm ($92\frac{1}{2}$ × $86\frac{3}{4}$ × 14ins)
Collection Jeanne-Claude Christo, New York
plate 177

D'ARCANGELO, Allan
32 *The Wedding (Unfinished)* 1962
acrylic on canvas 172.7 × 165.1cm (68 × 65ins)
Private Collection
plate 55

DINE, Jim
33 *Green Suit* 1959
oil, enamel and cotton 168 × 73cm (66 × $28\frac{3}{4}$ins)
Collection of the Artist
plate 10

DINE, Jim
34 *Car Crash* 1959–60
oil and mixed media on burlap 152.5 × 162.5cm (60 × 64ins)
Galerie Hans Mayer, Düsseldorf
plate 9

DINE, Jim
35 *Summer Tools* 1962
oil on canvas with objects, 3 panels each 213.7 × 91.7cm ($84\frac{1}{8}$ × $36\frac{1}{8}$ins)
Private Collection
plate 43

DINE, Jim
36 *Tennis Shoe* 1962
oil on panel, tennis shoe, paper 43 × 50.8 × 13.9cm (17 × 20 × $5\frac{1}{2}$ins)
Constance R. Caplan
plate 44

EQUIPO CRONICA
37 *Concentration or Quantity becomes quality (Concentración o La cantidad se transforma en calidad)* 1966
acrylic on canvas 160 × 160cm (63 × 63ins)
Private Collection
plate 194

FILLIOU, Robert (*see also Fluxus*)
38 *Poi Poi* 1961
glass and paper
Sohm Archive, Staatsgalerie Stuttgart

FLUXUS
39 *An Anthology*, Ed. Jackson Mac Low, La Monte Young, New York, 1963
Sohm Archive, Staatsgalerie Stuttgart

40 Ay-O, *Hand Tactile Box*, Ed. Fluxus, New York, *c.* 1964 (two versions)
Sohm Archive, Staatsgalerie Stuttgart

41 Ben, *Absolument n'importe quoi c'est art*, Nice, 1962 (flyer)
Sohm Archive, Staatsgalerie Stuttgart

42 Ben, *Art Total*, Nice, 1963 (poster)
Sohm Archive, Staatsgalerie Stuttgart

43 Ben, *Holes*, Ed. Fluxus, New York, 1964
Sohm Archive, Staatsgalerie Stuttgart

44 Ben, *Suicide Kit*, Ed. Fluxus, New York, 1967
Sohm Archive, Staatsgalerie Stuttgart

45 Brecht, George, *V TRE*, Ed. George Brecht, Metuchen, 1963
Sohm Archive, Staatsgalerie Stuttgart

46 Brecht, George, *Water Yam*, Ed. Fluxus, New York, 1963–72
Sohm Archive, Staatsgalerie Stuttgart
plate 182

47 Brecht, George, *Iced Dice*, Ed. Fluxus, New York, 1964
Sohm Archive, Staatsgalerie Stuttgart

48 Brecht, George, *Inclined Ball Puzzle*, Ed. Fluxus, New York, 1964–65 (two versions)
Sohm Archive, Staatsgalerie Stuttgart

49 Brecht, George, *Direction*, Ed. Fluxus, New York, *c.* 1965
Sohm Archive, Staatsgalerie Stuttgart

50 Brecht, George, *Deck*, Ed. Fluxus, New York, *c.* 1965
Sohm Archive, Staatsgalerie Stuttgart

51 *ccVTRE*, Ed. Fluxus, New York, 1964 ff.
Sohm Archive, Staatsgalerie Stuttgart

52 Christo, *Package*, Ed. Fluxus, New York, 1965
Sohm Archive, Staatsgalerie Stuttgart

53 *décoll/age No. 1–5*, Ed. Wolf Vostell, Cologne, 1962–66
Sohm Archive, Staatsgalerie Stuttgart

54 *Expanded Arts Diagram*, Ed. George Maciunas, *c.* 1968; mounted on wood
Sohm Archive, Staatsgalerie Stuttgart

55 Filliou, Robert with Brecht, George, *Banqueroute*, 1968
Sohm Archive, Staatsgalerie Stuttgart

56 Filliou, Robert, *Hand Show* (flyer)
Sohm Archive, Staatsgalerie Stuttgart

57 *FLUXFEST SALE*, Ed. Fluxus, New York, 1966
Sohm Archive, Staatsgalerie Stuttgart

58 *FLUXKIT*, Ed. Fluxus, New York, 1964
Hansjorg Mayer
plate 181

59 *FLUXSHOE*, 1972–73 (poster for UK exhibition)
Sohm Archive, Staatsgalerie Stuttgart

60 *FLUXUS 1*, Ed. George Maciunas, 1965
Sohm Archive, Staatsgalerie Stuttgart
plate 179

61 *FLUXUS*, 1962–63 (four posters for concerts in Wiesbaden, Copenhagen, Paris, Düsseldorf)
Sohm Archive, Staatsgalerie Stuttgart

62 *FLUXUS*, Hartmut Rekort, 1962 (six black and white photographs)
Sohm Archive, Staatsgalerie Stuttgart

63 *FLUXYEARBOX 2*, Ed. Fluxus, New York, 1968
Sohm Archive, Staatsgalerie Stuttgart

64 Flynt, Henry, *Communists Must Give Revolutionary Leadership in Culture*, 1965 (manifesto)
Sohm Archive, Staatsgalerie Stuttgart

65 Friedman, Ken, *A Flux Corsage*, Ed. Fluxus, New York, 1969
Sohm Archive, Staatsgalerie Stuttgart

66 Hendricks, Geoffrey, *A Flux Reliquiary*, Ed. Fluxus, New York, 1970
Sohm Archive, Staatsgalerie Stuttgart

67 Hi-Red-Center, *Canned Mystery*, collage on tin can (two versions)
Sohm Archive, Staatsgalerie Stuttgart

68 Hi-Red-Center, *Fluxus Printing*, 1965 (flyer)
Sohm Archive, Staatsgalerie Stuttgart

69 Higgins, Dick, *Invocation of Canyons and Boulders for Stan Brakhage*, Ed. Fluxus, New York
Sohm Archive, Staatsgalerie Stuttgart

70 Jones, Joe, *Mechanical Fluxorchestra*, Ed. Fluxus, New York, 1966
Sohm Archive, Staatsgalerie Stuttgart

71 Kirkeby, Per, *Flux Finger Sweater*, Ed. Fluxus, New York, 1969
Sohm Archive, Staatsgalerie Stuttgart

72 Knizak, Milan, *Flux Dreams*, Ed. Fluxus, New York, 1969
Sohm Archive, Staatsgalerie Stuttgart

73 Knowles, Alison, *Bean Rolls*, Ed. Fluxus, New York, 1964
Sohm Archive, Staatsgalerie Stuttgart

74 Kosugi, Takehisa, *Events*, Ed. Fluxus, New York, 1964
Sohm Archive, Staatsgalerie Stuttgart

75 Kubota, Shigeko, *Flux Napkins*, Ed. Fluxus, New York, 1967
Sohm Archive, Staatsgalerie Stuttgart

76 Maciunas, George, *Musica Antiqua et Nova*, 1961 (four invitation cards)
Sohm Archive, Staatsgalerie Stuttgart

77 Maciunas, George, *USA Surpasses All the Genocide Records . . .*, 1966 (flyer)
Sohm Archive, Staatsgalerie Stuttgart

78 Maciunas, George, *Burglary Flux Kit*, Ed. Fluxus, New York, 1971
Sohm Archive, Staatsgalerie Stuttgart

79 Maciunas, George, *Excreta Fluxorum*, Ed. Fluxus, New York, 1973
Sohm Archive, Staatsgalerie Stuttgart

80 Maciunas, George, *Fluxpost;* printed sheet of stamps, 28 × 22cm
Sohm Archive, Staatsgalerie Stuttgart

81 Oldenburg, Claes, *False Food Selection*, Ed. Fluxus, New York, 1966
Sohm Archive, Staatsgalerie Stuttgart

82 Ono, Yoko, *This Is Not Here*, 1971, de luxe edition, design by George Maciunas
Sohm Archive, Staatsgalerie Stuttgart

83 Paik, Nam June, *Fluxus Island in Décoll/age Ocean*, 1963 (flyer)
Sohm Archive, Staatsgalerie Stuttgart

84 Paik, Nam June, *Zen for Film*, Ed. Fluxus, New York, 1964
Sohm Archive, Staatsgalerie Stuttgart

85 Paik, Nam June, *Flux Sonata By Nam June Paik*, 1973 (posters)
Sohm Archive, Staatsgalerie Stuttgart

86 Patterson, Benjamin, *Exposition à Paris/Sneak Preview* (with Robert Filliou), 1962 (poster)
Sohm Archive, Staatsgalerie Stuttgart

87 Saito, Takako, *Fluxchess*, Ed. Fluxus, New York, 1966
Sohm Archive, Staatsgalerie Stuttgart

88 Schmit, Tomas, *Schreibmaschinengedicht*, 1964; drawing, 21 × 29cm
Sohm Archive, Staatsgalerie Stuttgart

89 Shiomi, Mieko (Chieko), *Spatial Poem No. 1* (word event), Ed. Fluxus, New York, 1965
Sohm Archive, Staatsgalerie Stuttgart

90 Spoerri, Daniel, *L'Optique moderne*, 1963
Sohm Archive, Staatsgalerie Stuttgart

91 Watts, Robert, *Events*, Ed. Fluxus, New York, 1964–65
Sohm Archive, Staatsgalerie Stuttgart

92 Watts, Robert, *Flux Atlas*, Ed. Fluxus, New York, 1973
Sohm Archive, Staatsgalerie Stuttgart

93 Watts, Robert, *Flux Stamps*
Sohm Archive, Staatsgalerie Stuttgart

94 Young, La Monte, *Compositions 1960, No 2*, Ed. Fluxus, New York, 1964
Sohm Archive, Staatsgalerie Stuttgart

95 Young, La Monte, *Compositions 1961*, Ed. Fluxus, New York, 1963
Sohm Archive, Staatsgalerie Stuttgart

GOODE, Joe
96 *Small Space* 1963
oil on canvas with painted glass 175.3 × 172 × 7cm, bottle: 21.6 × 8.6 × 8.6cm ($69\frac{1}{16} \times 67\frac{11}{16} \times 2\frac{3}{4}$ins, bottle: $8\frac{1}{2} \times 3\frac{3}{8}$ins)
Lent by the Whitney Museum of American Art, New York; Gift of the Frederick R. Weisman Art Foundation
plate 76

GOODE, Joe
97 *Untitled (Staircase)* *c.* 1966
wood and carpet 243.8 × 246.4 × 22.9cm (96 × 97 × 9ins)
Private Collection
plate 77

HAINS, Raymond
98 *Torn Poster (Affiche déchirée)* 1961
coloured paper on zinc 200 × 100cm ($78\frac{3}{4} \times 39\frac{7}{8}$ins)
Museum Ludwig, Cologne
plate 167

HAMILTON, Richard
99 *Just what is it that makes today's homes so different, so appealing?* 1956
collage on paper 26 × 25cm ($10\frac{1}{4} \times 9\frac{7}{8}$ins)
Kunsthalle Tübingen, Prof. Dr. Georg Zundel Collection
plate 106

HAMILTON, Richard
100 *Hommage à Chrysler Corp.* 1957
oil, metal, foil and collage on panel 122 × 81cm (48 × 32ins)
Private Collection
plate 110

HAMILTON, Richard
101 *Glorious Techniculture* 1961–64
oil and collage on asbestos panel 122 x 122cm (48 x 48ins)
Private Collection
plate 130

HAMILTON, Richard
102 *Towards a definitive statement on the coming trends in men's wear: Adonis in Y fronts* 1962
oil and collage on panel 61 x 81cm (24 x 32ins)
Private Collection, Courtesy of Mr Raymond Danowski
plate 129

HAMILTON, Richard
103 *Epiphany* 1964
cellulose on panel 112cm diam. (44in diam.)
Collection of the Artist
plate 138

HAMILTON, Richard
104 *I'm dreaming of a white Christmas* 1967–68
oil on canvas 106.5 x 160cm (50 x 63ins)
Oëffentliche Kunstsammlung Basel·Kunstmuseum
On loan from Sammlung Ludwig
plate 151

HAMILTON, Richard
105 *Swingeing London 67 II* 1968
oil and silkscreen on canvas 67 x 85cm ($26\frac{1}{2}$ x $33\frac{1}{2}$ins)
Museum Ludwig, Ludwig Donation, Cologne
plate 152

HAMILTON, Richard
106 *Soft Pink Landscape* 1971–72
oil on canvas 122 x 162.7cm (48 x 64ins)
Ludwig Museum in the Hungarian National Gallery, Budapest
plate 154

HAMILTON, Richard
107 *The Orangeman* 1988–90
oil on canvas, 2 parts, each 200 x 100cm ($78\frac{3}{4}$ x $39\frac{3}{8}$ins)
Collection of the Artist
plate 164 (NOT EXHIBITED)

HOCKNEY, David
108 *Adhesiveness* 1960
oil on board 127 x 101.6cm (50 x 40ins)
Collection Winnie Fung
plate 114

HOCKNEY, David
109 *Figure in a Flat Style* 1961
oil on canvas 178 x 85cm ($70\frac{1}{8}$ x $33\frac{1}{2}$ins)
Collection M. and E. Stoffel
plate 115

HOCKNEY, David
110 *I'm in the Mood for Love* 1961
oil on canvas 127 x 101.6cm (50 x 40ins)
Royal College of Art Collection
plate 116

HOCKNEY, David
111 *Domestic Scene, Broadchalke, Wilts* 1963
acrylic on canvas 183 x 183cm (72 x 72ins)
Mrs and Mr Herbert L. Lucas
plate 131

HOCKNEY, David
112 *Rocky Mountains and Tired Indians* 1965
acrylic on canvas 170.4 x 252.8cm (67 x $99\frac{1}{2}$ins)
Scottish National Gallery of Modern Art
plate 148

HOCKNEY, David
113 *A Bigger Splash* 1967
acrylic on canvas 242.6 x 243.8cm ($95\frac{1}{2}$ x 96ins)
Tate Gallery, Purchased 1981
plate 149

INDIANA, Robert
114 *Zig* 1960
oil, wood, wire, iron 165 x 45 x 41cm (65 x $17\frac{3}{4}$ x 16ins)
Museum Ludwig, Ludwig Donation, Cologne
plate 26

INDIANA, Robert
115 *American Gas Works* 1962
acrylic on canvas 152.5 x 122cm (60 x 48ins)
Museum Ludwig, Ludwig Donation, Cologne
plate 50

JACQUET, Alain
116 *Birth of Venus* 1963
oil on canvas 220 x 105cm ($86\frac{1}{2}$ x $41\frac{1}{2}$ins)
Collection Daniel Varenne, Geneva
plate 183

JACQUET, Alain
117 *Déjeuner sur l'Herbe* 1964–65
silkscreen on canvas 175 x 195cm ($68\frac{7}{8}$ x $76\frac{3}{4}$ins)
Arts Council Collection, South Bank Centre, London
plate 184

JESS
118 *Tricky Cad – Case 1* 1954
newspaper paste-up 19 x 24.1cm ($7\frac{1}{2}$ x $9\frac{1}{2}$ins)
Odyssia Gallery
plate 2

JESS
119 *Tricky Cad – Case IV* 1957
newspaper paste-up 24.1 x 14cm ($9\frac{1}{2}$ x $5\frac{1}{2}$ins)
Odyssia Gallery
plate 3

JOHNS, Jasper
120 *Flag above White* 1954
encaustic on canvas 59 x 51cm ($23\frac{1}{4}$ x 20ins)
Sonnabend Collection
plate 1

JOHNS, Jasper
121 *Gray Target* 1958
encaustic on canvas 106.5 x 106.5cm (42 x 42ins)
Sonnabend Collection
plate 15

JOHNS, Jasper
122 *Map* 1960
encaustic on paper on canvas 20.3 x 27.9cm (8 x 11 ins)
Robert Rauschenberg
plate 13

JOHNS, Jasper
123 *Painted Bronze (Ale Cans)* 1960
painted bronze 14 x 20.3 x 12.1cm ($5\frac{1}{2}$ x 8 x $4\frac{3}{4}$ins)
Museum Ludwig, Ludwig Donation, Cologne
plate 16

JOHNS, Jasper
124 *Painted Bronze (Savarin Can)* 1960
painted bronze 34.3cm high, 20.3cm diam. ($13\frac{1}{2}$ins high, 8ins diam.)
Collection of the Artist
plate 14

JOHNS, Jasper
125 *0 Through 9* 1961
oil on canvas 137.2 x 104.8cm (54 x $41\frac{1}{4}$ins)
Tate Gallery. Presented by the Friends of the Tate Gallery, 1961
plate 34

JOHNS, Jasper
126 *Good Time Charley* 1961
encaustic on canvas with objects 96.5 x 61 x 11cm (38 x 24 x $4\frac{3}{8}$ins)
Private Collection
plate 33

JOHNS, Jasper
127 *Double Flag* 1962
oil on canvas 249.5 x 183.5cm ($98\frac{1}{4}$ x $72\frac{1}{4}$ins)
Norman and Irma Braman
plate 53

JOHNSON, Ray
128 *Elvis Presley 2* 1955
ink, collage, paper on cardboard 27.3 x 19cm ($10\frac{3}{4}$ x $7\frac{1}{2}$ins)
William S. Wilson
plate 7

JOHNSON, Ray
129 *James Dean* 1958
ink, collage, paper on cardboard 30 x 24cm (12 x 9ins)
Henry Martin
plate 8

JOHNSON, Ray
130 *Shirley Temple* 1958
ink, collage, paper on cardboard 30 x 24 cm (12 x 9ins)
Henry Martin
plate 6

JOHNSON, Ray
131 *Untitled (Gymnastics)* 1958
ink, collage, paper on cardboard 27.9 x 19cm (11 x $7\frac{1}{2}$ins)
Massimo and Francesca Valsecchi Collection, Italy
plate 5

JONES, Allen
132 *Thinking about Women* 1961
oil on canvas 152 x 152cm (60 x 60ins)
Norfolk Contemporary Art Society
plate 119

JONES, Allen
133 *Bikini Baby* 1962
oil on canvas 184 x 184cm ($72\frac{1}{2}$ x $72\frac{1}{2}$ins)
Ford Motor Company Limited
plate 121

JONES, Allen
134 *2nd Bus* 1962
oil on canvas 122 x 155cm rhomboid (48 x 61ins), plus 2 canvases each 31 x 31cm ($12\frac{1}{4}$ x $12\frac{1}{4}$ins)
Granada Television
plate 120

JONES, Allen
135 *Perfect Match* 1966–67
oil on canvas 280 x 93cm ($110\frac{1}{4}$ x $36\frac{5}{8}$ins)
Museum Ludwig, Ludwig Donation, Cologne
plate 155

JONES, Allen
136 *Table* 1969
fibreglass, leather, hair, glass 61 x 144.8 x 83.8cm (24 x 57 x 33ins)
Ludwig Forum, Aachen
plate 157

JONES, Allen
137 *Bare Me* 1972
oil on canvas 244.5 x 121.5cm ($96\frac{1}{4}$ x $47\frac{3}{4}$ins)
Gothenburg Art Gallery
plate 156

KAPROW, Allan
138 *Stained Glass Window* 1956
collage 266 x 175cm ($104\frac{3}{4}$ x 69ins)
Ludwig Museum, Ludwig Donation, Cologne
plate 4

KIENHOLZ, Edward
139 *George Warshington in Drag* 1957
oil paint on plywood 82.6 x 91.4 x 7.6cm ($32\frac{1}{2}$ x 36 x 3ins)
Private Collection
plate 17

KIENHOLZ, Edward
140 *John Doe* 1959
assemblage: oil, paint on mannequin parts; perambulator, wood, metal, plaster, plastic, rubber
100.2 x 48.3 x 79.4cm ($39\frac{1}{2}$ x 19 x $31\frac{1}{4}$ins)
The Menil Collection, Houston
plate 19

KIENHOLZ, Edward
141 *Walter Hopps, Hopps, Hopps* 1959
mixed media 221 x 106.7 x 30cm (87 x 42 x 12ins)
Collection Lannan Foundation, Los Angeles
plate 18

KITAJ, R. B.
142 *A Student of Vienna* 1961–62
oil and collage on canvas 92 x 92cm ($36\frac{1}{4}$ x $36\frac{1}{4}$ins)
Waddington Galleries
plate 125

KITAJ, R. B.
143 *Good News for Incunabulists* 1962
oil on canvas 155 × 155cm (60 × 60ins)
Collection M. and E. Stoffel
plate 126

KITAJ, R. B.
144 *Junta* 1962
oil on canvas 91.4 × 213.4cm (36 × 84ins)
Private Collection
plate 124

KØPCKE, Arthur
145 *Reading Work Piece (principles no. 66-124-59-126)* 1964
painting and collage on canvas 66.5 × 85cm
(26$\frac{1}{8}$ × 33$\frac{1}{2}$ins)
Kunsthalle, Kiel

KØPCKE, Arthur
146 *What's the Time* 1969
clocks and watches on board 16.5 × 60.5 × 18cm
(6$\frac{1}{2}$ × 24 × 7ins)
Sohm Archive, Staatsgalerie Stuttgart

LICHTENSTEIN, Roy
147 *Popeye* 1961
oil on canvas 106.7 × 142.2cm (42 × 56ins)
David Lichtenstein
plate 23

LICHTENSTEIN, Roy
148 *Washing Machine* 1961
oil on canvas 141.5 × 171.5cm (55$\frac{3}{4}$ × 67$\frac{1}{2}$ins)
Richard Brown Baker Collection, Courtesy of the Yale University Art Gallery
plate 25

LICHTENSTEIN, Roy
149 *Blam* 1962
oil on canvas 170 × 200cm (67 × 78$\frac{7}{8}$ins)
Richard Brown Baker Collection, Courtesy of the Yale University Art Gallery
plate 46

LICHTENSTEIN, Roy
150 *Masterpiece* 1962
oil and magna on canvas 137.2 × 137.2cm (54 × 54ins)
Collection of Agnes Gund
plate 49

LICHTENSTEIN, Roy
151 *I Know . . . Brad* 1963
oil and magna on canvas 168 × 96cm (66$\frac{1}{8}$ × 37$\frac{3}{4}$ins)
Ludwig Forum, Aachen
plate 63

LICHTENSTEIN, Roy
152 *Torpedo . . . los!* 1963
oil on canvas 172.2 × 203.8cm (68 × 80ins)
Private Collection
plate 62

LICHTENSTEIN, Roy
153 *White Brushstroke #1* 1965
oil and magna on canvas 121.9 × 142.2cm (48 × 56ins)
Irving Blum, New York
plate 84

LICHTENSTEIN, Roy
154 *Rouen Cathedral II (seen at three different times of day)* 1969
magna on canvas, three panels each 160 × 106.8cm (63 × 42ins)
Museum Ludwig, Ludwig Donation, Cologne
plate 88

LICHTENSTEIN, Roy
155 *Entablature* 1971
oil on canvas 60 × 366cm (23$\frac{1}{2}$ × 144ins)
Collection Attilio Codognato
plate 87

LICHTENSTEIN, Roy
156 *Interior with Built-in Bar* 1991
oil and magna on canvas 290 × 417cm (114 × 164ins)
Private Collection
plate 98

MACIUNAS, George (*see also Fluxus*)
157 *Grinder Chess* 1965
ink on paper 30 × 21cm (12 × 8$\frac{1}{4}$ins)
Sohm Archive, Staatsgalerie Stuttgart

OLDENBURG, Claes (*see also Fluxus*)
158 *Cap* 1961
muslin, wire, plaster, enamel 16.8 × 48.3 × 41.6cm
(6$\frac{5}{8}$ × 19 × 16$\frac{3}{8}$ins)
Onnasch Collection, Berlin
plate 28

OLDENBURG, Claes
159 *Green Ladies' Shoes* 1962
muslin, wire, plaster, enamel 30.5 × 40.6 × 40.6cm
(12 × 16 × 16ins)
The Mayor Gallery Ltd, London, and Thomas Ammann Fine Art, Zurich
plate 32

OLDENBURG, Claes
160 *Plate of Meat* 1961
muslin, wire, plaster, enamel 95 × 138 × 10.2cm
(39 × 53 × 4ins)
Onnasch Collection, Berlin
plate 29

OLDENBURG, Claes
161 *Sewing Machine* 1961
plaster, enamel 115 × 158cm (45$\frac{1}{4}$ × 62$\frac{1}{4}$ins)
Onnasch Collection, Berlin
plate 30

OLDENBURG, Claes
162 *U.S. Flag Fragment* 1961
muslin, wire, plaster, enamel 82 × 101cm (32$\frac{1}{4}$ × 39$\frac{3}{4}$ins)
Marc Landeau
plate 31

OLDENBURG, Claes
163 *Banana Splits and Glaces en Dégustation* 1964
plaster, tempera; glass case 53 × 100 × 51cm
(21 × 39$\frac{3}{8}$ × 20ins)
Ludwig Forum, Aachen
plate 74

OLDENBURG, Claes
164 *Giant Soft Toothpaste* 1964
vinyl, canvas, kapok, metal, wood, silicone
43.2 × 167.6 × 64.7cm (17 × 66 × 25$\frac{1}{2}$ins)
Barbara and Richard S. Lane
plate 75

OLDENBURG, Claes
165 *Model (Ghost) Medicine Cabinet* 1966
canvas, kapok, wood, metal, acrylic
90.2 × 61 × 16.5cm (35$\frac{1}{2}$ × 24 × 6$\frac{1}{2}$ins)
Moderna Museet, Stockholm
plate 56

OLDENBURG, Claes
166 *Soft Medicine Cabinet* 1966
vinyl, kapok, wood, metal, acrylic 90.2 × 61 × 16.5cm
(35$\frac{1}{2}$ × 24 × 6$\frac{1}{2}$ins)
Michael D. Abrams
plate 57

OLDENBURG, Claes
167 *Giant Saw – Hard Version* 1969
wood, aluminium, urethane foam 235 × 105 × 261cm
(92$\frac{1}{2}$ × 41$\frac{3}{8}$ × 102$\frac{3}{4}$ins)
Collection of the Vancouver Art Gallery, Bloedel Foundation, Murrin Bequest and Endeavour Auction Fund purchase 1969
plate 89

OLDENBURG, Claes
168 *Geometric Mouse – scale A* 1973
steel, aluminium, enamel 365.8 × 457.2 × 213.4cm
(144 × 180 × 84ins)
Moderna Museet, Stockholm
plate 90

OLDENBURG, Claes and VAN BRUGGEN, Coosje
169 *Bottle of Notes (Model)* 1989–90
aluminium, expanded polystyrene, latex
271.8 × 124.4 × 99 cm (107 × 49 × 39ins)
Leo Castelli Gallery and the Artists
plate 91

PAOLOZZI, Eduardo
170 *Real Gold* 1950
collage on paper 36.2 × 24.8cm (14$\frac{1}{4}$ × 9$\frac{3}{4}$ins)
Tate Gallery, Presented by the Artist
plate 103

PAOLOZZI, Eduardo
171 *Popular Mechanics* 1951
collage on paper 24 × 36cm (9$\frac{1}{2}$ × 14$\frac{1}{4}$ins)
The Board of Trustees of the Victoria and Albert Museum
plate 105

PAOLOZZI, Eduardo
172 *You can't beat the Real Thing* 1951
collage on paper 36 × 24cm (14$\frac{1}{8}$ × 9$\frac{1}{2}$ins)
The Board of Trustees of the Victoria and Albert Museum
plate 102

PAOLOZZI, Eduardo
173 *Yours Till the Boys Come Home* 1951
collage on paper 36.2 × 24.8cm (14$\frac{1}{4}$ × 9$\frac{3}{4}$ins)
Tate Gallery, Presented by the Artist 1971
plate 104

PAOLOZZI, Eduardo
174 *Four Towers* 1962
painted aluminium 203.2 × 77.5 × 78.5cm
(80 × 30$\frac{1}{2}$ × 31ins)
Scottish National Gallery of Modern Art
plate 128

PAOLOZZI, Eduardo
175 *Solo* 1962
painted aluminium 169.5cm high (66$\frac{3}{4}$ins high)
Paul and Linda McCartney
plate 127

PAOLOZZI, Eduardo
176 *Moonstrips Empire News* 1967
screenprints [selection from a total of 100]
38 × 25.5cm each (15 × 10ins each)
Michael D. Abrams
plate 150

PAOLOZZI, Eduardo
177 *Portrait of an Actor (for Luis Buñuel)* 1984
bronze 35 × 27.5 × 19.5cm (13$\frac{3}{4}$ × 10$\frac{7}{8}$ × 7$\frac{5}{8}$ins)
Collection of the Artist
plate 163

PHILLIPS, Peter
178 *Purple Flag* 1960
oil, collage and wax on canvas 213 × 184cm
(83$\frac{7}{8}$ × 72$\frac{3}{4}$ins)
Private Collection, London
plate 112

PHILLIPS, Peter
179 *Forces Sweetheart – Synchronised* 1962
oil and collage on canvas 180 × 180cm (70$\frac{7}{8}$ × 70$\frac{7}{8}$ins)
Private Collection, Brussels
plate 122

PHILLIPS, Peter
180 *Random Illusion No. 6* 1969
acrylic and tempera on canvas with lacquered wood
228 × 401cm (89$\frac{3}{4}$ × 157$\frac{7}{8}$ins)
Galerie Neuendorf, Frankfurt
plate 158

PHILLIPS, Peter
181 *Art-O-Matic Cudacutie* 1972
acrylic on canvas 200 × 400cm (78$\frac{3}{4}$ × 157$\frac{1}{2}$ins)
Galerie Neuendorf, Frankfurt
plate 159

PISTOLETTO, Michelangelo
182 *The Stove of Oldenburg (La Stufa di Oldenburg)* 1965
painted tissue paper on polished stainless steel
200 × 120cm (78$\frac{3}{4}$ × 47$\frac{1}{4}$ins)
Sonnabend Collection
plate 178

POLKE, Sigmar
183 *Biscuits (Kekse)* 1964
oil on canvas 80 × 75cm (31$\frac{1}{2}$ × 29$\frac{1}{2}$ins)
Städtische Galerie im Lenbachhaus, Munich
plate 187

POLKE, Sigmar
184 *Vase II* 1965
oil on flannelette sheet 90 × 75cm (35$\frac{1}{2}$ × 29$\frac{1}{2}$ins)
Kunstmuseum im Ehrenhof, Düsseldorf
plate 188

POLKE, Sigmar
185 *Woman at the Mirror (Frau vor Spiegel)* 1966
acrylic on fabric 125 × 80cm ($49\frac{1}{4}$ × $31\frac{1}{2}$ins)
Private Collection, London
plate 189

POLKE, Sigmar
186 *Heron Painting II (Reiherbild II)* 1968
dispersion on flannel 190 × 150cm ($74\frac{3}{4}$ × 59ins)
Courtesy Thomas Ammann, Zurich
plate 190

RAMOS, Mel
187 *Batmobile* 1962
oil on canvas 124.5 × 112cm (52 × 44ins)
Museum Moderner Kunst, Vienna, Bequest of the Austrian Ludwig Foundation
plate 41

RAMOS, Mel
188 *Miss Cushion Air (Miss Firestone)* 1965
oil on canvas 178 × 178 × 4.5cm (70 × 70 × $1\frac{3}{4}$ins)
Courtesy of The Louis K. Meisel Gallery, New York
plate 85

RAUSCHENBERG, Robert
189 *Gift for Apollo* 1959
combine painting: oil, fabric, paper on wood, rubber, metal 111.1 × 74.9cm ($43\frac{3}{4}$ × $29\frac{1}{2}$ins)
The Museum of Contemporary Art, Los Angeles: The Panza Collection
plate 11

RAUSCHENBERG, Robert
190 *Pilgrim* 1960
combine painting: oil on canvas, collage, wood 200 × 143 × 45cm ($78\frac{3}{4}$ × $56\frac{1}{4}$ × $17\frac{3}{4}$ins)
Onnasch Collection, Berlin
plate 12

RAUSCHENBERG, Robert
191 *Dylaby* 1962
combine painting: oil, metal, fabric, wood on canvas 278 × 221 × 38cm ($109\frac{1}{2}$ × 87 × 15ins)
Sonnabend Collection
plate 45

RAUSCHENBERG, Robert
192 *Spot* 1963
oil and silkscreen on canvas 147.3 × 101.6cm (58 × 40ins)
Staatsgalerie Stuttgart
plate 69

RAUSCHENBERG, Robert
193 *Retroactive II* 1964
oil and silkscreen ink on canvas 213.4 × 152.4cm (84 × 60ins)
Stefan T. Edlis Collection
plate 82

RAUSCHENBERG, Robert
194 *Courtyard (Urban Bourbon Series)* 1989
acrylic and enamel on enamelled aluminium 304.8 × 365.8cm (112 × 144ins)
Collection of the Artist
plate 97

RAYSSE, Martial
195 *Rose* 1962
acrylic and neon on canvas 182 × 131cm ($71\frac{5}{8}$ × $51\frac{1}{2}$ins)
Onnasch Collection, Berlin
plate 186

RAYSSE, Martial
196 *Simple and Quiet Painting* 1965
photograph, cardboard, oil on canvas, plastic 130 × 195cm (51 × $76\frac{3}{4}$ins)
Museum Ludwig, Ludwig Donation, Cologne
plate 185

RICHTER, Gerhard
197 *Folding Clothes Horse (Faltbarer Trockner)* 1962
oil on canvas 105 × 70cm ($41\frac{3}{8}$ × $27\frac{1}{2}$ins)
Fröhlich Collection, Stuttgart
plate 191

RICHTER, Gerhard
198 *Alfa Romeo (with Text) (Alfa Romeo [mit Text])* 1965
oil on canvas 150 × 155cm (59 × 61ins)
Private Collection Frieder-Burda, Baden-Baden, Courtesy Runkel-Hue-Williams, London
plate 193

RICHTER, Gerhard
199 *The Swimmers (Schwimmerinnen)* 1965
oil on canvas 200 × 160cm ($78\frac{3}{4}$ × 63ins)
Fröhlich Collection, Stuttgart
plate 192

RIVERS, Larry
200 *Kings* 1960
oil on canvas 132 × 152.4cm (52 × 60ins)
Collection Robert Julius and Andrea Bollt, New York
plate 22

RIVERS, Larry
201 *Final Veteran: The Last Civil War Veteran in the Coffin* 1961
oil on canvas 203.2 × 129.5cm (80 × 51ins)
Waddington Galleries
plate 21

RIVERS, Larry and TINGUELY, Jean
202 *Turning Friendship of America and France* 1961
oil on canvas; metal 204 × 104 × 81cm ($80\frac{1}{4}$ × 41 × $31\frac{7}{8}$ins)
Onnasch Collection, Berlin
plate 20

ROSENQUIST, James
203 *Hey, Let's Go for a Ride* 1961
oil on canvas 91.4 × 91.4cm (36 × 36ins)
Private Collection
plate 35

ROSENQUIST, James
204 *I Love You with My Ford* 1961
oil on canvas 210.2 × 237.5cm ($84\frac{1}{2}$ × 95ins)
Moderna Museet, Stockholm
plate 42

ROSENQUIST, James
205 *Look Alive (Blue Feet, Look Alive)* 1961
oil on canvas with mirror 170.2 × 148.6cm (67 × $58\frac{1}{2}$ins)
Michael D. Abrams
plate 36

ROSENQUIST, James
206 *Star Thief* 1980
oil on canvas 518.2 × 1402.1cm (204 × 552ins)
Private Collection, Courtesy Richard L. Feigen and Co.
plate 96

ROTELLA, Mimmo
207 *Scotch Brand* 1960
decollage on canvas 146 × 114cm ($57\frac{1}{2}$ × 45ins)
Giò Marconi, Milan
plate 165

ROTELLA, Mimmo
208 *Viva America* 1963
decollage on canvas 85 × 89cm ($33\frac{1}{2}$ × 35ins)
Giorgio Marconi, Milan
plate 176

RUSCHA, Ed
209 *Flash, L.A. Times* 1963
oil on canvas 182.9 × 170.2cm (72 × 67ins)
Courtesy of the Mead Corporation
plate 60

RUSCHA, Ed
210 *Talk about Space* 1963
acrylic on canvas, pencil 181 × 170cm ($71\frac{1}{4}$ × 67ins)
Onnasch Collection, Berlin
plate 61

RUSCHA, Ed
211 *The Los Angeles County Museum of Art on Fire* 1965–68
oil on canvas 135.9 × 339.1cm ($53\frac{1}{2}$ × $133\frac{1}{2}$ins)
Hirshhorn Museum and Sculpture Garden, Smithsonian Institution. Gift of Joseph H. Hirshhorn, 1972
plate 86

RUSCHA, Ed
212 *Now Then, As I Was About To Say* 1973
shellac on waterfall rayon 91.4 × 101.6cm (36 × 40ins)
PaineWebber Group Inc., New York
plate 92

RUSCHA, Ed
213 *Pacific Coast Highway* 1987
acrylic on canvas 152.4 × 137.2cm (60 × 54ins)
Collection Winnie Fung
plate 93

SAINT PHALLE, Niki de
214 *St Sebastian or the Portrait of My Love (Saint-Sebastian ou le Portrait de mon amour)* 1960
oil, paper, fabric and darts 72 × 55 × 7cm ($28\frac{1}{2}$ × $21\frac{3}{4}$ × $2\frac{3}{4}$ins)
Collection of the Artist
plate 168

SEGAL, George
215 *Woman Standing in a Bathtub* 1964
muslin, plaster, wire mesh, porcelain, metal, linoleum, wood and razor 161.9 × 167.6 × 110.5cm ($63\frac{3}{4}$ × 66 × $43\frac{1}{2}$ins)
Courtesy Fred Hoffman Gallery, Santa Monica, CA and Martin Lawrence Limited Editions, Inc.
plate 58

SEGAL, George
216 *Artist in His Loft* 1969
porcelain and metal 225 × 172.5 × 150cm ($88\frac{1}{2}$ × 70 × 59ins)
Onnasch Collection, Berlin
plate 59

SELF, Colin
217 *Nuclear Bomber* 1963
mixed media 27.3 × 61 × 49.5cm ($10\frac{3}{4}$ × 24 × $19\frac{1}{2}$ins)
Collection of the Artist
plate 140

SELF, Colin
218 *Girl with a Popsicle* 1964
pencil on paper 43.2 × 34.9cm (17 × $13\frac{3}{4}$ins)
Private Collection
plate 139

SELF, Colin
219 *Cinema 11* 1965
pencil and silver paper collage on paper 38.2 × 57cm (15 × $22\frac{1}{2}$ins)
James Kirkman, London
plate 144

SELF, Colin
220 *Cinema 14* 1965
aerosol spray paint and pencil 55 × 76cm ($21\frac{5}{8}$ × 30ins)
Collection of the Artist
plate 143

SELF, Colin
221 *Hot Dog 3 (14.3.65)* 1965
graphite pencil and chalk on paper 35.5 × 53cm (14 × $20\frac{7}{8}$ins)
Collection of the Artist
plate 141

SELF, Colin
222 *Public Shelter 110* 1965
pencil, coloured crayon and collage 55.75 × 38cm (22 × 15ins)
James Kirkman, London
plate 142

SMITH, Richard
223 *Formal Giant* 1960
oil on canvas 213.5 × 213.5cm (84 × 84ins)
Knoedler Kasmin Limited
plate 113

SMITH, Richard
224 *Alpine* 1963
oil on canvas 114 × 147 × 56cm ($44\frac{7}{8}$ × $57\frac{5}{8}$ × 22ins)
Private Collection
plate 134

SPOERRI, Daniel (*see also Fluxus*)
225 *The Playpen (Le Parc de bébé)* 1961
found objects, assemblage 120 × 140 × 55cm
(47¼ × 55⅛ × 21⅝ins)
Peruz Collection, Milan
plate 170

THIEBAUD, Wayne
226 *Five Hot Dogs* 1961
oil on canvas 45.7 × 60.9cm (18 × 24ins)
Collection of John Bransten
plate 40

THIEBAUD, Wayne
227 *Cake Counter* 1963
oil on canvas 152.4 × 183cm (60 × 72ins)
Museum Ludwig, Ludwig Donation, Cologne
plate 72

THIEBAUD, Wayne
228 *Jawbreaker Machine (Bubble Gum Machine)* 1963
oil on canvas 65.7 × 80.3cm (25⅞ × 31⅝ins)
The Nelson-Atkins Museum of Art, Kansas City, Missouri (Gift of Mr and Mrs Jack Glenn through the Friends of Art)
plate 73

TILSON, Joe
229 *A–Z Box of Friends and Family* 1963
mixed media 233 × 152.4cm (91¾ × 60ins)
Waddington Galleries
plate 133

TILSON, Joe
230 *Nine Elements* 1963
mixed media on wood 259 × 182.8cm (102 × 72ins)
Scottish National Gallery of Modern Art
plate 132

TILSON, Joe
231 *P.C. from N.Y.C.* 1965
screenprint on paper 198.4 × 65.7cm (78⅛ × 25⅞ins)
Waddington Graphics
plate 145

TILSON, Joe
232 *Page 7, Snow White and the Black Dwarf* 1969
screenprint and oil on canvas 125 × 186cm
(49¼ × 73¼ins)
Waddington Galleries
plate 153

TINGUELY, Jean
233 *Flat Iron (Fer à repasser)* 1962
plastic, iron, electric motor 53 × 50 × 45cm
(20⅞ × 19⅝ × 17¾ins)
Fogal Legfashion
plate 169

VILLEGLE, Jacques de la
234 *Boulevard St Martin* 1959
collage 222 × 245cm (87½ × 96½ins)
Onnasch Collection, Berlin
plate 166

VOSTELL, Wolf (*see also Fluxus*)
235 *Marilyn Monroe (Marilyn Idolo)* 1963
collage and decollage 157 × 122cm (61⅞ × 48ins)
Museum moderner Kunst, Vienna, Bequest of the Hahn Collection, Cologne
plate 175

WARHOL, Andy
236 *Saturday's Popeye* 1960
synthetic polymer paint on canvas 108.5 × 98.7cm
(43 × 39ins)
Ludwig Forum, Aachen
plate 24

WARHOL, Andy
237 *80 2-Dollar Bills, Front and Rear* 1962
silkscreen ink on canvas 210 × 96cm (83 × 38ins)
Museum Ludwig, Ludwig Donation, Cologne
plate 52

WARHOL, Andy
238 *Big Campbell's Soup Can (19¢)* 1962
synthetic polymer paint and pencil on canvas
183 × 137cm (72 × 54ins)
Private Collection
plate 47

WARHOL, Andy
239 *Do It Yourself: Landscape* 1962
synthetic polymer paint and Prestype on canvas
178 × 137cm (70 × 54ins)
Museum Ludwig, Ludwig Donation, Cologne
plate 48

WARHOL, Andy
240 *Blue Liz as Cleopatra* 1963
silkscreen ink and synthetic polymer paint on canvas 209 × 165cm (82¼ × 65ins)
Courtesy Thomas Ammann, Zurich
plate 66

WARHOL, Andy
241 *Early Colored Liz* 1963
silkscreen on canvas 101.6 × 101.6cm (40 × 40ins)
Private Collection; Courtesy of BlumHelman Gallery, New York
plate 64

WARHOL, Andy
242 *White Car Crash 19 times* 1963
synthetic polymer paint and silkscreen ink on canvas 368.3 × 211.5cm (145 × 83¼ins)
Courtesy Thomas Ammann, Zurich
plate 67

WARHOL, Andy
243 *Boxes* 1964
silkscreen ink on wood 28 Brillo boxes, each
44 × 43 × 35.5cm (17⅜ × 17 × 14ins); 14 Campbell's boxes, each 25.5 × 48 × 24cm (10 × 18⅞ × 9½ins)
Museum Ludwig, Ludwig Donation, Cologne
plate 68

WARHOL, Andy
244 *Marilyn* 1964
synthetic polymer paint and silkscreen ink on canvas 101.5 × 101.5cm (40 × 40ins)
Courtesy Thomas Ammann, Zurich
plate 65

WARHOL, Andy
245 *Flowers* 1966
acrylic and silkscreen enamel on canvas
207.6 × 356.9cm (81¾ × 140½ins)
Saatchi Collection, London
plate 83

WARHOL, Andy
246 *Mao* 1973
acrylic and silkscreen on canvas 448.3 × 346.1cm
(176½ × 136¼ins)
Saatchi Collection, London
plate 94

WARHOL, Andy
247 *Dollar Signs* 1981
silkscreen on synthetic polymer paint on canvas
228.6 × 177.8cm (90 × 70ins)
Lent by the Andy Warhol Foundation for The Visual Arts, Inc., New York
plate 95

WARHOL, Andy
248 *Raphael 1 – $6.99* 1985
synthetic polymer paint on canvas 396.9 × 294.6cm
(156¼ × 92ins)
Lent by the Andy Warhol Foundation for The Visual Arts, Inc., New York
plate 101

WATTS, Robert (*see also Fluxus*)
249 *Stamp Machine No. 4* 1961
metal 41 × 20 × 14cm (16⅛ × 8 × 5½ins)
Sohm Archive, Staatsgalerie Stuttgart
see page 227

WESLEY, John
250 *Olympic Field Hockey Officials* 1962
oil on canvas 183 × 183cm (72 × 72ins)
Onnasch Collection, Berlin
plate 54

WESSELMANN, Tom
251 *Great American Nude #1* 1961
mixed media and collage on board 121.9 × 121.9cm
(48 × 48ins)
Claire Wesselmann
plate 39

WESSELMANN, Tom
252 *Bathtub Collage #2* 1963
oil, collage and objects on board 122 × 185.5 × 15cm
(48 × 73 × 6ins)
The Mayor Gallery Ltd, London and Daniel Varenne, Geneva
plate 70

WESSELMANN, Tom
253 *Interior #1* 1964
mixed media and collage on board
152.4 × 121.9 × 10.2cm (60 × 48 × 4ins)
Norman and Irma Braman
plate 71

WESSELMAN, Tom
254 *Big Blonde #2* 1988
enamel on cut-out aluminium 175.3 × 238.8cm
(69 × 94ins)
Waddington Galleries
plate 99

WESTERMANN, H. C.
255 *Swingin' Red King and Silver Queen* 1960
wood and metal 212 × 74 × 61cm (76¾ × 29 × 24ins)
Private Collection
plate 27

WESTERMANN, H. C.
256 *A Little Black Cage* 1965
walnut, enamel and copper wire screen
39.4 × 29.2 × 31.7cm (15½ × 11½ × 12½ins)
The Peter and Chrissy Blake Collection
plate 79

WESTERMANN, H. C.
257 *Bowling Trophy* 1967
wood and stone 43 × 33 × 31cm (17 × 13 × 12ins)
The Peter and Chrissy Blake Collection
plate 78

WILLIAMS, Emmett
258 *Alphabet Symphony* 1963
26 mounted photographs
Sohm Archive, Staatsgalerie Stuttgart

biographies

Arman

b Nice, 1928

Born Armand Fernandez, Arman studied at the Ecole Nationale des Arts Décoratifs in Nice (1946–49) and at the Ecole du Louvre in Paris (1949–51). He met Yves Klein in 1948 through Judo classes. The two became close friends and collaborators, and they exhibited with the Nouveaux Réalistes from the inception of the group in 1960. In his early paintings, *Cachets* (Stamps), Arman made abstract images using impressions of inked rubber-stamps and later, for the *Allures d'objets* (Appearances of objects), functional objects dipped in paint. By 1959 he relied solely on the expressive power of the objects themselves and began his series of *Accumulations,* gathering together large quantities of identical mass-produced objects including cog wheels, shoe-trees, cameras and violins, and sealing them in plexiglass. The *Poubelle* (Wastebin) series of apparently random collections of rubbish culminated in 'Le Plein' (Fullness) in 1960, for which Arman packed the Galerie Iris Clert with truckloads of assorted refuse in response to Klein's exhibition 'Le Vide' (Emptiness) held there two years previously. Arman has pursued his interest in the cycle of production and consumption throughout his career. Parallel to

the *Accumulations,* he has also explored various ways of destroying objects by slicing, burning and smashing them. Acts of 'conscious vandalism' have included the dynamiting of a white MG sportscar in 1963 and the axing of a suite of standard American furniture during a gallery performance in New York in 1974. Since the 1970s Arman has made several outdoor sculptures, including the monumental *Long Term Parking* (1982), in which 60 cars are embedded in a vertical concrete slab. He divides his time between New York, Paris and Nice. *J. S.*

O. Hahn, *Arman*, Paris, 1972
J. van der Marck, *Arman,* New York, 1984
B. Lamarche-Vadel, *Arman,* Paris, 1987

Eduardo Arroyo

b Madrid, 1937

Eduardo Arroyo was educated at the Lycée Français in Madrid after which he trained and worked briefly as a journalist, but he was largely self-taught as an artist, producing his first paintings in the mid-1950s. In 1958 he moved to Paris where in 1961 he had his first one-man show at the Galerie Claude Lévin. His works of the early 1960s were

crudely painted, almost naive, images satirising authoritarian figures such as Napoleon. In 1963 a one-man show of his work was closed in Madrid and this confirmed his intention not to return to Franco's Spain. From the mid-1960s he turned to famous artists such as Diego Velázquez as a source for his work, and in the late 1960s he parodied the paintings of Joan Miró. In the context of his exile, this repeated treatment of Spanish subjects and artists gave his paintings a political edge lacking in most Pop Art. In a broader attack on art, his painting *In Defence to Traditions* (1965) expressed his dissatisfaction with accepted conventions by presenting four separate images of the same sugary pastoral scene, each executed in a different established style. By the 1970s he had developed a sleek technique reminiscent of that of René Magritte, which he applied to thematically related series such as *Winston Churchill, Painter* (1970). In another series, *Among the Painters* (1975–78), Arroyo likened painters to the movie gangsters of the 1930s, suggesting a similar greed for money and power. He painted the faces as coloured patches and executed others in collage using sandpaper. In the late 1970s and into the 1980s he created a series of sandpaper collages and paintings of boxers. In 1980 he introduced the tragicomic chimney sweep figure in a series of sandpaper collages and bronze heads that dominated his work until 1982, although this figure reappeared later. Absurdly attired in evening dress, the chimney sweep emerged as Arroyo's equivalent to the traditional figure of the harlequin. In paintings and mixed media works of the 1980s Arroyo also returned to the image of the gangster. *P. C.*

Paris 1982, *Eduardo Arroyo,* exhibition catalogue by G. Aillaud, C. Derouet, G. Gassiot-Talabot and B. Pautrat, Centre Georges Pompidou, Paris, 1982
New York 1983, *Eduardo Arroyo,* exhibition catalogue by D. Bozo, C. Derouet and W. Spies, Leonard Hutton Galleries, New York, 1983
Dortmund 1987, *Eduardo Arroyo: Theater – Boxen – Figuration,* exhibition catalogue by W. Spies et al., Museum für Kunst und Kulturgeschichte der Stadt Dortmund, Dortmund, 1987

Richard Artschwager

b Washington, DC, 1923

After studying science at Cornell University, Richard Artschwager moved to New York in 1949 and studied for a year with the Purist painter Amédée Ozenfant. After various jobs, he began making furniture commercially in 1953, and in 1960 he was commissioned by the Catholic Church to make portable altars for the US Navy. It was the first time that he had made something that was functional and yet at the same time transcended its use. After meeting Claes Oldenburg, who encouraged him to 'take himself seriously', in 1961, he gradually made the transition from craftsman to artist. In *Portrait 1* (1962) he combined the two elements that have since characterised his work: seemingly functional, body-scaled objects and framed, grisaille paintings on celotex. After *Portrait 1*, in which he had used painted furniture, Artschwager began to fabricate abstract furniture, covering blocks of

plywood with thin veneers of formica. By using different coloured formica he was able to suggest a functional object while retaining the effect of illusion. Initially concentrating on simple tables and chairs, he gradually experimented with more elaborate construction techniques. Paintings such as *Apartment House* (1964), in which images taken from photographs are transposed onto coarse-grained celotex, also explore the fusion of sculptural reality and pictorial fiction. Artschwager began showing at the Leo Castelli Gallery, New York, in 1963 and had his first one-man show there in 1965. In recent years he has made greater use of colour and the works are more exuberant and less 'purist' in appearance. Artschwager lives and works in Charlottesville, NY. *J. S.*

Buffalo 1979, *Richard Artschwager's Theme(s)*, exhibition catalogue, essays by R. Armstrong, L. L. Cathcart and S. Delehanty, Albright-Knox Art Gallery, Buffalo, NY, 1979

Basel 1985, *Richard Artschwager*, exhibition catalogue, essay by J.-C. Ammann, Kunsthalle, Basel, 1985

New York 1988, *Artschwager, Richard*, exhibition catalogue by R. Armstrong, Whitney Museum of American Art, New York, 1988

Clive Barker

b Luton, Beds, 1940

Clive Barker studied painting at Luton College of Technology from 1957 to 1959, but he left before completing the course because it failed to meet his expectations, choosing instead to work for eighteen months on the assembly line of the Vauxhall Motors car factory. He moved to London in 1961 and worked in a jeweller and pawnbroker's shop on the Portobello Road while continuing to paint. In his early sculptures he used leather (from 1962) and chrome-plated metal, the materials he was familiar with at Vauxhall Motors. During the late 1960s he produced facsimiles of everyday objects, such as buckets, false teeth and Coca-Cola bottles cast in bronze and chrome-plated, of symbolically charged objects such as cowboy boots and of objects associated with art, notably a pair of paint-boxes in chrome-plated steel and gold-plated brass. By coating his objects in a uniform shiny surface, he distanced them from reality and gave them a new, more 'perfect' identity. He also produced tributes to favourite

painters, including versions of *Van Gogh's Chair* (1966) and *Van Gogh's Sunflowers* (1969) in bronze. These homages were among his most Pop works. During the 1970s Barker explored the theme of the human head, for example in a group of gas-masks shown in 1974 and a series of life-masks of Francis Bacon. His most notable works of the 1980s included a series of variations on the Venus de Milo. *C. O.*

London 1968, *Clive Barker: Recent Works*, exhibition catalogue, text by C. Finch, Robert Fraser Gallery, London, 1968

Sheffield 1981, *Clive Barker: Sculpture, Drawings and Prints*, exhibition catalogue, text by G. Melly, Mappin Art Gallery, Sheffield, 1981

London 1987, *Clive Barker Portraits*, exhibition catalogue, introduction by N. Lynton, National Portrait Gallery, London, 1987

Ben

b Naples, 1935

Born Ben Vautier, he was educated at various places in Turkey, Egypt and Greece and in 1949 settled in Nice. A self-taught artist, in 1958 he bought a shop in Nice where he sold records and organised small exhibitions, among them a group exhibition in 1959 that included work by Martial Raysse, and his own first one-man show in 1960. His original name for the gallery, Laboratoire 32, was later changed to Galerie Ben Doute de Tout (Ben doubts everything). In 1958 he began to produce his characteristic paintings, consisting of large handwritten words on a plain background, often white on black, using single words or brief sentences; the banality of both the style and the words themselves had a subversive intent. More openly expressing this attitude were a number of 'Vomit Pictures' of 1958, in which he vomited onto an otherwise untouched canvas. In 1962 he took part in the 'Festival of Misfits' in London, and thereafter he became closely involved with Fluxus and its activities. Among his performance works were a number of 'gestes' or actions, such as sleeping or sweeping the road at predetermined times and places. The most extreme of these occurred in 1969, when he beat his head against a wall until his forehead bled. Among his more permanent works were a series of Fluxus editioned objects, often containers filled with banal objects, such as *Dirty Water* (1964). Such appropriation of objects as art reached an extreme in *Fluxbox Containing God*

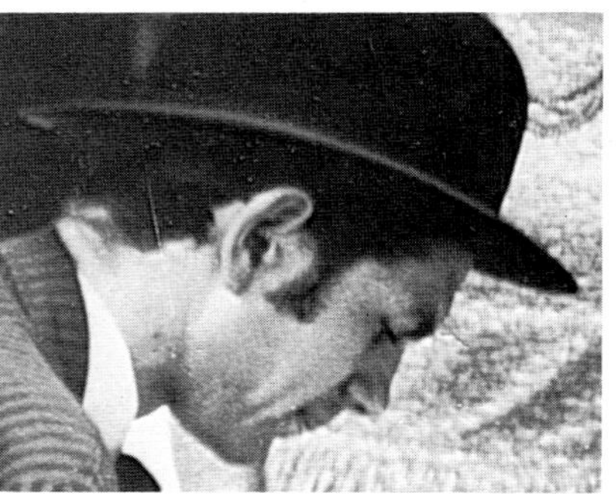

of 1961. Ben's concept of Total Art, proposed in 1965, expressed this attitude most fully by suggesting that all things – including objects and acts – were art. One of the most radical and nihilistic members of Fluxus, Ben participated in the activities of the movement into the 1970s. More recently, he has concentrated on producing word paintings in the style of his earlier works, visually relaying vague and negative messages, such as 'C'est sans importance'. *P. G.*

Amsterdam 1973, *Art=Ben: Ben Vautier*, exhibition catalogue by A. Petersen, Stedelijk Museum, Amsterdam, 1973

Ben Vautier, *Tout Ben*, Paris, 1974

Calais 1987, *Ben*, exhibition catalogue by G. Durozoï, Musée des Beaux-Arts, Calais, 1987

Billy Al Bengston

b Dodge City, 1934

Billy Al Bengston entered Los Angeles Junior College in 1953 to study ceramics and in 1955 moved to the California College of Arts and Crafts, Oakland, where he studied painting, printmaking and ceramics. From 1956 to 1957 he studied ceramics under Peter Voulkos at the Los Angeles County Art Institute but shortly afterwards abandoned the medium in favour of painting because of its craft connotation. His early canvases were abstract, showing the influence of Abstract Expressionism, and in 1958 he had his first one-man show at the Ferus Gallery in Los Angeles. While living in Europe from 1958 to 1959 he first saw reproductions of works by Jasper Johns. On his return to the USA his style radically altered; he adopted preconceived images, placing them at the centre of flatly painted backgrounds. The first motif was a 'Valentine' heart, followed by the 'sergeant-stripe' or chevron motif, as in *Clint* (1961), whose title was characteristically derived from the name of a Hollywood star. Though inevitably given a military interpretation, Bengston's intention with the 'sergeant-stripe', as with the heart, was to take a banal image and transform it into a work of art. The chevron was the dominant motif over the next ten years and by 1961 he began to use spraypaint to create complicated, brightly coloured backgrounds. There was a deliberate association with the 'customizing' of automobiles, a popular art form concentrated on

southern California. Some of the later examples were sprayed onto twisted aluminium sheets using car paint. He interrupted this series for a show at the Ferus Gallery in 1961, for which he painted works depicting parts of his BSA motorbike, such as *Carburetor Floatbowl* (1961). Again using banal, found imagery, this group of pictures, with its overt references to modern technology and youth culture, was an important contribution to nascent Pop Art. After its brief use in 1960, the 'Dracula' or iris motif dominated the works of the 1970s, often set against sensual, brightly coloured backgrounds in watercolour or acrylic. The works of the 1980s were flamboyant images of flowers, mask-like faces and the moon, inspired by a trip to Hawaii in 1978. *P. C.*

San Francisco 1968, *Billy Al Bengston: Motel Dracula*, exhibition catalogue by J. Monte, San Francisco Museum of Art, 1968
Los Angeles, Washington and Vancouver 1968–69, *Billy Al Bengston*, exhibition catalogue by J. Monte, County Museum of Art, Los Angeles, Corcoran Gallery, Washington, DC, Vancouver Art Gallery, 1968–69
Houston and Oakland 1988, *Billy Al Bengston: Painting of Three Decades*, exhibition catalogue by K. Tsujimoto et al., Contemporary Arts Museum, Houston, Oakland Museum, 1988

Peter Blake

b Dartford, Kent, 1932

Peter Blake trained as a graphic artist at Gravesend Technical College and School of Art (1946–49) and Gravesend School of Art (1949–51). As a teenager he developed an interest in folk art derived from the fairgrounds and wrestling matches he visited. During and just after his time at the Royal College of Art (1953–56) he painted his first pictures that could be described as Pop, such as *Siriol, She-Devil of Naked Madness* (1957), representing imaginary circus figures and painted to look like found pieces of fairground art. In 1956–57 Blake travelled around Europe on a Leverhulme scholarship, studying folk and popular art. From 1959, inspired by works he had seen in reproduction by Jasper Johns, Robert Rauschenberg and H. C. Westermann, he produced collage-based paintings of pop musicians, film stars and pin-up girls, such as *Kim Novak Wall* (1959), bold

Pop works that appeared to be quite different in technique from the meticulously painted works he had produced earlier. In these works he introduced subject matter that characterised British Pop during the next decade. In the late 1950s and early 1960s Blake dispensed with his drawing skills in favour of printed material, magazine photographs or postcards, which he collaged on to found or fabricated objects painted in bright colours. *Toy Shop* (1962) is an assemblage of cheap toys and ephemera arranged in a brightly-coloured shopfront constructed from a cupboard door and found window. In 1967 Blake produced the cover design for The Beatles' *Sergeant Pepper* album and made a multiple printed on tin, *Babe Rainbow*, which sold for £1. In 1969 he moved to Wellow, near Bath, forming the Brotherhood of Ruralists in 1975 with six friends. Over this period he returned to his earlier style of figurative realism, producing fairy pictures and paintings inspired by literary subjects. Since his return to London in 1979 he has painted both contemporary subjects and pictures rooted in fantasy. Elected ARA 1974, RA 1981. *C. O.*

Bristol 1969, *Peter Blake*, exhibition catalogue, introduction by R. Coleman, City Art Gallery, Bristol, 1969
London 1983, *Peter Blake*, exhibition catalogue by M. Compton, Tate Gallery, London, 1983
M. Vaizey, *Peter Blake*, London, 1986

Derek Boshier

b Portsmouth, Hants, 1937

Derek Boshier studied at Yeovil School of Art (1953–57), and at the Royal College of Art (1959–62) together with David Hockney, R. B. Kitaj, Allen Jones, Peter Phillips and Patrick Caulfield. His work differed from theirs in that it had a strong satirical edge. His paintings made frequent reference to current events, particularly those with a political dimension, and to the manipulation of people's lives through advertising. His paintings of consumer products such as Pepsi Cola appeared less a celebration of modern popular culture than an illustration of the Americanisation of British post-war society. A group of paintings made in 1962 on the theme of a new striped toothpaste examined the manipulative forces of advertising. Boshier's involvement with Pop Art was short-lived. In 1962 he went to India on a Commonwealth scholarship and produced a series of canvases,

most of them accidentally destroyed; they were related stylistically to his previous work, but the subject matter was centred on Hindu symbolism and mythology. On his return to England he painted hard-edge geometric abstracts. In 1966 he abandoned painting altogether and started making sculptures out of perspex and neon. For the next thirteen years he used photography, film and collage, though his work still had a strong political and social bias and a preoccupation with unmasking the more sinister sides of advertising. In 1979 Boshier started painting again. In 1980 he moved to Houston, as the Assistant Professor of Painting at the University of Houston. His paintings are rooted in the observation of people and their environment, now in the context of Texas. *C. O.*

Manchester 1975, *Derek Boshier: Work 1971–74*, exhibition catalogue by Derek Boshier, Whitworth Art

Gallery, Manchester, 1975
London 1982, *Derek Boshier: Texas Works*, exhibition catalogue by D. Brauer, Institute of Contemporary Arts, London, 1982
Liverpool, Edinburgh and Middlesbrough 1983, *Derek Boshier: Selected Drawings 1960–1982*, exhibition catalogue by M. Livingstone, Bluecoat Gallery, Liverpool, New 57 Gallery, Edinburgh, Cleveland Gallery, Middlesbrough, 1983

George Brecht

b Halfway, OR, 1925

George Brecht studied at the Philadelphia College of Pharmacy and Science (1946–50) and at the New School for Social Research in New York (1958–59). At the latter he studied musical composition with John Cage, his fellow students including Henry Flynt, Dick Higgins, Allan Kaprow and

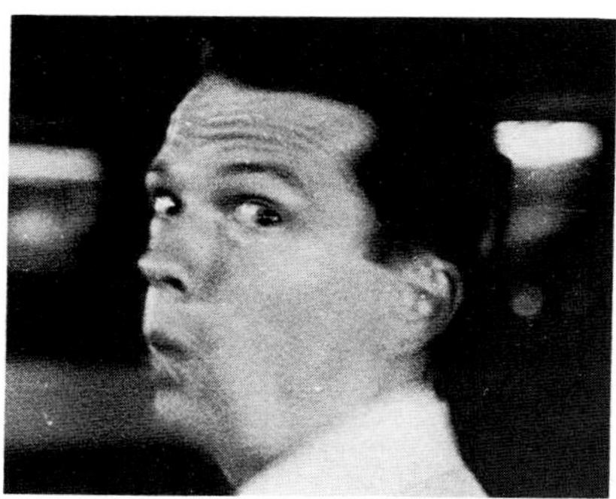

Jackson Mac Low. In the mid-1950s he was particularly interested in chance, experimenting with paint splashed onto canvas, folded and then allowed to blot. After working with Cage, however, he turned his attention to Events, some of them performance pieces, and these formed the basis of his first one-man show at the Reuben Gallery, New York, in 1959. The 'scores' for these were printed on small pieces of card, that for *Drip Music* (*Drip Event*), for example, stating 'For single or multiple performance. A source of dripping water and an empty vessel are arranged so that the water falls into the vessel'. Many of these cards were published as a Fluxus edition in 1963 in a box entitled *Water Yam*, and some were performed at Fluxus concerts. Together with Robert Filliou, from 1965 to 1968 he ran the shop La Cédille qui Sourit in Villefranche-sur-Mer, which sold small Fluxus works of art and other objects. He remained a central figure in Fluxus until its effective disintegration after the death of Maciunas in 1978. Having produced assemblages made from banal objets trouvés since *c.* 1960, in 1964 Brecht began a series of assemblages, often set in wooden boxes, which formed *The Book of the Tumbler on Fire*, a work still in progress. Divided into pages, chapters and volumes, Volume 1 was made from 1964 to 1969 in fourteen chapters, each consisting of a series of related assemblages. There were also 'Footnotes' comprising chairs with a few ordinary objects on them, many of which had an associated text from the *Guinness Book of Records*. More recently, as well as continuing the *Book*, he has produced a number of rocks carved with the word 'void' on them. Since 1972 he has lived in Cologne. *P. C.*

New York 1973, *George Brecht: Works 1957–1973*, exhibition catalogue by P. Frank et al., Onnasch Galerie, New York, 1973
Berne 1978, *Texte zu einer Heterospektive von George Brecht*, exhibition catalogue by H. Martin et al., Kunsthalle, Berne, 1978
H. Martin, *An Introduction to George Brecht's Book of the Tumbler on Fire*, Milan, 1978

Patrick Caulfield

b London, 1936

Patrick Caulfield studied at Chelsea School of Art (1956–60) and at the Royal College of Art (1960–63). He has mostly avoided using images from popular culture, painting instead landscapes, interiors and still lifes that are so traditional as to seem timeless.

Although familiar with American painting, in particular American Abstract Expressionism, the inspiration for his early work, such as *Engagement Ring* (1963), came primarily from European painters, such as Gris, Léger and Magritte. In spite of his protestations that he was not a Pop artist, he came close to the spirit of the movement in his use of a flat, graphic and impersonal style to portray mundane or corny subjects. In his search for anonymity through the use of familiar, even trite, images, he has created, paradoxically, a very personal style, capable of conveying with extreme subtlety a variety of moods and atmospheres. Until 1965 he painted on hardboard with glossy household enamel paints. In the early 1970s he produced large-scale paintings, many of them around 3 m (10 ft) in height, on the theme of domestic interiors, stripping down the composition to the essential elements of linear drawing over an expanse of a single colour. By the mid-1970s he began to elaborate this basic scheme by using different techniques within each painting, such as a precisely rendered trompe l'oeil realism, as in *Town and Country* (1979). Although never a prolific painter, since 1964 Caulfield has produced many screenprints, a medium well-suited to the flat areas of intense colour contained in uniform black lines characteristic of most of his work. *Buffet* (1987) shows his current aesthetic at its most extreme in its large format, in its virtual abstractness punctuated by trompe l'oeil details of extraordinary refinement and in its ability to convey both mood and a physically palpable atmosphere through apparently unpromising elements. *C. O.*

C. Finch, *Patrick Caulfield*, London, 1971
London 1981, *Patrick Caulfield: Prints 1964–81*, exhibition catalogue, introduction by B. Robertson, Waddington Galleries, London, 1981
Liverpool and London 1981–82, *Patrick Caulfield: Paintings 1963–81*, exhibition catalogue by M. Livingstone, Walker Art Gallery, Liverpool, Tate Gallery, London, 1981–82

César

b Marseilles, 1921

Born César Baldaccini, he studied at the Ecole des Beaux-Arts in Marseilles (1935–39) and at the Ecole Nationale Supérieure des Beaux-Arts in Paris (1943–48). Breaking from his academic training, by the late 1940s he was producing sculptures from iron wire and lead sheets. In 1952 he began making

welded sculpture from scrap iron and in 1954 had his first one-man show at the Galerie Lucien Durand in Paris. In the mid-1950s he concentrated on a series of sculptures made from welded scrap iron, representing angular, menacing birds and insects. In the late 1950s and early 1960s he produced a group of planar sculptures constructed from numerous small sections of welded iron. In 1958 he made the first of his *Compressions*, initially from pieces of metal. By 1960 he had turned to cars, which he crushed into rectangular blocks. The element of chance in this process and the appropriation of ready-made, commercial objects led César to become one of the founding members of the Nouveaux Réalistes in 1960. During the 1960s he continued to make *Compressions*, scrap metal works and distorted human figures in bronze, as well as sculptures representing grossly enlarged parts of the body, such as the thumb or breast, based on casts from life. As a counterpart to the *Compressions*, in 1967 he made his first *Expansion*, using a rapidly expanding, partially controllable, fluid polyurethane mixture that quickly solidified. From 1967 to 1970 he made *Expansions* in public as a sort of Happening and also extended the process by using molten glass and metal. In 1970 he began pouring foam or metal over objects such as busts or car doors. Early in the 1970s he made *Compressions* from plexiglass and later also from cardboard and paper. Since the 1980s he has continued to devise variations on all his earlier techniques, including a number of *Compression Portraits*, flattened compressions of objets trouvés so arranged as to suggest an illusionistic perspectival rendering of their three-dimensional equivalents. *P. C.*

D. Cooper, *César*, Amriswil, 1960
P. Restany, *César*, New York, 1976
P. Restany, *César*, Paris, 1988

Christo

b Gabrovo, Bulgaria, 1935

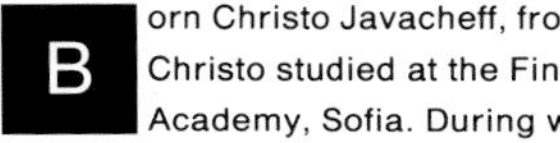

Born Christo Javacheff, from 1953 to 1956 Christo studied at the Fine Arts Academy, Sofia. During weekends he and fellow students worked for the state 'improving' the scenery along the route of the Orient Express by relocating farm equipment, stacking logs and covering haystacks with tarpaulins to demonstrate the apparent prosperity of the country. After six months in Prague, he ecaped to Vienna where he studied for a term at the Akademie der bildenden

Künste. He moved to Paris in 1958. There he came into contact with other artists who had joined together in 1960 to form the Nouveaux Réalistes, and he began wrapping found objects in cloth or polythene and tying them with string. Objects included bottles, cans, a Renault 4 car and copies of magazines such as *Der Spiegel* and *Look*. Although Christo shared the Pop artists' interest in consumer goods and their enhancement through packaging, in all his works the emphasis remains primarily on the fabric used for wrapping rather than the object wrapped. His first one-man exhibition was held in 1961 at the Galerie Haro Lauhus in Cologne, where he showed a variety of wrapped objects; at the same time he presented *Dockside Packages*, barrels covered by tarpaulins, in Cologne harbour. He moved to New York in 1964 and has since concentrated on increasingly ambitious projects, wrapping and transforming monuments, buildings, bridges and valleys. The most spectacular of these ephemeral works include *Running Fence* (1972–76), a white nylon fence, 39.6 km ($24\frac{1}{2}$ miles) long and 5.5 m (18 ft) high, stretching across northern California, and the *Surrounded Islands*, Biscayne Bay, FL (1980–83), for which he encircled 11 islands with 620,000 sq m (6.5 million sq ft) of pink polypropylene. *J. S.*

D. Bourdon, *Christo*, New York, 1970
J. Schellmann and J. Benecke, ed, *Christo: Prints and Objects, Catalogue Raisonné 1963–87*, introduction by W. Spies, Munich, 1988
Sydney and Perth 1990–91, *Christo*, exhibition catalogue, essays by A. Elsen, A. Bond, D. Thomas and N. Baume, Art Gallery of New South Wales, Sydney, 1990, Art Gallery of Western Australia, Perth, 1991

Allan D'Arcangelo

b Buffalo, NY, 1930

Allan D'Arcangelo studied writing at the New School for Social Research in New York (1953–54) and painting at Mexico City College (1957–59). He had his first show at

the Galería Genova, Mexico City, in 1958. His first Pop paintings concentrated on the human form, sometimes with a political charge or undercurrent of social satire. From these he developed the definitively Pop subject matter of auto-travel and road signs, as in the *U.S. Highway* series of 1963; but in his highly simplified and designed 'hard-edge' approach he is equally allied with Minimalism. Indeed, Nicholas Calas described the tree-edged parallel lines of *Landscape* (1967) as 'an abstract painting supported by a highway vocabulary'. The exclusion of detail and highly conventionalised perspective not only points up the banal and clichéd nature of the image but also increases the viewer's sense of a meaningless velocity, with the flatness of the picture bringing the horizon vertiginously close. As early as 1963 he used real materials such as wire fencing or Venetian blinds in conjunction with increasingly abstracted two-dimensional imagery. After a long prolific period, his output slowed to a near stop in the 1970s, when he returned to a more detailed and relatively naturalistic style. Power lines, a crop field and oil tanks were among the subjects of his 1982 one-man show at the Grace Borgenicht Gallery, New York, of which one critic observed a 'tendency to return to straight painting . . . the paintings could have been painted by a more brutal Georgia O'Keefe'. *E. B.*

Philadelphia and Buffalo 1971, *Allan D'Arcangelo: Paintings 1963–1970*, exhibition catalogue, essay by T. Towle, interview by S. Prokopoff, Institute of Contemporary Art, University of Pennsylvania, Philadelphia, Albright-Knox Art Gallery, Buffalo, NY, 1971
Purchase 1978, *Allan D'Arcangelo: Paintings of the Early Sixties*, exhibition catalogue, preface by Allan D'Arcangelo, Neuberger Museum, State University of New York at Purchase, 1978
Buffalo 1979, *The American Landscape: Paintings by Allan D'Arcangelo*, exhibition catalogue, introduction by D. Ashton, Burchfield Center, Western New York Forum for American Art, Buffalo, NY, 1979

Jim Dine

b Cincinnati, 1935

Jim Dine attended evening classes at the Art Academy of Cincinnati from 1951 to 1953 and from 1953 to 1957 studied at the University of Cincinnati and briefly at the Boston Museum School. He then attended Ohio University from 1957 to 1958 and in 1960 had his first one-man show at the Reuben Gallery in New York, during which he presented the Happening *Car Crash*, one of four performance works of that year. These Happenings, together with those performed at the time by Allan Kaprow, Claes Oldenburg and Red Grooms, were an important influence on the emergence of American Pop Art. Since the late 1950s Dine had incorporated real objects into his works, as in *Green Suit* (1959). Owing a debt to 'combines' by Rauschenberg such as *Bed* (1955), this savagely shredded and painted suit is a disquieting form of self-portrait. The use of clothing as a cypher for the self was repeated by Dine in the numerous *Robe* assemblages and paintings that he began to produce in 1964 and to which he has continued to return. Another extended theme, begun in 1962, was that of tools, which he used both as subjects for drawings and as found objects in assemblages such as *Summer Tools* (1962). Here, the vividly painted background has landscape connotations, while the tools themselves – as in all of Dine's work – are presented as extensions of the hand, emphasising the construction of the work of art as both a mundane and mysterious process. Such an interest in banal objects also

undermines the traditional limits on the subject matter of art. In 1963 Dine painted several works imitating commercial colour charts, further subverting questions about composition and subject matter, and in 1963–64 he produced a number of collage works using the form of an artist's palette. This recurrent reference to the artist in Dine's work sets it apart from the studied anonymity of most Pop Art. Furthermore he often drew attention to the hand-made quality of his works and to the role played by drawing, and he has displayed little interest in the style or subject matter of mechanically produced imagery. Apart from the tool and robe works, from the mid-1960s and into the 1980s he used a heart motif in a series of paintings, collages and sculptures, some of them also including tools. In the 1980s he added trees, gates and the Venus de Milo to his repertoire of favoured images. *P. C.*

D. Shapiro, *Jim Dine: Painting What One Is*, New York, 1981
Minneapolis 1984, *Jim Dine: Five Themes*, exhibition catalogue by G. W. J. Beal and R. Creeley, Walker Art Center, Minneapolis, 1984
C. W. Glenn, *Jim Dine: Drawings*, New York, 1985

Equipo Crónica

The Equipo Crónica ('Chronicle team') was formed in 1964 by the three Valencia-born artists Rafael Solbes (*b* 1940; *d* Valencia, 1981), Manuel Valdés (*b* 1942) and Juan Antonio Toledo (*b* 1940), although Toledo left in 1965. Solbes and Valdés had studied together at the Escuela de Bellas Artes de San Carlos in Valencia and in 1965 they had their first group show at the Galleria 'Il Centro' in Turin. The group's earliest works, from 1965, used repeated, graphic images in a grid format, reflecting the influence of American Pop Art. *America! America!* (1965), for example, uses the motif of Mickey Mouse's head on nineteen of the twenty panels, but the depiction on the remaining panel of the mushroom cloud following a nuclear explosion lends the work a barbed quality. Working in series, by 1967 the group began to use motifs and styles from widely-known artists. They favoured Spaniards such as Diego Velázquez, Picasso and Goya but also plundered the work of George Grosz, Kazimir Malevich, Ernst Ludwig Kirchner, René Magritte and others. *Guernica 69* (1969), for example, a series based on Picasso's mural size painting of 1937, presents Picasso's figures in an even more bloodied and mutilated state.

Often using their work to attack the Franco régime, in this series they make frequent allusion to sinister officials as a comment on the authoritarian climate of Spain at that time and to reinforce the message of Picasso's original. Violence and power were also evident in series such as *Police and Culture* (1971) and the *Black Series* (1972). The latter incorporated movie-type gangsters, as well as paint tubes and pencils, into compositions derived from artists such as Juan Gris and Yves Tanguy. The gangsters intrude into the seemingly hostile 'fine art' environments, suggesting the power of art and also the inextricable link between art and life. The group continued to work until Solbes's death in 1981, later series including *The Subversion of Signs* (1974–76), *The Game of Billiards* (1977) and *The Public and The Private* (1981). *P. C.*

T. Llorens, *Equipo Crónica*, Barcelona, 1972
Saint-Etienne, Rennes and Pau 1974–75, *Equipo Crónica*, exhibition catalogue by T. Llorens, Maison de la Culture, Saint-Etienne, 1974, Maison de la Culture, Rennes, 1974, Musée des Beaux-Arts, Pau, 1975
Valencia and Madrid 1989, *Equipo Crónica, 1965–1981*, exhibition catalogue by V. Bazal, M. Dalmace, Equipo Crónica and T. Llorens, IVAM Centre Julio González, Valencia, Centro de Arte Reina Sofia, Madrid, 1989

Robert Filliou

b Sauve, Gard, 1926; *d* 1987

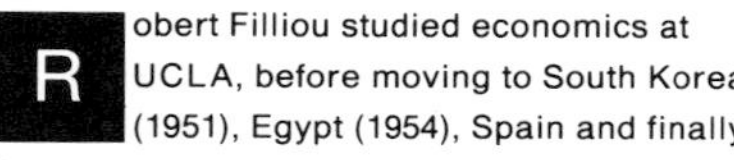

Robert Filliou studied economics at UCLA, before moving to South Korea (1951), Egypt (1954), Spain and finally Denmark, returning to France in 1959. In the streets of Paris in 1962 he started to exhibit works in a cap, which he called the Galerie Légitime. This held an exhibition of Benjamin Paterson's work in July and one of other Fluxus artists, including himself, in October. The single day 'Sneak Preview' Fluxus event was also organised under the auspices of the Galerie Légitime in Paris in July 1962. At the 'Festival of Misfits' in London in 1962 he performed his work *Bowling Game*, in which balls with labels such

as 'When you see Filliou' were rolled towards pins inscribed with such phrases as 'Think of Spoerri'. Filliou was also a participant in later Fluxus events, though not on a regular basis. In the early 1960s he was particularly interested in poetry and made a number of 'object poems' from pieces of wood hooked together, onto which he stuck printed lines of poetry and other objects. In the same period he made a number of *Poi-Poi Beer* works with Køpcke, each consisting of empty beer bottles appropriated as art by a label stuck on by the artists. During the 1960s several of his objects, such as *Fluxdust*, a plastic box full of dust, were issued as Fluxus editions. With George Brecht, from 1965 to 1968 he ran the shop La Cédille qui Sourit in Villefranche-sur-Mer, which sold jewellery, games and small works of Fluxus art. In 1970 he founded the République Géniale, a notional republic devoted to the cultivation of human genius, producing various assembled works as part of its activities. From the late 1960s up to the present Filliou has made assemblages of objets trouvés often incorporating related handwritten texts. Many of these form 'research projects', such as the *Research on Art and Astrology* (1969) and *9 Weeks of Research on Futurology* (1972). *P. C.*

Hanover, Paris and Berne 1984–85, *Das Immerwährende Ereignis zeigt/The Eternal Network Presents/La Fête Permanente présente: Robert Filliou*, exhibition catalogue by Robert Filliou, Sprengel-Museum, Hanover, 1984, Musée d'Art Moderne de la

Ville de Paris, 1984, Kunsthalle, Berne, 1985
Düsseldorf 1987, *Robert Filliou 1926–1987 zum Gedächtnis*, exhibition catalogue by H. W. Schmit et al., Städtische Kunsthalle, Düsseldorf, 1987
J. Hendricks, *Fluxus Codex*, New York, 1988, pp. 238–46

Joe Goode

b Oklahoma City, 1937

In 1959 Joe Goode followed his childhood friend, Ed Ruscha, to Los Angeles to study advertising design at the Chouinard Art Institute where he stayed until 1961. In 1962, together with Wayne Thiebaud, Mel Ramos and others, Goode and Ruscha were included in 'New Painting of Common Objects', a prescient 'Pop' exhibition at the Pasadena Art Museum. Goode exhibited a series of *Milk Bottle Paintings* influenced by Jasper Johns, which were also shown in his first solo show at the Dilexi Gallery, Los Angeles, the same year. These works, which an early reviewer called 'the loneliest paintings imaginable', combine a painterly monochrome abstraction with a Pop engagement with the found object. In his *House* series of 1963 the artist isolated a pencil drawing of a typical American dwelling on a disproportionately large painted ground, as if to comment on the isolation of suburban life. By 1964 he had begun a series of *Staircases* akin to the ready-mades of Duchamp: constructed of plywood and covered with carpet, they appear real but are merely illusions since they are non-functional and rely on the surrounding wall to act both as field and support. Much of Goode's work is introspective; in the 1960s he used household or commonplace objects to probe our visual perception, rather than to glorify consumerism. Since the early 1970s Goode's

work has moved away from Pop, but he has continued to explore notions of perception. He lives in California, dividing his time between Springville in the Sierra Nevada and his studio in the Los Angeles suburb of Venice. *S. F.*

Fort Worth 1972, *Joe Goode: Work Until Now*, exhibition catalogue by H. T. Hopkins, Fort Worth Art Center, 1972
Newport Beach et al. 1989, *LA Pop in the Sixties*, exhibition catalogue, Newport Harbor Art Museum, Newport Beach, 1989, pp. 107–15
Santa Monica 1990, *Joe Goode: Waterfall Paintings*, exhibition catalogue by N. Halpern Brougher, James Corcoran Gallery, Santa Monica, 1990

Raymond Hains

b Saint-Brieuc, France, 1926

Raymond Hains studied sculpture at the Ecole des Beaux-Arts in Rennes in 1945, where he met Jacques de la Villeglé, but left after only a few months. In 1946 he produced his first abstract photographs and the following year experimented with a distorting lens which had wide, parallel grooves on its surface. The effect of using this was to splinter objects photographed through it, resulting in what Hains called 'hypnogogic' photographs. In 1947 he had his first one-man show, of photographs, at the Galerie Colette Allendy in Paris. Over the next few years he developed his 'hypnogogic' process applying it to the production of abstract films as well as photographs. In collaboration with Villeglé, he published *Hépérile éclaté* (Paris, 1953), using his 'hypnogogic' process to produce a series of splintered, typographic images of Camille Bryen's phonetic poem *Hépérile*. This rendered the text illegible and further atomised the language into a series of marks as opposed to phonetic sounds. He continued to use the

'hypnogogic' process into the 1960s. Pursuing a similar theme, since 1949 he had been gathering torn posters, *affiches lacérées* (*décollages*), finding in these the same mutilation of image he contrived in his photography. Together with Villeglé he displayed a selection of these in the 1957 exhibition 'Loi du 29 Juillet 1881' at the Galerie Colette Allendy, named after the date of the law banning posters. In 1960 he became a member of the Nouveaux Réalistes and later participated in exhibitions of *affiches lacérées* with Dufrêne, Rotella and Villeglé. Since 1959 he has also exhibited *affiches lacérées* on their original wood or metal hoardings. Constructing Pop sculptures from consumer objects, in 1965 he exhibited a number of vast matchboxes at the Galerie Iris Clert in Paris. More recently, while continuing to produce *affiches lacérées*, he has also produced photographs of them in situ, as well as photographs of shop signs and other commercial images. *P. C.*

Paris 1976, *Raymond Hains et la photographie*, exhibition catalogue, Centre National d'Art Moderne, Paris, 1976
Saint-Etienne 1976, *Beautés Volées*, exhibition catalogue by B. Cesson, Musée d'Art et d'Industrie, Saint-Etienne, 1976, pp. 19–32
Paris 1990, *Guide des Collections Permanentes ou mises en plis: Raymond Hains*, exhibition catalogue by C. David et al., Centre Georges Pompidou, Paris, 1990

Richard Hamilton

b London, 1922

After a varied career, both academic and practical, Richard Hamilton became from 1952 a leading member of the Independent Group, which analysed the products of mass culture. His collage *Just what*

is it that makes today's homes so different, so appealing?, made in 1956 as the design for the poster for the Whitechapel Gallery exhibition 'This is Tomorrow', is now recognised as one of the earliest Pop works. This was followed by paintings such as *$he* (1958–61) and *Hommage à Chrysler Corp* (1957), in which he made direct use of a large range of images culled from advertising, making reference to such presentation techniques but painting them in the modernist tradition of Cézanne and early Cubism. He has often produced works in series, such as *Towards a definitive statement on the coming trends in men's wear* (1962). In 1963 he made his first screenprint, and he subsequently translated the images of many of his most important Pop paintings into this medium. Screenprinting gave him the chance to enlarge the technical vocabulary of the paintings by incorporating fragments from different sources, including photography, with wit and ingenuity, as in the *Swingeing London* series (1968–69), screenprinted from a newspaper photograph showing Mick Jagger and the art dealer Robert Fraser being arrested on drugs charges. Actual photographs were also collaged to the surface of certain paintings such as *My Marilyn* (1965), while *I'm dreaming of a white Christmas* (1967–68) was painted by hand but based on the colour negative of a film still. Hamilton taught in the fine art department of the University of Newcastle-upon-Tyne from 1953 to 1966; among the many students whose work he influenced were Rita Donagh, Mark Lancaster, Tim Head, Stephen Buckley, Tony Carter and Bryan Ferry. A prolific writer, Hamilton has produced articulate texts on all his major works. *C. O.*

London, Eindhoven and Berne 1970, *Richard Hamilton*, exhibition catalogue by R. Morphet, Tate Gallery, London, Stedelijk van Abbemuseum, Eindhoven, Kunsthalle, Berne, 1970
Richard Hamilton, *Collected Words, 1953–82*, London, 1982
Winterthur, Hanover and Valencia 1990–91, *Richard Hamilton: Exteriors, Interiors, Objects, People*, exhibition catalogue by D. Schwarz, S. Bann, R. Hamilton, L. Cooke and S. Maharaj, Kunstmuseum, Winterthur, Kestner-Gesellschaft, Hanover, IVAM, Centre Julio González, Valencia, 1990–91

David Hockney

b Bradford, West Yorks, 1937

David Hockney studied at Bradford College of Art (1953–57). He had already acquired a national reputation by the time he left the Royal College of Art with the gold medal for his year in 1962. He studied there with R. B. Kitaj, Allen Jones, Peter Phillips, Derek Boshier and Patrick Caulfield. Before he had left the Royal College he was approached by the dealer John Kasmin and he had his first exhibition with him in 1963 when he was 26. His

relationship to Pop Art was somewhat marginal, but his games with style and references to graffiti and packaging in works such as *Adhesiveness* (1960) and *I'm in the Mood for Love* (1961) led him to be identified with the movement. In late 1963 Hockney moved to Los Angeles, making it his base until his return to London in 1967. The life of southern California, with its open spaces, rectilinear architecture, sensuous life style, vivid light and bright colour had an overwhelming effect on the works he produced during this period. His style became more naturalistic and he began to work more from photographs and drawings made directly from life. Increasingly he drew attention to his use of the camera by producing images, painted in acrylic, within a bare canvas border which made them look like greatly enlarged photographs. Since 1974 Hockney has designed sets and costumes for a number of opera productions, for example for Glyndebourne and for the Metropolitan Opera in New York. Although he has long distanced himself from Pop Art, preferring in recent years to cite Picasso as his greatest inspiration, in his fascination with technological development – with Polaroid photography, photocopying, four-colour reproduction and images sent by Fax machine – he has continued to pursue a line of investigation particularly associated with the movement. Since 1979 he has again made Los Angeles his main home. Elected ARA 1985, RA Elect 1991. *C. O.*

N. Stangos, ed., *David Hockney by David Hockney*, London, 1976
M. Livingstone, *David Hockney*, London and New York, 1981 and 1987
Los Angeles, New York and London 1988–89, *David Hockney: A Retrospective*, exhibition catalogue, ed. M. Tuchman and S. Barron, Los Angeles County Museum of Art, The Metropolitan Museum of Art, New York, Tate Gallery, London, 1988–89

Robert Indiana

b New Castle, IN, 1928

Born Robert Clark, he trained from 1949 to 1953 at the Art Institute of Chicago, followed by a summer at Skowhegan School of Painting and Sculpture, Maine, in 1953. He spent a year at the University of Edinburgh from 1953 to 1954 and on his return to the USA he settled in New York. In 1955 he met Ellsworth Kelly, whose hard-edge abstraction helped shape his style in the late 1950s. When he moved to a new studio at Coenties Slip in 1956 his

neighbours included not only Kelly and other abstract painters such as Jack Youngerman and Agnes Martin but also another future Pop artist, James Rosenquist. From 1960 to 1962 Indiana produced constructions made predominantly of wood and other objets trouvés, in particular a series of *Herms* which, like their Classical predecessors, had large wooden phalluses and often metal wheels, suggestive of a chariot, as in *Hole* (1960). In this case, the arrows pointing to the hole counteract the male symbolism through tautology. In 1961 Indiana started producing austere paintings using large stencilled letters and hard-edged designs, further confirming the impact of Kelly's work. Indiana's adoption in these works of the minimal appearance of signs and commercial imagery demonstrated his desire to capture the experience of modern America, a goal also reflected in his decision to change his name to that of his native state. Their reference is often personal as well, however, as in *Eat/Die* (1962), which refers in part to the fact that his mother's last word was 'Eat'. Several of the sign works of 1961 and 1962 related to his love for American writers such as Herman Melville, while a number of works from 1963 using the figure five were homages to *I Saw the Figure Five in Gold* (1928) by Charles Demuth, an artist he greatly admired. In 1966 he initiated a series of paintings consisting of the word 'Love', an embodiment of the idealism of that decade. He also extended these into three dimensions in large aluminium sculptures. Indiana has continued to develop the sign works of the 1960s in paintings, aluminium sculptures, occasional constructions and public *Love* sculptures in steel. *P. C.*

Philadelphia, San Antonio and Indianapolis 1968, *Robert Indiana*, exhibition catalogue by J. W. McCoubrey, Institute of Contemporary Art, Philadelphia, Marion Kooger McNay Art Institute, San Antonio, TX, Herron Museum of Art, Indianapolis, 1968
Washington 1984, *Wood Works: Constructions by Robert Indiana*, exhibition catalogue by V. M. Mecklenburg, National Museum of American Art, Smithsonian Institute, Washington, DC, 1984
C. J. Weinhardt, Jr, *Robert Indiana*, New York, 1990

Alain Jacquet

b Neuilly, France, 1939

Alain Jacquet attended the University of Grenoble and afterwards studied architecture at the Ecole Nationale des Beaux-Arts in Paris from 1959 to 1960. In 1961 he had his first one-man show at the Galerie Breteau in Paris. Among these early works was the brightly coloured *Jeu de Jacquet* (*Game of Backgammon*) of 1961, a pun on his surname in the form of a backgammon board. In 1962 he initiated a series of 'camouflage' works, spreading brightly coloured designs over objects such as sculpted heads, whose form declared them to be works of art. He then used banal, commercial images as a camouflage by superimposing them over images of famous paintings, thus forcing a deliberate clash of styles and cultures. In 1963 he painted a large camouflaged version of a painting of a hot dog by Roy Lichtenstein, which he then cut up and sold in pieces as a provocative comment on the art market as just another form of consumerism. In 1964 he painted the first of a series, *Le*

Déjeuner sur l'Herbe, based on a photographic recreation of Manet's famous painting with the critic Pierre Restany and other friends as models. Enlarging and manipulating the image to reveal the constituent colour dots, he produced a blurred effect suggestive of a massively magnified printed surface. These and related works, to which the term 'Mec Art' was applied in 1965, were made in a variety of ways: for example by screenprinting, by painting on plexiglass or by projecting the image onto photo-sensitised canvas. Such methods, adapted from techniques of mass reproduction, also allowed him to replicate the motif in endless variations. In some cases he enlarged details to make the image virtually abstract. In the late 1960s he began to produce sculptures in deceptive materials, such as a plank of wood made from plexiglass and printed wood designs, further emphasising the deceptive nature of art and, by implication, of the perceived world. In his paintings since the 1980s he has continued to investigate contemporary imagery, for instance in a series of paintings of Earth taken from outer space, and to experiment with alternative modes of mechanical reproduction such as laser-printing. *P. C.*

Zurich 1965, *Alain Jacquet*, exhibition catalogue by O. Hahn, City-Galerie, Zurich, 1965
Paris 1978, *Alain Jacquet: Donut Flight 6078*, exhibition catalogue by S. Pagé and L. Bossé, Musée d'Art Moderne de la Ville de Paris, 1978
D. Smith, *Alain Jacquet*, Paris, 1990

Jess

b Long Beach, CA, 1923

Born Jess Collins, he worked as a radiochemist and then went to the California School of Fine Arts in 1949, where he studied under Clyfford Still, Hassel Smith and Edward Corbett. His partnership with the poet Robert Duncan began in 1951 and in 1953 they ran the King Ubu Gallery in San Francisco, along with Harry Jacobus. Jess had his first one-man show of 'paste-up collages' and 'junk assemblages' in1954 at The Place, a San Francisco 'beat' bar and gallery, and during that period also developed both figurative and abstract oil paintings along what he has termed 'romantic-mythopoetic' lines. Frustrated by what he perceived as his lack of figurative mastery, he was attracted to collaging ready-made imagery. In works such as the *Tricky Cad* paste-up series of 1954–59, culled from the Dick Tracy

comic strip and using an anagram of the name as the title, he shows a characteristic precision in disorder which extends to his later interest in jigsaw imagery. He regarded the intricacy and density of his own work as presenting a network of narrative choices for the viewer, rather in the manner of Max Ernst's collages. In 1959 he began the first painting of his 'self-initiatory quest', the *Translations* series, which 'translate' a found image into a thick impasto painting. Although Jess has made use in his work of popular imagery, his aesthetic is on the fringes of Pop. It is the spiritual work of a sentimental collector, a deeply private romantic, rather than a public ironist. He has recently worked on an elegiac monochrome paste-up series *Emblems for Robert Duncan*, and on *Narkissos*, a large composite *Translation* on a homoerotic theme. *E. B.*

Dallas 1977, *Translations, Salvages, Paste-Ups by Jess*, exhibition catalogue, introduction by R. Duncan, Dallas, Museum of Fine Arts, 1977
Sarasota 1983, *Jess: Paste-ups and Assemblies 1951–1983*, exhibition catalogue by M. Auping, foreword by R. B. Kitaj, John and Mable Ringling Museum of Art, Sarasota, FL, 1983

Jasper Johns

b Augusta, GA, 1930

After studying from 1947 to 1948 at the University of South Carolina, Jasper Johns moved to New York in 1949, where he briefly attended a commercial art school before being drafted into the US army, with which he was stationed in Japan. After returning to New York in 1952 he attended Hunter College for two days and then supported himself by working in a bookshop and making display work for department stores. In 1954 he met Robert Rauschenberg, who became a close friend and important influence. The first *Flag, Target* and *Number* paintings were made in the mid-1950s and were shown in Johns's first one-man exhibition at the Leo Castelli Gallery, New York, in 1958. The seemingly impassive reproduction of familiar, two-dimensional objects had a tremendous impact, and Johns's dissociation of painting from self-expression unwittingly marked the arrival of Pop and the end of the Abstract Expressionist reign. Although widely acknowledged as an important precursor of Pop, Johns has always tried to distance himself from the movement in order to preserve the ambiguity of his works. By using bold, commonplace imagery, 'things which the mind already knows', Johns was able to 'work

on other levels', to explore the function of paint on canvas and to draw attention to the subtle changes made by the artist in producing variations of the same image. In 1960 he began making a number of small sculptures, casting lightbulbs, ale cans and flashlights in bronze, emphasising their ordinariness through the use of a revered medium. Since the 1960s drawing and printmaking have been important aspects of his work, as have his collaborations with the composer John Cage and choreographer and dancer Merce Cunningham. Johns lives and works in Stony Point, NY. Elected Honorary RA 1989. *J. S.*

M. Kozloff, *Jasper Johns*, New York, [1969]
M. Chrichton, *Jasper Johns*, New York and London, 1977
D. Shapiro, *Jasper Johns Drawings 1954–1984*, New York, 1984

Ray Johnson

b Detroit, 1927

Ray Johnson studied at the Art Students League in New York (1944–45) and then attended Black Mountain College in North Carolina (1945–48), studying under Josef Albers, Robert Motherwell, Ossip Zadkine and others. In 1948 he had his first one-man show at the One Wall Gallery in New York. From 1949 to 1952 he was a member of American Abstract Artists, exhibiting abstract works alongside painters such as Ad Reinhardt. By the mid-1950s, however, influenced by Robert Rauschenberg and Cy Twombly, he started to produce 'moticos'. These were small collages with additions in ink and paint made over magazine and newspaper photographs. Some of them

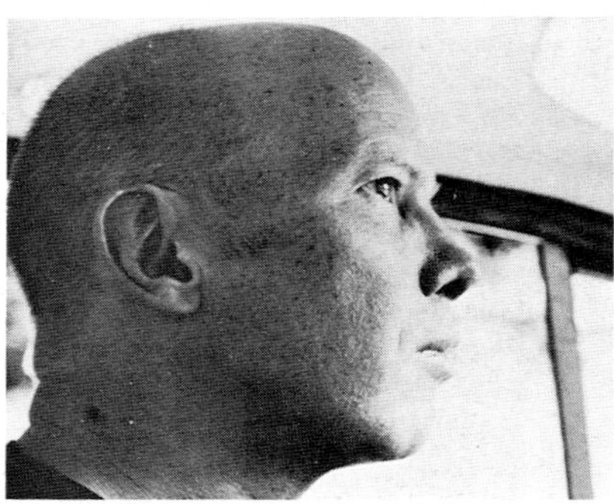

were centred on cult figures, as in *Elvis Presley 2* (1955) and *James Dean* (1958), in which he used the collage and other added elements to poke fun at revered personalities. His use of mass imagery and concern with the icons of the star system prefigured later Pop Art developments. Also in the late 1950s he made a number of small collages from overpainted printed images cut into strips and then rearranged and mounted, as in *Hand Marilyn Monroe* (1958). In the early 1960s he started producing 'mail art' works in which collages and other cuttings were sent by mail, the contents having some reference to the recipient. After his one-man show at the Marian Willard Gallery in New York in 1965 his collages increased in both size and complexity, often including earlier recycled collages and using photographs, handwritten texts and painted board. Sometimes these were mocking homages to past artists such as Leonardo da Vinci, Mondrian or Magritte. From 1968 to 1973 he founded and ran the New York Correspondence School of Art, which sent out works of 'mail art'. Through the 1970s and since, Johnson has continued to produce collage and 'mail art' works, relating the former to all aspects of culture: writers, artists and actors. *P. C.*

Raleigh 1976, *Correspondence: An Exhibition of the Letters of Ray Johnson,* exhibition catalogue, introduction by W. Wilson, North Carolina Museum of Art, Raleigh, 1976

W. Wilson, ed., *Ray Johnson Ray Johnson,* New York, 1977

Roslyn Harbor 1984, *Works by Ray Johnson,* exhibition catalogue by D. Bourdon, Nassau County Museum of Fine Art, Roslyn Harbor, NY, 1984

Allen Jones

b Southampton, Hants, 1937

Allen Jones entered the Royal College of Art in 1959 with R. B. Kitaj, Peter Phillips, David Hockney and Derek Boshier, but after a tempestuous relationship with the college authorities he was expelled at the end of his first year. He returned to Hornsea College of Art in London, where he had previously studied, to do a teacher training course. However, the friendships that he had made at the Royal College and the sense of involvement he felt in the early stages of a new

movement gave him the determination to pursue the new direction he had already found for himself. His paintings *The Artist Thinks* (1960) and *Thinking about Women* (1961) were among the earliest paintings to include reference to comic strips. These were followed in 1962 by a series of *Bus* paintings, a sustained investigation of the relationship between the shape of the canvas and implied movement. In 1964–65, while living in New York, Jones developed his full-blown Pop style, moving from a painterly technique to a harder, more graphic, style and from a gentle eroticism to openly fetishistic images. In 1969 he produced a set of fibreglass sculptures of life-size women dressed in high leather boots and bondage wear in the posture of a piece of furniture. These were his most extreme statements as a Pop artist. In 1970 he designed the set and costumes for part of the production of *O Calcutta* in London. Since the early 1970s he has taught at various art schools in America, Canada and Germany. He has now returned in his paintings and sculptures to a more formal and stylised approach to the figure, though colour and the human form remain his fundamental concerns. Elected ARA 1981, RA 1986. *C. O.*

Allen Jones, *Figures,* Berlin and Milan, 1969

M. Livingstone, *Allen Jones Sheer Magic,* New York, 1979

Liverpool et al., 1979, *Allen Jones: Retrospective of Paintings 1957–78,* exhibition catalogue by M. Livingstone, Walker Art Gallery, Liverpool, 1979

Allan Kaprow

b Atlantic City, NJ, 1927

After studying art at New York University (1945–49), Allan Kaprow studied painting under Hans Hoffman at the Hans Hoffman School of Fine Arts in New York (1947–48) and art history at Columbia University under Meyer Schapiro (1950–52). He co-founded the Hansa Gallery in New York in 1952 and had his first one-man show there in 1953. He started to make collages in 1953 and in 1955–56 he painted a number of canvases in a gestural style indebted to Jackson Pollock. These were followed in 1956–57 by 'action-collages' incorporating a variety of materials, such as newspaper, straw and wire, overpainted in an Abstract Expressionist manner. From 1957 to 1959 he studied at the New School for Social Research in New York under John Cage, whose interest in the role of chance had a great effect on his work. From this time onwards Kaprow

gave up traditional fine art forms and turned to Environments and Happenings, producing his first such Environment in 1957. These varied in complexity, some involving lights and music as well as objects. One of the simplest but most effective was *The Yard* (1961), which consisted of a delimited space filled with tyres. In 1959 he presented *18 Happenings in Six Parts* at the Reuben Gallery in New York, publicly establishing the new art form. This involved six players and a fairly detailed script for both participants and audience. Kaprow stopped making Environments in 1965 to concentrate on Happenings, which after 1968 he modified to 'Activities'. These were less theatrical than the Happenings and were enacted from simple scripts. Breaking with the established traditions of art by his unconventional, conceptual approach, Kaprow has continued to perform his Activities around the world. *P. C.*

Pasadena 1967, *Allan Kaprow,* exhibition catalogue by B. Berman, Pasadena Art Museum, Pasadena, CA, 1967

Bremen 1976, *Allan Kaprow,* exhibition catalogue by J. Diedrichs, Kunsthalle, Bremen, 1976

Dortmund 1986, *Allan Kaprow,* exhibition catalogue, Museum am Ostwall, Dortmund, 1986

Edward Kienholz

b Fairfield, WA, 1927

A self-taught artist, Edward Kienholz had his first one-man show at the Café Galeria in Los Angeles in 1955. In 1956 he opened the Now Gallery in Los Angeles, one of the first avant-garde galleries in that city. It closed the following year and he and Walter Hopps then opened the Ferus Gallery, where Ed Ruscha and Billy Al Bengston later had their first one-man shows. After initially producing paintings in oil and watercolour, in 1954 he began producing his first wooden relief paintings. Deliberately ugly, these consisted of pieces of wood nailed to a panel and then painted with a broom in dark, unappealing colours. By the end of the 1950s he had begun to produce assemblages using junk materials. In 1961 he made his first 'tableau', or environmental assemblage, *Roxy's*, which recreated an entire brothel in a series of furnished rooms filled with assemblages of figures and other objects. The figures were made from disturbing juxtapositions of incongruous materials, including animal heads, recalling earlier Surrealist objects. In contrast to the studied neutrality of much Pop Art, Kienholz invariably used his tableaux to make social and

political comments; their emphasis on narrative further distinguished them from the majority of Pop Art. In the mid-1960s he introduced the 'concept tableau' as a way of minimising the production costs of large tableaux. These could be bought as a concept and realised later at additional cost if desired by the buyer. He has continued to produce tableaux since the 1960s, often casting the constituent figures from live models. Since 1973 he has divided his time between Berlin and Hope, ID. In the 1970s his experience of Germany led to many tableaux obliquely referring to the Nazi past as well as to Wagner's *Ring*. His tableaux from the 1980s onwards have, like the earlier ones, been more overt and hard-hitting. *P. C.*

Los Angeles 1966, *Edward Kienholz*, exhibition catalogue by M. Tuchman, Los Angeles County Museum of Art, 1966

Düsseldorf 1989, *Kienholz*, exhibition catalogue by J. Harten, Kunsthalle, Düsseldorf, 1989

R. L. Pincus, *On a Scale that competes with the World: The Art of Edward and Nancy Reddin Kienholz*, Berkeley, 1990

R. B. Kitaj

b Cleveland, OH, 1932

R. B. Kitaj came to London in his mid-20s after travelling a great deal as a seaman and after studying at Cooper Union in New York (1950–51) and at the Akademie der bildenden Künste in Vienna (1951–52). He later attended the Ruskin School of Art in Oxford (1958–59) and then studied at the Royal College of Art (1959–61). He was five years older than the other students and had first-hand knowledge of a wide range of modern European and contemporary American art, including Abstract Expressionism and the work of Robert Rauschenberg. As the subjects for his paintings were mainly taken from literary or historical sources rather than from popular culture, he never felt comfortable within the framework of Pop, but he nevertheless exerted an influence on other artists in his year at the Royal College, notably on Hockney. He remained closest to Pop in his use of images based on photographs or frame enlargements from films. From 1961 to 1967 Kitaj taught at art schools in London, and in 1967–68 he was Visiting Professor at the University of California, Berkeley. From 1963 to 1975 he was a prolific maker of screenprints. He selected a major exhibition in 1976 for the Hayward Gallery, London, of works purchased by him for the Arts

Council of Great Britain, 'The Human Clay'. It signalled his increasing concern with the human figure and with his Jewish heritage. Elected ARA 1984, RA Elect 1991. *C. O.*

Hanover 1970, *R. B. Kitaj*, exhibition catalogue, ed. W. Schmied, Kestner-Gesellschaft, Hanover, 1970

Washington, Cleveland and Düsseldorf 1982, *R. B. Kitaj*, exhibition catalogue, ed. J. Shannon, Hirshhorn Museum, Washington, DC, Museum of Art, Cleveland, OH, Kunsthalle, Düsseldorf, 1982

M. Livingstone, *R. B. Kitaj*, London and New York, 1985

Arthur Køpcke

b Hamburg, 1928; *d* Copenhagen, 1977

Arthur (or Addi) Køpcke (Koepcke or Köpcke) moved to Copenhagen in 1953 and in 1958 opened the Galerie Køpcke, where he had his first one-man show in 1961. He held one-man shows there of work by Dieter Roth, Piero Manzoni and Daniel Spoerri, among

others, before closing the gallery in 1963. From 1960 to 1968 he was a member of the Maj-Udstillingen (May-Exhibition) group in Copenhagen. At the Fluxus 'Festival of Misfits' in London in 1962 he performed *Music While You Work*, which involved carrying out a task accompanied by a faltering record. In November 1962 he organised a Fluxus festival, the first to take place in Copenhagen, and all the principal members of Fluxus took part. Apart from his performance works he produced a number of collages, assemblages and other objects. Since 1952 he had been making collages from torn fragments of advertisements and other mass images partly obliterated by overpainting. By the late 1950s these collages included additional materials such as string. From the early 1960s he produced objects that had undergone 'treatment'. These were usually books in which he had either glued the pages together or inserted objects. Stamped with messages such as 'Fill: With Own Imagination' and distinctive Køpcke labels, such works, appropriated as art by only minimal alteration, displayed the Fluxus interest in found objects. In 1961 he began making assemblages from junk objects and printed matter, many of them spray-painted in silver. He began producing 'Rebus' pictures and drawings in 1963 which, though unique, were rapidly made and so accorded with the Fluxus demand for mass-produced art. From 1964 until his death Køpcke concentrated on oil, felt-tip and collage works that used advertising and cartoon imagery and incorporated handwritten suggestions for various nonsensical activities. *P. C.*

H. Ruhé, *Fluxus: The Most Radical and Experimental Art Movement of the Sixties*, Amsterdam, 1979, section 3. Køp

Berlin et al. 1988, *Arthur Køpcke: Bilder und Stücke*, exhibition catalogue by J. Cladders et al., Daadgalerie, Berlin, 1988
J. Hendricks, *Fluxus Codex*, New York, 1988, pp. 301–5

Roy Lichtenstein

b New York, 1923

Roy Lichtenstein graduated from the School of Fine Arts at Ohio State University with an MA in 1949 but stayed on to teach until 1951. Between 1951 and 1957 he worked in Cleveland, OH, and made small-scale paintings on themes related to American history and the Wild West. Towards the end of the 1950s, while teaching in New York, he made drawings of characters from Walt Disney and also inserted hidden references to Mickey Mouse, Donald Duck and Bugs Bunny into paintings executed in a loose Abstract

Expressionist style. In 1960 he was appointed Assistant Professor at Douglass College, Rutgers University, New Brunswick, NJ. Through a fellow instructor, Allan Kaprow, he was introduced to Happenings and to the artists Jim Dine, Claes Oldenburg and George Segal. He began his first Pop paintings in 1961, transferring cartoon characters from comic books or bubble-gum wrappers (*Look Mickey* and *Popeye*) directly onto primed canvas with minor but telling changes. His brazen use of bold outline, primary colours and speech bubbles, and his imitation in the paintings that followed of the printing technique of Benday dots, caused a mixture of excitement and shock when the paintings were first shown at the Leo Castelli Gallery, New York, in 1962. Later that year, he was also included in the 'New Realists' exhibition at the Sidney Janis Gallery. Apart from the violent and 'glandular' emotions exaggerated in cartoon strips, Lichtenstein's subjects have also included the works of modern artists, and in the 1970s he made a series of pictures that parodied other styles in painting, including Fauvism, Surrealism and Expressionism. Since the first Pop paintings Lichtenstein has retained his bold style and mechanical method of reinterpreting images, adapting his technique for sculptures and later murals. He divides his time between New York and Southampton, NY. *J. S.*

J. Coplans, ed., *Roy Lichtenstein*, New York, 1972
L. Alloway, *Lichtenstein*, New York, 1983
New York 1987, *The Drawings of Roy Lichtenstein*, exhibition catalogue by B. Rose, MOMA, New York, 1987

George Maciunas

b Kaunas, Lithuania, 1931; *d* Boston, MA, 1978

In 1960 George Maciunas attended classes in electronic music run by Richard Maxfield at the New School for Social Research in New York. There he met the composer La Monte Young as well as a number of artists later associated with Fluxus who had studied under John Cage, such as George Brecht, Henry Flynt, Allan Kaprow and Jackson Mac Low. In 1961, at his own AG Gallery in New York, he held a series of lecture – demonstrations entitled *Musica Antiqua et Nova*, at which the first mention of Fluxus was made. After taking a job as a graphic artist with the US Air Force, in November 1961 he was sent to West

Germany, returning to New York in mid-1963. During this period abroad he started organising Fluxus as a movement. Following single events earlier that year, in 1962 he planned a series of worldwide Fluxus concerts that were to begin in Berlin and end in New York. These were partially realised in the concerts that began in Wiesbaden and then, as Festum Fluxorum, travelled to other European centres from September to December 1962. Most of the constituent works were performances of 'action music' in which various actions, often banal, were carried out according to a 'score'. One such was Maciunas's *In Memoriam to Adriano Olivetti*, the score of which was a used roll from an adding machine. In 1963 he wrote the bombastic Fluxus manifesto, part of which stated the intention of Fluxus as to 'purge the world of bourgeois sickness, "intellectual", professional and commercialised culture'. Apart from his 'scores' and writings Maciunas produced several Fluxus objects; some of them were lighthearted, such as the *Venus de Milo Barbeque Apron* (1967), while others were aggressively political, such as the 1966 flag poster *USA Surpasses All the Genocide Records*, which refers to the American involvement in Vietnam and the decimation of the American Indians. Maciunas organised and participated in most of the Fluxus festivals. As he was the movement's main driving force, the movement effectively ended when he died. *P. C.*

Bloomfield Hills 1981, *Fluxus etc.*, exhibition catalogue by J. Hendricks, Cranbrook Academy of Arts, Bloomfield Hills, MI, 1981, pp. 141–68
J. Hendricks, *Fluxus Codex*, New York, 1988, pp. 317–96
S. Home, *The Assault on Culture and Utopian Currents from Lettrisme to Class War*, London, 1988, chaps 9 & 10

Claes Oldenburg

b Stockholm, 1929

Claes Oldenburg came to the USA as an infant, settling with his family in Chicago in 1936. After studying art and literature from 1946 to 1950 at Yale University, he attended evening classes at the Art Institute of Chicago from 1950 to 1952 while working as a trainee reporter for the Chicago News Bureau. After moving to New York in 1956, he came into contact with the artists Red Grooms, Allan Kaprow and Jim Dine and took part in several Happenings centred around the Judson Gallery. His early works, influenced by Jean Dubuffet and his concept of 'Art Brut', were made from cheap, low-grade materials such as cardboard or burlap soaked in paste and modelled into crude shapes

of figures and junk objects found in the streets. These were followed by brightly coloured plaster sculptures made for his installation *The Store* in 1961, in which he blurred the distinction between art and commerce by displaying his wares, mainly food and clothing, in a rented shop front and encouraging purchasers to take works away with them. His over life-size soft sculptures of fast foods, such as *Floor Cake* and *Floor Cone*, first made an appearance in his one-man exhibition at the Green Gallery, New York, in 1962. Since then Oldenburg has fabricated different versions of household furniture, appliances and 'edibles': 'hard' versions in painted wood, 'soft' versions made in cloth or vinyl and 'ghost' versions that are replicas of the original object drained of colour. In 1965 he began a series of drawings and collages in which he proposed giant, three-dimensional versions of ordinary, often absurd objects, such as the baked potato or frankfurter, as civic monuments. The first to be realised was *Lipstick Ascending on Caterpillar Tracks*, installed at Yale University in 1969. Since 1976 Oldenburg has collaborated on commissions for public sculptures with his second wife, Coosje van Bruggen. His many realised projects include a giant baseball bat of welded steel bars for Chicago (1977). *J. S.*

B. Rose, *Claes Oldenburg*, New York, 1970
Pasadena 1971, *Claes Oldenburg: Object into Monument*, exhibition catalogue by B. Haskell, Pasadena Art Museum, 1971
Sunderland 1988, *A Bottle of Notes and Some Voyages*, exhibition catalogue, essays by Claes Oldenburg, G. Celant, C. van Bruggen and G. Storck, Northern Centre for Contemporary Art, Sunderland, 1988

Nam June Paik

b Seoul, Korea, 1932

Nam June Paik studied music and art history at Tokyo University from 1952 to 1956 and then spent two years studying music at various institutions in West Germany. Most significantly, in 1958 he attended the International Summer Course for New Music at Darmstadt, where he met John Cage, who proved an important influence on his work. In that year Paik settled in Cologne and began work at the WDR Studio für elektronische Musik with the composer Karlheinz Stockhausen, remaining there until 1963. In 1959 he began producing 'action music', performing *Hommage à John Cage* in that year at Galerie 22 in Düsseldorf. In 1961 he founded the University of Avant-Garde Hinduism, of which he was the only member and for which he published a monthly review. The same year he met George Maciunas, through whom he became drawn into the Fluxus group, remaining associated with it throughout its existence. At the proto-Fluxus event 'Neo-Dada in der Musik' in Düsseldorf in June 1962 he performed various works, including the action music piece *One For Solo Violin*, in which he slowly raised a violin and then smashed it onto a table. In the early 1960s he also made a number of assemblages using banal objets trouvés and occasionally musical instruments. He returned to Japan in 1963 to learn about video and collaborated with the electronic engineer Shuya Abe in the construction of *Robot K-456*, a remote controlled robot-sculpture. He moved in 1964 to New York, where he met Charlotte Moorman, a musician with whom he has since collaborated on various action music works. One of the most famous of these was performed at the Film-makers Cinematheque in New York City in 1967. Moorman played Paik's *Opéra sextronique* in the nude with a cello and

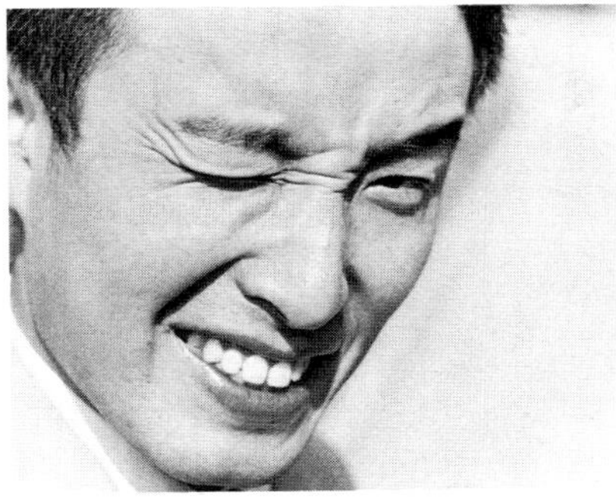

bunch of flowers, and both were arrested during the performance for indecency. Since the late 1960s Paik has concentrated on video art and TV sculptures, distorting the video images either by directly altering the TV sets or by prior manipulation of the video tapes. *P. C.*

New York 1982, *Nam June Paik*, exhibition catalogue by J. B. Hannardt et al., Metropolitan Museum of Art, New York, 1982
W. Herzogenrath, *Nam June Paik: Fluxus-Video*, Munich, 1983
London 1988, *Nam June Paik: Video Works 1963–1988*, exhibition catalogue by W. Herzogenrath, Hayward Gallery, London, 1988

Eduardo Paolozzi

b Leith, Scotland, 1924

Eduardo Paolozzi was born in Scotland to Italian parents. He took evening classes at Edinburgh College of Art (1943) and studied from 1944 to 1947 at the Slade School of Art in London. From 1947 to 1950 he lived in Paris, where he met artists associated with Dada and Surrealism, such as Hans Arp, as well as Braque, Léger, Giacometti and Dubuffet. On his return to England he became involved with the Independent Group, for whom he presented a lecture in 1952 of slides made from scrapbook images, fragments from comic books, postcards, advertisements, popular magazines and other material that he had collected for his own reference. These collages were published in facsimile in 1972 as a portfolio of screenprints, *Bunk*, and have retrospectively been considered forerunners of Pop. Paolozzi's bronze sculptures of the 1950s had elements that presaged his later Pop works, such as references to robots and the incorporation of found objects into the maquette before casting. In 1962 he emerged as a Pop artist when he began to produce abstracted, robot-like figures cast in various metals, such as *Four Towers* (1962) and *Solo* (1962). In the mid-1960s he began to give them glossy industrial finishes or to paint them in bright primary colours. It was at this time that Paolozzi began to produce the collage-based screenprints which are among his most important contributions to Pop, such as *As Is When* (1965) and *Moonstrips Empire News* (1967). In the late 1960s Paolozzi began to explore a more abstract formal language, again using aluminium, stainless steel and chromed

steel. Although he continued to make reference to the mass media and to work on the collage principle in his prints and sculptures alike, he was never again so closely involved with Pop. Elected ARA 1972, RA 1979. *C. O.*

D. Kirkpatrick *Eduardo Paolozzi*, London, 1970
Edinburgh et al. 1984, *Eduardo Paolozzi Recurring Themes*, exhibition catalogue by R. Spencer, R. Seitz and C. Frayling, Royal Scottish Academy, Edinburgh, 1984
W. Konnertz, *Eduardo Paolozzi*, Cologne, 1984

Peter Phillips

b Birmingham, W. Midlands, 1939

Peter Phillips entered art school at the age of thirteen, spending two years at the Moseley Road Secondary School of Art in Birmingham (1953–55). Here he was taught painting and decorating, sign-writing, heraldry, silversmithing, graphic design and technical draughtsmanship. This training left its mark and influenced his style. He studied at the Royal College of Art from 1959 to 1962 along with Hockney, Kitaj, Allen Jones, Boshier and Caulfield. Friction between him and his tutors in the Painting School caused him to transfer to the Television School in 1961, but he received his Diploma in Painting in June 1962. His early work in the 1960s was influenced by his American counterparts, such as Jasper Johns. He used such imagery as board games, funfairs, pin-ups and comic books, painted in a bold, flat style. He gained a Harkness Fellowship in 1964 and lived in New York from 1964 to 1966. In 1965 he travelled around North America by car with Allen Jones. While in New York he produced works on a much larger scale, though still based

on the same Pop images. He also started to use the airbrush, which produced a flat painted surface that looked glossy and machine-made. Before leaving New York he worked on a series called *Custom Paintings* using the airbrush. He completed this in 1967 after he had moved to Zurich, where he lived until moving to Mallorca in 1988. During the 1980s his paintings have become more contemplative in mood and more abstract in appearance, although they continue to be based on fragments of found images culled from photographs in magazines and similar sources. *C. O.*

Münster 1972, *Peter Phillips*, exhibition catalogue, introduction by C. Finch, Westfälischer Kunstverein, Münster, 1972
E. Crispolti, *Peter Phillips, Works/Opere 1960–1974*, Milan, 1977
Liverpool 1982, *Retrovision Peter Phillips: Paintings 1960–82*, exhibition catalogue by M. Livingstone, Walker Art Gallery, Liverpool, 1982

Michelangelo Pistoletto

b Biella, Italy, 1933

Michelangelo Pistoletto grew up in Turin and worked for his father, a restorer and fresco painter, from 1947 to 1958. At the age of twenty, after studying advertising, he set up his own advertising agency but continued to work with his father and to experiment with his own paintings, mainly self-portrait studies. Impressed by an exhibition of Francis Bacon's work in 1958, he began to concentrate on single full-length figures set against monochrome backgrounds of metallic gold or silver, or varnished black, and these were shown in his first one-man exhibition at the Galleria Galatea, Turin, in 1960. The burnished surfaces of the paintings caught the reflection of the viewer, appearing and disappearing in the void around the painted figure, which led in 1962 to his characteristic mirror paintings. In these Pistoletto pasted images of life-size figures (traced on tissue paper, or later in the form of silk-screened photographs) onto polished stainless steel plates. Described as 'permanent happenings', the mirror-like surfaces recorded the viewer and his surroundings, combining reality and the present with representation and the past. The paintings, which established his international reputation, were included in the exhibitions 'Dessins Pop' at the Ileana Sonnabend Gallery,

Paris, in 1963 and 'Pop Art Nouveau Réalisme' at the Palais des Beaux-Arts, Brussels, in 1965. Since his mirror paintings, Pistoletto has explored a wide variety of media and initiated several collaborative performances, consciously avoiding a particular style. As a result his work is extremely diverse, and groups of works such as the *Oggetti in meno* (Minus objects; 1965–66), though conceptually coherent, remain stylistically independent. The disparity between objects and materials and the integration of past and present within one work has continued to interest Pistoletto. In *Venus with Rags* (1967) he juxtaposed a cast of a Classical nude with a pile of brightly coloured rags, and in the 1980s he began a series of large roughly carved figures and torsos, 'recollections of sculpture', using the contrast between marble and polyurethane as another way of making reference to the relationship between tradition and the transitory. *J. S.*

Florence 1984, *Pistoletto*, exhibition catalogue, essay by G. Celant, Forte di Belvedere, Florence; published Milan, 1984
Baden-Baden 1988, *Michelangelo Pistoletto*, exhibition catalogue, essays by J. Poetter and R. E. Pahlke, Staatliche Kunsthalle, Baden-Baden, 1988
G. Celant, *Pistoletto*, New York, 1989

Sigmar Polke

b Oels, Germany, 1941

Sigmar Polke moved from East to West Germany in 1953 and from 1961 to 1967 studied at the Staatliche Kunstakademie in Düsseldorf, where he was taught by Joseph Beuys, Gerald Hoehme and Karl-Otto Goetz. In 1966 he had his first one-man show at the Galerie René Block in West Berlin. Together with Gerhard Richter and Konrad Lueg he founded the Kapitalistischer Realismus (Capitalist Realism) movement in 1963. Though prompted by American Pop Art it took a more distanced and political approach to mass imagery and products. Many of the resulting works such as *Biscuits* (1964) depicted banal consumer objects in a wry reference to the pleasures of capitalist society. This was also intended as a half-hearted taunt at Socialist Realism and the failed economic society from which it arose, where even objects as basic as this were difficult to obtain. In other Capitalist

Realist works Polke applied a print dot technique derived from Roy Lichtenstein to banal images, but instead of merely imitating the mechanical process he blurred and dissarranged some of the dots, ironically suggesting the 'fault' of human intervention, as in *Vase II* (1965). In the mid-1960s he began creating works that made mocking allusions to contemporary and past artists, including casual recreations of works by Dürer or Kandinsky as well as imitations of Arte Povera and Conceptual art. These were often painted on cloth, sometimes on patterned fabrics, subverting the contemporary fashion for exotic materials and stylistic development. Continuing to use unusual materials, in the early 1970s Polke took his inspiration from the late, at that time, discredited paintings of Francis Picabia, producing kitsch erotic works. In the late 1970s he incorporated cartoon imagery in some of his paintings. In his works since the 1980s he has adopted an iconography taken from magic and diabolism as well as more overtly political imagery of prison camps and watch towers. Still working in a variety of styles and devising new techniques, most recently he has shown 'paintings' made exclusively from trails of smoke. *P. C.*

Cologne 1984, *Sigmar Polke*, exhibition catalogue by H. Szeeman et al., Josef-Haubrich-Kunsthalle, Cologne, 1984
Rotterdam and Bonn 1984, *Sigmar Polke*, exhibition catalogue by W. Beeren and D. Stemmler, Museum Boymans-van Beuningen, Rotterdam, Städtisches Kunstmuseum, Bonn, 1984
Paris 1988, *Sigmar Polke*, exhibition catalogue by B. Lamarche-Vadel et al., Musée d'Art Moderne de la Ville de Paris, 1988

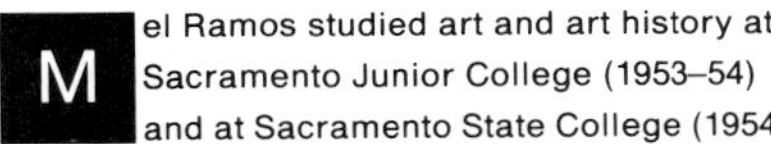

Mel Ramos

b Sacramento, CA, 1935

Mel Ramos studied art and art history at Sacramento Junior College (1953–54) and at Sacramento State College (1954–58), where he was taught by Wayne Thiebaud. By the late 1950s, influenced by Bay Area painters such as Nathan Oliveira and David Park, he was painting sombre, virtually abstract works relieved by occasional patches of bright colour. In 1961 he began to paint comic-strip characters, as in *Batmobile* (1962), sometimes representing them close to life size to make them believable. His technique, like Thiebaud's, involved prominent brushwork, a legacy of Abstract Expressionism, and he also used an unmodelled monochrome background to emphasise the flat canvas surface. These first Pop paintings, made by him in 1961 and 1962 without knowledge of the comic-strip pictures made at the same time

by Warhol and Lichtenstein, were all of male characters. In 1963 he concentrated on female comic-strip characters such as Wonder Woman, introducing a note of provocative female sexiness that became central to his work. Ramos had his first one-man show at the Bianchini Gallery in New York in 1964. In the same year he began a series of single female figures derived from pin-up magazines and from advertisements in which they were used as enticements to sell products, as in *Miss Cushion Air* (*Miss Firestone*) (1965). As in some of the earlier comic-strip works, large-scale lettering was used, sometimes lifted straight from advertisements. The brushstrokes in these paintings, absorbed into a harsh graphic style, were less visible and tactile than before. Developing this subject, from 1972 Ramos painted nudes based on images by other artists including Ingres, Modigliani, Manet and de Kooning, replacing their eroticism with the more vulgar and direct sexuality of the pin-up. As with the preceding pictures these were intended as ironic comments on the exploitative treatment of women in society, though similar accusations have been made of his own work. In the 1980s Ramos turned to landscape subjects and a series of works entitled *The Artist in his Studio*. *P. C.*

E. Claridge, *Mel Ramos*, London, 1975
Mel Ramos, *Watercolours*, Berkeley, 1979
Waltham 1980, *Mel Ramos: A Twenty Year Survey*, exhibition catalogue by C. Belz, Rose Art Museum, Brandeis University, Waltham, MA, 1980

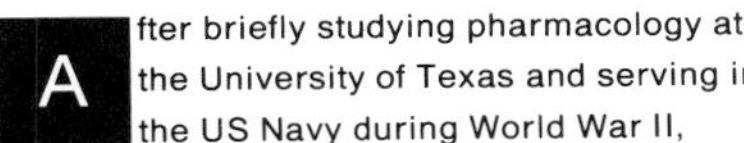

Robert Rauschenberg

b Port Arthur, TX, 1925

After briefly studying pharmacology at the University of Texas and serving in the US Navy during World War II, Rauschenberg first studied art at the Kansas City Art Institute. He attended the Académie Julian in Paris in 1948 and in 1949 he studied at Black Mountain College, NC. There he met Merce Cunningham, John Cage and Cy Twombly and participated in the first Happening, Cage's *Theatre Piece 1*, a multi-media event including dance, music and slide projections. He moved to New York in 1949 and attended the Art Students League. The painted assemblages incorporating objets trouvés produced by him from the mid-1950s, which he called 'combines',

were influenced by Kurt Schwitters and by the Cubists' use of collage. In *Rebus* (1955), he combined a patchwork of sports photographs, strip cartoons and colour samples with Abstract Expressionist sweeps and runs of paint. For *Bed* (1955), perhaps his most notorious 'combine', he painted over unmade bedclothes, including a quilt, pillow and sheets, and presented them vertically as a painting. Like Johns, a close friend who had a studio in the same building, Rauschenberg during this period often explored in his paintings the confrontation between the subjectivity of his personal style of execution and the neutrality or anonymity of mass-produced images. In *Factum I* and *Factum II* (1957), he duplicated the same found images and brushmarks in both canvases while retaining sufficient subtle differences between them for each to remain a 'unique work of art'. Rauschenberg has continued to explore new ideas and techniques, introducing audience participation in *Black Market* (1961) and later experimenting with electronics. He has travelled widely and worked in many different countries, collaborating with foreign print publishers and touring with dance and theatre companies, designing sets and costumes. *J. S.*

A. Forge, *Rauschenberg*, New York, 1969
Washington 1976, *Robert Rauschenberg*, exhibition catalogue, essay by L. Alloway, Smithsonian Institution, Washington, DC, 1976
M. L. Kotz, *Rauschenberg/Art and Life*, New York, 1990

Martial Raysse

b Golfe-Juan, France, 1936

A self-taught artist, Martial Raysse had his first one-man show at the Galerie Longchamp in Nice in 1957. His works from 1959 to 1960 were assemblages of garish manufactured objets trouvés such as detergent boxes, plastic brushes, beauty products and other ephemera, emphasising the pointless breadth of choice and artificiality of modern society. He was one of the founders in 1960 of Nouveau Réalisme, and he participated in their subsequent group exhibitions. In 1962, together with Niki de Saint Phalle, Spoerri, Tinguely, Rauschenberg and others, he was invited to take part in the 'Dylaby (Dynamic Labyrinth)' show at the Stedelijk Museum in Amsterdam. For this he constructed the environmental

assemblage *Raysse Beach*, in which he created a beach scene using female mannequins, large photographs of women and plastic beach toys. The installation pointed to the synthetically glamorous modern ideal of happiness. Soon after this he began to produce paintings, such as *Rose* (1962), invariably of female figures, spray-painted in bright synthetic colours over a photographic or screenprinted base. The lips and eyelashes were often retouched as if to beautify the image, so making an ironic reference to modern standards of taste. Pressing the point further, he applied a similar process to reproductions of paintings by masters such as Ingres and Cranach, again using bright colours. *Simple and Sweet Picture* (1965), for example, was derived from François Gérard's *Psyche Receiving Cupid's First Kiss* (1798), and the incorporation of a small neon heart vulgarly emphasised the previously discreet eroticism. On the same theme were mixed media sculptures deliberately appearing artificial and modern, which often used neon lights as symbols of brash, capitalist society. After abandoning painting in 1968, since the mid-1970s he has returned to conventional forms, producing pictures inspired by mythology, tradition and the Classical past. *P. C.*

Amsterdam 1965, *Martial Raysse: maître et esclave de l'imagination*, exhibition catalogue by P. Restany, Stedelijk Museum, Amsterdam, 1965
Los Angeles 1967, *Martial Raysse*, exhibition catalogue by O. Hahn, Dwan Gallery, Los Angeles, 1967
Paris 1981, *Martial Raysse 1970–1980*, exhibition catalogue, Centre Georges Pompidou, Paris, 1981

Gerhard Richter

b Dresden, 1932

Gerhard Richter studied at the Hochschule für bildende Künste in Dresden (1952–57) and then at the Staatliche Kunstakademie in Düsseldorf (1961–64). Settling in Düsseldorf, in 1963 he was one of the founders of the Kapitalistischer Realismus (Capitalist Realism) group with Sigmar Polke and Konrad Lueg. In the same year he organised, with Lueg, the *Demonstration for Capitalist Realism*, a performance in a furniture store in Düsseldorf lasting an entire evening, with the two artists sitting in a living room in which all the furniture had been raised on white

pedestals. Presenting themselves as living sculptures in counterpoint with the furniture as works of art, they created an event inspired by the same spirit as Duchamp's ready-mades. Since about 1962 Richter had used photographs as the basis for his paintings, copying them by hand onto canvas; in many of these the imagery appears to be out of focus, thus accentuating its air of casualness. Derived from photographic portraits, snapshots and images of such mundane objects as chairs and curtains, these paintings deliberately shunned normal expectations of compositional finesse and self-conscious style. In league with this apparent artlessness, the arbitrary, banal subjects reflect the monotony of the consumer culture from which they derive. The blurring and lack of detail suggest that while photographs might be compared with reality, paintings, especially within modernism, are thought of as autonomous entities independent of their representational function. The photo-based works, like the abstract monochromes produced by Richter in the same period, were all painted in grey, of which Richter said: 'Of all colours, only grey has the quality of representing nothing'. Richter used bright colours in a series of very different works based on commercial colour charts, such as *Fifteen Colours* (1966), but avoided any emotive connotations by again presenting them as objets trouvés. In the 1970s and 1980s Richter continued to work in what seemed very different manners, producing both bright and sensual abstract paintings and conventional-looking landscapes in a muted realist style. As in his previous work, however, in both groups of pictures he has continued to explore the interplay between photography and painting, replication and artifice. *P. C.*

Düsseldorf 1986, *Gerhard Richter: Bilder/Paintings 1962–1985*, exhibition catalogue, ed. J. Harten, Städtische Kunsthalle, Düsseldorf, 1986
R. Nasgaard, *Gerhard Richter*, London, 1988
Rotterdam 1989, *Gerhard Richter*, exhibition catalogue by A. Tilroe and B. H. D. Buchloh, Museum Boymans-van Beuningen, Rotterdam, 1989

Larry Rivers

b New York, 1923

Born Yitzroch Loiza Grossberg, Rivers studied music from 1944 to 1945 at the Juilliard School of Music, and painting in 1945 at Hans Hoffman's School, both in New York. From 1948 to 1951 he studied art education at New York University and he had his first one-man show at the Jane Street Gallery, New York, in 1949. After painting works influenced by Pierre

Bonnard and Henri Matisse in the late 1940s, in the early 1950s he reworked pictures by past artists, including Cézanne and Courbet, in an Abstract Expressionist style. The most famous of these was *Washington Crossing the Delaware* (1953), based on the patriotic picture of the same title painted in 1851 by Emmanuel Leutze. By the late 1950s, playing on the implications of the flag and target paintings by Jasper Johns, he was using found images from playing cards, cigarette packets, menus, money and other familiar flat objects in an impulsive gestural style, as in *Kings* (1960). While living in Paris from 1961 to 1962 he met Jean TInguely, with whom he collaborated on *Turning Friendship of America and France* (1961), which incorporated a motorised canvas based on a French cigarette packet. This was followed in 1963 by collages and oils rephrasing Rembrandt's *The Syndics* (1662) as reproduced on the boxes of Dutch Master cigars, a sort of double found image. From 1962 to 1964 he worked on a series of drawings, paintings and sculptures in which parts of the female anatomy were labelled with stencilled words in various languages. These parodied text book diagrams while contrasting the sensual subject matter with the neutral look of the stencilled lettering. In 1965 he produced a vast painted construction, *The History of the Russian Revolution: from Marx to Mayakovsky*, in which he combined objets trouvés such as rifles and photographs with painted images to form a kaleidoscopic survey of the Russian Revolutions. Rivers has continued to develop his techniques of the 1960s, using either collage elements or fragmentary painted images sometimes applied to narrative or historical subjects, as in his examination of Jewish identity, *The History of Matzoh*, in 1983. *P. C.*

Larry Rivers and C. Brightman, *Drawings and Digressions*, New York, 1979
H. A. Harrison, *Larry Rivers*, New York, 1984
S. Hunter, *Larry Rivers*, Berkeley, 1989

James Rosenquist

b Grand Forks, ND, 1933

From 1953 to 1954 James Rosenquist studied painting techniques at the University of Minnesota while supporting himself as a billboard painter. In 1955 he attended the Art Students League in New York and over the next four years he painted small abstract works. He again worked as a billboard painter from 1957 to 1960 and in 1962 had his first one-man show at the Green Gallery in New York. In 1960 he began to incorporate commercial images into his works, interlacing incongruous fragmented sections, as in *I Love You with My Ford* (1961). This technique mirrored the mass of sensory inputs jostling for attention in modern society. Such fragmentation is even more extreme in *Look Alive* (*Blue Feet, Look Alive*) (1961), where apparently arbitrary juxtapositions of elements and contrasts of scale are further complicated by the transient reflections of a mirror. While many of

Rosenquist's paintings incorporated commercial motifs, others, such as *Untitled* (*Blue Sky*) (1962) relied on the Surreal effect achieved by incongruous combinations of familiar images. In 1965 he executed the monumental *F-111*, a 26 m (86 ft) wide panorama of images gathered around that of an F-111 fighter plane. At each end are reflective aluminium panels pulling the viewer into the composition as well as emphasising the harsh, metallic style of the painting. The diverse collection of images included spaghetti, a tyre, a girl under a hairdryer and a nuclear explosion, thus contrasting the innocuous and the lethal in a pointed condemnation of American politics. In 1967 he experimented with transparent mylar sheet as a support for images presented as if suspended in mid-air. Since the 1960s he has

developed his use of commercial imagery, turning increasingly to lithography and etching in the 1970s while retaining his cool graphic style. In his more recent work he has interleaved splintered images, again suggesting the role of simultaneity in contemporary life. *P. C.*

Cologne 1972, *James Rosenquist: Gemälde, Räume, Graphik*, exhibition catalogue by E. Weiss, Kunsthalle, Cologne, 1972
New York 1972, *James Rosenquist*, exhibition catalogue by M. Tucker, Whitney Museum of American Art, New York, 1972
J. Goldman, *James Rosenquist*, New York, 1985

Mimmo Rotella

b Catanzaro, Italy, 1918

Mimmo Rotella studied at the Accademia di Belle Arti in Naples during World War II and moved to Rome in 1945, holding his first one-man show there in 1951 at the Galleria Chiurazzi. In 1949 he had started writing phonetic poems, which he called 'epistalici', some of which he recorded while at Kansas City University on a Fulbright Scholarship from 1951 to 1952. After returning to Rome, he began in 1953 to create *décollages* by tearing down posters and mounting them on canvas. He exhibited some of these in 1954 at a group show of young artists' work in Rome, this being the first public appearance of the *décollage* technique anywhere. Until 1957 he tore and rearranged the *décollages* after they were mounted but later abandoned this manipulation in favour of using them as objets trouvés. He was a founder member of Nouveau Réalisme in 1960. His *décollages* were similar to those made by other members, François Dufrêne, Hains and Villeglé, with whom he took part in group exhibitions of *décollages* in the 1960s. From 1961 to 1962 he also experimented with assemblages made from junk objects. In 1963 Rotella developed what he called 'Mec Art', in which photographic images were mechanically reproduced by projecting them onto photo-sensitised canvas. This technique denied any painterly aspects to the works as well as locking into the prevailing culture of mass-produced imagery. For these works he photographed either images in newspapers, to make 'reportages', or typographic proofs, to produce 'artypos', and then transferred these onto canvas as found or by multiple superposition.

Together with Alain Jacquet, Pol Bury and others he took part in the exhibition 'Hommage à Nicéphore Niépce' at the Galerie J in Paris, which publicly launched Mec Art in 1965. Having continued these works into the 1970s, in the 1980s he returned to both paint on canvas and *décollage*, the latter overpainted with graffiti-like images since 1987. *P. C.*

T. Trini, *Rotella*, Milan, 1974
S. Hunter, *Rotella: Décollages 1954–1964*, Milan, 1986
A. Bonito Oliva et al., *Mimmo Rotella: 'Lamière'*, Milan, 1989

Ed Ruscha

b Omaha, NB, 1937

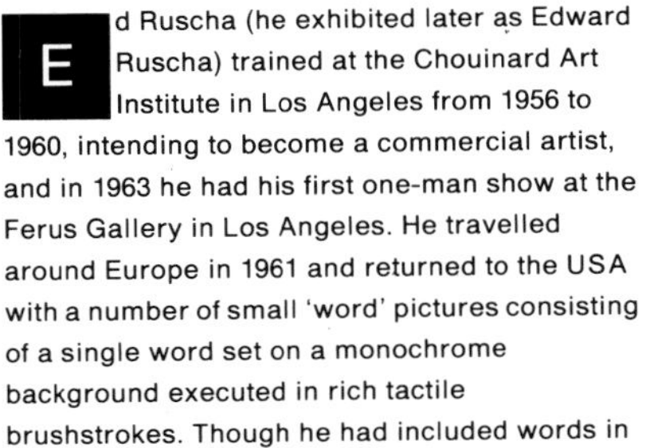

Ed Ruscha (he exhibited later as Edward Ruscha) trained at the Chouinard Art Institute in Los Angeles from 1956 to 1960, intending to become a commercial artist, and in 1963 he had his first one-man show at the Ferus Gallery in Los Angeles. He travelled around Europe in 1961 and returned to the USA with a number of small 'word' pictures consisting of a single word set on a monochrome background executed in rich tactile brushstrokes. Though he had included words in works made in 1959, these were much more sparing in colour and design. By 1962 the brushwork had dissolved into a hard-edged, graphic style, as in *Flash L.A. Times* (1963), absorbing bright commercial imagery. His book *Twentysix Gasoline Stations* of 1963 was the first of several in which he documented banal features of urban America, in this case consisting of photographs of petrol stations along Route 66 between Los Angeles and Oklahoma. In a similar spirit, throughout the 1960s he executed paintings of such motifs as petrol stations, fires, apartment blocks and birds in the harsh style of the word pictures. By the late 1960s the words in his oil paintings became more overtly reified and were often painted in trompe-l'oeil as if made from liquid poured onto the surface. These made a play between the word as a mere abstract sign and its potential as an aesthetic object. The words themselves, such as 'Hey', 'Eye' and 'Cut', were enigmatic and without clear reference. In the late 1960s Ruscha turned increasingly to lithography and screenprinting and also to drawing. In the early 1970s he reverted to a flatter presentation of lettering, using substances such as vegetable

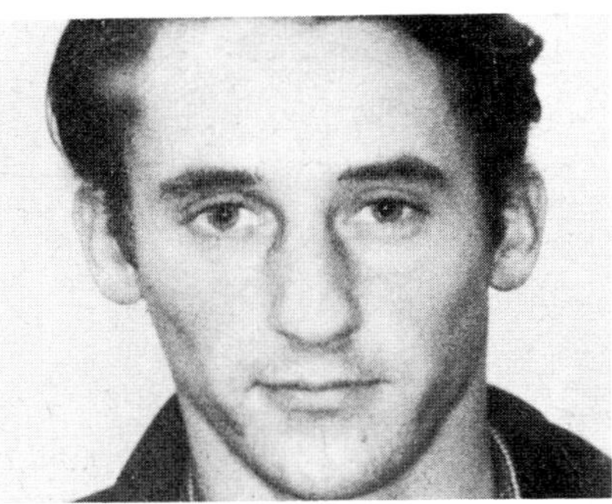

colours, ketchup, tea and egg yolk instead of paint on fabrics such as satin and moiré. The words themselves remained mysterious, announcing messages like 'People Getting Ready to Do Things'. Since then Ruscha has continued to produce word pictures, often setting them on sky-like backgrounds. In the late 1980s he has also produced diffusely-lit black-and-white paintings of such images as sailing ships and cars in silhouette. *P. C.*

Buffalo 1976, *Ed Ruscha*, exhibition catalogue by L. L. Cathcart, Albright-Knox Art Gallery, Buffalo, NY, 1976
San Francisco 1982, *The Works of Edward Ruscha*, exhibition catalogue, essays by D. Hickey and P. Plagens, introduction by A. Livet, foreword by H. T. Hopkins, Museum of Modern Art, San Francisco, and New York [as book], 1982
Rotterdam, London and Los Angeles 1990, *Edward Ruscha: Paintings*, exhibition catalogue by P. Hulten, D. Cameron and B. Blistène, Museum Boymans-van Beuningen, Rotterdam, Serpentine Gallery, London, Museum of Contemporary Art, Los Angeles, 1990

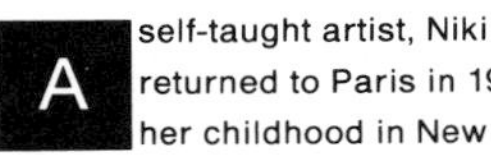

Niki de Saint Phalle

b Paris, 1930

A self-taught artist, Niki de Saint Phalle returned to Paris in 1951 after spending her childhood in New York and began to paint in that year. She had her first one-woman show, of brightly coloured paintings in a naive style, in St Gallen, Switzerland in 1956. From 1960 she worked, and lived, with Jean Tinguely, and she exhibited with the Nouveaux Réalistes from 1961 to 1963. In 1961 she produced her first *Shot-reliefs,* in which a relief assemblage of found materials was coloured by shooting with a rifle at bags of paint attached to the surface, a mocking reference to Action Painting. Concurrent with these were assemblages of human figures made from clothes with dart board heads. The dart board suggested chance and the arbitrary, which were important themes for the Nouveaux Réalistes. Having earlier made a series of disturbing female figures from junk materials, in 1964 she produced the first of her *Nana* figures. These were voluptuous, rotund females constructed from papier-mâché or plaster on wire netting and then brightly painted. The most spectacular and public of these was

She: A Cathedral, a 25 m (82 ft) long reclining *Nana* built in collaboration with Tinguely and Per-Olof Ultvedt at the Moderna Museet, Stockholm, in 1966. The visitors could enter between her legs and walk around inside, where there were machines, film shows and other installations. Since then she has continued making brightly coloured sculptures, some of human figures and others in amorphous, organic forms. Many of these have been large outdoor sculptures or architectural projects, including the *Stravinsky Fountain,* built with Tinguely for the Place Igor Stravinsky outside the Centre Georges Pompidou in Paris from 1982 to 1983. These Surreal, fantastic works embody a variety of influences from Pre-Columbian and Indian Art to the work of Joan Miró, Picasso and the architect Antoni Gaudí. *P. C.*

Paris 1980, *Niki de Saint Phalle,* exhibition catalogue by P. Hulten et al., Centre Georges Pompidou, Paris, 1980

Munich 1987, *Niki de Saint Phalle; Bilden—Figuren—Phantastische Gärten,* exhibition catalogue by C. Schulz-Hoffman et al., Kunsthalle der Hypo-Kulturstiftung, Munich, 1987

Roslyn Harbor 1987, *Fantastic Vision: works by Niki de Saint Phalle,* exhibition catalogue by D. Bourdon et al., Nassau County Museum of Fine Art, Roslyn Harbor, NY, 1987

George Segal

b New York, 1924

George Segal took a foundation art course at Cooper Union in New York (1941–42) and studied a number of subjects part-time at Rutgers University, New Brunswick, NJ (1942–46). He then studied art education at the Pratt Institute of Design in Brooklyn (1947–48), followed by a similar course at New York University (1948–49). Although he continued until 1958 to operate a chicken farm, in 1953 he began to paint seriously, holding his first one-man show at the Hansa Gallery in New York in 1956. He started to experiment with sculpture in 1958, producing representations of the human figure from wire netting, burlap and plaster in a roughly finished style. In 1961 he first began to cast his sculptures from live models, wrapping them in bandages and then covering them in plaster. Once dry the plaster was removed to form the basis of the finished work, a method that captured the essential features of the model without becoming involved with the illusionistic replication of detail. At the same time he decided to incorporate his figures into environments. In addition to portrait

sculptures, Segal produced works sympathetically portraying the banality of modern life, such as *The Farm Worker* (1962–63), in which both the pose and environment seem to express a deadening monotony. There were also works of intimate, usually private, activities such as bathing or dressing, as in *Woman Standing in a Bathtub* (1964), and occasionally overtly political subjects. The emotional engagement evident in his work distinguishes it from mainstream Pop Art, though his use of modern, 'found' subjects does relate him obliquely to the movement. From the mid-1970s his technique changed; he used the plaster cast as a mould into which he poured liquid plaster, so forming a more detailed rendering of the figure, often painted in a single bright colour. Some of these works were then re-cast in bronze. Continuing this method, in the 1980s he made Cézannesque still lifes. Since 1976 he has produced several public sculptures, including *The Rush Hour* (1983), erected in 1987 in Finsbury Avenue Square, Broadgate, London. *P. C.*

J. van der Marck, *George Segal,* New York, 1979

P. Tuchman, *George Segal,* New York, 1983

S. Hunter and D. Hawthorne, *George Segal,* Barcelona, 1984

Colin Self

b Norwich, Norfolk, 1941

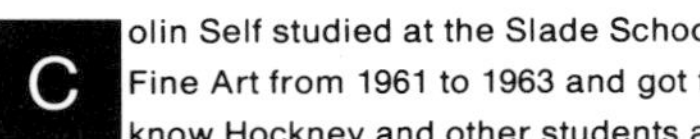

Colin Self studied at the Slade School of Fine Art from 1961 to 1963 and got to know Hockney and other students at the Royal College of Art at that time. Although he had reservations about the Pop label because of its implied celebration of modern materialist society, he applauded the movement as a working-class affront to traditional fine art elitism. His works of the 1960s were often darker in mood than those of his contemporaries. His early works included meticulous and haunting drawings of armchairs and sofas, sometimes with figures, drawn with an unreal intensity against bare backgrounds. Other series were devoted to the American hot dog, to the modern architecture of cinema interiors and to the trappings of fashion. Convinced of the world's imminent destruction by nuclear war and conscious of the violence of society, he produced obsessively worked drawings in ballpoint pen such as the *Mortal Combat* series begun in 1963, often using animals as a metaphor of the aggressive and self-destructive forces that rule human behaviour. In 1962 and 1965 he travelled widely in the USA and Canada.

In *Fall-out Shelter,* a series of drawings made as a result of visiting New York, he used pencil, coloured pencil, fluorescent paper and glitter to create an atmosphere of foreboding. Self was not drawn to the technology favoured by many of the Pop artists, working mostly in pencil and pen, but he did produce striking etchings enlarged from photographs, the *Power and Beauty* series (1968). He also made sculptures in the 1960s, the most startling of them again on the theme of nuclear destruction (*The Nuclear Victim*, 1966). Since returning to Norwich in 1965 he has continued to produce a large number of highly personal drawings in a variety of styles. *C. O.*

C. Finch, 'Colin Self', *Art International*, XI, 4, 20 April 1967, pp. 27–31
Colin Self, 'Colin Self and David Hockney Discuss their Recent Work', *Studio International*, CLXXVI, December 1968, pp. 277–8
London 1986, *Colin Self's Colin Selfs*, exhibition catalogue preface by J. Lingwood, Institute of Contemporary Arts, London, 1986

Richard Smith

b Letchworth, Herts, 1931

Richard Smith studied at the Royal College of Art from 1954 to 1957, with Peter Blake and Joe Tilson as fellow students. At a large exhibition of contemporary American painting held at the Tate Gallery in 1956 he first saw works by such abstract painters as Mark Rothko, Jackson Pollock and Sam Francis, which had a powerful and lasting effect on him. In 1959 he moved to New York for two years on a Harkness Fellowship, and it was there that he first produced works such as *Formal Giant* (1960), inspired by the large scale of billboards and the sumptuous colour of glossy magazines. He began to paint on an ambitious scale, using imagery that was generalised, as if

he was reluctant to abandon pure abstraction altogether, but that was clearly drawn from advertising, consumer products and magazines. He had his first one-man exhibition in 1961 in New York at the Green Gallery. He returned to London in 1961 and continued to produce works on a large scale inspired by the packaging of commodities, such as cigarette packs, using shaped canvases and, from 1963, three-dimensional constructions, such as *Alpine* (1963). From 1963 to 1965 Smith worked again in New York, where he once more stressed formal abstract values while continuing to make reference to consumer goods. In the 1970s he worked on a series of kite-like stretcherless canvases. He has lived in New York since 1976. *C. O.*

London 1966, *Richard Smith: Paintings 1958–1966*, exhibition catalogue by B. Robertson, Whitechapel Art Gallery, London, 1966
London, 1975, *Richard Smith: Seven Exhibitions 1961–75*, exhibition catalogue by B. Rose, Tate Gallery, London, 1975

Daniel Spoerri

b Galati, Romania, 1930

Born Daniel Isaac Feinstein, Spoerri emigrated to Switzerland in 1942, where he lived with his uncle Théophile Spoerri. Training as a classical dancer in Zurich and then in Paris, he was principal dancer for the Berne Opera from 1954 to 1957. After working in avant-garde theatre he turned to art in 1959 and had his first one-man show at the Galleria Schwarz in Milan in 1961. In 1960 he was one of the founders of Nouveau Réalisme, exhibiting with them thereafter. The same year he began to make his *tableaux-pièges* ('snare-pictures'), in which a random collection of used, often jaded, objects, such as crockery and cutlery on a table, would be 'snared', i.e. glued down, and exhibited. Sometimes he presented the objects in such a way as to give the illusion that they had been found, as in *The Playpen* (1961). Occasionally the *tableaux-pièges* originated from the debris of public events, as in those made from what was left in the restaurant set up at the City-Galerie in Zurich in 1965. Harnessing chance arrangements and non-artistic materials, this aesthetic was further developed at the exhibition 'L'Epicerie' at the Galerie Køpcke in Copenhagen in 1961. Though otherwise unchanged, ordinary groceries were labelled 'Caution Work of Art' and signed by Spoerri, an activity close in spirit to that of Duchamp's ready-mades. Similarly, his book *Topographie anecdotée du hasard* (Paris, 1962)

is a mock-scholarly description and appreciation of banal objects found all over the world. Concurrent with the *tableaux-pièges* were several 'détrompe-l'oeil' works, in which the illusionism of a painting would be deliberately undermined by the attachment of a real object. His 'word-snares' of the mid-1960s were bizarre relief assemblages illustrating proverbs or sayings. Spoerri has continued to produce reliefs and assemblages up to the present: since 1985 he has made 'ethno-syncretic' assemblages using objects that have or have had magical significance. *P. C.*

Zurich 1966, *Daniel Spoerri*, exhibition catalogue by Daniel Spoerri, City-Galerie, Zurich, 1966
Zurich 1972, *Daniel Spoerri*, exhibition catalogue by C. Bremer and M. Bloem, Helmhaus, Zurich, 1972
Paris 1990, *Petit Lexique sentimental autour de Daniel Spoerri*, exhibition catalogue by A. Kambler et al., Centre Georges Pompidou, Paris, 1990

Wayne Thiebaud

b Mesa, AZ, 1920

Wayne Thiebaud began his career as a cartoonist and graphic designer. After working briefly in the animation department of Walt Disney Studios in Los Angeles and studying commercial art, he worked for ten years as a free-lance cartoonist and illustrator. In 1949 he decided to become a

painter and studied at San José State College and later at California State College, graduating in 1953 with an MA. Ordinary objects such as gum-ball dispensers and food counters appear in his work as early as 1953 but veiled beneath layers of Abstract Expressionist brushstrokes. Influenced by the paintings of Edward Hopper, he gradually adopted a more impassive, realist style and concentrated on consumer goods, usually food, isolated against a monochrome background. Single or multiple images of hot dogs, cream cakes, lipsticks and ice-cream cones are depicted in thick, shiny paint often resembling the substance portrayed, whether icing or ketchup. His celebration of all-American junk food and adherence to traditional painting techniques led to Thiebaud being nicknamed the 'Carbohydrate Morandi' when the works were first shown in San Francisco. Though largely ignored at that time, the paintings received critical acclaim when included in his first one-man exhibition in New York, at the Allan Stone

Gallery in 1962, and soon afterwards in the 'New Realists' group exhibition at the Sidney Janis Gallery. In 1963 he turned his attention to figures and their relationship to one another or to other objects, but continued to depict them in the same impassive, 'consumer appealing' style. Since the 1970s Thiebaud has concentrated more on cityscapes of San Francisco, landscapes and pastels of animals, but he also continues to paint images of mass-produced consumer goods. He lives and works in Sacramento and San Francisco. *J. S.*

Pasadena 1968, *Wayne Thiebaud,* exhibition catalogue by J. Coplans, Pasadena Art Museum, 1968
Phoenix 1976, *Wayne Thiebaud: Survey 1947–1976,* exhibition catalogue, essay by G. Cooper, Art Museum, Phoenix, AZ, 1976
San Francisco 1985, *Wayne Thiebaud,* exhibition catalogue by K. Tsujimoto, Museum of Modern Art, San Francisco, 1985

Joe Tilson

b London, 1928

Joe Tilson studied in London at St Martin's School of Art (1949–52) and at the Royal College of Art (1952–55). Although he painted figuratively as a student, the Abstract Expressionist paintings shown at an exhibition of contemporary American art at the Tate Gallery in 1956 had a powerful effect upon him, and he began to experiment with abstract painting. By 1961 he had abandoned this approach in favour of constructed objects fabricated with attention to the carpentry skills he had acquired before going to art school. The earliest of these works, such as *For Jake and*

Anna (1961), coincided with the new directions being established by the next generation of students at the Royal College of Art. Incorporating elements that soon became integral to his work – bright colours, bold, simplified structures and stencilled lettering – these wooden constructions of the early 1960s were among his most personal contributions to Pop. He and his wife Jos also played an important role in bringing artists together at informal gatherings at their home, as testified by his *A–Z Box of Friends and Family* (1963), a collection of small works specially commissioned from a number of Pop artists and other colleagues. From the mid-1960s Tilson used screenprinting to produce quintessentially Pop works, such as *P.C. from N.Y.C.* (1965). By 1972, when he moved with his family from London to Wiltshire, he was becoming disenchanted with the mechanical methods of production. Taking up etching and also returning to wooden constructions, he became increasingly involved with political and ecological concerns, with alchemy, with our relationship to nature and with subjects drawn from pre-Classical mythology. Elected ARA 1985, RA Elect 1991. *C. O.*

London 1970, *Joe Tilson Pages,* exhibition catalogue, Marlborough Fine Art Ltd, London, 1970
Rotterdam 1973, *Joe Tilson,* exhibition catalogue, ed. R. Hammacher-van den Brande, Museum Boymans-van Beuningen, Rotterdam, 1973
A. C. Quintavalle, *Tilson,* Milan, 1977

Jean Tinguely

b Fribourg, Switzerland, 1925

Naturally inventive, Jean Tinguely began making water-wheels and wire constructions after irregular attendance at the Basel School of Arts and Crafts between 1941 and 1945. He also experimented with 'dematerialisation', suspending household objects from the ceiling and rotating them at high speed using electric motors. He collaborated with Daniel Spoerri on a kinetic

backdrop for the ballet *Prisma* in 1953, and later he began making painted reliefs combining fixed and moving parts. His interest in movement and the role of chance led him to 'sound reliefs' in 1955, in which moving objects such as hammers made various noises as they hit against other objects, and in 1959 to frenetic drawing machines. In 1960 he visited New York, where he came into contact with Jasper Johns and Robert Rauschenberg. While there he presented, in the courtyard at MOMA, his first sculpture to self-destruct, thus helping to inaugurate a new art form: auto-destructive art. On returning to Paris he learnt electrical welding techniques and began a series of sculptures using scrap metal, some of which later incorporated junk objects. After teaming up in Nouveau Réalisme with other artists, including his friends Yves Klein and Daniel Spoerri, Tinguely returned to New York at the end of 1960 to live with the French artist Niki de Saint Phalle. Together they took part in several Happenings in the early 1960s with Johns, Rauschenberg and the choreographer and dancer Merce Cunningham. Tinguely made his first fountain in 1960 and has since worked on several public sculptures, often in collaboration with Niki de Saint Phalle. These include the giant, walk-in sculpture (made also in collaboration with Per-Olof Ultvedt) of a reclining woman for an exhibition at the Moderna Museet, Stockholm, in 1966 (complete with bar, aquarium and mini-cinema) and the *Stravinsky Fountain* in 1982–3 for the Place Igor Stravinsky outside the Centre Georges Pompidou in Paris. *J. S.*

C. Bischofberger, *Jean Tinguely: Catalogue Raisonné, Sculptures and Reliefs 1954–1968,* Zurich, 1982
London 1982, *Tinguely,* exhibition catalogue, introduction by R. Calvocoressi, Tate Gallery, London, 1982
P. Hultén, *Jean Tinguely: A Magic Stronger than Death,* Milan, 1987

Jacques de la Villeglé

b Quimper, 1926

Jacques de la Villeglé entered the Ecole des Beaux-Arts in Rennes in 1944, first studying painting and then, from 1945, architecture, and it was there that he met Raymond Hains. After this he pursued his architectural studies at the Ecole Nationale Supérieure des Beaux-Arts in Nantes from 1947 to 1949. In St Malo in 1947 he started to form a collection of objets trouvés from the sea and elsewhere. Moving to Paris in 1949 he began to collaborate with Hains in making photographs, abstract films and *affiches lacérées* (*décollages*). Together they published the book *Hépérile éclaté* (Paris, 1953), which used Hains's

'hypnogogic' photographic process to produce a series of splintered, typographic images of Camille Bryen's phonetic poem *Hépérile*. They jointly organised the 'Loi de 29 Juillet 1881' show at the Galerie Colette Allendy in Paris in 1957, exhibiting a series of *affiches lacérées* (torn poster fragments) collected around Paris. In June 1959 Villeglé organised his first one-man show, in François Dufrêne's studio in Paris. Entitled 'Lacéré Anonyme' (Anonymous Tear), it consisted of a series of soirées in which participants were invited to 'create' *affiches lacérées* under Villeglé's guidance.The show was designed to subvert the idea of the work of art as a personal product and also ironically referred to the studios run by the great artists of the past. Though often appearing as if they had been torn down and exhibited untouched, the fragments in his *affiches lacérées* are in fact manipulated to provide the most suitable image for his purposes. He soon became acquainted with the Nouveaux Réalistes, becoming a member of the group on its foundation in 1960. He participated in several group exhibitions of *affiches lacérées* organised by Pierre Restany in the 1960s together with Hains, Rotella and Dufrêne and has continued to produce these works up to the present. *P. C.*

Stockholm 1971, *Villeglé: retrospektivt 1949–1971*, exhibition catalogue by O. Hahn and Jacques de la Villeglé, Moderna Museet, Stockholm, 1971
Saint-Etienne 1976, *Beautés volées*, exhibition catalogue by B. Cesson, Musée d'Art et d'Industrie, Saint-Etienne, 1976, pp. 45–6, 53–60
Paris 1988, *Jacques Villeglé*, exhibition catalogue by Jacques de la Villeglé, Galerie du Génie, Paris, 1988

Wolf Vostell

b Leverkusen, Germany, 1932

Wolf Vostell studied lithography in a print works in Cologne from 1950 to 1953 and painting and typography at the Werkkunstschule in Wuppertal in 1954. In 1954 he started to produce his first *décollages* by tearing up posters, typographic designs and photographs and mounting them. From 1955 to 1957 he studied at the Ecole des Beaux-Arts in Paris and in 1957 attended the Kunstakademie

in Düsseldorf. He organised his first street Happening in Paris in 1958, entitled *Theatre is in the Street*, inspired by A. M. Cassandre's book of the same name. As was the case for his subsequent public events, this was based on Vostell's belief that art and life are inextricably united. His first one-man show, at the Salones Educación y Descanso in Cáceres, Spain, also took place in 1958 and from 1962 he became involved with the Fluxus movement. The largest of his Happenings was *In Ulm, About Ulm, Around Ulm* (1964), which took place in Ulm Theatre and 24 other locations in the city. This and his other Happenings incorporated, among other things, noise, concrete, cars and numerous participants, and in contrast to similar events in the USA they had a detailed 'score'. Concurrently with the public activities, Vostell continued to make *décollages*. By the early 1960s he had begun to manipulate the found images and also to efface them by overpainting. In 1965 he started using photographs from magazines and newspapers, often of a violent nature, as collage elements or transferred onto canvas by screenprinting. These were again partly obliterated by overpainting or sometimes paired with real objects as part of a brutal process that further enhanced the violence of the imagery. He continued to organise Happenings into the 1970s as well as producing relief assemblages such as the *Mania* series of 1973. From the 1980s up to the present he has concentrated more on painting and photomontage, frequently using pornographic imagery. *P. C.*

Berlin 1975, *Vostell: Retrospektive 1958–1974*, exhibition catalogue by W. Schmied et al., Neue Nationalgalerie, Berlin, 1975
Braunschweig 1980, *Wolf Vostell: Dé-Coll/agen, Verwischungen, Schichtenbilder, Bleibilder, Objektbilder, 1955–1979*, exhibition catalogue by J. Schilling and K. Höweler, Kunstverein, Braunschweig, 1980
Strasbourg 1985, *Wolf Vostell: Environnement-Video-Peintures-Dessins, 1977–1985*, exhibition catalogue by N. Lehni et al., Musée d'Art Moderne, Strasbourg, 1985

Andy Warhol

b McKeesport, PA, 1928; *d* New York, 1987

Andy Warhol studied commercial art from 1945 to 1949 at the Carnegie Technical College in Pittsburgh and worked throughout the 1950s as a successful commercial illustrator and window designer in New York. His early Pop paintings, including *Saturday's Popeye* and *Superman* (both 1960) were first used as backdrops for window display at Bonwit Teller department store in 1961. On discovering that Lichtenstein had also adopted comic strip heroes as his subjects, he turned to consumer products, producing his first multiple repetitive images of *Campbell's Soup Cans* and *Coca-Cola Bottles* in 1962. Warhol's method of reproducing identical images, echoing the assembly-line production of the objects depicted, gradually became technically more efficient and a standard feature of his work. He introduced the

process of screenprinting in 1962 and encouraged the impression that works were churned out from the Factory, as his studio was known, by his entourage of assistants. Throughout the 1960s, Warhol selected images which epitomised both the glamour and the violence of American life, mass-producing publicity shots of *Marilyn Monroe* and *Liz Taylor* at the same time as his disturbing images of the *Electric Chair*. Towards the end of the 1960s he concentrated almost entirely on making films (his most famous include *Kiss* and *Chelsea Girls*), and he also promoted the rock group The Velvet Underground in live multi-media performances. He became New York's society portrait artist in the 1970s, producing images of the rich and famous, often on commission. He returned to the theme of money in his *Dollar Signs* of the early 1980s and welcomed the arrival of a new generation of artists working in the spirit of Pop, even collaborating on two series of paintings with the graffiti artist Jean Michel Basquiat. He died after a routine gall-bladder operation, a cult figure and 'Pope of Pop'. *J. S.*

J. Coplans, *Andy Warhol*, New York, 1970
D. Bourdon, *Warhol*, New York, 1989
New York 1989, *Andy Warhol: A Retrospective*, exhibition catalogue, ed. K. McShine, MOMA, New York, 1989

Robert Watts

b Burlington, IA, 1923; *d* 1987

Robert Watts studied mechanical engineering at the University of Louisville, KY (1942–44), and attended the Art Students League in New York (1946–48). He also received an MA from Columbia University in 1951 after studying ceramics, drawing and art history. From 1946 to 1958 he produced abstract paintings, receiving his first one-man show at Douglass College Art Gallery, Rutgers University, New Brunswick, NJ, in 1953. He then developed an interest in chance, which resulted in a number of electrical, kinetic works harnessing seemingly random effects. At the same time he also experimented with film. In 1960 he performed his first Event, leading to his association with the Fluxus movement from 1962. In addition to his regular participation in Fluxus festivals he produced ephemeral objects, such as a series of sheets of fake stamps, many bearing erotic imagery, made from 1961 to 1964. These were connected to the Fluxus fascination with the postal system as a means of propagating their ideas and art objects. At the Yam Festival of 1963, for example, Watts and George Brecht organised a 'Delivery Event', advertised thus: 'Robert Watts and/or George Brecht will

assemble a work and arrange delivery to you or an addressee of your choice' upon receipt of money. Also in the early 1960s Watts made several works from stones bearing numbers stating their weight or volume. By their banality and ready-made nature these fulfilled the Fluxus desire to attack 'high' art. In the 1970s Watts made a number of shallow box assemblages incorporating curious objects (for example, a nest, a mouse skeleton and rose branches) that reflected his interest in archaeology, science and nature. From the 1970s until his death he also made prints, the last of which were based on collages. *P. C.*

Madrid 1987, *Robert Watts: Flux Med, Obra Grafica,* exhibition catalogue by K. Friedman et al., Estudio del Joan Guaita, Madrid, 1987
J. Hendricks, *Fluxus Codex,* New York, 1988, pp. 525–79
New York 1990, *Robert Watts,* exhibition catalogue by B. H. D. Buchloch, Leo Castelli Gallery, New York, 1990

John Wesley

b Los Angeles, 1928

Before graduating from high school in 1946, John Wesley attended evening classes at the Los Angeles City College and the University of California in Los Angeles. Having worked as an aircraft riveter, from 1953 to 1958 he was employed as an illustrator in the engineering department of Northrop Aircraft. During this time he began to paint, contributing to group shows in California in 1958 and 1959. He moved to New York in 1960 and in 1963 had his first one-man show there at the Robert Elkon Gallery. Many of the paintings he produced in 1962 and 1963 were based on photographs of the 1932 Los Angeles Olympics, the figures painted in stark black outlines and unmodelled colour. Through such works, in a cool style suggestive of cartoons or comic strips, he soon became associated with Pop Art, participating in some of the movement's major early exhibitions. In contrast to hard-core Pop artists, however, he rarely employed imagery from the mass media, although he occasionally made reference to the American flag and more generally to emblematic motifs. Though he remained faithful to his flat, linear style, over the succeeding years his subject matter gradually changed, and by the mid-1960s he was using animals and repeated images, often set within a framing design. In 1971 he produced an edition of screenprints entitled *Panoply,* based

on the events of World War I. By the 1970s his preference was for more enigmatic imagery, closer in some ways to Surrealism than to Pop Art, although in 1973–74 he made reference to Gig Young's comic strip *Blondie* for the series *Searching for Bumstead,* inspired by childhood memories of haunting, empty spaces. In 1976, in honour of the American Bicentennial, he painted a number of *Patriotic Tableaux,* using the American flag as a motif. In the late 1970s and early 1980s he spent much time in the south of France. In his most recent pictures he has maintained a suggestive ambiguity while using repeated images to decorative effect. *P. C.*

Berlin 1982–83, *Cheep! John Wesley: Bilder aus den Jahren 1962–1982,* exhibition catalogue by H. Green, Reinhard Onnasch Galerie, Berlin, 1982–83
Tokyo et al. 1987, *Pop Art, USA–UK,* exhibition catalogue by L. Alloway and M. Livingstone, Odakyu Grand Gallery, Tokyo, 1987, pp. 74–6, 153
M. Livingstone, *Pop Art: A Continuing History,* London, 1990, pp. 82–3, 208

Tom Wesselmann

b Cincinnati, 1931

Tom Wesselmann studied psychology at the University of Cincinnati from 1951 to 1952 and 1954 to 1956, during the latter period also attending the Art Academy of Cincinnati. He then studied at Cooper Union in New York from 1956 to 1959 and had his first one-man show at the Tanager Gallery, New York, in 1961. In 1959 and 1960 he made a number of small collages, mostly representing figures in interiors, which led in 1960 to a series of nudes and in 1961 to the *Little Great American Nude* series. Feeling he should make larger works, he used one of these collages as the basis for *Great American Nude #1,* a collage-based painting restricted to the colours red, blue and white. The title of the series was an ironic reference to other Great American creations, such as the Novel or Dream. Both in style and colouring it suggests a reference to Matisse, especially through the simplification and pose of the nude figure. He added to the *Great American Nude* series throughout the 1960s and beyond, always retaining the deliberately overt and sometimes shockingly frank eroticism. In 1962 he began a series of *Still Life* assemblages, using modern objects and advertising imagery, as in *Still Life #39* (1962). In a similar vein, the *Interiors* series

of 1964 again used emphatically modern, synthetic materials, as in *Interior #1.* The *Bathtub Collage* series, begun in 1963, pushed the depiction of intimate scenes to an extreme, vulgarly emphasising the implicit voyeurism by the use of real objects, as in *Bathtub Collage #2* (1963). He initiated many other series in the late 1960s, such as the *Bedroom Paintings, Seascapes* and *Smokers,* continuing to develop them into the 1970s. During the 1970s he occasionally produced large canvas works using several free-standing sections, so dissolving the barrier between painting and sculpture. Since 1983 Wesselmann has concentrated on brightly painted 'drawings', massively enlarged from quick sketches and cut from sheets of aluminium or steel. *P. C.*

Long Beach 1974, *Tom Wesselmann: The Early Years, Collages 1959–1962,* exhibition catalogue by C. W. Glenn, California State University Art Galleries, Long Beach, 1974
S. Stealingworth, *Tom Wesselmann,* New York, 1981
London 1988, *Tom Wesselmann: Paintings 1962–1986,* exhibition catalogue by J. McEwen, The Mayor Gallery and the Mayor Rowan Gallery, London, 1988

H. C. Westermann

b Los Angeles, 1922; *d* Danbury, CT, 1981

In 1947, after serving in the US Marine Corps and working as an acrobat, H.C. Westermann entered the School of the Art Institute of Chicago, where he studied advertising and design. He re-enlisted in the Marine Corps in 1950 and served in Korea, returning to Chicago in 1952 and re-entering the School of the Art Institute. He studied Fine Art under Paul Weighardt and began to exhibit paintings in 1953. In 1954 he stopped painting to concentrate entirely on sculpture and in 1955 he sold his first construction to the architect Mies van der Rohe. Throughout the 1950s Westermann supported himself as a handyman and carpenter, the possible source of the meticulous craftsmanship of his eccentric wooden assemblages, which combine American folk with Dada and Surrealism, the names of Duchamp and Cornell being regularly invoked in connection with his work. He had his first one-man show at the Allan Frumkin Gallery in Chicago in 1958, and when Frumkin opened a gallery in New York in 1959, Westermann gained access to a New York art audience. He also showed at the 1959 'New Images of Man' exhibition at MOMA, New York, where he and fellow Chicago artists Leon Golub and Cosmo

Campbell were dubbed the 'Chicago Monster Roster'. In 1956, developing his explorations of architectural forms, he began a series of suggestive, curious miniature buildings, including *The Madhouse* (1958) and *The Mysterious Yellow Mausoleum* (1958), in which the viewer peeps through the windows to observe disturbing scenes within, and *About a Black Magic Maker* (1959–60). Although Westermann stressed the optimism of his work, he was scarred by his war experiences, from which he derived a Dadaist perception of the purposelessness of civilisation. The sometimes sinister quality of his sculptures, such as *Swingin' Red King and Silver Queen* (1960), has caused him to be seen as a precursor of 'funk' art. Westermann's assemblages should be seen as autonomous objects rather than representations, and are often punning, paradoxical and inscrutably non-functional. His later work reveals an increasingly abstract orientation and a concern with the nature of materials. He also worked with bronze and produced lithographs and drawings, which displayed to the full his sense of humour. *E. B.*

New York et al. 1978, *H. C. Westermann*, exhibition catalogue by B. Haskell, Whitney Museum of American Art, New York, 1978

London 1981, *H. C. Westermann*, exhibition catalogue, Serpentine Gallery, London, 1981

B. Barrett, ed., *Letters from H. C. Westermann*, New York, 1988

Emmett Williams

b Greenville, SC, 1925

After studying poetry at Kenyon College with John Crowe Ranson, Emmett Williams moved to Europe in 1949, living first in Paris, then Lugano and finally Darmstadt.

In Darmstadt in the mid-1950s he met Daniel Spoerri and Claus Bremer, who were interested, like Williams, in concrete poetry; through Spoerri he met Robert Filliou, Dieter Roth and Jean Tinguely. Williams's poetry was first published in the magazine *Material*, founded by Spoerri, and it later appeared in the important Fluxus publication *An Anthology* edited by La Monte Young and Jackson Mac Low. Associated with the movement from its inception, Williams participated in the large Fluxus festival in Wiesbaden in September 1962, during which he presented his work *An Opera*, a fragmented poem written on long rolls of paper. At the 'Festival of Misfits' in London in 1962 he presented his *Alphabet Symphony*. In this work he 'performed' the alphabet using objects and actions, chosen largely by chance, in place of the letters. After organising a performance in Paris in 1963 that involved Fluxus artists but was not called a Fluxus festival, he was banished from the movement by its leader George Maciunas. Nevertheless, his work was still performed and published by the Fluxus group well into the 1970s. He returned in 1966 to America, where until 1970 he was editor of The Something Else Press, through which he published works by Spoerri, himself and others, including Spoerri's *An Anecdoted Topography of Chance* in 1966. Since the 1970s he has concentrated on making prints. Some, such as the *Variations upon a Spoerri Landscape* (1973), were figurative, in this case based on photographs and inspired by Spoerri's *tableaux-pièges* ('snare-pictures'). Others, such as *Letters to Ay-O* (1976–77), were poems in which brightly coloured words were set out in an ordered symmetric design. More recently he has continued producing prints, some of them brightly coloured abstract works. *P. C.*

H. Ruhé, *Fluxus: The Most Radical and Experimental Art Movement of the Sixties*, Amsterdam, 1979, section 3. Wil

Emmett Williams, *Schemes and Variations*, Stuttgart, 1981

J. Hendricks, *Fluxus Codex*, New York, 1988, pp. 579–82

Biographies compiled by:
E.B. Elizabeth Brooks
P.C. Philip Cooper
S.F. Simonetta Fraquelli
C.O. Caroline Odgers
J.S. Joanna Skipwith

chronology

history

cultural events

	history	AMERICA	UK	CONTINENTAL EUROPE AND ELSEWHERE
1951	*UK* End of Marshall Aid *UK* Winston Churchill re-elected as Prime Minister (Conservative Party in power until 1964)	'Robert Rauschenberg', first solo exhibition, Betty Parsons Gallery, New York 'Roy Lichtenstein', first solo exhibition, Carlebach Gallery, New York First colour broadcasts by CBS television **Books:** Marshall McLuhan, *The Mechanical Bride: Folklore of Industrial Man*; J. D. Salinger, *The Catcher in the Rye*	Festival of Britain opens 'Growth and Form', Institute of Contemporary Arts (ICA), London	● ● ●
1952	*USA* Dwight D. Eisenhower elected President, with Richard Nixon as Vice-President (Republican Party in power until 1960)	'Andy Warhol: Fifteen Drawings based on the Writings of Truman Capote', first solo exhibition, Hugo Gallery, New York Rauschenberg, Merce Cunningham and John Cage collaborate at Black Mountain College, North Carolina **Films:** *Niagara* (with Marilyn Monroe)	'Young Sculptors', ICA, London Formation of the 'Young Group', later known as the Independent Group, with Reyner Banham as its secretary Joe Tilson enters Royal College of Art, London	● ● ●
1953	*USSR* Joseph Stalin dies. Nikita Khrushchev becomes First Secretary *UK* Coronation of Queen Elizabeth II Korean War ends *FRG* Konrad Adenauer re-elected Chancellor	'Willem de Kooning: Paintings on the Theme of the Woman', Sidney Janis Gallery, New York Larry Rivers' *George Washington Crossing the Delaware* exhibited at Tibor de Nagy Gallery, New York 'Dada 1916–1923', Sidney Janis Gallery, New York 'Robert Rauschenberg' exhibition of White Paintings and Black Paintings, Stable Gallery, New York 'Allan Kaprow', first solo exhibition, Hansa Gallery, New York First issue of *Playboy* Cinemascope first used **Films:** Fred Zinnemann, *From Here to Eternity* (with Frank Sinatra, Montgomery Clift), *How to Marry a Millionaire* (with Marilyn Monroe), *Gentlemen Prefer Blondes* (with Marilyn Monroe and Jane Russell)	'Parallel of Life and Art', ICA, London Peter Blake enters Royal College of Art BBC Radio presents The Goon Show	Raymond Hains and Jacques de la Villeglé collaborate Arman and Yves Klein collaborate on Happenings Jean Tinguely and Daniel Spoerri collaborate on ballet, *Prisma* **Films:** Luchino Visconti, *Senso* **Books:** Roland Barthes, *Le Degré Zéro de l'écriture*
1954	*UK* End of rationing *USA* Senator Joseph McCarthy criticised by Congress for his anti-communist investigations over last four years	'Jess', first solo exhibition, The Place, San Francisco Marilyn Monroe marries ex-baseball player Joe DiMaggio 55% of US homes have TV sets **Films:** Elia Kazan, *On the Waterfront* (with Marlon Brando) and *East of Eden* (with James Dean)	'Man versus Machine', Building Centre, London 'Collage and Objects', ICA, London Richard Smith and Robyn Denny enter Royal College of Art	'César' first solo exhibition, Galerie Lucien Durand, Paris
1955	*UK* Winston Churchill resigns as Prime Minister. Anthony Eden appointed in his place *UK* General Election won by Conservative Party *UK* Hugh Gaitskell elected leader of Labour Party Eastern Bloc nations form military alliance, the Warsaw Pact, in response to creation of NATO by Western countries in 1949	'Ed Kienholz', first solo exhibition, Café Galleria, Los Angeles Rauschenberg and Jasper Johns meet Richard Bellamy runs the Hansa Gallery in New York (until 1959); co-directed with Ivan Karp 1956–57 James Rosenquist moves to New York, meets Robert Indiana James Dean killed in a car crash Disneyland opens in Anaheim, California **Films:** Nicholas Ray, *Rebel Without a*	'Richard Hamilton', Hanover Gallery, London 'Man, Machine and Motion', Hatton Gallery, Newcastle-upon-Tyne, touring to ICA, London Lawrence Alloway becomes Assistant Director of ICA, London	● ● ●

	AMERICA	UK	CONTINENTAL EUROPE AND ELSEWHERE
	Cause (with James Dean, Natalie Wood); George Stevens, *Giant* (with Rock Hudson, Elizabeth Taylor, James Dean); Delbert Mann, *Marty* (with Ernest Borgnine); Richard Brooks, *The Blackboard Jungle* (with Glenn Ford); Billy Wilder, *The Seven Year Itch* (with Marilyn Monroe) **Hits:** Bill Haley and the Comets' first hit, *Rock around the Clock*		
1956 *USSR* Khrushchev denounces Stalin's 'cult of personality' *UK* Khrushchev and Bulganin visit Britain *Egypt* nationalises Suez Canal; provokes the Suez crisis (Israel, Britain, France invade); establishment of United Arab Republic *Hungary* Soviet troops invade *USA* Eisenhower re-elected President	'George Segal', first solo exhibition, Hansa Gallery, New York Claes Oldenburg moves to New York Edward Kienholz opens Now Gallery in Los Angeles (closes after a year) Elvis Presley appears on Ed Sullivan Show Marilyn Monroe marries playwright Arthur Miller Jackson Pollock dies in car crash **Films:** Fred M. Wilcox, *Forbidden Planet* (with Walter Pidgeon) **Hits:** Elvis Presley, *Heartbreak Hotel*, Chuck Berry, *Roll over Beethoven*, Little Richard, *Tutti Frutti*	'Modern Art in the United States', Tate Gallery, London 'This is Tomorrow', Whitechapel Art Gallery, London John Osbourne's *Look Back in Anger* first peformed at Royal Court **Books:** Colin Wilson, *The Outsider*	'Arman', first solo exhibition, Galerie du Haut-Pavé, Paris 'Niki de Saint Phalle', first solo exhibition, St Gallen, Switzerland
1957 *UK* Harold Macmillan becomes Prime Minister Treaty of Rome; establishment of European Economic Community (EEC) *USSR* First Sputnik satellite launched	Leo Castelli Gallery opens in New York Kienholz and Walter Hopps open Ferus Gallery, Los Angeles Elvis Presley called up by US Army **Films:** *And God Created Woman* (with Brigitte Bardot), *Jailhouse Rock* (with Elvis Presley) **Hits:** Buddy Holly, *Peggy Sue*, The Everly Brothers, *Bye Bye Love* **Books:** Vance Packard, *The Hidden Persuaders*; Jack Kerouac, *On the Road*	Hamilton teaches part-time at Royal College of Art in department of Interior Design (until 1961) Bill Haley and the Comets concert in London Television audiences overtake radio	'Martial Raysse', first solo exhibition, Galerie Longchamp, Nice **Books:** Roland Barthes, *Mythologies*
1958 *UK* Campaign for Nuclear Disarmament (CND) founded; march to Atomic Weapons Research Establishment at Aldermaston Coup in Algiers *France* General Charles de Gaulle returns as Prime Minister, later elected President	'Jasper Johns', first solo exhibition, Leo Castelli Gallery, New York 'Robert Rauschenberg', 'combine' paintings exhibition, Leo Castelli Gallery, New York 'Billy Al Bengston', first solo exhibition, Ferus Gallery, Los Angeles 'Red Grooms', first solo exhibition, Sun Gallery, Provincetown, MA 'H. C. Westermann', first solo exhibition, Allan Frumkin Gallery, Chicago 'Allan D'Arcangelo', first exhibition, Galería Genova, Mexico City Jim Dine arrives in New York where he meets Tom Wesselmann and Oldenburg **Films:** *The Young Lions* (with Marlon Brando) **Hits:** Eddie Cochran, *Summertime Blues*, The Teddy Bears, *To Know Him is to Love Him*	'Five Young Painters', ICA, London 'Eduardo Paolozzi', Hanover Gallery, London Anthony Donaldson enters Slade School of Fine Art, London Peter Blake and Clive Barker meet Nicholas Monro enters Chelsea School of Art, London, where he meets Patrick Caulfield R. B. Kitaj moves to England; he collaborates with Paolozzi in Oxford **Books:** John Kenneth Galbraith, *The Affluent Society*	'Le Vide,' Yves Klein exhibition, Galerie Iris Clert, Paris Christo arrives in Paris Daniel Spoerri settles in Paris Arthur Køpcke opens Galerie Køpcke in Copenhagen (closes 1963) **Books:** Robert Frank, *Les Américains* (US edition published 1959)
1959 *Cuba* Dictator Fulgencio Batista flees; Fidel Castro becomes new leader *USA* 'Kitchen debate' between Nixon and Khrushchev televised live from Moscow on American television *USA* Khrushchev visits United States *USSR* Soviet spaceship photographs far side of the moon	'Allan Kaprow, 18 Happenings in Six Parts', Reuben Gallery, New York 'Sixteen Americans', Museum of Modern Art, New York 'George Brecht', first solo exhibition, Reuben Gallery, New York Ivan Karp works at the Leo Castelli Gallery (until 1969) Anna Reuben opens Reuben Gallery, New York Buddy Holly dies in plane crash TV series of *Mickey Mouse* **Films:** Billy Wilder, *Some Like it Hot* (with Jack Lemmon, Tony Curtis, Marilyn Monroe) **Books:** Vance Packard, *Status Seekers: An Exploration of Class Behavior in America*	'The New American Painting', Tate Gallery, London 'The Developing Process', ICA, London 'Place', ICA, London Kitaj, David Hockney, Allen Jones, Peter Phillips, Derek Boshier enter Royal College of Art The Club opens at 100 Oxford Street, London **Hits:** Cliff Richard, *Living Doll*	'Biennale de Paris', Musée d'Art Moderne de la Ville de Paris, Paris (includes 'combine' paintings by Robert Rauschenberg) 'Robert Rauschenberg', Galleria La Tartaruga, Rome 'Jasper Johns', solo exhibition, Galerie Rive Droite, Paris **Films:** Federico Fellini, *La Dolce Vita* (with Marcello Mastroianni); François Truffaut, *Les Quatre Cents Coups*

	AMERICA	UK	CONTINENTAL EUROPE AND ELSEWHERE
1960 *USA* John F. Kennedy elected President (Democratic Party in power until 1968) *USA* Oral contraceptives approved for sale	'Ray Gun', 'Claes Oldenburg, The Street' and 'Jim Dine, The House', Judson Gallery, New York 'New Forms – New Media', Martha Jackson Gallery, New York 'New Forms – New Media, Version II', Martha Jackson Gallery, New York 'Jim Dine', first solo exhibition, Reuben Gallery, New York *The Smiling Workman*, Jim Dine Happening, Judson Gallery, New York Series of Happenings by Jim Dine, Reuben Gallery, New York: *Car Crash, Jim Dine's Vaudeville, The Shining Bed* Bellamy opens Green Gallery in New York; funded by collector Robert Scull Jean Tinguely visits New York, presents *Hommage à New York*, Museum of Modern Art; he comes into contact with Rauschenberg and Johns; settles in New York with Niki de Saint Phalle Roy Lichtenstein and Allan Kaprow teach at Rutgers University, New Brunswick, NJ Kaprow introduces Lichtenstein to Dine, Oldenburg and Segal Eddie Cochran and Gene Vincent die in car crash 87% of US homes have TV sets	Caulfield enters Royal College of Art Jones expelled from Royal College of Art Gerald Laing enters St Martin's School of Art, London **Films:** Karel Reisz, *Saturday Night and Sunday Morning* (with Albert Finney) **Books:** Reyner Banham, *Theory and Design in the First Machine Age*	'Le Plein', Arman exhibition, Galerie Iris Clert, Paris 'Les Nouveaux Réalistes', Galleria Apollinaire, Milan 'A 40 degrés au-dessus de Dada', Galerie J, Paris 'Le Nouveau Réalisme à Paris et à New York', Galerie Rive Droite, Paris 'Michelangelo Pistoletto', first solo exhibition, Galleria Galatea, Turin Nouveau Réalisme is founded; the members include Arman, François Dufrêne, César, Hains, Klein, Raysse, Pierre Restany, Mimmo Rotella, Spoerri, Tinguely, Villeglé Johns, Rauschenberg, Saint Phalle and Tinguely take part in a performance of John Cage's *Variation II* in Paris Arman meets Rivers, Rauschenberg and Johns in Paris **Films:** Luchino Visconti, *Rocco and his brothers* (with Alain Delon)
1961 *USSR* Yuri Gagarin becomes first man in space *USA/Cuba* Bay of Pigs: failed invasion by Cuban exiles Dag Hammarskjöld, Secretary-General of the United Nations, killed in plane crash while seeking peace in Congo *GDR* Wall erected between East and West Berlin *UK* Oral contraceptives approved for sale	'Environments, Situations, Spaces', Martha Jackson Gallery, New York 'The Art of Assemblage', The Museum of Modern Art, New York 'Yves Klein', Leo Castelli Gallery, New York (also seen at Dwan Gallery, Los Angeles) 'Tom Wesselmann, Great American Nude', first solo exhibition, Tanager Gallery, New York 'Richard Smith', first solo exhibition, Green Gallery, New York 'Arman', Cordier-Warren Gallery, New York Oldenburg opens *The Store*, *Ray Gun Mfg. Co.* on East 2nd Street, New York in cooperation with Green Gallery George Maciunas holds lecture-demonstrations, *Musica Antiqua et Nova*, at his AG Gallery, New York Yoko Ono holds pre-Fluxus concerts in her Chambers Street loft, Manhattan Richard Artschwager and Oldenburg meet Lawrence Alloway appointed curator at Guggenheim Museum, New York David Hockney visits New York Bob Dylan causes excitement in New York **Films:** Boris Leven, *West Side Story* (with Natalie Wood, Richard Beymer, Russ Tamblyn; music by Leonard Bernstein) **Hits:** Fats Domino, *I Hear You Knocking*	'Young Contemporaries', RBA Galleries, London (including Caulfield, Hockney, Jones, Kitaj and Phillips) Lawrence Alloway resigns as Programme Director at ICA, London, moves to New York Blake meets Boshier and Phillips Hamilton gives prizes to Kitaj and Hockney at Royal College of Art Colin Self enters the Slade	'Christo', first solo exhibition, Galerie Haro Lauhus, Cologne 'Alain Jacquet', first solo exhibition, Galerie Breteau, Paris '2e Biennale des Jeunes', Musée d'Art Moderne de la Ville de Paris, Paris (includes works by Hockney, Jones, Smith and Tilson) 'Jasper Johns', Galerie Rive Droite, Paris 'Robert Rauschenberg', Galerie Daniel Cordier, Paris 'Daniel Spoerri', first solo exhibition, Galleria Schwarz, Milan 'Arthur Køpcke', first solo exhibition, Galerie Køpcke, Copenhagen 'Eduardo Arroyo', first solo exhibition, Galerie Claude Lévin, Paris Saint Phalle joins Nouveau Réalisme Pierre Restany presents the Nouveaux Réalistes, Arman, Dufrêne, Hains, Klein, Saint Phalle and Tinguely on the French television programme, *En Français dans le texte* George Maciunas, as graphic artist with US Air Force, sent to Germany; there between 1962 and 1963 he organises Fluxus concerts Maciunas meets Nam June Paik and Wolf Vostell **Films:** Francois Truffaut, *Jules et Jim* (with Jeanne Moreau)
1962 *USA* John Glenn becomes first man to orbit earth Cuban missile crisis *South Africa* Nelson Mandela's trial begins	'James Rosenquist', first solo exhibition, Green Gallery, New York 'Roy Lichtenstein', cartoon images, Leo Castelli Gallery, New York 'The New Painting of Common Objects', Pasadena Art Museum, CA Claes Oldenburg, second version of *The Store* at Green Gallery, New York 'Andy Warhol, Paintings of Campbell's Soup Cans', Ferus Gallery, Los Angeles 'International Exhibition of the New Realists', Sidney Janis Gallery, New York 'My Country 'Tis of Thee', Dwan Gallery, Los Angeles 'Joe Goode', first solo exhibition, Dilexi	'Peter Blake', first solo exhibition, Portal Gallery, London 'Joe Tilson', Marlborough Fine Art, London 'Image in Progress', Grabowski Gallery, London Jann Haworth enters the Slade Sunday Times first colour supplement (features on Pop Art and Mary Quant) Marshall McLuhan lectures at ICA, London *Pop Goes the Easel*, Ken Russell monitor film for BBC Television shown (25 March), features Blake, Boshier, Pauline Boty and Phillips	'Dylaby' (Dynamic Labyrinth), Stedelijk Museum, Amsterdam Christo and Gerard Deschamps join Nouveau Réalisme Robert Filliou exhibits works in a cap, called the 'Galerie Légitime', in the streets of Paris, Frankfurt and London Fluxus Festival in Wiesbaden, Copenhagen, Paris Klein dies

	AMERICA	**UK**	**CONTINENTAL EUROPE AND ELSEWHERE**
	Gallery, Los Angeles 'Andy Warhol', Stable Gallery, New York 'Robert Indiana', first solo exhibition, Stable Gallery, New York 'Wayne Thiebaud', Allan Stone Gallery, New York Ferus Gallery now directed by Irving Blum Marilyn Monroe found dead **Books:** Joseph Heller, *Catch 22*		
1963 *UK* Death of Gaitskell *UK* Profumo Affair (sex scandal with Christine Keeler causes John Profumo, Secretary of State for War, to resign) *FRG* Kennedy visits Berlin, delivers 'Ich bin ein Berliner' (I am a Berliner) speech *USA* Martin Luther King leads peaceful civil-rights march to Washington, DC, delivers 'I have a dream' speech *USA* Kennedy assassinated, Lyndon B. Johnson becomes President	'Americans 1963', Museum of Modern Art, New York 'Six Painters and the Object', The Solomon R. Guggenheim Museum, New York 'The Popular Image Exhibition', Washington Gallery of Art, Washington DC 'Popular Art', Nelson-Atkins Museum of Art, Kansas City 'Pop Goes! The Easel', Contemporary Arts Museum, Houston 'Six More' (in conjunction with 'Six Painters and the Object', New York), Los Angeles County Museum of Art 'Pop Art USA', Oakland Art Museum 'Mixed Media and Pop Art', Albright-Knox Art Gallery, Buffalo 'Edward Ruscha', Ferus Gallery, Los Angeles 'Robert Rauschenberg' (Retrospective), The Jewish Museum, New York 'John Wesley', first solo exhibition, Robert Elkon Gallery, New York Warhol studio becomes known as the Factory Richard Hamilton meets Warhol at the 'By or of Marcel Duchamp or Rose Selavy' retrospective, Pasadena Art Museum Hockney lives in Los Angeles **Films:** *Cleopatra* (with Elizabeth Taylor, Richard Burton); Alfred Hitchcock, *The Birds*; Andy Warhol, *Sleep, Kiss* and *Blow Job* **Hits:** The Crystals, *Da Doo Ron Ron*, Beach Boys, *Surfin' USA*, The Ronettes, *Be my Baby*	'David Hockney', first solo exhibition, Kasmin Gallery, London 'Allen Jones', first solo exhibition, Arthur Tooth & Sons, London 'R. B. Kitaj with commentary, Pictures without commentary', Marlborough Fine Art, London 'The Popular Image', ICA, London The Beatles' first LP, *Please Please Me* is released; they appear at the Royal Variety Performance **Hits:** The Beatles, *She Loves You*	'Les Nouveaux Réalistes' and Festival of Nouveau Réalisme, Neue Galerie im Künstlerhaus, Munich 'Robert Rauschenberg', Galerie Ileana Sonnabend, Paris 'Jim Dine', Galerie Ileana Sonnabend, Paris '3e Biennale des Jeunes', Musée d'Art Moderne de la Ville de Paris, Paris (includes work by Hockney, Boshier, Jones, Phillips) Fluxus Festival in Düsseldorf Gerhard Richter, Konrad Lueg, Sigmar Polke and Manfred Kuttner organise a show in an empty shop in Düsseldorf, entitled *Pop Art? Kapitalistischer Realismus? Nouveau Réalisme?* Richter and Lueg stage a Happening in a Düsseldorf furniture store, entitled *A Demonstration for Capitalist Realism* **Films:** Federico Fellini, $8\frac{1}{2}$ (with Marcello Mastroianni)
1964 *South Africa* Nelson Mandela sentenced to life imprisonment *USSR* Khrushchev falls, Leonid Brezhnev becomes First Secretary *UK* Harold Wilson elected Prime Minister (Labour Party in power until 1970)	'Jasper Johns' (Retrospective), The Jewish Museum, New York 'The American Supermarket', Bianchini Gallery, New York 'Mel Ramos', first solo exhibition, Bianchini Gallery, New York Christo moves to New York World Fair opens in New York The Beatles perform on Ed Sullivan Show First record releases on the Motown label **Hits:** The Shangri-Las, *Leader of the Pack*	'The New Generation: 1964', Whitechapel Art Gallery, London Radio Caroline makes its first broadcast from North Sea *Ready, Steady, Go* on television **Films:** The Beatles, *A Hard Day's Night* **Hits:** The Animals, *House of the Rising Sun*	'Andy Warhol', Galerie Ileana Sonnabend, Paris 'Claes Oldenburg', Galerie Ileana Sonnabend, Paris 'Michelangelo Pistoletto', Galerie Ileana Sonnabend, Paris 'Nieuwe Realisten (Nieuw Realisme, Nieuwe figuratie, Object schildering, Pop art, Nouveau Realisme, Traditioneel realisme, Sociaal realisme)', Gemeentemuseum, The Hague 'Amerikansk pop-kunst', Moderna Museet, Stockholm Rauschenberg receives the Grand Prize at the Venice Biennale; Johns, Dine and Oldenburg also exhibit; Joe Tilson exhibition in British Pavilion Rotella settles in Paris
1965 *USA* Murder of Malcolm X of Black Power Muslims *USA* Johnson orders large-scale bombing of North Vietnam *Rhodesia* Ian Smith declares UDI (Unilateral Declaration of Independence) *China* Cultural Revolution begins (ends 1969)	'Richard Artschwager', first solo exhibition, Leo Castelli Gallery, New York 'Andy Warhol' (Retrospective), ICA, University of Pennsylvania 'The New American Realism', Worcester Art Museum, Worcester, MA	'Patrick Caulfield', first solo exhibition, Robert Fraser Gallery, London 'Peter Phillips', first solo exhibition, Kornblee Gallery, New York 'Colin Self', first solo exhibition, Piccadilly Gallery, London Bob Dylan plays at Albert Hall Mini skirts are the height of fashion	'Pop Art, Nouveau Réalisme, etc,' Palais des Beaux-Arts, Brussels 'Roy Lichtenstein', Galerie Ileana Sonnabend, Paris 'James Rosenquist', Galerie Ileana Sonnabend, Paris 'Allan D'Arcangelo', Galerie Ileana Sonnabend, Paris 'Andy Warhol', Galleria Gian Enzo

	AMERICA	UK	CONTINENTAL EUROPE AND ELSEWHERE
	'Pop Art and the American Tradition', Milwaukee Art Center, Milwaukee 'Ray Johnson', solo exhibition, Willard Gallery, New York	**Films:** The Beatles, *Help*, Richard Lester, *The Knack* (with Rita Tushingham) **Hits:** Rolling Stones, *(I Can't Get No) Satisfaction*, The Who, *My Generation*	Sperone, Turin 'Equipo Crónica', first group show, Galleria 'Il Centro', Turin Brecht and Filliou run the shop, *La Cedille qui Sourit*, Villefranche-sur-Mer (until 1968)
1966 *USA/UK* Protests against Vietnam War *USA* Emergence of Hippie movement	'The Other Tradition', Institute of Contemporary Art, University of Pennsylvania, Philadelphia **Films:** Andy Warhol, *The Chelsea Girls* and *The Velvet Underground*	'Marcel Duchamp', exhibition at Tate Gallery, London (with Richard Hamilton's reconstruction of the *Large Glass*) London becomes fashion centre: King's Road, Chelsea, Kensington Church Street, Carnaby Street **Hits:** The Beatles, *Day Tripper*, *Paperback Writer*, *Eleanor Rigby*	'Sigmar Polke', first solo exhibition, Galerie René Block, West Berlin 'Hon', Moderna Museet, Stockholm 'Michelangelo Pistoletto', Galleria La Bertesca, Genoa **Films:** Michelangelo Antonioni, *Blow Up*
1967 Arab-Israeli Six-Day War *Bolivia* Death of Ernesto 'Che' Guevara	'Claes Oldenburg, Projects for Monuments', Museum of Contemporary Art, Chicago 'Homage to Marilyn Monroe', Sidney Janis Gallery, New York **Films:** *The Graduate* (with Dustin Hoffman, Anne Bancroft, Katharine Ross), *Bonnie and Clyde* (with Warren Beatty, Faye Dunaway), *Guess who's coming to Dinner* (with Spencer Tracy, Katharine Hepburn, Sidney Poitier) **Hits:** The Doors, *Light my Fire*	Mick Jagger and gallery owner Robert Fraser appear in court on drugs charges The Beatles go to India to see the Maharishi Mahesh Yogi The Beatles' manager, Brian Epstein, found dead Festival of Flower Children **Hits:** The Beatles, *Sergeant Pepper's Lonely Hearts Club Band* (LP with cover by Peter Blake)	'Tom Wesselmann', Galerie Ileana Sonnabend, Paris
1968 *USA* Martin Luther King assassinated *USA* Robert F. Kennedy assassinated *France/Germany* Fierce student unrest and riots in Paris and throughout Germany, the 'month of barricades' *USSR* invades Czechoslovakia *USA* Nixon elected President (Republican Party in power until 1976)	'Assemblage in California', Art Gallery, University of California, Irvine Warhol is shot and seriously hurt by the actress Valerie Solanis **Films:** *Barbarella* (with Jane Fonda)	'Clive Barker', first solo exhibition, Robert Fraser Gallery, London 'The Obsessive Image 1960–68', ICA, London 'Roy Lichtenstein' (Retrospective), Tate Gallery, London, and European tour The Beatles open Apple boutique in London American musical *Hair* opens in London	John Lennon and Yoko Ono 'bed in' for peace at the Hilton Hotel, Amsterdam
1969 *UK* Civil unrest in Northern Ireland leading to direct rule from London *USA* Apollo 11 space mission; Neil Armstrong becomes first man to walk on the moon *FRG* Willy Brandt elected Chancellor *Italy* Terrorist bombings in Milan and Rome	'New York Painting and Sculpture: 1940–1970', Metropolitan Museum of Art, New York 'Claes Oldenburg' (Retrospective), MOMA, New York 'New York, The Second Breakthrough 1959–64', Art Gallery, University of California at Irvine First issue of Warhol's *Interview* is published Woodstock Music Festival, New York State **Films:** *Easy Rider* (with Peter Fonda, Dennis Hopper)	'Pop Art', Hayward Gallery, London Brian Jones of Rolling Stones found dead Rolling Stones play for free in Hyde Park Isle of Wight Pop Festival Biba department store opens in London **Films:** Stanley Kubrick, *2001: A Space Odyssey*	• • •
1970 *USA* Nixon sends US troops into Cambodia *USA* Anti-war protestors shot at Kent State University, Ohio *UK* Edward Heath elected Prime Minister (Conservative Party in power until 1974) *France* Death of de Gaulle *Chile* Salvador Allende elected President	Jimi Hendrix dies of overdose Janis Joplin dies of overdose	'David Hockney' (Retrospective), Whitechapel Art Gallery, London 'Richard Hamilton' (Retrospective), Tate Gallery, London Beatles officially split up Second Isle of Wight Pop concert	'Nouveau Realisme 1960–1970', Rotonda della Besana, Milan; organised by Centre Apollinaire 'Fluxus and Happenings', Kunstverein, Cologne
1971 *FRG* Brandt receives Nobel Peace Prize	'Multiples. The First Decade', Philadelphia Museum of Art, Philadelphia Jim Morrison dies of overdose	'Eduardo Paolozzi' (Retrospective), Tate Gallery, London **Hits:** Rolling Stones, *Sticky Fingers* LP (cover by Andy Warhol)	• • •
1972 Nixon visits China *FRG* Arrest of Ulrike Meinhof and Andreas Baader, leaders of the	• • •	• • •	'Peter Phillips' (Retrospective), Westfälischer Kunstverein, Munster

	AMERICA	UK	CONTINENTAL EUROPE AND ELSEWHERE
Baader–Meinhof terrorist group *FRG* Arab guerrillas murder Israeli athletes at Munich Olympics *USA* Nixon re-elected President			
1973 Britain, Ireland and Denmark become members of EEC Peace Treaty in Paris calls for complete withdrawal of US troops from Vietnam *USA* Watergate Affair Yom Kippur War ('October War'); Egypt and Syria defeated following their attack on Israel World Oil crisis *Chile* President Allende overthrown and killed by military junta led by General Pinochet	● ● ●	● ● ●	'Tilson' (Retrospective), Museum Boymans-van Beuningen, Rotterdam
1974 *UK* Wilson re-elected Prime Minister (Labour Party in power until 1979) *FRG* Brandt resigns after one of his personal assistants, Guillaume, is discovered to be a GDR spy *USA* Nixon forced to resign over Watergate Affair, Gerald Ford becomes President	'American Pop Art', Whitney Museum of American Art, New York	● ● ●	● ● ●
1975 *UK* Margaret Thatcher becomes leader of the Conservative Party Fall of Saigon and end of Vietnam War *UK* Two thirds of population vote to stay in EEC *Spain* Death of General Franco *Spain* Juan Carlos becomes King	● ● ●	'Richard Smith: Seven Exhibitions 1961–75', Tate Gallery, London	● ● ●
1976 *China* Death of Chairman Mao Tse-tung *USA* Jimmy Carter elected President (Democratic Party in power until 1980)	'American Pop Art and Culture of the Sixties', New Gallery of Contemporary Art, Cleveland, OH 'Robert Rauschenberg', Smithsonian Institute, Washington DC	● ● ●	'Pop Art in England: Beginnings of a New Figuration 1947–63', Kunstverein, Hamburg, Städtische Galerie im Lenbachhaus, Munich, York City Art Gallery
1977 *Spain* Democracy returns; Adolfo Suárez elected Prime Minister *South Africa* Steve Biko killed *Rhodesia* Ian Smith accepts black majority rule	'Jasper Johns' (Retrospective), Whitney Museum, New York and tour Elvis Presley dies	● ● ●	'Paris–New York', Musée National d'Art Moderne, Centre Georges Pompidou, Paris
1978 *USA* Camp David Talks: Anwar Sadat, President of Egypt, and Menachem Begin, Prime Minister of Israel, meet with President Carter to discuss Middle East peace settlement *Italy* Polish cardinal, Karol Wojtyla elected Pope as John Paul II, the first non-Italian Pope for over 500 years *Italy* Aldo Moro, former Prime Minister, is murdered by Red Brigades	● ● ●	● ● ●	● ● ●
1979 *Iran* The Shah driven into exile; Ayatollah Khomeini becomes leader *USA* Egypt and Israel sign Peace Treaty *UK* Margaret Thatcher elected Prime Minister *Iran* takes US hostages *Rhodesia* renamed Zimbabwe *Afghanistan* Soviet troops invade	● ● ●	'Allen Jones' (Retrospective), Walker Art Gallery, Liverpool	● ● ●
1980 *UK* Three gunmen sieze 20 hostages at the Iranian Embassy, London, and demand freedom for 91 Arabs in Iran	John Lennon shot dead **Books:** Andy Warhol and Pat Hackett, *POPism: The Warhol '60s*	● ● ●	● ● ●

	AMERICA	UK	CONTINENTAL EUROPE AND ELSEWHERE
Poland Lech Walesa leads strike at Gdansk shipyards; founds Solidarity trade union *USA* Ronald Reagan elected President (Republican Party in power to date)			
1981 *Egypt* Sadat assassinated Greece becomes member of EEC	● ● ●	'Patrick Caulfield', Walker Art Gallery, Liverpool and Tate Gallery, London	● ● ●
1982 Falklands War *USSR* Brezhnev dies; succeeded by Yuri Andropov	● ● ●	'Peter Phillips' (Retrospective), Walker Art Gallery, Liverpool and tour	'Arroyo' (Retrospective), Musée National d'Art Moderne, Centre Georges Pompidou, Paris
1983 *UK* Conservative Party elected for second term	● ● ●	'Peter Blake' (Retrospective), Tate Gallery, London and tour	● ● ●
1984 *UK* IRA bomb blasts Conservative Party conference hotel in Brighton *India* Indira Gandhi assassinated Famine in Ethiopia	'Blam! The Explosion of Pop, Minimalism, and Performance, 1958–64', Whitney Museum of American Art, New York Warhol collaborates on paintings with Jean Michel Basquiat and Francesco Clemente	● ● ●	'Sigmar Polke' (Retrospective), Josef-Haubrich-Kunsthalle, Cologne
1985 *USSR* Mikhail Gorbachev becomes leader of Soviet Union following death of Konstantin Chernenko Reagan and Gorbachev hold talks in Geneva	'James Rosenquist' (Retrospective), Denver Art Museum and tour	● ● ●	'Pop Art 1955–70', Art Gallery of New South Wales, Sydney (and tour of Australia)
1986 *USSR* Chernobyl disaster *USSR* Gorbachev first uses term 'Glasnost' (openness) *Libya* US Air Force bombs Tripoli Spain and Portugal become members of EEC	● ● ●	● ● ●	'1960 Les Nouveaux Réalistes', Musée d'Art Moderne de la Ville de Paris, Paris 'Die 60er Jahre. Kölns Weg zur Kunstmetropole. Von Happening zum Kunstmarkt', Kunstverein, Cologne
1987 *UK* Violent storms sweep country *UK* Stock market collapses on Black Friday	'Made in USA. An Americanization in Modern Art, The '50s & '60s', University Art Museum, University of California, Berkeley Warhol dies following gall-bladder surgery	● ● ●	'Pop Art America Europa dalla Collezione Ludwig', Forte Belvedere, Florence (exhibition tour) 'Pop USA–UK: American and British artists of the '60s in the '80s', Odakyu Grand Gallery, Tokyo (and tour of Japan)
1988 End of Iran–Iraq War *USA* George Bush elected President	'Artschwager, Richard', Whitney Museum, New York and tour	● ● ●	Jasper Johns wins first prize at Venice Biennale
1989 *China* Tiananmen Square massacre in Peking Political reform in Eastern Europe (Czechoslovakia, Poland, Hungary, Romania) Berlin Wall taken down	'Andy Warhol: A Retrospective', Museum of Modern Art, New York and world tour 'LA POP in the Sixties', Newport Harbor Art Museum, Newport Beach	● ● ●	● ● ●
1990 Germany reunited *South Africa* Release of Nelson Mandela *Kuwait* Iraqi troops invade *UK* Thatcher resigns; John Major becomes Prime Minister	'High & Low: Modern Art and Popular Culture', Museum of Modern Art, New York	'The Independent Group: Postwar Britain and the Aesthetics of Plenty', ICA, London (exhibition tour)	'Art et Pub (Art et Publicité 1890–1990)', Musée National d'Art Moderne, Centre Georges Pompidou, Paris 'Richard Hamilton' (Retrospective), Kunstmuseum, Winterthur and tour
1991 Gulf War Famine in Ethiopia Cyclone in Bangladesh	● ● ●	'The Pop Art Show', Royal Academy of Arts, London	● ● ●

select **bibliography**

GENERAL SURVEYS

A. Bony, *Années 60's*, Paris, 1984

N. Calas, *Art in the Age of Risk and Other Essays*, New York, 1968

N. Calas and E. Calas, *Icons and Images of the Sixties*, New York, 1971

A. Hansen, *A Primer of Happenings & Time/Space Art*, New York, 1965

A. Henri, *Environments and Happenings*, London, 1974

U. Kultermann, *Art-Events and Happenings*, London, 1971

BOOKS ON POP

M. Amaya, *Pop as Art: A Survey of the New Super-Realism*, London and New York, 1965

E. Bailey, *Pop Art*, London, 1976

J. Becker and W. Vostell, *Happenings, Fluxus, Pop Art, Nouveau Réalisme*, Hamburg, 1965

M. Compton, *Pop Art*, London, 1970

E. Crispolti, *La pop art*, Milan, 1966

R.-G. Dienst, *Pop-Art: Eine Kritische Information*, Wiesbaden, 1965

C. Finch, *Pop Art: Object and Image*, London and New York, 1968

J. Hermand, *Pop International: Eine Kritische Analyse*, Frankfurt, 1971

J.-P. Keller, *Pop Art et évidence du quotidien: pour une sociologie du regard ésthetique*, Lausanne, 1979

J.-L. Lebel, *Le Happening*, Paris, 1966

E. Leffingwell and K. Marta, eds, *Modern Dreams: The Rise and Fall and Rise of Pop*, Cambridge, MA, 1988

L. Lippard, *Pop Art*, London and New York, 1966, rev. 1970

M. Livingstone, *Pop Art: A Continuing History*, London and New York, 1990

W. Noth, *Strukturen des Happenings*, Hildesheim, 1972

H. Ohff, *Pop und die Folgen*, Düsseldorf, 1969

T. Osterwold, *Pop Art*, Cologne, 1989

J. Pierre, *An Illustrated Dictionary of Pop Art*, Paris 1975; Eng. edn London, 1977

J. Russell and S. Gablik, *Pop Art Redefined*, London and New York, 1969

P. Taylor, ed., *Post-Pop Art*, Cambridge, MA, 1989

C. Tomkins, *The Bride and the Bachelors: The Heretical Courtship in Modern Art*, New York and London, 1965

Y. Tono, *The Pop Image of Man*, Tokyo, 1971

J. Walker, *Cross-overs: Art into Pop, Pop into Art*, London and New York, 1987

J. Weber, *Pop-Art, Happenings und Neue Realisten*, Munich, 1970

S. Wilson, *Pop*, London, 1974, repr. in *Modern Art: Impressionism to Post-Modernism*, ed. D. Britt, London, 1989

EXHIBITION CATALOGUES

Paris 1961, *Le Nouveau Réalisme à Paris et à New York*, preface by P. Restany, Galerie Rive Droite, Paris, 1961

New York 1962, *New Realists*, texts by J. Ashbery, P. Restany and S. Janis, Sidney Janis Gallery, New York, 1962

Berlin 1964, *Neue Realisten & Pop Art*, intro. by W. Hofmann, Akademie der Künste, Berlin, 1964

The Hague 1964, *Nieuwe Realisten*, Gemeentemuseum, The Hague, 1964

Brussels 1965, *Pop Art, Nouveau Réalisme, etc*, texts by J. Dypréau and P. Restany, Palais des Beaux-Arts, Brussels, 1965

Paris 1965, *La Figuration narrative dans l'art contemporain*, texts by G. Gassiot-Talbot, Galerie Creuze, Paris, 1965

London 1968, *The Obsessive Image*, intro. by M. Amaya, Institute of Contemporary Arts, London, 1968

London 1969, *Pop Art*, intro. by J. Russell and S. Gablik, Hayward Gallery, London, 1969

Knokke-le-Zoute 1970, *Pop Art: Nieuwe figurative/Nouveau Réalisme*, essays by J. Russell, G. Bekaert and P. Restany, Casino Communal, Knokke-le-Zoute, 1970

Paris 1977, *Paris–New York*, texts by A. Pacquement and P. Hultén, Centre Georges Pompidou, Paris, 1977

West Berlin 1978, *Aspekte der 60er Jahre: Aus der Sammlung Reinhard Onnasch*, interview with Onnasch by D. Honisch, Nationalgalerie, West Berlin, 1978

Sydney et al. 1985, *Pop Art 1955–70*, text by H. Geldzahler, Art Gallery of New South Wales, Sydney, 1985

Florence 1987, *Pop Art America Europa dalla Collezione Ludwig*, Forti di Belvedere, Florence, 1987

London, Dublin and Manchester 1987, *Comic Iconoclasm*, Institute of Contemporary Arts, London, Douglas Hyde Gallery, Dublin, Cornerhouse, Manchester, 1987

Tokyo et al. 1987, *Pop Art U.S.A.–U.K.*, texts by L. Alloway and M. Livingstone, Odakyu Grand Gallery, Tokyo, 1987

New York, Chicago and Los Angeles 1990, *High & Low: Modern Art & Popular Culture*, Museum of Modern Art, New York, Art Institute of Chicago, Museum of Contemporary Art, Los Angeles, 1990

ARTICLES

L. Alloway, '"Pop Art" since 1949', *The Listener*, 27 Dec. 1962, pp. 1085–7

L. Alloway, 'Popular Culture and Pop Art', *Studio International*, clxxviii, July/August 1969, pp. 17–21

L. Cooke, 'The Independent Group: British and American Pop Art, a "Palimpsestuous Legacy"', *Modern Art and Popular Culture: Readings in High and Low*, eds K. Varnedoe and A. Gopnik, New York, 1990, pp. 192–216

S. Gablik, 'Protagonists of Pop: Five Interviews Conducted by Suzi Gablik', *Studio International*, clxxviii, July/August 1969, pp. 9–16

D. Hebdige, 'In Poor Taste: Notes on Pop', *Block*, 8, 1983, pp. 54–68

M. Levy, 'Pop Art for Admass', *Studio International*, clxi, Nov. 1963, pp. 184–9

J. Reichardt, 'Pop Art and after', *Art International*, 7, Feb. 1963, pp. 42–7

B. Rose, 'The New Realists, Neo-Dada, Le Nouveau Réalisme, Pop Art, the New Vulgarians, Common Object Painting, Know-nothing Genre', *Art International*, vii, 1, Jan 1963, pp. 22–8

J. Russell, 'Pop Reappraised', *Art in America*, 57, July/August 1969, pp. 78–89

D. Sylvester, 'Art in a Coke Climate', *Sunday Times Magazine*, 26 Jan. 1964, pp. 14–23

N. Whiteley, 'Throw-away Culture in the 1950s and 1960s', *Oxford Art Journal*, x, 2, 1987, pp. 3–27

AMERICA

GENERAL SURVEYS

L. Alloway, *Topics in American Art since 1945*, New York, 1975

G. Battcock, ed., *The New Art: A Critical Anthology*, New York, 1973

L. de Coppet and A. Jones, *The Art Dealers: The Powers behind the Scene Talk about the Business of Art*, New York, 1984

H. Geldzahler, *New York Painting and Sculpture 1940–1970*, New York, 1970

A. Kaprow, *Assemblage, Environments and Happenings*, New York, 1966

M. Kirby, *Happenings*, New York, 1965

J. Lipman and R. Marshall, *Art about Art*, New York, 1978

I. Sandler, *American Art of the 1960s*, New York, 1988

S. Stich, *Made in U.S.A.: An Americanization in Modern Art, the '50s and '60s*, Berkeley, 1987

BOOKS ON POP

L. Alloway, *American Pop Art*, New York and London, 1974

A. Boatto, *Pop Art*, Rome, 1983

A. Codognato, ed., *Pop Art: evoluzione di una generazione*, Milan, 1980

N. Dubreuil-Blondin, *La Fonction critique dans le Pop Art américain*, Montreal, 1980

B. Haskell, *Blam! The Explosion of Pop, Minimalism, and Performance 1958–1964*, New York and London, 1984

D. Herzka, *Pop art one*, New York, 1965

C. A. Mahsun, *Pop Art and the Critics*, Ann Arbor, 1987

C. A. Mahsun, ed., *Pop Art: The Critical Dialogue*, Ann Arbor, 1988

J. Rublowsky, *Pop Art: Images of the American Dream*, New York, 1965

A. Warhol with P. Hackett, *POPism: The Warhol '60s*, New York, 1980

EXHIBITION CATALOGUES

New York 1960, *New Forms–New Media I*, texts by L. Alloway and A. Kaprow, foreword by M. Jackson, Martha Jackson Gallery, New York, 1960

New York 1961, *Environments, Situations, Spaces*, Martha Jackson Gallery, New York, 1961

Los Angeles 1962, *My Country 'Tis of Thee*, text by G. Nordland, Dwan Gallery, Los Angeles, 1962

Pasadena 1962, *New Paintings of Common Objects*, text by J. Coplans, Pasadena Art Museum, 1962

Los Angeles 1963, *Six More*, text by L. Alloway, Los Angeles County Museum of Art, 1963

New York 1963, *Americans 1963*, Museum of Modern Art, New York, 1963

New York 1963, *6 Painters and the Object*, text by L. Alloway, Solomon R. Guggenheim Museum, New York, 1963

Oakland 1963, *Pop Art USA*, intro. by J. Coplans, Oakland Art Museum, 1963

Washington, DC 1963, *The Popular Image*, text by

A. Solomon, Washington Gallery of Modern Art, Washington, DC, 1963
Stockholm 1964, *Amerikanste Pop-Kunst*, texts by A. Solomon and B. Kluver, Moderna Museet, Stockholm, 1964
Irvine 1965, *New York: The Second Breakthrough 1959–1964*, text by A. Solomon, Art Gallery, University of California at Irvine, 1965
Milwaukee 1965, *Pop Art and the American Tradition*, text by T. Atkinson, Milwaukee Art Center, 1965
Worcester 1965, *The New American Realism*, texts by D. Catton Rich and M. Carey, Worcester Art Museum, MA, 1965
Frankfurt 1967, *Kompass, Paintings after 1945 in New York*, text by J. Leering, Kunstverein, Frankfurt, 1967
Philadelphia 1971, *Multiples: The First Decade*, text by J. L. Tancock, Philadelphia Museum of Art, 1971
Cleveland 1976, *American Pop Art and the Culture of the Sixties*, New Gallery of Contemporary Art, Cleveland, OH, 1976
Newport Beach et al. 1989, *LA Pop in the Sixties*, Newport Harbor Art Museum, Newport Beach, CA, 1989

ARTICLES
C. R. Baldwin, 'On the Nature of Pop', *Artforum*, 12, June 1974, pp. 34–8
H. Geldzahler, 'The Art Audience and the Critic', *The Hudson Review*, 18, Sept. 1965, pp. 105–9
H. Geldzahler and K. Moffett, 'Pop Art: Two Views', ART*news*, lxxiii, May 1971, pp. 30–2
B. Glaser, 'Oldenburg, Lichtenstein, Warhol: A Discussion', *Artforum*, 4, Feb. 1966, pp. 20–4
E. H. Johnson, 'The Image Duplicators – Lichtenstein, Rauschenberg and Warhol', *Canadian Art*, 23, Jan. 1966, pp. 12–19
A. Kaprow, 'Pop Art: Past, Present and Future', *The Malahat Review*, 3, July 1967, pp. 54–76
E. T. Kelly, 'New-Dada: A Critique of Pop Art', *Art Journal*, 23, Spring 1964, pp. 199–201
M. Kozloff, 'Pop Culture, Metaphysical Disgust and the New Vulgarians', *Art International*, vi, 2, March 1962, pp. 34–6
D. B. Kuspit, 'Pop Art: A Reactionary Realism', *Art Journal*, 36, Fall 1976, pp. 31–8
J. Perrault, 'Classic Pop Revisited', *Art in America*, 64, March/April 1974, pp. 64–8
P. Plagens, 'Golden Days', in *Modern Art and Popular Culture: Readings in High and Low*, eds K. Varnedoe and A. Goplik, New York, 1990, pp. 219–29
P. Restany, 'Pop Art, un nouvel humainisme américain', *Aujourd'hui*, 55–56, Jan. 1967, pp. 121–2
J. A. Richardson, 'Dada, Camp, and the Mode Called Pop', *The Journal of Aesthetics and Art Criticism*, 24, Summer 1966, pp. 549–58
B. Rose, 'ABC Art', *Art in America*, 53, Oct. 1965, pp. 57–69
B. Rose, 'New York Letter: Pop Art Revisited', *Art International*, 8, Dec. 1964, pp. 47–51
B. Rose, 'Pop in Perspective', *Encounter*, 25, August 1965, pp. 59–63
R. Rosenblum, 'Pop Art and Non-Pop Art', *Art and Literature*, Summer 1965, pp. 80–93
J. Sandberg, 'Some Traditional Aspects of Pop Art', *Art Journal*, 26, Sept. 1967, pp. 228–34, 245
I. Sandler, 'New Cool Art', *Art in America*, 53, Feb. 1965, pp. 96–101
D. G. Seckler, 'Folklore of the Banal', *Art in America*, 50, Winter 1962, pp. 52–61
P. Selz, 'A Symposium on Pop Art', *Arts Magazine*, 37, April 1963, pp. 36–45
G. R. Swenson, 'The New American Sign Painters', ART*news*, lxi, 61, Sept. 1962, pp. 45–7, 61–2
G. R. Swenson, 'What is Pop Art?', ART*news*, lxii, Nov. 1963, pp. 24–7, 61–5; Feb. 1964, pp. 40–3, 62–7
S. Tillim, 'Further Observations on the Pop Phenomenon', *Artforum*, 3, Nov. 1965, pp. 17–19
P. Tuchman, 'Pop! Interviews with George Segal, Andy Warhol, Roy Lichtenstein, James Rosenquist and Robert Indiana', ART*news*, lxxiii, May 1974, pp. 24–9
A. Warhol and P. Hackett, 'In the Beginning: On the Origins of Pop Art and Other Matters', *New York*, 13, March 1980, pp. 60–2, 64–6, 69–71

BRITAIN

GENERAL SURVEYS
C. Frayling, *The Royal College of Art: One Hundred and Fifty Years of Art and Design*, London, 1987
P. Huxley, ed., *Exhibition Road: Painters at the Royal College of Art*, Oxford, 1988
J. Lewinski, *Portrait of the Artist: 25 Years of British Art*, Manchester, 1988
B. Robertson, J. Russell and Lord Snowdon, *Private View*, London, 1965

BOOKS ON POP
C. Finch, *Image as Language–Aspects of British Art 1950–1968*, Harmondsworth, 1969
G. Melly, *Revolt into Style: The Pop Arts in Britain*, Harmondsworth, 1972
D. Robbins, ed., *The Independent Group: Postwar Britain and the Aesthetics of Plenty*, Cambridge, MA, and London, 1990
N. Whiteley, *Pop Design from Modernism to Mod: Theory and Design in Britain 1955–72*, London, 1987

EXHIBITION CATALOGUES
London 1956, *This is Tomorrow*, texts by L. Alloway, D. Lewis and R. Banham, Whitechapel Art Gallery, London, 1956
London 1962, *Image in Progress*, Grabowski Gallery, London, 1962
London 1964, *The New Generation: 1964*, Whitechapel Art Gallery, London, 1964
Geneva 1965, *Jeune peinture anglaise: Pop-Art, op-art et autres tendances*, intro. J. Damase, Galerie Motte, London, 1965
Minneapolis et al. 1965, *London: The New Scene*, texts by M. Friedman and A. Bowness, Walker Art Center, Minneapolis, 1965
Karlsruhe 1969, *Information: Joe Tilson, Peter Phillips, Allen Jones, Eduardo Paolozzi, Ronald B. Kitaj, Richard Hamilton*, text by P. Althews, Badischer Kunstverein, Karlsruhe, 1969
Hamburg 1976, *Pop Art in England: Beginnings of a New Figuration 1947–63*, texts by U. Schneede and F. Whitford, Kunstverein, Hamburg, 1976
London 1987, *British Art in the 20th Century: The Modern Movement*, Royal Academy, London, 1987

ARTICLES
M. Livingstone, 'New! Improved! Varieties of British Pop Sculpture', *Art & Design*, iii, 11–12, 1987, pp. 5–12
M. Livingstone, 'Prototypes of Pop', *Exhibition Road: Painters at the Royal College of Art*, ed. P. Huxley, Oxford, 1988, pp. 41–53
A. Massey, 'The Independent Group: Towards a Redefinition', *Burlington Magazine*, cxxix, 1009, April 1987, pp. 232–42
R. Melville, 'English Pop', *Quadrum*, 17, 1964, pp. 23–38, 182–3
R. Smith, 'New Readers Start here . . .', *Ark*, 32, Summer 1962

NOUVEAU REALISME, FLUXUS & POP IN EUROPE

BOOKS
Association d'Art Moderne Genève, ed., *Fluxus International & Co. à Genève*, Geneva, 1989
P. Couperie et al., *Bande dessinée et figuration narrative*, Paris, 1967
J. Hendricks, *Fluxus etc./Addenda I. The Gilbert and Lila Silverman Collection*, New York, 1983
J. Hendricks, *Fluxus Codex*, New York, 1988
S. Home, *The Assault on Culture and Utopian Currents from Lettrisme to Class War*, London, 1988
P. Restany, *Les Nouveaux Réalistes*, Paris, 1968, rev. as *Le Nouveau Réalisme*, Paris, 1978
H. Ruhé, *Fluxus: The Most Radical and Experimental Art Movement of the Sixties*, Amsterdam, 1979
R. Wick, *Zur Soziologie Intermediärer Kunstpraxis Happening, Fluxus, Aktionen*, Cologne, 1975

EXHIBITION CATALOGUES
Milan 1960, *Les Nouveaux Réalistes*, preface P. Restany, Galerie Apollinaire, Milan, 1960
Munich 1963, *Les Nouveaux Réalistes*, preface P. Restany, Neue Galerie im Künstler Haus, Munich, 1963
Paris 1964, *Mythologies quotidiennes*, Musée d'Art Moderne de la Ville de Paris, 1964
Cologne 1970, *Fluxus and Happenings*, eds H. Szeemann and H. Sohm, Kunstverein, Cologne, 1970
Milan 1970, *Nouveau Réalisme 1960–1970*, preface P. Restany, Rotonde de la Besana, Milan, 1970
Paris 1970, *Nouveau Réalisme 1960–1970*, preface P. Restany, Galerie Mathias Fels, Paris, 1970
Paris 1974, *Fluxus, éléments d'informations*, A.R.C.2, Musée d'Art Moderne de la Ville de Paris, 1974
Bloomfield Hills 1981, *Fluxus etc.*, text by J. Hendricks, Cranbrook Academy of Art, Bloomfield Hills, MI, 1981
Berlin 1982, *1962–Wiesbaden–Fluxus–1982. Eine Kleine Geschichte in drei Teilen, Wiesbaden, Kassel, Berlin*, ed. René Block, DAAD, 1982
Vienna 1982, *Paris 1960–1980*, text by W. Drechsler, Museum Moderner Kunst, Vienna, 1982
Pavia 1983, *Il Pop art e l'Italia*, texts by R. Bossaglio and S. Zatti, Castello Visconteo, Pavia, 1983
Cologne 1986, *Die 60er Jahre. Kölns Weg zur Kunstmetropole. Vom Happening zum Kunstmarket*, ed. W. Herzogenrath and G. Lueg
Paris 1986, *Les Nouveaux Réalistes 1960*, ed. B. Contensou, interview and poems by P. Restany, chronology by A. Bodet and S. Lecombre, Musée d'Art Moderne de la Ville de Paris, 1986
New York 1988, *Fluxus: Selections from the Gilbert and Lila Silverman Collection*, text by C. Phillpot and J. Hendricks, Museum of Modern Art, New York, 1988
Venice 1990, *Ubi Fluxus ibi motus 1962–1990*, ed. A. Bonito Oliva, Granai della Repubblica, Venice, 1990
Vienna 1990, *Fluxus Subjektive*, texts by K. Friedman et al., Galerie Krinzinger, Vienna, 1990

ARTICLES
D. Abadie, 'Le Nouveau Réalisme', *25 Ans d'art en France 1960–1985*, Paris, 1986
B. Altshuler, 'Fluxus redux', *Arts Magazine*, 64, Sept. 1989, pp. 66–70
P. Moore, 'Fluxus Focus', *Artforum*, 21, Oct. 1982, pp. 33–7
P. Restany, 'Le Nouveau Réalisme à la Conquête de New York', *Art International*, vii, 1, Jan. 1963, pp. 29–36

LENDERS TO THE EXHIBITION

Aachen, Ludwig Forum (cat 136, 151, 163, 236)
Michael D. Abrams (cat 27, 166, 176, 205)
Eduardo Arroyo (cat 3)

Basel, Kunstmuseum, on loan from the Ludwig Collection (cat 104)
Billy Al Bengston (cat 12, 13)
The Peter and Chrissy Blake Collection (cat 20, 21, 256, 257)
Irving Blum, New York (cat 153)
Collection Robert Julius and Andrea Bollt, New York (cat 200)
Pat Booth (cat 17)
Norman and Irma Braman (cat 127, 253)
Collection of John Bransten (cat 226)
Hermann and Marietta Braun, Remscheid (cat 23)
Richard Brown Baker Collection, Courtesy of the Yale University Art Gallery (cat 148, 149)
Budapest, Ludwig Museum in the Hungarian National Gallery (cat 106)

Constance R. Caplan (cat 36)
Leo Castelli (cat 7)
Central Selling Organisation's Contemporary Art Collection (cat 26)
Collection Jeanne-Claude Christo, New York (cat 31)
Collection Attilio Codognato (cat 155)
Cologne, Museum Ludwig (cat 6, 19, 98, 105, 114, 115, 123, 135, 138, 154, 196, 227, 237, 239, 243)

Jim Dine (cat 33)
Düsseldorf, Hans Mayer Gallery (cat 34)
Düsseldorf, Kunstmuseum (cat 184)

Edinburgh, Scottish National Gallery of Modern Art (cat 112, 174, 230)
Stefan T. Edlis Collection (cat 193)

Fogal Legfashion (cat 233)
Ford Motor Company Limited (cat 133)
Frankfurt, Galerie Neuendorf (cat 180, 181)
Private Collection Frieder-Burda, Baden-Baden (cat 198)
Fröhlich Collection, Stuttgart (cat 197, 199)
Collection Winnie Fung (cat 108, 213)

Gothenburg Art Gallery (cat 137)
Granada Television (cat 134)

Collection of Agnes Gund (cat 150)

Richard Hamilton (cat 103, 107)
Houston, The Menil Collection (cat 140)

Jasper Johns (cat 124)

Kansas City, Nelson-Atkins Museum of Art (cat 228)
Kiel, Kunsthalle (cat 145)
James Kirkman, London (cat 219, 222)
Kasper König Frankfurt am Main (cat 5)

Marc Landeau (cat 162)
Barbara and Richard S. Lane (cat 164)
David Lichtenstein (cat 147)
London, Arts Council Collection, South Bank Centre (cat 117)
London, Knoedler Kasmin Limited (cat 223)
London, The Mayor Gallery Ltd and Thomas Ammann Fine Art, Zurich (cat 159)
London, The Mayor Gallery Ltd and Daniel Varenne, Geneva (cat 252)
London, Royal College of Art (cat 15, 25, 110)
London, Tate Gallery (cat 14, 18, 113, 125, 170, 173)
London, The Board of Trustees of the Victoria and Albert Museum (cat 171, 172)
London, Waddington Galleries (cat 28, 142, 201, 229, 232, 254)
London, Waddington Graphics (cat 231)
Los Angeles, Collection Lannan Foundation (cat 141)
Los Angeles, Museum of Contemporary Art: The Panza Collection (cat 189)
Mr and Mrs Herbert L. Lucas (cat 111)

Paul and Linda McCartney (cat 10, 175)
Giò Marconi, Milan (cat 207)
Giorgio Marconi, Milan (cat 208)
Henry Martin (cat 129, 130)
Hansjorg Mayer (cat 58)
Courtesy of the Mead Corporation (cat 209)
Munich, Städtische Galerie im Lenbachhaus (cat 183)

New York, Courtesy Mary Boone Gallery (cat 8)
New York, Leo Castelli Gallery, Claes Oldenburg and Coosje van Bruggen (cat 169)
New York, Courtesy of The Louis K. Meisel Gallery (cat 188)
New York, Odyssia Gallery (cat 118, 119)
New York, Private Collection, Courtesy of BlumHelman Gallery (cat 241)
New York, Private Collection, Courtesy of Richard L. Feigen and Co (cat 206)
New York, Andy Warhol Foundation for The Visual Arts, Inc (cat 247, 248)
New York, Whitney Museum of American Art (cat 96)
Norfolk, Contemporary Art Society (cat 132)

Onnasch Collection, Berlin (cat 158, 160, 161, 190, 195, 202, 210, 216, 234, 250)

PaineWebber Group Inc, New York (cat 212)
Sir Eduardo Paolozzi (cat 177)
Paris, Galerie Beaubourg, Marianne and Pierre Nahon (cat 29)
Paris, Musée National d'Art Moderne, Centre Georges Pompidou (cat 4)
Peruz Collection, Milan (cat 225)

Robert Rauschenberg (cat 122, 194)

Saatchi Collection, London (cat 245, 246)
Niki de Saint Phalle (cat 214)
Santa Monica, CA, Courtesy Fred Hoffman Gallery and Martin Lawrence Limited Editions, Inc (cat 215)
Colin Self (cat 217, 220, 221)
Sheffield, City Art Galleries (cat 22)
Sonnabend Collection (cat 1, 30, 120, 121, 182, 191)
Frank Stella Collection, New York (cat 2)
Stockholm, Moderna Museet (cat 165, 168, 204)
Collection M. and E. Stoffel (cat 109, 143)
Stuttgart, Staatsgalerie (cat 192)
Stuttgart, Staatsgalerie, Sohm Archive (cat 11, 24, 38, 39, 40, 41, 42, 43, 44, 45, 46, 47, 48, 49, 50, 51, 52, 53, 54, 55, 56, 57, 59, 60, 61, 62, 63, 64, 65, 66, 67, 68, 69, 70, 71, 72, 73, 74, 75, 76, 77, 78, 79, 80, 81, 82, 83, 84, 85, 86, 87, 88, 89, 90, 91, 92, 93, 94, 95, 146, 157, 249, 258)

Tübingen, Kunsthalle, Prof. Dr Georg Zundel Collection (cat 99)

Collection Massimo and Francesca Valsecchi (cat 131)
Vancouver Art Gallery (cat 167)
Collection Daniel Varenne, Geneva (cat 116)
Vienna, Museum Moderner Kunst (cat 187, 235)

Washington, Hirshhorn Museum and Sculpture Garden, Smithsonian Institute (cat 211)
Claire Wesselmann (cat 251)
William S. Wilson (cat 128)

Zurich, Courtesy Thomas Ammann (cat 186, 240, 242, 244)

Also many lenders who prefer to remain anonymous.

PHOTOGRAPHIC AND ANTHOLOGY ACKNOWLEDGEMENTS

Photographs reproduced in this volume have been provided, in the majority of cases, by the owners or custodians of the works, indicated in the captions, or from the authors' archives. The following list applies to photographs for which a separate acknowledgement is due.

Catalogue Plate Illustrations
Peter Accettola cat 32
Michael Agee cat 148, 149
Artothek cat 151
Peter Brenner Photography cat 111
Leo Castelli Gallery, New York cat 150, 155
Geoffrey Clements, New York cat 96, 119, 193
Color Fotolabor Dr Parisini, Vienna cat 187, 235
Colorfoto Hans Hinz cat 104
A. C. Cooper Ltd cat 16, 144
Prudence Cuming Associates Ltd cat 10, 20, 21, 27, 133, 166, 175, 176, 218, 219, 222, 229, 231, 256, 257
D. James Dee cat 118
Courtesy Jeffrey Deitch cat 127
Courtesy Anthony d'Offay Gallery, London cat 103, 107
Joachim Fliegner cat 216
Brian Forrest cat 12, 13
Patrick Goetelen cat 102
Paula Goldman cat 189
Richard Goodbody, New York cat 17
Hansjorg Henn, Zurich cat 233
Hickey & Robertson, Houston, Texas cat 139
Salvatore Licitra, Milan cat 131
J. Littkemann, Berlin cat 250
Robert McKeever cat 156
Trevor Mills cat 167
Ann Munchow, Aachen cat 136
William Nettles, Los Angeles cat 108, 213
Kevin Noble cat 128
Courtesy Pace Gallery, New York cat 33
Alan Pettigrew cat 217, 220, 221
Courtesy of the Philadelphia Museum of Art cat 124
Eric Pollitzer, New York cat 126, 251
Antonia Reeve, Edinburgh cat 174
Rheinisches Bildarchiv, Cologne cat 6, 19, 98, 105, 114, 115, 123, 135, 138, 154, 227, 237, 239, 243
F. Rosenstiel, Cologne cat 161, 198
Tom Scott, Edinburgh cat 112
F. J. Thomas, Hollywood, California cat 140
Paolo Vandrasch, Milan cat 207, 208, 225
Wolfgang Volz, New York cat 31
Courtesy of Waddington Galleries cat 100, 109, 143, 255
John Webb cat 117
Willard Associates Photography, Miami cat 253
Dorothy Zeidman cat 164, 169
Uli Zeller, Cologne cat 197

Text Illustrations
Brian Albert p. 261 (fig. 2)
Ernst A. Busche p. 31 (fig 1)
Rudolph Burckhardt p. 21 (fig 4)
Prudence Cuming Associates Ltd p. 32 (fig 2)
Institute of Contemporary Art, London p. 16 (fig 7); p. 148 (fig 1)
Courtesy Allan D'Arcangelo p. 15 (fig 5)
Bill Jacobson Studio p. 13 (fig 3)
Courtesy Sidney Janis Gallery, New York p. 12 (fig 1); p. 35 (fig 6)
Courtesy Roy Lichtenstein p. 17 (fig 8); p. 21 (fig 4)
Courtesy Lisson Gallery, London p. 266 (fig 9)
Museum Ludwig, Cologne p. 222 (figs 1 & 2)
Norton Simon Museum p. 34 (fig 5)
Alan Pettigrew p. 153 (fig 9)
Photo Studios Limited p. 152 (fig 7)
Courtesy Mel Ramos p. 14 (fig 5)
Hartmut Rekort p. 226 (fig 2 & 3)
Rheinisches Bildarchiv, Cologne p. 220 (fig 1 & 2)
Thomas Ruff p. 265 (fig 8)
Service Photographique, Centre Georges Pompidou p. 216 (fig 2)
Courtesy Sonnabend Gallery, New York p. 20 (fig 2); p. 21 (fig 3)
Studio Marconi p. 18 (fig 9)
Tate Gallery, London p. 20 (fig 1)
Zindman/Fremont p. 263 (fig 3); p. 265 (fig 7)

Photographs of the Artists (Details)
Eduardo Arroyo: Gamarra y Garrigues, Madrid
Richard Artschwager: Courtesy Leo Castelli Gallery, New York
Clive Barker: David Courts
Billy Al Bengston: Walter Urie
George Brecht: Dick Higgins
Patrick Caulfield: Guglielmo Galvin
César: André Morain
Christo: Wolfgang Volz
Allan D'Arcangelo: R. D'Allesandro
Jim Dine: Nancy Dine (Courtesy Pace Gallery, New York)
Robert Filliou: Peter Moore
Raymond Hains: Harry Shunk
Richard Hamilton: Timothy Greenfield Sanders (Courtesy Anthony d'Offay Gallery, London)
David Hockney: Jim McHugh
Robert Indiana: Theodore Beck
Alain Jacquet: Gregoire Müller
Jasper Johns: Richard Lesley Schulman (Courtesy Leo Castelli Gallery)
Allen Jones: Jill Kennington
Edward Kienholz: Sidney B. Felsen (Courtesy LA Louver Gallery, Venice, CA)
R. B. Kitaj: Prudence Cuming Associates Limited
Arthur Køpcke: Archiv Sohm
Roy Lichtenstein: Liz Murray
George Maciunas: Archiv Sohm
Claes Oldenburg: Herbert Tinz, Sydsvenskan, Malmö, Sweden
Nam June Paik: Archiv Sohm
Eduardo Paolozzi: Frank Thurston
Mel Ramos: Leta Ramos
Robert Rauschenberg: Courtesy Leo Castelli Gallery, New York
Martial Raysse: Courtesy Samy Kinge Gallery, Paris
Larry Rivers: Camilla McGrath
James Rosenquist: Russ Blaise (Courtesy Richard L. Feigen & Co, New York and London)
Niki de Saint Phalle: Laurent Condominas
George Segal: Allan Finkelman (Courtesy Sidney Janis Gallery, New York)
Colin Self: Jessica Prendergast
Richard Smith: Rob Huber
Daniel Spoerri: Harry Shunk
Wayne Thiebaud: Matt Bult
Ben Vautier: George Maciunas
Jacques de la Villeglé: Harry Shunk
Andy Warhol: Richard L. Schulman (Courtesy Andy Warhol Foundation for the Visual Arts, Inc., New York)
Robert Watts: Archiv Sohm
Emmett Williams: Bruce Fleming

Every effort has been made to trace and acknowledge the source of illustrations and copyright holders. The organisers and publishers sincerely apologise for any inadvertent errors or omissions and will be happy to correct them in any future edition.

Anthology Acknowledgements
Copyright of the extracts belongs to the author except in the following cases:

American Craft p. 41 (Richard Artschwager); p. 51 (Claes Oldenburg)
Architectural Design Magazine p. 154 (Lawrence Alloway)
Art in America p. 53 (Robert Rauschenberg, 1966)
Art International p. 53 (Mel Ramos); p. 62 (H. C. Westermann)
ARTnews p. 42 (Jim Dine); p. 44 (Robert Indiana); p. 45 (Jasper Johns); p. 49 (Allan Kaprow); p. 49 (Roy Lichtenstein); p. 56 (James Rosenquist); p. 59 (Andy Warhol); p. 61 (Tom Wesselmann)
Arts Magazine p. 40 (A Symposium on Pop Art)
David Bourdon p. 48 (Ray Johnson)
Harcourt Black Jovanovich p. 60 (Andy Warhol, 1980)
Museum of Modern Art p. 53 (Robert Rauschenberg, 1959)
Newport Harbor Art Museum p. 44 (Joe Goode)
Norton Simon Museum p. 58 (Wayne Thiebaud)
Jaiser Reichardt p. 157 (David Hockney); p. 158 (Allen Jones)
Royal College of Art p. 156 (Derek Boshier); p. 158 (David Hockney)
Mrs G. L. T. Sackler p. 57 (James Rosenquist, 1968); p. 155 (Peter Blake); p. 160 (Eduardo Paolozzi); p. 161 (Richard Smith)
Thames & Hudson p. 157 (Richard Hamilton, 1982)
The Trustees of the Whitechapel Art Gallery p. 160 (Peter Phillips)

index of names

Numbers in italics refer to illustration page numbers

THE ROYAL ACADEMY TRUST

The Trustees of the Royal Academy Trust wish to express their gratitude to the many companies and individuals who have already given their support to the appeal. In particular they would like to extend their thanks to:

H.M. The Queen
H.R.H. Princess Alexandra
The Hon. Angus Ogilvy
Air Seychelles Limited
Russell Aitken
Allied-Lyons PLC
American Airways
American Associates of the Royal Academy Trust
American Express Europe Limited
The Arthur Andersen Foundation
Mrs John W. Anderson II
Anglia Television Limited
The Hon. Walter and Mrs Annenberg
James Archibald
Mr and Mrs Tobin Armstrong
The Astor Foundation
Atlantic Richfield Company
Mr and Mrs J. Evans Attwell
Mr and Mrs Stanton Avery
Mrs Henry Bagley
Mr and Mrs Alan Bain
Nancy Balfour
The Bank of England
Bankers Trust Company
Barclays Bank PLC
The Baring Foundation
B.A.T. Industries PLC
B-CH 1971 Charitable Trust
The Suzanne Beadle Charitable Trust
Tom Bendhem
Mr and Mrs James Benson
BICC plc
In Memoriam: Ida Rose Biggs
Elizabeth Blackadder RA
Norman Blamey RA
The BOC Group
Bollinger Champagne
Mr and Mrs Gerrit P. van de Bovenkamp
C. T. Bowring & Co. Limited
Peter Bowring
British Airways
British Caledonian Airways
The British Electric Traction Company PLC
British Gas Corporation
British Gypsum
British Olivetti Limited
The British Petroleum Company PLC
Britoil plc
Brixton Estate
Brooke Bond Group
The Brown Foundation, Inc
Gilbert Brown
BT
BTR plc
Bulgari Jewellers
Bunzl PLC
Mr and Mrs Walter Burke
Capel Charitable Trust
The Capital Group Inc.
Carlton Communications
Mrs Winifred Carter
Mr and Mrs John Edgar Chapoton
Christie's
Citibank NA
The Cleary Foundation
The Trustees of the Clore Foundation
The Worshipful Company of Clothworkers
The John S. Cohen Foundation
Mr and Mrs Terence Cole
Joseph Collier Charitable Trust
Commercial Union Assurance Company plc
Ernest Cook Trust
Mrs Jan Cowles
Crown Decorative Products Ltd
Culra Charitable Trust
Mr and Mrs Marvin Davis
Mr and Mrs James Dean
Roger de Grey PRA
The De La Rue Company plc
The Hon. C. Douglas and Mrs Dillon
The Distillers' Company
Mr and Mrs Harry Djanogly
Mr and Mrs Gaylord Donnelly
Alfred Dunhill Limited
The Durrington Corporation
Eagle Star Insurance Group
The Gilbert & Eileen Edgar Charitable Trust
Miss Jayne Edwardes
The Ells Will Trust
English Heritage
Roberta Entwistle
Esso UK plc
Mr and Mrs T. M. Evans
Anthony Eyton RA
The Esmée Fairbairn Charitable Trust
Mr and Mrs Donald R. Findlay
The Hon. Leonard and Mrs Firestone
The Worshipful Company of Fishmongers
Mr Christopher Forbes
Forbes Magazine
The Henry Ford II Fund
Joseph Strong Frazer Trust
Ms Maud Frizon
John Frye Bourne
Gallaher Limited
The Garfield Weston Foundation
Mrs Pat H. Gerber
The Getty Grant Program
The J. Paul Getty Jr. Trust
Glaxo Holdings (1972) Charity Trust
Mr Guilford Glazer
Gleneagles Hotel
The Jack Goldhill Charitable Trust
The Horace W. Goldsmith Foundation
The Worshipful Company of Goldsmiths
Mr John Gore
Frederick Gore RA
Her Majesty's Government
The Greentree Foundation
Mr Lewis Grinnon
The Worshipful Company of Grocers
Mr and Mrs Wallace Grubman
Guest, Keen & Nettlefolds plc
Calouste Gulbenkian Foundation
The Worshipful Company of Haberdashers
Mr and Mrs Melville Wakeman Hall
Donald Hamilton-Fraser RA
Dr and Mrs Armand Hammer
Mrs Sue Hammerson OBE
The Hammerson Group of Companies
The Lord Hanson
Philip and Pauline Harris Charitable Trust
Mrs John Hay Whitney
The Hayward Foundation
Hayward Tyler
Hazlitt, Gooden & Fox
Hedley Foundation
H. J. Heinz Charitable Trust
Mr Henry J. Heinz II
Norman Hepple RA
Herring Son & Daw Rating Ltd
Hertz (UK) Ltd
Mr and Mrs Norman Hickman
High Winds Fund
Hill Samuel Group PLC
Hilton Hotel Corporation
David Hockney BBC Radio 4 Appeal
Mrs James Stewart Hooker
Ken Howard ARA
IBM United Kingdom Limited
The Idlewild Trust
Imperial Chemical Industries PLC
Imperial Tobacco Limited
Inchcape Charitable Trust
Inter Continental Hotels Corporation
International Thompson Organisation
The Worshipful Company of Ironmongers
Elin and Lewis Johnson
R. J. Kiln Limited
Mrs D. King
Kodak
The Kress Foundation
Ladbroke Group plc
Maurice Laing Foundation
Ilias Lalounis Gallery
John S. Latsis
Mr and Mrs Larry Lawrence
Roland P. Lay
Miss R. A. Le Bas
Leading Hotels of the World
The Leche Trust
Mr and Mrs Panagiotis Lemos
Mr and Mrs William M. Lese
Lord Leverhulme's Charitable Trust
Mr and Mrs Leon Levy
John Lewis Partnership plc
Lex Services PLC
Sir Sydney and Lady Lipworth
Lloyds Bank PLC
The Corporation and Members of Lloyd's and Lloyd's Brokers
Mr and Mrs Jack Lyons
MacDonald-Buchanan Trust
McKenna & Co.
McKinsey and Company Inc
The Manifold Trust
The Manor Charitable Trust
Mr and Mrs John L. Marion
Marks & Spencer plc
Sir George Martin Charitable Trust
Mr and Mrs Jack C. Massey
Matheson & Co. Limited
MB Group plc
Paul Mellon KBE
The Anthony and Elizabeth Mellows Charitable Trust
The Mercers' Company
The Merchant Taylors' Company
Meridian Hotels Limited
Midland Bank plc
The Miller and Tiley Charitable Trust
Millichope Foundation
Mobil Oil Company Limited
The Moorgate Trust Fund
Morgan Grenfell & Co. Ltd
The National Magazine Co.
National Westminster Bank plc
Mrs Mary Newman
News International plc
Stavros S. Niarchos
Occidental International Oil Inc.
Olympia and York
Mr and Mrs Peter O'Donnell
Oppenheimer Charitable Trust
Orrin Charitable Trust
The Otemae College
H. R. Owen Limited
P & O Steam Navigation Company
Pearson plc
Peerless Pump
Mr and Mrs Milton Petrie
Petrofina UK Ltd.
P.F. Charitable Trust
Pilgrim Trust
The Plessey Company plc
Mr and Mrs Loring G. Pratt
The Private Capital Group
Prudential Assurance Company Ltd
Mr and Mrs J. A. Pye's Charitable Settlement
The Radcliffe Trust
The Rank Foundation
The Rank Organisation plc
Ranks Hovis McDougall PLC
The Rayne Foundation
Reed International PLC
Mr Laurance S. Rockefeller
The Ronson Charitable Foundation
The Jacob Rothschild Charitable Trust
Rowntree Macintosh
The Royal Bank of Scotland
RTZ Services Limited
Dr and Mrs Arthur M. Sackler
The Sainsbury Family Charitable Trust
Jean Sainsbury Charitable Trust
Mrs Jean Sainsbury
Peter Samuel Charitable Trust
Save and Prosper
Mrs Frances Scaife
Mr and Mrs Sam Scali
Mr and Mrs Benno C. Schmidt
J. Henry Schroder Wagg & Co. Ltd.
Sea Containers Limited
Shell UK Limited
Harry & Abe Sherman Foundation
Dr Francis Singer
The Skinners' Company
The Sloane Club
The Sloane Street Trust
Mr Marvin Sloves

Mr and Mrs Edward Byron Smith
Mrs Frederick Stafford
Standard Chartered Bank
Standard Telephones & Cables PLC
Mr and Mrs Dennis C. Stanfill
The Starr Foundation
Sterling Guarantee PLC
Robert L. Sterling Jr.
The Bernard Sunley Charitable Foundation
Tarmac plc
Mr and Mrs A. Alfred Taubman
Technical Indexes Limited
Thames Television Limited
Mr Bruce E. Thompson Jr.
Sir Jules Thorn Charitable Trust
THORN EMI plc
Thomas Tilling plc
Trafalgar House Public Limited Company
Ware and Edythe Travelstead
The Triangle Trust (1949) Fund
Trident Television plc
Trustees Saving Bank (Holdings) Limited
TWA
The Twenty Seven Foundation
The 29th May 1961 Charitable Trust
Unilever PLC
Venice Simplon-Orient Express
Vorwerk
The Wales Foundation
S. G. Warburg & Company Limited
The Weldon U.K. Charitable Trust
Westminster City Council
Mr and Mrs Garry H. Weston
Anthony Whishaw RA
Whitbread & Company PLC
Wilde Sapte
The Willard Intercontinental
HDH Wills 1965 Charitable Trust
HH Wingate Foundation
Winsor & Newton (part of the Reckitt & Colman Group)
The Wolfson Foundation
Mr Lawrence Wood
Mr and Mrs William Wood Prince
Mr Ian Woodner
Sir John Woolf
Mr Charles Wrightsman
Dr Tomozo Yano

CORPORATE MEMBERS

Patron: Mrs Margaret Thatcher
Arthur Andersen & Co.
A. T. Kearney Limited
BAT Industries plc
British Alcan Aluminium plc
British Gas Plc
BT
Bunzl PLC
Campbell's
Chesterton International
Chubb Insurance Company of Europe
Cookson Group plc
The Diamond Trading Company (Pty) Limited
J. W. Falkner and Sons Ltd
Goldman Sachs International Limited
Grand Metropolitan plc
Griffiths McGee Demolition Co Ltd
Haden Young Limited
Hill and Knowlton
Hill Samuel Bank Limited
Hillier Parker
ICI plc
Intercontinental Hotel Group
Jaguar Cars Limited
John Laing plc
Lehman Brothers International
Lex Service PLC
London & Edinburgh Trust PLC
Marks and Spencer p.l.c.
Midland Group
MoMart Limited
Mountleigh Group plc
The Nikko Securities Co., (Europe) Ltd
P & O Steam Navigation Company
Reed International P.L.C.
Reuters Limited
Rosehaugh PLC
Rothmans International p.l.c.
Rothmans International Tobacco (UK) Limited
St James Place Capital Plc
Salomon Brothers International Limited
The Daily Telegraph
THORN EMI PLC
TI Group plc
Unilever PLC

CORPORATE ASSOCIATES

3i plc
Thos. Agnew & Sons Ltd
Alexandra Rose Day
Allen & Overy
American Express Europe Limited
Amery Parkes
The Arts Club
Ashurst Morris Crisp
A T & T (UK) Ltd
Bankers Trust Company
Banque Paribas
Barclays Bank Plc
Barclays de Zoete Wedd Ltd
Belron International BV
BET PLC
BMP DDB Needham
BMW (GB) LTD
The BOC Group
Booker plc
Boston Safe Deposit and Trust Company (UK) Ltd
Bovis Construction Limited
BP Chemicals Limited
BP International
Brixton Estate plc
H. P. Bulmer Holdings plc
Burmah Castrol Trading Limited
Cable and Wireless plc
Capital & Counties plc
Carlton Beck
Charles Scott & Partners
Charterhouse plc
The Chase Manhattan Bank NA
Chevron U.K. Limited
Christie's
CIGNA RE Corporation
CJA (Management Recruitment Consultants) Limited
Clifford Chance
Coca-Cola Northwest Europe
Courage Charitable Trust
Coutts & Co
The De La Rue Company p.l.c.
Deutsche Bank AG
Dowty
Durrington Corporation
Eagle Star Insurance Company Limited
Richard Ellis
Enterprise Oil plc
Ernst and Young
Esso UK plc
Fiat UK Ltd
Fina plc
Financial Group of North Atlantic
Gardiner & Theobald
Gartmore Investment Management Limited
General Accident
The General Electric Company plc
Girobank plc
Gleeds
Global Asset Management
Granada Group
Greycoat PLC
Guardian Royal Exchange plc
Guinness Mahon Holdings plc
Halecrest – Design & Build
The Hammerson Group
Hawker Siddeley Group plc
Hay Management Consultants Ltd
Heidrick and Struggles International Inc
H. J. Heinz Company Limited
IBM UK Limited
Inchcape plc
Johnson Wax Ltd
KHBB
The Kleinwort Benson Group
Kodak Ltd
Kumagai Gumi U.K. Limited
Laing + Cruickshank
John Lewis Partnership plc
London Weekend Television
Y. J. Lovell (Holdings) PLC
Macfarlanes
E. D. & F. Man Ltd. Charitable Trust
The Manufacturers Life Insurance Company (UK) Ltd
Marlborough Fine Art (London) Ltd
The Mars group of companies in the U.K.
Martini & Rossi
The Worshipful Company of Mercers
Morgan, Lewis & Bockius
Morgan Stanley International
Motion Picture Enterprises Ltd
Nabarro Nathanson
National Westminster Bank plc
National Power plc
NCR Limited
NEC (UK) Ltd
The Nestlé Charitable Trust
Nihon Keizai Shimbun Europe Ltd
Occidental Petroleum (Caledonia) Ltd
Olivetti Systems & Networks Limited
Olympia & York
Ove Arup Partnership
Pearson plc
Pentagram Design Ltd
Pentland Group plc
The Post Office
Publicis
Rayner Essex
Renton Howard Wood Levin (Partnership)
Richardson Greenshields of Canada Limited
The Royal Bank of Scotland plc
Royal Insurance Holdings plc
RTZ Limited
J. Sainsbury
Santa Fe Exploration
Save & Prosper Educational Trust
Schroder Investment Management Ltd
J. Henry Schroder Wagg & Co Limited
Sears plc
The Sedgwick Group plc
Slough Estates plc
W. H. Smith & Son Limited
Smith & Williamson
SmithKline Beecham
Smiths Industries PLC
SONY UK Limited
Sotheby's
Speyhawk Public Limited Company
S R U Group
Stanhope Properties plc
Sun Life Assurance Society plc
Sir Richard Sutton's Settled Estates
Tate & Lyle plc
Taylor Joynson Garrett
Tenneco Europe Limited
Thames Television PLC
Tomkins PLC
Trafalgar House Construction Holdings Ltd
Trusthouse Forte
TVS Entertainment
United Biscuits (UK) Limited
S. G. Warburg Group plc
The Wellcome Foundation Ltd
Wickes plc
Williams Lea Group Limited
Wood & Wood International Signs Limited
Yamaichi International (Europe) Ltd

FRIENDS OF THE ROYAL ACADEMY

BENEFACTORS
The Lady Brinton
Sir Nigel and Lady Broackes
Keith Bromley Esq
The John S. Cohen Foundation
The Colby Trust
Michael E. Flintoff Esq
The Lady Gibson
Jack Goldhill Esq
Mrs Mary Graves
D. J. Hoare Esq
Irene and Hyman Kreitman
D. E. Laing Esq
The Landmark Trust
Roland Lay Esq
The Trustees of the Leach Fourteenth Trust
Sir Hugh Leggatt
Sir Sydney and Lady Lipworth
Jack Lyons Esq
Mrs T. S. Mallinson
The Manor Charitable Trustees
Lieut. Col. L. S. Michael OBE
Jan Mitchell Esq
The Lord Moyne
The Lady Moyne
Mrs Sylvia Mulcahy
G. R. Nicholas Esq
Mrs Vincent Paravicini
Richard Park Esq
Phillips Fine Art Auctioneer
Mrs Denise Rapp
Mrs Adrianne Reed
The Late Anne M. Roxburgh
Mrs Basil Samuel
Lord Sharp CBE
The Very Reverend E. F. Shotter
Dr Francis Singer
The Spencer Charitable Trust
Miss K. Stalnaker
Lady Daphne Straight
Mrs Pamela Synge
Harry Teacher Esq
The Henry Vyner Charitable Trust
A. Witkin Vacuum Instruments & Products Ltd
Charles Wollaston Esq

INDIVIDUAL SPONSORS
Gerald M. Abrahams Esq
Mrs C. P. L. Adlington
Kent Alessandro Esq
Richard B. Allan Esq
Richard Alston Esq
I. F. C. Anstruther Esq
Mrs Ann Appelbe
J. R. Asprey Esq
Edgar Astaire Esq
Lady Attenborough

B. A. Bailey Esq
W. M. Ballantyne Esq
J. M. Bartos Esq
Mrs Robin Behar
M. G. Bell Esq
Mrs Olive Bell
P. F. J. Bennett Esq
Mrs Susan Besser
Mrs John Bibby
P. G. Bird Esq
Mrs L. Blackstone
Mrs C. W. T. Blackwell
Peter Boizot Esq
C. T. Bowring (Charities Fund) Ltd.
Mrs J. M. Bracegirdle
Mrs Susan Bradman
John H. Brandler Esq
Cornelius Broere Esq
Lady Brown
Jeremy Brown Esq
Mrs Susan Burns
Richard Butler Esq

Mrs A. Cadbury
Mr and Mrs R. Cadbury
Mrs C. A. Cain
Mrs L. Cantor
Carroll Foundation
Miss E. M. Cassin
R. A. Cernis Esq
W. J. Chapman Esq
Miss A. Chilcott Fawcett
M. Chowen Esq
Ian Christie Esq
Mrs Joanna V. Clarke
Clarkson Jersey Charitable Trust
B. R. Clifton Esq
Mrs R. Cohen
Mrs N. S. Conrad
Mrs Elizabeth Corob
C. Cotton Esq
Mrs O. Cox-Fill

Mrs Saeda H. Dalloul
Philip Daubeny Esq
John Denham Esq
The Marquess of Douro
Ian Dunlop Esq

Mrs A. Edwards
Kenneth Edwards Esq
Miss Beryl Eeman

Gerry Farrell Esq
Mrs K. W. Feesey MSc.
Mrs B. D. Fenton
Mrs John N. Ferguson
P. Ferguson Esq
Dr Gert-Rudolf Flick
J. G. Fogel Esq
Miss C. Fox
Mrs Jeremy Francis
Mrs Myrtle Franklin

R. P. Gapper Esq
Graham Gauld Esq
M. V. Gauntlett Esq
Robert Gavron Esq
Stephen A. Geiger Esq
Lady Gibberd
Mrs E. J. Gillespie
Anthony Goatman Esq
Michael I. Godbee Esq
Mrs H. D. Goddard
Mrs P. Goldsmith
Michael P. Goodman Esq
Lady Gosling
P. G. Goulandris Esq
Gavin Graham Esq
Mrs J. M. Grant
Mrs J. Green
R. Wallington Green Esq
R. W. Gregson-Brown Esq
Mrs M. Griessmann
Mrs O. Grogan
Mrs W. Grubman

M. Haber Esq
J. A. Hadjipateras Esq
Mrs L. Hadjipateras
Jonathan D. Harris Esq
Robert Harris Esq
R. M. Harris Esq
Mogens Hauschildt Esq
Miss Julia Hazandras
R. Headlam Esq
M. Z. Hepker Esq
Malcolm Herring Esq
Mrs Penelope Heseltine
Mrs K. S. Hill
R. J. Hoare Esq
Reginald Hoe Esq
Mrs A. Hoellering
Mrs Joann Honari
Charles Howard Esq
Mrs Annemarie Howitt
Ms J Huber
John Hughes Esq
Christopher R. Hull Esq
Norman J. Hyams Esq
David Hyman Esq

Mrs Manya Igel
C. Ingram Esq
Mrs H. Irgens-Larsen
S. Isern-Feliu Esq
Ms Karen B. Isman

J. P. Jacobs Esq
Miss Angela Jackson
Mrs J. C. Jaqua
Alan Jeavons Esq
Mrs Sonya Jenkins
H. Joels Esq
Mrs A. Johnson
K. K. Jonietz Esq
Mrs T. Josefowitz

Mr and Mrs Kahan
Mr and Mrs S. H. Karmel
Mrs M. Kidd
Mr D. H. Killick
Peter W. Kininmonth Esq
James Kirkman Esq
Mrs L. Kosta

Mrs E. Landau
Andria Thal Lass
Thomas Leaver Esq
Ronald Lee Esq
Morris Leigh Esq
Mrs P. Leighton
Mr and Mrs R. Leiman
R. H. Leming Esq
Mr and Mrs N. S. Lersten
Owen Luder Esq
Mrs Graham Lyons

Mrs S. McGill
Mrs G. M. S. McIntosh
Malcolm McIntyre Esq
Ms Heather Mackay
Peter McMean Esq
Stuart MacWhirter Esq
Mrs Susan Maddocks
Dr Abraham Marcus
The Hon. Simon Marks
Mrs Veronika Marlow
Mr and Mrs Vincent J. Marmion
B. P. Marsh Esq
J. B. H. Martin Esq
R. C. Martin Esq
C. Mason-Watts Esq
Mrs C. H. Maunsell
Dr D. S. J. Maw
A. Mehta Esq
M. H. Meissner Esq
Ms Pia C. Miller
The Hon. Stephen Monson
Mrs Alan Morgan
Mrs Angela Morrison
The Jocelyn & Katharine Morton Charitable Trust
Miss L. Moule
A. H. J. Muir Esq

The Oakmoor Trust
Ocean Group plc (P. H. Holt Trust)
Jeffery P. Onions Esq
Mrs E. M. Oppenheim Sandelson
Brian R. Oury Esq

Mrs Jo Palmer
N. S. Palmer Esq
R. A. Parkin Esq
H. H. Pattisson Esq
Dr L. G. Petty
Mrs M. C. S. Philip
Ralph Picken Esq
G. B. Pincus Esq
William Plapinger Esq

Mrs Margaret Reeves
Mrs Janice Rich
P. J. Richardson Esq
Dr A. P. Ridges
Chris Rigler Esq
Mrs. J. R. Ritblat
D. Robertson Esq
Robinson Charitable Trust
F. Peter Robinson Esq
D. Rocklin Esq
Mrs A. Rodman
The Rt. Hon. Lord Rootes
Baron Elie de Rothschild
Mr and Mrs Oliver Roux
The Rufford Foundation
The Hon. Sir Steven Runciman CH
Mrs Margaret Rymer

The Worshipful Company of Saddlers
Sir Robert Sainsbury
G. Salmanowitz Esq
Lady Samuel
Mrs Bernice Sandelson
Ms L. Schiff
Mrs L. Schwartz
Mrs Bern L. Schwartz
Ms S. Shah
Christopher Shaw Esq
Shell U.K. Ltd.
Mark Shelmerdine Esq
Mrs Pamela Sheridan
Mohamed Shourbaji
Desmond de Silva Esq QC
R. J. Simia Esq
R. J. Simmons Esq
Mrs E. Slotover
Dr and Mrs Leonard Slotover
Mrs Smiley's Charity Trust
James S. Smith Esq
M. J. Souhami Esq
The Spencer Wills Trust
Mr & Mrs Gunter Z. Steffens
Cyril Stein Esq
James Q. Stringer Esq
Mrs B. Stubbs
Mrs A. Susman
Robin Symes Esq

J. A. Tackaberry Esq
Nikolas D. Tarling Esq
G. C. A. Thom Esq
Anthony H. Thornton Esq
Ms Britt Tidelius
Herbert R. Towning Esq
Mrs Andrew Trollope

A. J. Vines Esq

Mrs C. R. Walford
Mr D. R. Walton Masters
Mrs C. Warburg
Neil Warren Esq
Miss J. Waterous
Mrs R. Watson
J. B. Watton Esq
Mrs C. Weldon
Mr Gilman Welply
Frank S. Wenstrom Esq
W. Weston Esq
Miss L. West Russell
R. A. M. Whitaker Esq
J. Wickham Esq
Wilde Sapte
Graham V. Willcox Esq
Colin C. Williams Esq
David Wilson Esq
Sir Brian Wolfson
Mrs I. Wolstenholme
W. M. Wood Esq
R. M. Woodhouse Esq
Fred S. Worms Esq

D. Young Esq

F. Zangrilli Esq

SPONSORS OF PAST EXHIBITIONS

The Council of the Royal Academy thanks sponsors of past exhibitions for their support. Sponsors of major exhibitions during the last ten years have included:

ALITALIA
Italian Art in the 20th Century 1989

AMERICAN EXPRESS FOUNDATION
Masters of 17th-Century Dutch Genre Painting 1984
'Je suis le cahier': The Sketchbooks of Picasso 1986

ARTS COUNCIL OF GREAT BRITAIN
A New Spirit in Painting 1981
Gertrude Hermes 1981
Carel Weight 1982
Elizabeth Blackadder 1982
Allan Gwynne Jones 1983
The Hague School 1983
Peter Greenham 1985

AUSTRIAN AIRLINES
Egon Schiele and his contemporaries from the Leopold Collection, Vienna 1990

BANQUE INDOSUEZ
Gauguin and The School of Pont-Aven: Prints and Paintings 1989

BAT INDUSTRIES PLC
Murillo 1983
Paintings from the Royal Academy US TOUR 1982/4, RA 1984

BECK'S BIER
German Art in the 20th Century 1985

BOVIS CONSTRUCTION LTD
New Architecture 1986

BRITISH ALCAN ALUMINIUM
Sir Alfred Gilbert 1986

BRITISH GYPSUM LTD
New Architecture 1986

BRITISH PETROLEUM PLC
British Art in the 20th Century 1987

CANARY WHARF DEVELOPMENT CO
New Architecture 1986

W. I. CARR
Gauguin and The School of Pont-Aven: Prints and Paintings 1989

THE CHASE MANHATTAN BANK
Cézanne: The Early Years 1988

THE DAI-ICHI KANGYO BANK, LIMITED
222nd Summer Exhibition 1990

DEUTSCHE BANK AG
German Art in the 20th Century 1985

DIGITAL EQUIPMENT CORPORATION
Monet in the '90s: The Series Paintings 1990

THE ECONOMIST
Inigo Jones Architect 1989

EDWARDIAN HOTELS
The Edwardians and After
Paintings and Sculpture from the Royal Academy's Collection 1900–1950 1990

ELECTRICITY COUNCIL
New Architecture 1986

ESSO PETROLEUM COMPANY LTD
Summer Exhibition 1988

FIAT
Italian Art in the 20th Century 1989

FINANCIAL TIMES
Inigo Jones Architect 1989

FIRST NATIONAL BANK OF CHICAGO
Chagall 1985

FORD MOTOR COMPANY LIMITED
The Fauve Landscape: Matisse, Derain, Braque and their Circle 1991

FRIENDS OF THE ROYAL ACADEMY
Elizabeth Blackadder 1982
Carel Weight 1982
Allan Gwynne Jones 1983
Peter Greenham 1985
Sir Alfred Gilbert 1986

GAMLESTADEN
Royal Treasures of Sweden 1550–1700 1989

JOSEPH GARTNER
New Architecture 1986

J. PAUL GETTY JR CHARITABLE TRUST
The Age of Chivalry 1987

GLAXO HOLDINGS P.L.C.
From Byzantium to El Greco 1987
Great Impressionist and other Master Paintings from the Emil G. Bührle Collection, Zurich 1991

GREYCOAT PLC
Sir Christopher Wren and the Making of St Paul's 1991

GUINNESS PLC
Twentieth-Century Modern Masters: The Jacques and Natasha Gelman Collection 1990
223rd Summer Exhibition 1991

DR ARMAND HAMMER & THE ARMAND HAMMER FOUNDATION
Honoré Daumier 1981
Leonardo da Vinci: Nature Studies Codex Hammer 1981

THE HENRY MOORE FOUNDATION
Henry Moore 1988

HOECHST (UK) LTD
German Art in the 20th Century 1985

IBM UNITED KINGDOM LIMITED
215th Summer Exhibition 1983

THE INDEPENDENT
The Art of Photography 1839–1989 1989

INTERCRAFT DESIGNS LIMITED
Inigo Jones Architect 1989

THE JAPAN FOUNDATION
The Great Japan Exhibition 1981

JOANNOU & PARASKEVAIDES (OVERSEAS) LTD
From Byzantium to El Greco 1987

THE KLEINWORT BENSON GROUP
Inigo Jones Architect 1989

LLOYDS BANK
The Age of Chivalry 1987

LOGICA
The Art of Photography 1839–1989 1989

LUFTHANSA
German Art in the 20th Century 1985

MARTINI & ROSSI LTD
Painting in Naples from Caravaggio to Giordano 1982

MELITTA
German Art in the 20th Century 1985

MERCEDES-BENZ
German Art in the 20th Century 1985

MIDLAND BANK P.L.C.
The Great Japan Exhibition 1981
The Art of Photography 1839–1989 1989

MITSUBISHI ESTATE COMPANY UK LIMITED
Sir Christopher Wren and The Making of St Paul's 1991

MOBIL
Treasures from Ancient Nigeria 1982
Modern Masters from the Thyssen-Bornemisza Collection 1984
From Byzantium to El Greco 1987

NATIONAL WESTMINSTER BANK
Reynolds 1986

THE OBSERVER
The Great Japan Exhibition 1981

OLIVETTI
The Cimabue Crucifix 1983

OTIS ELEVATORS
New Architecture 1986

OVERSEAS CONTAINERS LIMITED
The Great Japan Exhibition 1981

PARK TOWER REALTY CORPORATION
Sir Christopher Wren and the Making of St Paul's 1991

PEARSON P.L.C.
Eduardo Paolozzi Underground 1986

PILKINGTON GLASS
New Architecture 1986

PRINGLE OF SCOTLAND
The Great Japan Exhibition 1981

REED INTERNATIONAL P.L.C.
Toulouse-Lautrec: The Graphic Works 1988
Sir Christopher Wren and the Making of St Paul's 1991

ROBERT BOSCH LIMITED
German Art in the 20th Century 1985

ARTHUR M. SACKLER FOUNDATION
Jewels of the Ancients 1987

SALOMON BROTHERS
Henry Moore 1988

SEA CONTAINERS & VENICE SIMPLON-ORIENT EXPRESS
The Genius of Venice 1983

THE SHELL COMPANIES OF JAPAN
The Great Japan Exhibition 1981

SIEMENS
German Art in the 20th Century 1985

SILHOUETTE EYEWEAR
Egon Schiele and his contemporaries from the Leopold Collection, Vienna 1990

SWAN HELLENIC
Edward Lear 1985

JOHN SWIRE
The Great Japan Exhibition 1981

TEXACO
Selections from the Royal Academy's Private Collection 1991

THE TIMES
Old Master Paintings from the Thyssen-Bornemisza Collection 1988

TRAFALGAR HOUSE
Elisabeth Frink 1985

TRUSTHOUSE FORTE
Edward Lear 1985

UNILEVER
The Hague School 1983
Frans Hals 1990

WALKER BOOKS LIMITED
Edward Lear 1985